CONTENTS

FOREWORD

This is a story of passion. It is the right word to describe the devotion of citizen activists who fight for preservation of rapidly disappearing wilderness. Passion is also the right word to describe the outstanding team of students and their mentors from The Evergreen State College who created this remarkable book. It is a story of conflict and partnership, of lawsuits and compromise, and of recognition that the job of conservation has just begun.

A tiny band of environmental student activists started, early in the last century, to demand protection of our unique landscape. Their numbers exploded after World War II when the detritus of uncontrolled growth became starkly visible.

Almost all were galvanized into action by personal experience. My own epiphany occurred on a Boy Scout hike into the Olympic Mountains. It was my first extended adventure and included a memorable climb of Mt. Deception. The huge trees of dark and silent forests gave way to endless meadows of wildflowers as we left the trail and scrambled toward the mountaintop. From the peak I saw rank on rank of mountains clothed in endless green forests. In that moment I realized "This is how it was before humans touched the earth." That began a love affair with the mountains that continues to this day. Now I am ready to show these remarkable places to my grandchildren. But what will they show to their grandchildren? That is the challenge which must motivate today's generation.

Washington State in the 20th Century grew from 500,000 people to over 6 million, and 2 million more will arrive in the next 20 years. Urbanization of our state separated most people from the wilderness around them and few experienced the escalating destruction of our natural heritage.

A few lonely activists, horrified by what they saw, declared war on the status quo. Each sought to protect a favorite place. They wrote, spoke, and protested, relentlessly. Most importantly, they gathered followers, built coalitions, and saved precious fragments of our disappearing wild places. Their stories are told here to honor their efforts and to inspire those who follow.

As the new century begins, the experiences of the past speak to us. Tools of environmental activism are often scalpel-sharp but occasionally blunt and misdirected. Ecoterrorism may thrill some but seldom produces lasting positive results. Organizational political partisanship divides environmental enthusiasts and can make those organizations irrelevant. Interminable lawsuits may temporarily protect unique lands but often lead to negative reactions in the courts or in Congress.

The best examples of environmental success evolve out of cooperation and even constructive compromise. Instead of zealously sitting in trees, conservationists are now buying them. Where tribes once fought with state game agents over fishing rights, tribal leaders and state officials are now co-managing fisheries resources and restoring salmon runs.

Environmental protection is far too important for eternal conflict. Activists can identify endangered places and propose new protection, but cannot legislate and seldom have the money to protect those endangered places. Legislators rarely initiate new environmental ideas but often carry activists' ideas to fruition. They too, seldom have enough money. Citizen "angels" (generous private donors) are -captivated by the ideas and ideals of citizen activists and contribute their money to preserve special places.

This triumvirate of environmental activists, responsive legislators, and generous citizen angels will typify the success stories of the 21st Century. Their successes will be insufficient however, unless we all adopt a basic human ethic.

None of us really owns the land. We are renters of space and time but will eventually transfer our legacy to the next generation. The ultimate lesson of this important book to the human race is "tread lightly and leave your camp spot better than when you came."

by Former Washington State Governor Daniel J. Evans

ACKNOWLEDGMENTS

The citizens' movement to preserve Washington's wildness has an impressive history of accomplishments, as this book demonstrates. None of these accomplishments could have been achieved without the hundreds, sometimes thousands, of citizens who worked together to realize common goals and dreams. On a smaller scale, that is how the research and writing of this book has been. To the extent that the authors' goals and dreams for this book are realized, it will be due to the tremendous collaboration and generosity of many people who went out of their way for us.

Inspiration and initial guidance for this project came from Dr. Daniel McCool and his students at the University of Utah, who showed us that a good book about wilderness preservation could be written by an undergraduate class.[1] The Evergreen State College provided the ideal institutional environment for our project plus essential financial and logistical support. Our successful start owed much to the assistance of Bill Ransom, Eddy Brown, Karen Fant, Don Parks, Ruthel Wynn, Sandra Estefania Lazo-Herencia, Viktoria Sinex, Jeffrey Brenan, Cathleen Christiansen, Ashley Towanda, and Gwen Ockenlaender. Evergreen faculty member Oscar Soule was an indispensable mentor, guide, companion, and instructor, whose unique combination of generosity, wisdom, and bonhomie helped to move the project from dream to reality. We are similarly indebted to others at The Evergreen State College: Alan Parker and Jennifer Scott of the Northwest Indian Applied Research Institute for advice and guidance in the conduct of our research; Ken Tabbutt for his cartographic and geologic expertise; Rip Heminway for guidance in map production; Sandy Yannone and her tireless team of tutors at the Evergreen Writing Center; Liza Rognas and Randy Stilson for assistance with library and archive usage; Julie Douglass and Penny Hinojosa for invaluable staff support; and Deborah Holmes for her expert computer assistance. Although Ben Shaine is one of the authors of this book, we wish to acknowledge his central importance to the program that produced this book. Besides working as a visiting faculty member for the program in the winter quarter, he volunteered a tremendous amount of his time in the fall and the spring, joining us for practically all field trips and peer-review sessions and working above and beyond the call of duty to help all of the students in the program at any time.

Many notable guests in class were essential, including Anne Kilgannon, Polly Dyer, John Gamon, Steve Herman, Doug Scott, Linda Moon Stumpff, Bonnie Phillips, Martha Henderson Tubesing, David Knibb, Jasmine Minbashian, David Jennings, Ira Spring, Kevin Marsh, and Mitch Friedman.

Those who gave generously of their time to speak with us in their offices included John Leary, Jennifer Eckstrom, Jon Owen, Jill Smith, Michael Closson, Elliot Marks, Maggie Coon, Bob Freimark, Amy Schlachtenhaufen, the researchers at the Center for Landscape Analysis, and Governor Dan Evans. Field trips throughout Washington's wild areas were immeasurably enriched by guides and instructors such as Ken Wilcox, Rick McGuire, Harvey Manning, Bob Wilson, Mark Skatrud, Frank Davis, Dale Swedburg, Georgiana Kautz, Florian Leischner, Ann Marie Finan, Bruce Higgins, John Squires, and Jonathan Guzzo. We wish to also thank Bonnie Phillips for providing us with the opportunity to test our ideas and share our information at the conference she organized, "Models for Protecting National Forests," on May 10, 2003, at The Evergreen State College.

For their hospitality, their photographs and maps, their books and files, their time, their wisdom, and their inspiration, as well as for their expert reviews of drafts—all of which were indispensable to this book—we thank Andy Stahl, Ann Marie Finan, Ben Hayes, Bill Arthur, Bob Dick, Bob Wilson, Bonnie Phillips, Bruce Higgins, Charles Crisafulli, Charlie Raines, Chase Davis, Daniel Evans, David Jennings, Diane Lloyd, Dick Ford, Don Parks, Donna Osseward, Doug Scott, Douglas Deur, Dr. Jack Winjum, Dr. John Osborn, Elliot Marks, Emily Platt, Eric Erler, Florian Leischner, Georgiana Kautz, Harvey Manning, Heather Brinton, Helen Ross-Pitts, Jasmine Minbashian, Jenifer Eckstrom, Jill Smith, Jim DiPeso, Joann Harper, Janet Way, John Gamon, John Leary, Jon Owen, John Perkins, John Spring, Jon and Sally Soest, Justin James, Karen Fant, Ken Wilcox, Kevin Marsh, Lauren Danner, Maggie Coon, Mark Lawler, Mark Skatrud, Martha Henderson Tubesing, Mike Lilga, Mike Petersen, Mitch Friedman, Oscar Soule, Pat Pringle, Patrick Goldsworthy, Patti Happe, Pete Nelson, Peter Frenzen, Peter Morrison, Phillip and Laura Zalesky, Polly Dyer, Rich Steele, Rick Leaumont, Rick McGuire, Roger Anderson, Sharon Parker, Susan Jane Brown, Susan Saul, Thomas M. Power, Tim Coleman, Tim McNulty, and Susan Zwinger. We were honored to have received the assistance of such an illustrious group of individuals and experts.

Finally, we feel blessed to have had the most supportive and enthusiastic publisher and staff imaginable at The Mountaineers Books. It was truly a pleasure and a tremendous education working with Helen Cherullo, Kathleen Cubley, Laura Drury, and many others at the press, along with our remarkable editor, Julie Van Pelt.

CHAPTER 1

Preservation and Regeneration of Wildness at the Close of the Frontier

◆ *Edward Whitesell* ◆

In 1893, one of the most influential of all U.S. historians, Frederick Jackson Turner, established his own place in history with a seminal article on the closing of the American frontier.[1] His essay explored the significance of the Census Bureau's determination that the U.S. frontier ended in 1890. In that year, the census showed that there was no longer a clearly defined line of settlers advancing across the United States, with settlements behind them and "free" land before them for the taking. The frontier was hardly closed, however, in what had officially become Washington State in 1889. Although following no single line of advance, twentieth-century settlement and the accompanying logging, ranching, mining, irrigated agriculture, and hydro-electric dams were all incursions into wild Washington by people, corporations, and government agencies, filling in the vast "empty" spaces left when Native peoples had been forced to relinquish their rightful claims to this land.

It is only at the turn of the present century that Washington is defini-tively saying goodbye to its frontier days and making the transition to a postfrontier way of living with its natural environment. During this difficult transition, while many private enterprises still look for new forests to fell, wetlands to fill, and deserts to flood, increasing numbers of Washington residents are experimenting with ways to live compatibly with the remaining wild places and wildlife.[2] More and more residents are making a commitment to long-term stewardship by protecting their open spaces rather than filling them in with the works of modern society. These citizen conservationists are devoted to salvaging the pieces of their state that remain in a condition approximating what Native peoples enjoyed before the frontier period began. They are working to create a postfrontier way of life in which there is ample space for the wild to flourish. This book was written for those citizen conservationists and for all citizens who wish to become involved in defending what remains of wild Washington at this historic juncture.[3]

CONSERVATION DURING AND AFTER THE FRONTIER

Conservationists work to protect environmental quality and, in so doing, to protect our quality of life.[4] An important goal within that broad conservation agenda has long been to preserve wild places: to guarantee that, at least in some places, native species, ecological processes, and undeveloped landscapes will remain largely unaltered by humans. A growing majority in the United States sees the further erosion of our remaining wildlands as an unacceptable degradation of our natural heritage and a crippling impoverishment of our lives. Furthermore, regardless of what people think about wild places, the fact remains that they are essential to the very survival of many other species who were inhabitants of this land long before any of us.

Most political campaigns advocating areas off-limits to intensive human use warn of impending and possibly irreversible losses should such areas not be set aside. Comparing present and future environmental conditions in this way is important in order to see what we might lose and to consider what kind of world we might be leaving to our children and to all those who come after them. However, our understanding of environmental issues is incomplete unless we also look into the past, to compare the quality of the environment we have inherited with that of our predecessors. If we compare the state of the wild in Washington today with what it was even two generations ago, it is clear that the issue of wildlands protection is best understood not just as a problem of impending loss. Twenty-first-century residents who work for the protection of Washington's wild places also have the tragic distinction of being the first generation of conservationists to live here in the aftermath of the state's extravagant frontier.

Pre-twentieth-century Native peoples and non-Native settlers could not possibly have imagined the magnitude of the changes that would be wrought here between their time and ours. Some of the most powerful creatures of the wild, such as grizzly bears and wolves, have been nearly eradicated from our state. The churning hordes of wild salmon that annually clogged our rivers since time immemorial have been placed on the endangered species list. Only 1 percent of the rolling, fertile hills and native grass-lands of eastern Washington has escaped plows, cows, and invasive, alien grasses, making the Palouse Prairie one of our country's most endangered ecosystems.[5] More than two-thirds of Washington's old-growth forests were cut down within the second half of the twentieth century alone. A mere 30 percent of Puget Sound's coastal marshes is left and intensive urban growth continues to pollute and diminish what remains. As if these statistics were not bad enough, the sizes, shapes, and locations of what is left of wild Washington paint an even bleaker picture. The aggregate acreage of the remaining grasslands, forests, and marshes is actually chopped up and scattered across the landscape in fragments that are often of little use to the species that depend upon them for survival. Anyone who has flown over the state has seen firsthand the patchwork that has been made of our land. Majestic volcanic cones or rocky peaks are scandalously clad in mini-skirts of subalpine forests amidst a landscape of cleared forestland, pastures, and highways. This landscape is our inheritance from the frontier.

It is certainly true that beautiful, biologically and culturally important places are still with us. As a minimum, these must be preserved against the threat of future losses. As compared to the environment of this region only a few generations ago, however, the magnitude of what we have already lost is truly astounding. A clear view of the natural heritage we have been denied leads many citizen conservationists to see the preservation of the fragmented wild places that remain as only a first, essential step. We are also faced with the need for regeneration of major portions of the wild Washington we have lost. This book is a tool for citizens to effectively lead the campaign for the preservation and regeneration of the wild in our times.

For over one hundred years, citizens of Washington State have taken the lead in political struggles to protect wild places. The seeds of these political campaigns, however, were planted during the earliest days of Euro-American settlement in this land. The settler society that created the United States was deeply divided for centuries about the elimination of its wilderness. On the one hand, the dominant ideology of this country extols the transformation of wilderness into farms, ranches, tree plantations, mines, railroads, highways, cities, factories, and shopping centers. This, we have been told, is development, and development is progress. On the other hand, there is a lesser-known history of this settler society and its relationship with the wilderness. In spite of the fact that development-as-progress is often portrayed as the only ideology of this country, several generations of U.S. citizens struggled in their own hearts and with each other over what was the proper way to live amidst vast tracts of wilderness.

Historian Lee Clark Mitchell has found that "issues that we assume are modern—conservation, protection of endangered species, native rights, and questioning the price of progress—actually originated early in the nineteenth century."[6] According to Mitchell's research, the historical record is full of North Americans "of all classes and occupations" who expressed time and again—in diaries, letters, newspaper editorials, and scientific papers—concern that a precious natural heritage was slipping rapidly away.[7] They worried about what would be left to us of the natural landscapes that they knew and loved. The most foresighted of them proposed vast reserves to be set aside for all future generations. In 1832, the famous lawyer and painter George Catlin proposed the establishment of a park to protect the Great Plains from Canada to Mexico, preserving its wild character and securing the freedom of its Native peoples. Other influential, talented individuals such as George Perkins Marsh (1801–82) and John Muir (1838–1914) have become well-known representatives of this part of conservation history. But the point that is missed in nearly all versions of this history is that the views of such prominent citizens were not aberrations in a society otherwise insensitive to the destruction of the wilderness. Such historical figures ultimately became influential precisely because they articulated growing apprehensions and feelings of loss among a sizeable portion of the citizenry.

As early as the 1890s, there was openly expressed public support in Washington State for shielding some parts of the frontier landscape from the increasingly obvious ravages of settlement and natural resource exploitation. In that decade, the mountains that framed intensive development along Puget Sound were identified for preservation. (Olympic National Park was proposed in 1890 and Mount Rainier National Park was established in 1899.) Reminiscent of Catlin's visionary proposal for the Great Plains, the entire Cascade Range was proposed in 1937 as a "super park" that came to be called Ice Peaks, and which would have protected the mountains all the way from the Canadian border to Oregon (see map 6.1).

Unfortunately, the momentum of frontier development in Washington State continued to overpower the forces of conservation. As conservationists became increasingly influential during the twentieth century, they saw all around them the demise of the wilderness that they were fortunate to have known in their childhood. Within the short span of one lifetime in the twentieth century, the mighty Columbia River was dammed from top to bottom and much of the surrounding shrub-steppe ecosystem was plowed over. The major estuaries of Puget Sound were nearly all sacrificed to farms, ports, factories, and cities, and the giant forests of western Washington were chopped into fragments. The warnings of early western settlers had gone unheeded. San Francisco journalist Henry George was right when he wrote in 1871, "our children will look with astonishment at the recklessness with which the public domain has been squandered. It will seem to them that we must have been mad."[8] For those of us alive in Washington at the tail end of 150 years of rapid settlement and exploitation of the land, the preservation of wild Washington has been reduced to picking up the pieces that remain.

Much of what remains wild is with us because it has yet to prove economically profitable as a source of raw materials. However, there are places that have been spared because of the tremendous efforts and sacrifices of citizen conservationists who worked, mostly as volunteers, to protect Washington's wild places for future generations. These conservationists succeeded against tremendous odds to leave us a lasting legacy of some of the most outstanding protected areas in the world. Conservationists who carry on this task today find plenty of work cut out for their generation. For some, this means incrementally expanding the existing National Wilderness Preservation System in Washington in places where previous conservation efforts did not succeed. For others, it means recovering that earlier visionary sense of what is desirable and possible, following the lead of George Catlin. Instead of focusing only on protecting isolated roadless areas on public lands, why not stitch together our fragmented wild areas by preserving them within extensive swaths of habitat set aside through a combination of public protected areas, private easements, land trusts, zoning regulations, and the like? Why not bring our major waterways back to pre-twentieth-century conditions through habitat restoration projects, including the removal of major dams? The modern citizen preservation and regeneration agenda ranges from the modest to the visionary.

While comprehensive visions for large-scale preservation and regeneration of Washington's wildness are nothing new (as the Ice Peaks proposal demonstrates), what is new is a clear consensus of opinion that more of our lands and waters should be preserved.[9] This is obvious in the state of Washington, as evidenced by the ongoing work of its congressional delegation to enact preservation proposals supported by diverse sectors of society. The designation of more wilderness areas, the protection of more old-growth forests, and the restoration of free-flowing rivers from the mountains to the sea will, however, continue to be marked by litigation, civil disobedience, fervent and acrimonious exchanges in the media and at public meetings, and, of course, a great deal of lobbying. Although the majority of citizens support wildlands preservation, for the foreseeable future there will continue to be social contestation over the fundamental questions of where, how much, and by what means this shall be done.

Many are troubled by the continuation of this controversy, feeling that it would be best to quickly settle these questions with some finality, so as to end the acrimony and provide a more stable and predictable climate for commerce and for resource management. It might seem logical to suppose that some negotiated compromise could be reached in which the major issues of land and water usage in the remaining wild areas of the state could be resolved through legislation and land-use planning measures. Logic and rational calculation, however, have proven to be necessary but insufficient tools in an emotional struggle over the lands where we live, work, and play. This is as it should be in a society founded upon a commitment to democratic procedures for choosing between competing moral principles. The wildlands and waterways of our state provide more than natural resources and transportation corridors, more than playgrounds and scenic vistas, more than fish and wildlife habitat to be managed according to scientific and technical prescriptions. We will continue to argue with one another over the future of wildlands and waterways in our state because, in the foreseeable future, we will continue to maintain strongly held differences of opinion about what constitutes a proper relationship between people and this place we call home.

Natural resource specialists and land-use planners can present an array of choices to the citizens of this state but they can never decide for us how many wilderness areas, old-growth forests, intact sagebrush ecosystems, or free-flowing rivers we or our descendents need or how many such places should be preserved for ethical reasons independent of human needs. In the territorial clashes between indigenous tribes of old and in the subsequent clashes between Native Americans and non-Natives, one central component has been the desperate struggle of different groups to maintain ties with the places and activities that are a central part of who they are as a people. Although those who are not Native American have a very different set of claims to the land, they too clash with others over territory and land uses as part of more fundamental struggles over who they are and what kind of world they wish to bequeath to their descendents. That is why wild places in Washington will continue to inspire social struggle so long as there are people here who value wild places—places where the human imprint is held in check by a society wise enough to exercise a measure of self-restraint.

WHY AND HOW THIS BOOK WAS WRITTEN

Defending Wild Washington is intended to contribute to effective resolutions of the continuing struggles over Washington's wildness. It is based upon the premise that wild places are preserved in the United States through effective political action by an informed and dedicated citizenry. We derived this premise from historical observations. Part 2 of this book demonstrates that the protected areas we currently enjoy would not be here now in anything like their present form if it had not been for the tremendous efforts of citizen conservationists, most of whom were self-taught, volunteer activists. As will be explained in our description and analysis of current citizen activism, it can be difficult now for volunteer activists to become engaged and to wield as much influence as their predecessors. This means that either wild areas may have to be protected differently in the future or concerted efforts will have to be made to reverse these trends in order to assure that an inclusive, accessible, and grassroots citizen movement continues to take the lead in protecting Washington's wildness.

There are several reasons why it is more difficult for many citizens to participate in and achieve results in conservation matters today. The number and variety of struggles over wild places in Washington can appear confusing and difficult to engage with for those who are not already deeply immersed in the associated political battles and scientific arguments. Despite the increasingly wide range of conservation agendas today, no single organization offers the public a comprehensive view of objectives and strategies to preserve and restore wild Washington. In the state there are different citizen campaigns for more congressional wilderness designations; administrative protection of all remaining national forest roadless areas; the prohibition of logging in the remaining, public, old-growth forests; the prohibition of all logging and grazing on public lands; and the restoration of many rivers and wetlands by removing dams and dikes. There are scores of nongovernmental, governmental (including tribal), and business organizations advocating, resisting, or attempting to modify these initiatives, and there are disagreements between the advocates themselves over goals and tactics. Although small grassroots groups continue to arise, medium-sized to large conservation organizations have matured into professional institutions with specialized staff members. It is easier to look up their Web pages and respond to action alerts than it is to walk into their offices and be put to work as a volunteer. Among active participants in the movement to protect Washington's wildness, there is increasing concern about imbalances within their ranks along the lines of geographic location, political affiliation, age, class, race, and gender.

Thus, for the public at large, it is increasingly difficult to understand the complexities of the debates and to influence them in ways that rise above the simplistic rhetoric of postcards or e-mail messages to politicians. For an individual citizen who knows and deeply loves a wild place in contention, this is frustrating and alienating. For the collective citizenry, it means less democratic participation in struggles over land use, over our sense of identity as different peoples, and over our moral responsibilities to the natural world and to our descendents. If the premise of this book is true—that wild places are preserved through effective political action by an informed and dedicated citizenry—then obstacles to meaningful citizen participation will both weaken the democratic process and produce land-use policies that neglect public demands for more wildlands protection.

That is what convinced us of the need to write the first comprehensive assessment of citizen preservation and regeneration efforts throughout Washington State. This book aims to increase the ability of contemporary citizen conservationists to be part of the informed and dedicated citizenry that we, the editor and authors of this book, hold to be fundamental to the preservation and regeneration of the wild. To be informed requires information. To be dedicated requires inspiration. This book contains ample quantities of both. It provides an overview of the wild landscapes and ecosystems of this state as they have changed over time, an historical account of how some of it has been set aside, an original examination and analysis of past and current citizen movements for preservation and regeneration of the wild, and an array of reference information to facilitate effective, citizen-led conservation.

One of the distinguishing characteristics of this book is its constructive criticism of the citizen movement for preservation and regeneration of the wild. Much that passes for constructive criticism is actually a philosophical critique of the idea of wilderness preservation, with no practical utility for citizens who need information with which to challenge threats to the places they cherish.[10] Conservation organizations, for their part, have been reticent to publish honest self-criticism. Discussion of past and continuing mistakes happens internally, but even this is not as common and instructive as it should be and, of course, the vast majority of citizen conservationists are excluded from such conversations because conservation organizations must protect their standings in highly competitive political and financial arenas.

Defending Wild Washington was jointly written by college students who dedicated an entire academic year (fall 2002 through spring 2003) to conducting full-time research, analysis, and writing. Their work was of a breadth and depth that would have been a luxury to citizen conservationists, who are constantly staving off threatening policies and developments and advancing their own proposals. These undergraduate students at The Evergreen State College in Olympia, Washington, have different backgrounds and beliefs but they are united in their support for the majority opinion in our country that more wildlands should be preserved. They are also united in their belief that an honest depiction and analysis of the great accomplishments as well as the limitations of the citizen movements for preservation and regeneration is needed now, in what seems to be a time of increasingly complicated preservation politics.

Beginning with discussions of the book outline and proceeding through all the stages of research and writing, this was a collaborative and largely student-led project. Washington State was chosen as the unit of analysis, as opposed to focusing on an ecological or geographical region, with full recognition of the limitations that this entails. Since wildlife and wild processes do not recognize political boundaries, our view of the region is admittedly constrained. Nevertheless, a focus on Washington State has the advantage of providing a more coherent story about citizen activism than could be told by including the rather different histories of activism in British Columbia, Idaho, and Oregon. Readers should recognize, however, that neighboring ecological regions and political activities are important parts of Washington State's history of action for the wild.

Research methods included a review of published and unpublished printed material, including historical archives. Many field trips were taken throughout the state. Original oral history recordings and countless hours of other interviews were carried out with citizen activists. A great deal of research material from this project has been archived in The Evergreen State College library, including maps, documents, research notes, and many hours of video and audio tape recordings with key figures in Washington wildlands campaigns, past and present. Inspirational stories of remarkable accomplishments were gathered and difficult questions about the citizen movements were discussed. Issues addressed included the changes in many conservation organizations toward more professional, more specialized groups less accessible to volunteers and more reliant on large foundations or corporations for funding. Questions also investigated the racial, cultural, gender, age, geographic, and class make-up of conservation organizations' staff and members as well as the diversity of interests served by the organizations' policies. All of the information gathered and the analysis resulting were shared and subjected to continual peer review and revision by all of the students and faculty, working as a team. In the end, we have prepared what we believe to be a useful aid to meaningful citizen engagement in the collective social endeavor to preserve and regenerate the wild.

WHAT FOLLOWS

Defending Wild Washington consists of three parts. The first portrays the physical, biological, and human landscape of the place that became Washington State just a little more than a century ago, showing that on any time scale—geological or historic—this place on Earth has almost always been wild and has always been a dynamic, evolving landscape. Chapter 2 provides a broad outline of the transformations—some subtle, others cataclysmic—experienced by inhabitants of this wilderness for the past 800 million years. Major players in this story have included members of our own species during the most recent tens of thousands of years, according to archaeologists. The first peoples not only experienced but also contributed to changes in some aspects of the

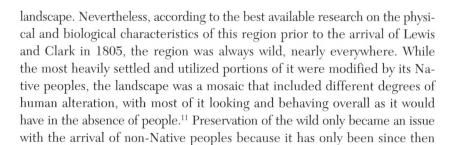

landscape. Nevertheless, according to the best available research on the physical and biological characteristics of this region prior to the arrival of Lewis and Clark in 1805, the region was always wild, nearly everywhere. While the most heavily settled and utilized portions of it were modified by its Native peoples, the landscape was a mosaic that included different degrees of human alteration, with most of it looking and behaving overall as it would have in the absence of people.[11] Preservation of the wild only became an issue with the arrival of non-Native peoples because it has only been since then that the landscape has been so radically altered that some residents have felt compelled to take corrective measures by setting aside nature reserves.

When non-Native peoples and the foreign socioeconomic system that they imported started making their marks on the landscape, a strategy of containment emerged, which we know as protected areas (for example, national parks and wilderness areas). If the landscape of Washington had always been a mosaic before this, now that mosaic was being disassembled, its component pieces torn apart and scattered, many of them lost forever. Chapter 3 describes what the modern conservation movement in Washington has achieved so far through the erection of legal and administrative walls around special parts of the former mosaic in order to defend these areas from bulldozers, chainsaws, and dynamite. The chapter briefly displays and explains the systems of protected areas that currently exist and, using the tools of conservation biology, it assesses the adequacy and viability of such protected spots within the contemporary, fragmented landscape.

Chapter 4 completes the portrayal of the landscape in broader terms, describing and assessing the social and political landscape as it pertains to the demands and opportunities for preservation and regeneration of the wild. Major, ongoing changes in regional, national, and global economies, the growth and diversification of Washington's population, and important shifts in patterns of civic participation are all vital to the success or failure of citizen conservation efforts. Among the changes is a shift from an economy based primarily upon resource extraction to one in which significant economic value is attached to open spaces and a healthy, attractive natural environment. Important population patterns include both the rapid growth of the Puget Lowlands region and the ethnic and racial diversification of the state. Among many other implications, such demographic changes challenge conservationists to secure preservation and to foster regeneration of wildness by focusing more on issues of transportation and urban sprawl and by making serious efforts to diversify membership as well as leadership. An examination of shifts in civic participation throughout U.S. society summarizes what is known about trends in volunteerism and about the number of young people who are seriously engaged in public affairs. Chapter 4 shows that familiarity with this human landscape is just as vital for navigating the uncertain terrain of conservation politics as is knowledge of the physical landscape.

Civic participation is what most of this book is about. The protected areas described in chapter 3 received their protection largely because of the citizen action recounted in part 2. Chapter 5 introduces this part of the book by presenting conceptual tools for understanding and evaluating different approaches to working collectively for a better world. Chapters 6 through 9 recount the history of citizen action for wild Washington within the twentieth century and the first years of the present century. As a rule, the history of citizens and nonprofit organizations is poorly recorded. Many of the people and organizations that safeguarded wild Washington remain anonymous. They did not struggle and sacrifice for years in order to gain personal fame but did so because they could not sit by and permit the destruction of the places that they knew and loved. Their stories deserve to be told not only to give them the recognition they deserve but also because these stories are our history as citizen conservationists. Ignorance of history condemns the present generation to repeat past mistakes and deprives us of important lessons. It also inhibits the construction of a powerful movement, inspired and informed by all that has gone before. Volunteer organizations have notoriously limited institutional memories and so do many of the modern, professional conservation groups. Part 2 addresses this serious shortcoming.

Chapters 6 through 9 proceed in chronological order, beginning in chapter 6 with a history of Washington's organized wilderness-preservation campaigns from the latter part of the nineteenth century into the 1970s. Chapter 8 continues the story of organized citizen work to protect Washington's wildness, showing how the movement considerably expanded its goals and strategies beyond the traditional emphasis on congressional designation of parks and wilderness areas. Chapters 7 and 9 add a more personal dimension to this history by relating the voices of some of the principal individuals in the movement, drawing from extensive, original oral-history research conducted by the authors of these chapters. What makes years of self-sacrifice worth the effort for citizen conservationists is not only the policy changes they ultimately obtain but also the thrill, camaraderie, and personal enrichment gained along the way through working alongside remarkable and inspiring individuals. Their stories and their personalities come across best in their own voices, which are found not only in these two chapters but also sprinkled throughout much of the rest of parts 2 and 3.

Chapter 10 concludes part 2 with a summary assessment of the citizen movement for Washington's wild places. This chapter argues that accomplishments of lasting value have been achieved by persons of modest means and often with no special past experience. The inspiration that this provides can motivate and inform other citizens who follow their lead. Another crucial dimension of this chapter is its discussion of the strengths and weaknesses of the conservation movement and its recommendations for future improvements. The chapter authors examine the ways in which the movement's organizations have evolved in size, structure, and dynamics; how these groups have or have not worked together; problems of membership composition, distribution, and inclusion in decision making; the effects of varying funding and publicity strategies; and the uses of science in the formation and pursuit of goals and strategies.

Part 3 returns to a portrayal of Washington's landscapes, describing specific conservation visions, plans, and actions for the wild in the state as a whole and for its major regions. Doing so, it draws together the information and analyses of parts 1 and 2, showing how citizen conservationists operate within the geographical, historical, environmental, social, and political contexts in which they find themselves. Chapter 11 provides an initial overview of conservationists' future visions and current approaches, ranging from localized protected-area campaigns around the state to regional efforts to establish coordinated land-use designations and policies for the preservation and regeneration of the wild. The remainder of part 3 provides statewide examples of some of the important work that is being done by citizen conservationists to implement such ideas. We hope that this sampling of conservation efforts proves useful to citizens confronting comparable challenges in other places.

Chapter 12 describes lesser-known and innovative efforts underway in the Cascades, the Coast Range, and the Olympics that supplement western Washington's national parks and wilderness areas. These include regeneration and recovery at Mount St. Helens, the use of private funding to save critical habitat in the Cascades and the Coast Range, and species reintroduction and dam removal in the Olympics. The chapter shows that wildness in the western mountains requires preservation through a variety of protective designations along with regeneration through measures allowing the return of native fish, wildlife, and natural ecological processes.

Chapter 13 shows that wildness has still not been eliminated even from the most heavily populated region of Washington State. The Puget Lowlands, which once harbored perhaps the richest environment of the state, is now plagued with Superfund sites and other areas that are seriously contaminated with toxic waste. It is polluted by landfills, noxious surface runoff from streets and farms, plus ubiquitous air pollution. It has been extensively paved and is constantly driven over by millions of people, day in and day out. And yet, one can still watch a few wild salmon spawn in some of its waterways. One can still see the occasional bald eagle or great blue heron flying over its industrial landscapes. One can even dive down into the salty wilderness of the Sound and find a wealth of wild marine life.

The Puget Lowlands is where most Washington wilderness activists live, but the vast majority of Washington wilderness campaigns have been focused on the highlands of western Washington. This is understandable, if only because these mountainous areas compose most of the federal lands that are eligible for wilderness designation. Nevertheless, it is somewhat surprising that relatively little attention has been paid to the remnant wildness of the Puget Lowlands. This region harbors ecologically unique pieces of the state that, within the memory of some conservation movement elders, included a great deal of biologically productive, lowland wilderness. Chapter 13 shares the encouraging news that, in parts of the Puget Lowlands, Native peoples, government agencies, land trusts, and conservation organizations are working together for the preservation and regeneration of wildness in some of the region's estuaries, unoccupied urban spaces, rural areas, and marine environments.

The final regional chapter examines the Columbia Basin and the eastern mountain ranges of the Rocky Mountains (in the northeast) and the Blue Mountains (in the southeast). As in the Puget Lowlands, settlers heavily impacted this once-wild landscape. Yet, as chapter 14 shows, creative and persistent citizen campaigns have protected part of what remains wild and promise to protect even more in the foreseeable future. The cases discussed in this chapter will describe a mixture of approaches to wildlands protection, including national monument and wilderness designations. This chapter recommends increased grassroots organizing and emphasis among citizen groups on protecting and restoring a variety of ecosystems that are more endangered than many of the more celebrated ecosystems in the western half of the state.

The concluding chapter summarizes the inspiring legacy of citizen conservation action in Washington State and the work remaining. Drawing on the lessons learned from the preceding chapters, it suggests a path toward a reconstituted social and natural environment in which people and wildness might coexist in broad regions of the state. Finally, it serves as a call to this and future generations to never forget that a dedicated and informed citizenry is the best guardian of Washington's wildness.

PART I

THE GEOGRAPHY OF WASHINGTON'S WILDNESS

CHAPTER 2

A History of Washington's
Landscape Transformations

◆ *Molly Arrandale, Travis Keron, and Raelynn Rinehart* ◆

Washington is a mosaic of contrasting landscapes, with an array of greens, grays, browns, and blues characterizing the region's distinct features. Swaths of evergreen forests color nearly half of the state, while muted shrubbery and grassland lighten the palette. Towering mountains, rugged valleys, chiseled canyons, broad plains, rolling hills, and windswept plateaus all add depth and texture to Washington's canvas. Rivers and roads transect the state, connecting distant sections while simultaneously creating new ones, and human settlements range from small to massive.

Even in such a simple portrayal, the complexity of Washington's landscapes is apparent. The colors and textures seen today are the mark of dynamic and intricate systems of life interacting at every level, and many forces influence this constantly changing mosaic. Geologic and climatic events have been the primary architects of its basic form, crafting mountains, plateaus, valleys, waterways, and more. The influx and retreat of species has brought a diverse and varying array of inhabitants, each of which contributes to the landscape's characteristics. Of Washington's vast floral and faunal assembly, humans are but one member. However, humans have dramatically increased the rate and degree of landscape alteration within the last 150 years of their approximately 15,000-year occupation. The intensified transformation of the land has created new contrasts within Washington. Areas exist that humans have

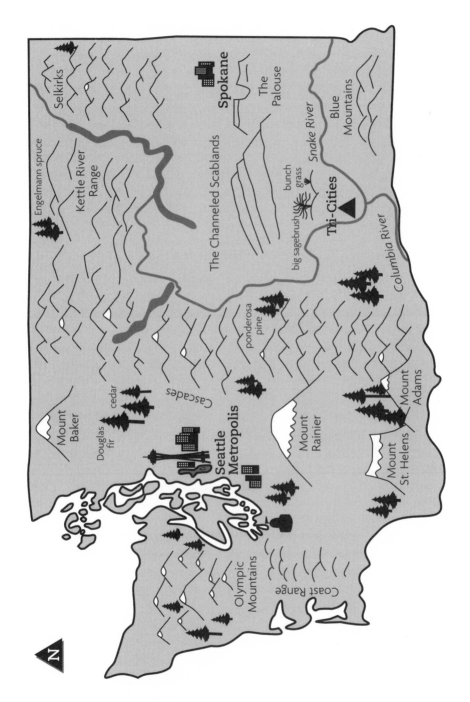

Map 2.1. *Diversity within the state's borders. From the windswept Columbia Plateau to the temperate rainforests of the Olympics, the state encompasses an amazing array of landscapes.* (Based on drawings by Anthony Bush)

significantly altered while others are relatively untouched, and the distinction between these contrasts has fueled an ongoing debate over what is "wild."

Behind the contrasting landscapes, there is a story to be told encompassing the history of how Washington came into its present state and the series of events that created those contrasts. Its present landscapes are not static; rather, various forces continually shape the terrain. Examining these forces chronologically provides a greater understanding of these landscapes and serves to compare human induced change in the last 150 years to the processes of the past. The complexity of Washington's wild character and the extent of human alteration to that character have fueled citizen action to protect the state's remnant wild places.

PRESENT-DAY WASHINGTON

An aerial view of Washington today highlights the state's multifaceted nature. From its eastern border with Idaho to the Pacific Ocean at its western edge, the state is an assortment of colors and textures influenced by topography and climate. Shielded from the moist Pacific air by the Cascade mountains, Washington's eastern half exists as an arid to semi-arid environment. Average annual precipitation ranges from 10 to 30 inches per year. Temperatures vary wildly, averaging between 80 and 90 degrees Fahrenheit during the day and plunging to 50 degrees at night in the summer. Winter can be brutally cold, with an overall average temperature of 20 to 30 degrees Fahrenheit and extremes dipping to minus 30 degrees.

In the southeastern corner of the state are the forested slopes of the Blue Mountains. A sliver of this range reaches into Washington from Oregon. Adapted to the dry conditions, the Blues' coniferous forests are a patchwork of thick tracts of Douglas fir, lodgepole pine, and true fir intermixed with stands of ponderosa pine with open, grassy understories. Formerly extensive, the open stands of ponderosa have been impacted by fire suppression and livestock grazing, resulting in dense fir forests.

Wrapped around the Blues are the Palouse Hills, a belt of deep, fertile soils that once harbored extensive swaths of native grasses. Now, wheat, lentils, and peas thrive in the dry, sunny days and cooler summer nights. Ninety-nine percent of the region has been converted to agricultural land. Millions of acres of dryland crops carpet the flat-to-rolling terrain, interspersed with small agricultural communities. Roads plait the Palouse, following its gentle curves and drawing connections between its populated areas. Interwoven with this seasonally brown-to-gold tapestry are threads of the soft green grasslands that once mantled its hills. Few large patches of native grasses remain and residual pieces are widely scattered.

An eastern view of the Blue Mountains in Washington's southeastern corner
(Photo by Raelynn Rinehart)

To the north, the city of Spokane rests on the border between the Palouse and the Okanogan Highlands. Washington's third-largest city, home to almost 200,000 people, is the major urban center of the lumber, mining, and farming area of eastern Washington, northern Idaho, and western Montana. The buildings and concrete of the city blend into the moderate slopes and rounded summits of the Okanogan Highlands to the north. Composed of the Kettle River Range and Selkirk Mountains, the Highlands lie in green folds across the upper corner of the state. Like the Blues to the south, a myriad of green hues cloak these slopes. Logging has left brown patches stripped of trees and dense, dark stands unchecked by fire.

The heart of eastern Washington is the Columbia Plateau. Underlying the Palouse, this basin spreads westward, bounded by the Okanogan Highlands to the north. Much of the Plateau is a scarred, erosional landscape, known as the Channeled Scablands. It is scored with ragged ridges and linear buttes broken by canyons and canals. On its surface, occasional glimpses of a soft gray-green are testament to the region's history. Shrub-steppe, an association of sagebrush and bunchgrasses that once covered the Plateau, survives only in small, remnant patches. A few larger sections still exist, but grazing and invasive grasses threaten the integrity of the entire ecosystem.

Hikers traverse the Kettle Crest Trail in the Kettle River Range in the Okanogan Highlands. (Photo by Tim Coleman; reprinted by permission)

The subdued colors of the shrub-steppe are all but lost in a sea of agricultural hues. Fields of potatoes, hay, asparagus, spearmint, and peas, as well as apple orchards and vineyards, bring a burst of bright green to the region seasonally. A network of roads stretches across the countryside, forming a grid of cultivated fields and agricultural communities. At the western edge of the Plateau, the green intensifies. A thick band of farmland follows the curve of the Columbia River, stretching as far from its banks as irrigation canals will reach. The Tri-Cities of Pasco, Kennewick, and Richland make up the major urban center of the area, harboring over 110,000 people at the juncture between the Columbia, Yakima, and Snake Rivers.

Over its 1,214-mile course, the Columbia River is sluggish—broken and fattened by a series of dams. It seeps through the Okanogan Highlands from Canada before curving around the western edge of the Plateau. In the south, it leaves its semicircular track and doubles back on itself, heading west along the southern border of Washington. Along this path, it meets the Cascades, a mountain range extending from Oregon into Canada. From where the Columbia crosses them, the Cascades of Washington stretch northward as a wall of forested slopes and snowcapped volcanic peaks, splitting the state lengthwise. Rising from the Columbia Plateau, the forests of the Cascades progress from ponderosa pine in the eastern valleys and lowlands through lodgepole pine, Douglas fir, and finally subalpine fir and Engelmann spruce in the higher elevations. As in the Blues, Kettles, and Selkirks, logging has brought a collage of brown and green hues to the Cascades' eastern slopes.

A relatively intact parcel of the shrub-steppe ecosystem of the Columbia Plateau exists on the Hanford Nuclear Site. (Photo by Lin Skavdahl)

The 1,214-mile Columbia River winds its way from Canada south across eastern Washington before crossing the Cascades to the Pacific Ocean. The Hanford Reach is the river's only remaining free-flowing section in the United States. (Photo by Lin Skavdahl)

The Cascade mountains are home to snow-covered peaks and evergreen forests, as here near South Chinook Pass. (Photo by Lin Skavdahl)

As the Columbia River flows west through the Cascade Range, it enters a world dominated by evergreens. The Cascades trap moist marine air moving inland from the coast. As the air moves up to cross the mountains, cooling causes it to drop its moisture as rain or snow, resulting in a mild and moist climate. Temperatures rarely fall below 30 degrees Fahrenheit in winter and rarely exceed 90 degrees in the summer, while annual precipitation in the Puget Lowlands and western Cascade foothills ranges from 30 to 80 inches. These moist and mild conditions created the dense, vast, and towering forests that led to Washington's designation as the Evergreen State. A variation of the North American boreal forests, they provide the base coloration for the western portion of the mosaic, but they are far from uniform; the forests are a patchwork of various shapes and shades, from the dark greens of older stands to the lighter greens and browns of those stands most newly disturbed.

The western border of the state is 150 miles of coastline along the Pacific Ocean. Along the southern shores are gently rolling sand dunes and mixed shore grasses, which form a narrow, sandy border at the edge of the trees. Salt marshes and estuaries, painted with waterfowl, native rushes, and invasive species, dot the coastline. Moving north into the Olympic Peninsula, the sandy border narrows gradually as the undulating dunes rise to rocky headlands topped with trees gnarled by high coastal winds. The thin border continues east, forming the northern edge of the Olympic Peninsula, where the land meets the blue-gray of the Strait of Juan de Fuca.

Cape Flattery, where the northwestern tip of the Olympic Peninsula meets the Pacific Ocean, exemplifies Washington's rocky northern coast. (Photo by Vantage Point Photography; source, Washington State Department of Ecology)

Much of the Peninsula's forest is heavily colored with large patches of brown and light green, often denoting recently logged or planted monocultures. Toward the center of the Peninsula, an island of dark green forests emerges, showing the boundary between the national forest and national park. Traveling up the flanks of the Olympic Mountains, the green forests give way to a splash of white and gray as the mountains rise into a crescent of rugged snow-capped peaks. Like the Cascades, the Olympics retain much of the moisture carried by ocean winds to the western slopes, and as the first range encountered by such moisture-laden air, the western slopes of the Olympics constitute the wettest environment in the state: precipitation as rain and snow can exceed 125–200 inches in the western foothills and interior of the Olympics, resulting in unique temperate rain forests and glaciers at low elevations. By way of contrast, the eastern portion of the peninsula is within the Olympic rain shadow and receives as little as 15 inches of rain annually. The extreme of this effect is represented by a golden plain on the northeastern tip of the Peninsula amid the surrounding forest.

The Olympic Mountains from Six Ridge Pass in southeastern Olympic National Park (Photo by Darin Heinemann; reprinted by permission)

Immediately east of this golden plain begins the bluish-gray streak known as Puget Sound. It flows south, reaching into the forest with fingerlike inlets, including the hook-shaped Hood Canal, which forms the eastern border of the Olympic Peninsula. At its southernmost point, where it cuts nearly halfway through the length of the state, the Sound sweeps back on itself. Now heading north to the Canadian border, the eastern shores of Puget Sound border the Puget Lowlands.

Composed of islands, river valleys, prairies, and rolling hills, the Puget Lowlands are a dramatic contrast to the rest of western Washington. Instead of legions of evergreen trees, much of the scene is dominated by Washington's metropolis, a labyrinth of streets, buildings, markets, parks, and nearly one-half of the Pacific Northwest's total population. This web expands to the foothills of the Cascades and to the peninsulas and islands in Puget Sound, with the major arterial being the Interstate 5 corridor that runs the length of western Washington connecting the major cities of Olympia, Tacoma, Seattle, Everett, and Bellingham, near the Canadian border. Moving farther from the metropolis, urban development loses prominence as it intermingles with forests, prairies, rivers, and agricultural lands.

Washington's present appearance represents only a snapshot of its existence. For millions of years it has been changing from one landscape to another. In fact, nearly 800 million years ago, the lands that compose Washington today did not even exist.

AN OCEAN IN RETREAT

Standing in present-day Spokane, oceans are not likely to be on one's mind. The nearest is the Pacific, some 320 miles to the west. Puget Sound, the next best thing, is only slightly closer. Towering mountain ranges and broad expanses of rough, arid terrain separate both from the inland city. Nonetheless, 800 to 700 million years ago, an ocean lapped at Spokane's shores, brought by forces almost as unimaginable as the sight itself.

The ground that presently separates Spokane from the Pacific is ostensibly seamless in its basic form; plateaus sweep gracefully into surrounding mountain ranges, which in turn meld with adjacent lowlands. In reality, Washington's expanse is a hodgepodge of rock assemblages, brought together by the movements of the earth's crust over millions of years. This concept works from the geologic theory of plate tectonics, which holds that the earth's crust is broken into massive slabs of rock. Known as plates, the size and position of these slabs change over time as they move across the earth's surface and interact with one another. Interpretations about details of the state's formation are not agreed upon by all and may give way to different tectonic models as new evidence surfaces. What follows is one account of events that laid the foundations of Washington.[1]

The event that made the area of present-day Spokane a seashore was the breaking apart of a supercontinent. Eight to seven hundred million years ago, when life was still made up of simple organisms, a rift appeared in a giant conglomeration of continents. As a single mass, what later became North America, Europe, and Asia split off as the eastern half. What would become Washington spent the next 600 million years as a small outcrop on the ragged western edge of this new continent. By the time this tectonic fragment would see additions to its landmass, single-celled organisms had evolved into dinosaurs.

Half a world away from the narrow strip that would become part of Washington, another ocean began to play a part in creating the land seen today. At the start of the Jurassic period, 205 million years ago, the Atlantic Ocean began to open, a process that continues to this day. Along a ridge that runs down the center of the ocean, the North American and Eurasian Plates began to separate. Basalt lava welled up into the opening between them, creating new oceanic crust as it hardened. As the Atlantic grew in the east, the Pacific Ocean began to lose ground along the western edge of the North American continent. The denser oceanic crust underlying the Pacific began sliding beneath the more buoyant crust of the advancing continent in a process known as subduction.

Several inches of oceanic crust were disappearing beneath the North American Plate each year during subduction. Along the western coast, the broad coastal plain of sedimentary rock that had accumulated over the past 600 million years was too buoyant to follow suit. Instead, it crumpled against the advancing North American Plate, forming the Kootenay Arc. A belt of these furrowed and folded rocks extends today from north of Spokane into British Columbia. The force of the colliding plates also stressed the crust of the continent, causing it to fracture and stack upon itself. This thickening of the crust was the first step in the formation of the Rocky Mountains, a process that continued for the next 100 million years.

The rising Rockies jutted into what is now northeastern Washington, forming the base for the present-day Selkirk range. Their summits likely reached 20,000 feet, towering above the flat inland landscape to the east. West of the mountains, the folds of the Kootenay Arc met the Pacific Ocean in present-day Stevens and Ferry Counties. It is unknown whether forests cloaked the rough terrain and towering slopes. However, one could imagine the immense peaks catching moisture from air coming off the ocean and fostering a seaward swath of thick vegetation much as the Cascades do today.

BETWEEN A ROCK AND A HARD PLACE

Off the west coast of the Kootenay Arc, islands dotted the horizon. Slowly but surely, the ocean between these scraps of continental crust and the advancing North American Plate was shrinking. Riding in on the sinking plate, a series of these terranes (an assemblage of rocks that share a more or less common history) collided with the West Coast. One by one, they fused with the continent, adding to its landmass. Multiple terranes docked in the Northwest, laying the foundation for much of what would become Washington.

The first to arrive were the Intermountain Terranes, slamming into the Kootenay Arc only 30 million years after the spreading Atlantic Ocean first started to push North America to the west. In what would become Washington, these newly arrived rocks stretched from the Kootenay Arc west across the Okanogan Highlands to the Methow Basin and reached from far northern British Columbia south to the edge of the Columbia Plateau. Seventy-five million years later, during the Cretaceous period, the North Cascades Terrane joined the western edge of the Intermountain Terranes, laying the base for the Cascades north of Snoqualmie Pass, as well as depositing a chain of fragments that would become the San Juan Islands. As the North Cascades Terrane joined with the northern landmass, subduction farther south brought the Blue Mountain volcanic archipelago to what would become northeastern Oregon. Ushered in by the Pacific Plate's swift descent beneath North America, these islands successively coupled with the continent to form the foundation of the Blue Mountains that jut into present-day southeastern Washington.

Aside from rafting in microcontinents to the growing coast, the interaction between the shifting plates altered the region's topography. The diving plate took the ocean floor miles beneath the earth's surface, subjecting it to such heat and pressure that the saturated oceanic crust released its water. This decreased the melting point of minerals in the earth's mantle, producing a partial melt of these rocks. The resulting magma swelled into the Rocky Mountains above, weakening them and causing them to fracture into gigantic slabs. Enormous blocks of granite slid tens of miles to the east, exposing older rocks beneath. The deep rocks laid bare by this colossal landslide would become the Selkirk Mountains.

Nearing the end of the Cretaceous period, what would become Washington had seen additions and alterations caused by the steady subduction of the oceanic plate beneath North America. Around 80 million years ago, it appears that the northern part of the plate underlying the Pacific broke loose and began a more rapid, northbound dive. The aberrant plate ground against the westbound edge of North America as the plate vanished beneath the continent's mass. The slab's grating descent produced significant tensional forces that contributed to the rise of the Okanogan and Kettle Domes in what would become northeastern Washington, as older rocks beneath the crust of the Okanogan Highlands pushed younger layers to either side and surfaced. To the south, the Blue Mountains rotated clockwise, pushed almost 90 degrees off center. Throughout the region, the shearing motion of the subducting plate fractured the earth's crust in a series of faults that allowed rocks on either side to move against one another along a north–south axis.

These same forces tore the ocean floor, creating rifts where outpourings of lava formed a chain of undersea volcanoes. Their peaks broke the surface of the Pacific in a string of low islands. In the Eocene epoch, 55 to 35 million years ago, the sinking oceanic plate ushered these submerged volcanoes in to what are now Washington and Oregon, where the volcanoes fused with the continent while they were still mainly underwater and became the foundation of the Coast Range and the Olympic Mountains. Along a coastline that curved from what is now Coos Bay to the future Puget Lowlands, these mountains remained hidden beneath the waves for another 25 million years.

Forty million years ago, subduction of the oceanic plate began again and magma rose through the North American Plate to give birth to a new chain of volcanoes known as the Early Cascades. Rising in a line south of the North Cascades Terrane, the new peaks overlooked a broad swampy plain that stretched west over the submerged Coast Range. Basins developed as sections of crust dropped down along faults, and these depressions filled with lakes and swamps. Streams and rivers dissected the landscape, running west into wide deltas in the shallow sea. Heronlike birds stalked the wetlands amidst broadleaf oak, palm, figs, palmetto, and swamp cypress. Offshore, whales and sharks cruised the waters of an ocean in retreat.

As it rose steadily out of the waves, the Coast Range displaced the ocean to the west and the sinking oceanic plate shoved slabs of continental crust beneath the incipient range. The more buoyant continental material floated the oceanic crust above sea level, a process that spanned at least 20 million years. To the east, the uplift of the range produced a tilting effect, depressing the lowlands of Puget Sound and the Willamette Valley. Toward the end of the Coast Range's uplift, continental sediments brought in by the subducting plate forged the Olympic Mountains at the northern tip of the present-day Olympic Peninsula. Perhaps due to sheer mass, the sedimentary rocks and basalts that make up the imposing range refused to be subducted. Instead, the North American continent scraped them from the ocean plate as it sank.

To the east, the Early Cascades continued to spew lava and ash. These peaks dominated the skyline until about 17 million years ago, when they apparently experienced a sharp decrease in output.[2] According to some, an interruption at their source caused their sudden decline. It is theorized that the subducting ocean slab broke as it descended, sending the lower half into the depths of the earth at a faster rate than the upper piece. Rock from the mantle welled into the gap between them, cutting off the stream and heat driving the volcanic chain.[3]

 HOT SPOT

As lava and ash from the Early Cascades declined, eruptions of a different sort were inundating the heart of the state with basalt. From cracks that penetrated the earth's crust, lava poured out across parts of the area now composed of Washington, Oregon, and Idaho in a series of massive flows beginning roughly 17 million years ago. More than three hundred separate flows have been documented, varying in volume and extent. Largest by far were the Grande Ronde basalt flows, accounting for nearly 90 percent of the total volume of flows. At its maximum, the Grande Ronde released enough lava in one second to cover twenty-four football fields with an inch of basalt.[4]

Spreading out across what is now south central Washington, the basalt filled the natural depression of the Columbia Plateau. Under the weight of the massive Grande Ronde flows, the plateau sank, forming a basin that subsequent flows filled with basalt. At the same time as these eruptions, the uplift of mountains in Idaho gently lifted the inland edge of the inundated plateau. Following the incline of the tilted terrain, the lavas flowed farther west and north. They reached the Pacific Ocean by following the course of the ancestral Columbia River through the Cascades. As the basalt covering the plateau cooled, it pushed the Columbia to its modern channel, well to the north of its ancestral path.

The floods of basalt were not continuous, and thousands of years passed between eruptions. During these intervals, eroded soil built up around bodies of water that formed where the lavas dammed streams and rivers. The climate was warm and rainy with mild winters, and forests and grasslands developed. On gentle slopes, mixed forests of spruce, fir, oak, maple, and beech were host to deer, bear, and strange, piglike animals called oredons. Camels, miniature three-toed horses, and mastodons grazed in the grassy meadows. Near the water, giant beavers downed willows and bald cypress, while diminutive aquatic rhinoceros swam amongst cattails and sedges.

The moist, warm climate experienced during the 2 million years of basalt flows was most likely a direct result of the flows themselves. Prior to their eruption, the area had experienced a dry climate east of the rising Cascades. Much as the modern Cascades do today, the volcanoes would have blocked moist air coming in from the Pacific. However, flows of lava as extensive as those in what would become southeastern Washington could have emitted enough carbon dioxide and methane to produce a greenhouse effect. Further, hot air rising off a sea of molten basalt would create an intense low-pressure area strong enough to pull moist air past the mountain barrier. Together, these two effects could have resulted in the heat and humidity that fostered the period's mix of strange and familiar species.

As the basalt flows dried up, so too did the heavy rainfall. Locally, a new chain of volcanoes was rising, fortifying the barrier to wet ocean air. These were the Modern Cascades, surfacing parallel to their predecessors, the Early Cascades. The broken plate beneath the Pacific was again fueling an active chain of volcanoes. From this chain emerged the Cascade peaks of present-day Washington: Glacier Peak and Mounts Baker, Rainier, St. Helens, and Adams. They tower above the remains of the Early Cascades, whose peaks dropped down along faults as the rocks beneath them cooled.

Although the Cascades had begun their lifelong western detainment of moisture, larger forces of dehydration were at work. Worldwide, the climate

The Cascade Range splits Washington down the middle with its volcanic peaks and crests. Here, Mount Rainier dominates the foreground, with her sisters Mount Adams (left) and Mount St. Helens (right, prior to the 1980 eruption) standing to either side. (Source: Washington State Department of Transportation)

was again becoming drier. In what would become Washington, modern-looking mammals such as raccoons, badgers, and coyotes appeared, inter-mingling with ancestral horses and camels. The swampy setting gave way to deciduous hardwoods and then to a semi-arid white oak forest. As plant cover declined, the infrequent rains could have induced flash floods. Streams were inconsistent and unconnected, unable to carry sediment to the ocean. They left broad deposits of gravel across valleys and lowlands. The mighty Columbia River, however, was still flowing. Had it dried up in these arid times, the climbing Cascades would have blocked its way to the sea. The river persevered, carving its way through the mountains as they rose.

 **ADVANCING ICE**

As the earth's climate became more arid, it also grew colder. When rainfall finally picked up again, around 2 million years ago, the temperatures stayed low. In the wetter and cooler environment, winter snowfall began to exceed summer snowmelt. Mountain peaks began to harbor huge sheets of ice that grew thicker with each passing year. As the sheets increased in size, they began to move, crossing the boundary from perennial ice patch to glacier. Moving into surrounding valleys and lowlands, the glaciers buried existing landscapes in ice. The land would remain obscured for thousands of years until the climate experienced a warming trend. Then the glaciers would retreat to the mountaintops, waiting for the temperatures to drop again.[5]

This was the start of the Pleistocene epoch, in which the earth experienced a series of ice ages. Glaciers advanced as many as twenty times, covering major portions of the earth in ice. With so much water frozen in glaciers, global sea levels dropped by several hundred feet, at times revealing land bridges between continents. Several times during the Pleistocene, the Bering Land Bridge surfaced and provided a migratory pathway between eastern Asia and Alaska. Along this corridor, species such as mammoths, bison, jaguars, and musk oxen moved into North America. Humans were also among the colonizers, although whether or not they followed the route of other immigrants is uncertain. Small groups of nomadic hunters could have followed game across the land bridge into present-day Alaska. Another theory of migration that is gaining popularity is that groups of people traveled by watercraft along the coast, assuming the coast was free of glaciers. The land bridge is thought to have been accessible periodically beginning 70,000 years ago, with the final exposure of the land bridge between approximately 14,000 and 10,000 years ago. Humans could have crossed into North America during any of these periods, with successive generations migrating south through ice-free corridors along the coastline, inland, or both, reaching the present-day lower United States and inhabiting every region of North America by 12,000 years before present.[6]

Tribes of the region also have stories explaining how humans came to be in their respective regions of the state and how the landscape was shaped. Many of these accounts feature a Creator, Changer, or Transformer, and the First Peoples, including Coyote, Raven, and others. These characters lived in this world in a different time, when animals, humans, and spirits were not separate. These beings prepared the land for the Human peoples by shaping it and leaving gifts in the form of food sources, and at one point the Creator turned them all into the forms recognizable today as ravens, coyotes, mountains, humans, and so on. These stories have been passed down orally through generations.[7]

"Elders relate that the world was not created; it always existed. However, at the Time of Beginnings, a Changer known as K'wati went around transforming features of the landscape and living things into the forms they have today. This Changer was short and bald and could conceal his identity so he would not be recognized. He had the power and imagination to make the world as wondrous as it is. K'wati made the rivers of the Olympics and the features of the coastline while he was being chased around by wolves. Carrying only a container of sea mammal oil and a comb, K'wati tried to slow down and elude the wolves by dumping oil here and there, which flowed downhill and turned into the rivers. He also used his comb to make great divots in the beach sand, which grew into headlands, so that the wolves had to swim around them, which allowed the Changer to escape. Later K'wati came back and near the mouth of the Quillayute River changed the wolves into the ancestors of the Quileute. So the Quileute have lived here since the Time of Beginnings."

From Chris Morganroth III, "Quileute," in *Native Peoples of the Olympic Peninsula: Who We Are*, ed. Jacilee Wray, 136 (Norman: University of Oklahoma Press, 2002); reprinted by permission of the University of Oklahoma Press.

The most recent glacial advance reached its maximum around 15,000 years ago, when a third of North America was under ice. Centered over Hudson Bay, the Laurentide Ice Sheet made up the majority of glacial ice on the continent, but it was the smaller Cordilleran Ice Sheet that covered the Northwest. From as far north as Alaska, it extended into what are now northern Washington, Idaho, and western Montana. In what would become Washington, ice filled the present-day Strait of Juan de Fuca, then wrapped around the Olympics to fill what would become Puget Sound. Seattle would have been buried beneath nearly 3,000 feet of ice, Olympia beneath 1,000 feet. From the Sound, the ice receded northward, dodging all but the northernmost section of the Cascades before pressing south again to flood the Okanogan Highlands. Here, the ice reached some 85 miles into the state, stopping 30 miles northeast of present-day Wenatchee (see map 2.2 on page 39).

 ## GOODBYE ICE, HELLO FLOODS

Ice coverage began to decline after reaching its maximum extent and had shrunk nearly to present levels by 10,000 years ago. Humans were definitely in what is now Washington during the period of glacial retreat. A mastodon

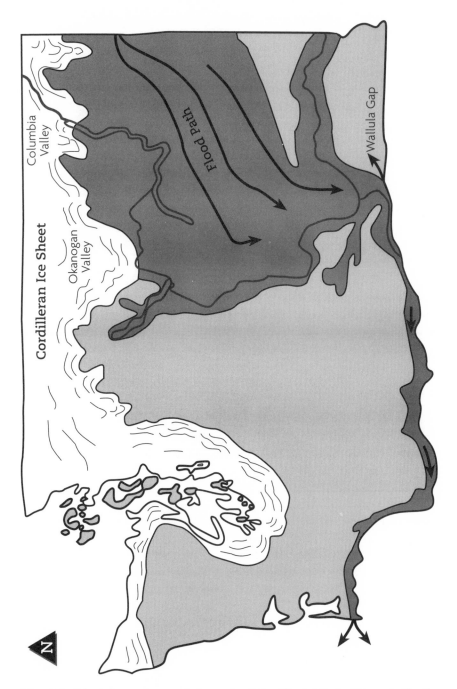

Map 2.2. *Glacial coverage and the path of the Glacial Lake Missoula floods around 15,000 years ago, during the last ice age* (Based on drawings by Anthony Bush and adapted from Jim Lichatowich, *Salmon Without Rivers: A History of the Pacific Salmon Crisis* [Washington, D.C.: Island Press, 1999]; © 1999 James A. Lichatowich; reprinted by permission of Island Press)

butcher site on the Olympic Peninsula, dated to 12,000 years ago, is the earliest archaeological evidence to date. Little is known about the people associated with the site, except that they appear to have been nomadic hunters, and possibly scavengers, traveling in small groups and dependent mostly on terrestrial mammals for food. At the time of the mastodon kill, the ice sheet had retreated north of present-day Seattle. Huge lakes hugged the edge of the ice, filling the glacially carved valleys and chasms of what would become the southern half of Puget Sound. Overflow from the lakes combined with diverted rivers to inundate the Chehalis River. The swollen river modified the huge valley through which the modern, diminutive Chehalis flows.

In what would become eastern Washington, thick layers of wind-blown silt dominated the landscape south of the retreating ice. The origin of the silt is unclear. Winds may have carried it off piles of gravel and rocks left behind by previous glaciers, but the orientation of its dunes suggest a southwest source. Either way, as much as 200 feet of silt obscured the underlying basalt throughout most of what is now southeastern Washington, and gray rivers plaited the surface of the region, flowing through sparse vegetation of low plants.

Glacial lakes similar to those in the Puget Lowlands backed up against the ice where it blocked the flow of rivers. In what would become eastern Washington, both the Columbia and Spokane Rivers formed lakes behind ice dams; west of the Cascades, smaller lakes were dammed against the Puget Ice Lobe. The presence and subsequent emptying of these bodies of water had important impacts on the region's landscapes. It was a lake in western Montana, however, that played the most dramatic role in altering what would become Washington. Glacial Lake Missoula, resulting from ice blockage of the Clark Fork River, filled and drained as many as forty times between 15,000 and 12,500 years ago. Each time the ice dam was breached, waters roared across what are now the Idaho panhandle and southeastern Washington, rushing into the Pacific along the route of the Columbia. Glacial Lake Missoula's final flood followed suit, obscuring the marks of its predecessors with its own scars upon the region's canvas.

The chances that any witness of the flood's commencement, human or otherwise, could have survived the experience are slim to none. Weakened by a stream of water tunneling through its base, the dam would have suddenly failed with a deafening explosion of cracking ice. Surging from the icy gates, a wall of churning, muddy water 2,000 feet high and laden with icebergs and boulders was unleashed onto the unsuspecting landscape. In two days, the lake would be completely empty, its waters raging west and south across the land. Near Grand Coulee, the flood plunged over what is now Dry Falls, a series of five horseshoe-shaped falls 4.7 times wider and 2.4 times higher than Niagara. Coursing at 60 miles per hour, the torrent swept away the deep soils of what is now southeastern Washington, save for the patch that comprises the Palouse Hills. The underlying basalt splintered under the force of the flood; the current gouged out depressions and rifts in the dark rock. Anyone lucky enough to make it to high ground would have seen the land to either side washed away, leaving them standing on an island of earth described by geologist Richard Waitt as a "battleship facing upstream."[8]

Stranded on high ground, survivors could have only watched as the roiling waters ripped across the land. Roaring into the Pasco basin, the floodwaters would have met the Wallula Gap, a mile-wide crack near the confluence of the Snake and Columbia Rivers. Here, 200 cubic miles of water a day tried to pass through a hole that could only discharge one fifth of that volume.[9] Behind the bottleneck, temporary Lake Lewis spread

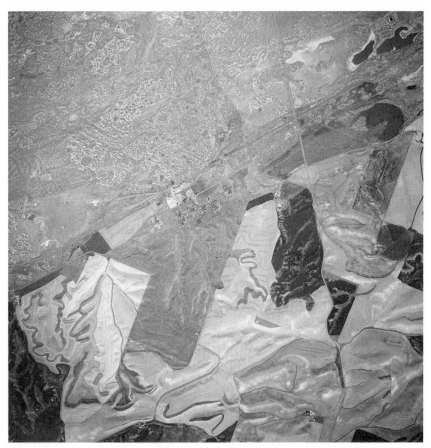

Near the town of Lamont, in northwest Whitman County, the scarred surface of the Channeled Scablands (top) is in marked contrast with the undulating Palouse Hills (bottom). (Source: Washington State Department of Transportation Aerial Photography)

out across 3,500 square miles. As the water jostled its way through the Columbia River Gorge, the flood reached heights 1,000 feet above the present river level, washing away the walls of the canyon. Waterfalls that now cascade down the steep rock faces to the Columbia are in fact tributary streams that lost their beds due to this rapid erosion.

In less than a week, Glacial Lake Missoula had lost all of its waters to the Pacific Ocean. Across the newly eroded countryside lay melting icebergs, immense boulders, vast gravel ripple marks, and tons of mud. Untouched by the floodwaters, the Palouse Hills in the southeastern corner of the state are a reminder of the thick soils and rolling topography that once dominated the Columbia Plateau. Now, the raw landscape known today as the Channeled Scablands lies in the flood's wake.

With the southeast ravaged by multiple floods and glaciers retreating northward, the region's landscapes were primed for repopulation. In the Columbia Plateau, the sagebrush and bunchgrasses that make up today's shrub-steppe ecosystem filled in the relatively sparse, low vegetation seen prior to flooding. With the retreat of the ice, the shrub-steppe pushed past its modern northern edge, invading dry forests around 10,000 years ago. The advance would last 5,000 years before the present-day grassland/forest border was established. Across the northern part of the region, areas freed from the smothering ice began a transition from tundra-like conditions towards modern environments. In northeastern and north-central areas, ponderosa and lodgepole pine crept into first moist sites, then drier areas, replacing the grasslands with open forests. West of the Cascades, trees that presently dominate higher-elevation forests prevailed in lowland areas at the end of the Pleistocene. Subalpine fir, Engelmann spruce, and mountain hemlock gradually moved up mountain slopes, replaced in lower elevations by open Douglas fir forests. Six thousand years ago, these open woodlands gave way to the modern closed forests of Douglas fir, western hemlock, and western red cedar.[10]

The faunal populations were also changing. The few Pacific salmon that survived the ravages of glaciers and post-glacial floods slowly repopulated the region's rivers, and developing forests fostered ideal habitat for spawning salmon. Species forced south by the ice moved back into the northern landscapes as the glaciers retreated. Many large terrestrial mammals, such as the mastodon, mammoth, dire wolf, musk ox, sabertooth cat, horse, camel, short-faced bear, and ancient bison became extinct during this time. The role of humans in this megafaunal extinction is unknown, yet hotly debated. The extinction correlates with both an influx of humans into North America and the changing climate at the end of the Ice Age. Consequently, both events are looked to as possibly playing a role in the extinction.

HUMANS SETTLE IN

As the landscape changed, humans adapted with it. At the end of the Ice Age, the people of what would become Washington were largely hunter-gatherers. The Columbia Plateau groups relied heavily on big game, while those near the Columbia River may have already developed a reliance on fishing. Along the coast, the people seem to have been highly mobile generalists as well, utilizing a wide variety of marine and terrestrial resources. Populations are thought to have been small throughout the region, and since they traveled widely, resource depletion was limited. As time progressed, the people learned about their surroundings and adjusted hunting and gathering practices to most effectively utilize available resources. They became dependent on shellfish, salmon, and other fish, as well as on plants, animals, and insects that all developed as the climate changed.[11]

In the coastal region, the higher dependence on salmon and other local resources fostered a transition to more sedentary lifestyles starting 4,000 to 6,000 years ago, possibly 8,000 years ago along major salmon-bearing rivers. Increasingly efficient food gathering and storage strategies and rising populations allowed for more intricately organized social systems, which contributed to the development of a more settled lifestyle. Human population increased around 3,000 to 4,000 years ago along the coast, which placed more strain on resources. Higher population density, combined with a gradually developing cultural view that surplus food was a status symbol, further increased the exploitation of coastal marine and terrestrial life. This led to the intensified use and maintenance of a system of secondary resource sites, which is evident in the seasonal cycle of travel between the more permanent winter village and more temporary hunting, fishing, and gathering sites used at other times of the year.

Adaptation and specialization continued over time and regional groups developed distinct characteristics. While peoples west of the Cascades developed more sedentary marine-based cultures, as described above, peoples east of the Cascades maintained a highly mobile lifestyle resulting from the scattered distribution, both spatially and temporally, of resources. For example, in order to obtain the same balanced diet available in a concentrated area of the coast, inland peoples traveled widely, following the maturation of bitterroot, cous, camas, berries, and salmon.[12] Within both coastal and inland groups, there were also many subgroups, ethnolinguistic groups defined by commonalities in language and customs rather than by "tribes."

Although the eastern and western cultures differed significantly, their impacts on the land did not. By the time Columbus first stumbled upon the Americas in 1492, both coastal and inland peoples had developed a seasonal resource gathering cycle and both had permanent villages, trail systems, and temporary resource sites.

 ## THE NATIVE AMERICAN LANDSCAPE

Imagine the Washington of 1492. Unobstructed rivers snaked through valleys of a tree-covered western Washington to Puget Sound and the Pacific Ocean. Along the coast, giant Sitka spruce intermixed with western hemlock and western red cedar, while deciduous bigleaf maple and red alder lined streams and rivers. Moving inland, the forest was similar, but gigantic mature western hemlock trees replaced the spruce. The only breaks in the blanket of forest were waterways, the Olympic and Cascade peaks, and the prairies and meadows that dotted the lowland valleys and subalpine zones. Down the eastern side of the Cascades, towering ponderosa pine and Douglas fir dominated. Nearing the base of the mountains the trees thinned out, then gave way to a sea of sagebrush and grasses that was broken by the soaring ponderosa forest of the Okanogan Highlands and Blue Mountains, and by rivers, lakes, and wetlands.

In this 66,572-square-mile expanse of land, there were perhaps fewer than 350,000 people.[13] However, close inspection would have been required to see their evidence. The overarching sign of people was the presence of permanent villages throughout the region's watersheds. Along the Pacific coast and Puget Sound, longhouses crafted from mature western red cedar trees were nestled at the outlets of major rivers, including the Columbia, Quinault, Hoh, Skokomish, Skagit, and many others. Settlements were not limited to the mouths of the rivers; there were also occasional villages upriver. Most watersheds hosted several villages. For example, the Quinault people inhabited more than forty sites throughout the Quinault River watershed, with only five permanent villages at the river's mouth.[14] The central longhouses that made up each village were typically 30 feet in width and 60 to 100 feet in length, and they housed multiple family groups. Small buildings for storage and other purposes sat behind the main lodges.

East of the Cascades the villages also concentrated near water, especially at the mouths of the largest tributaries of the Columbia River.[15] These villages consisted of multiple conical and domelike structures dug partly into the ground, with layers of woven tule (similar to a reed) and cattail mats draped over sturdy poles. The structures, often covered with earth to increase insulation, looked like earthen domes. In the Okanogan Highlands, lodges were also draped with tule mats, but the bases were rectangular, so the structures appeared like the roofs of common gabled houses set upon the ground without the walls. The diameters of the conical structures varied from 15 to 30 feet, and the oblong lodges ran from 15 to 60 feet long. Smaller secondary structures, like sweat lodges, completed the village. In both the coastal and inland villages, multiple family units lived in each lodge and averaged 30 to 55 square feet of living space per person.[16]

The waste accumulated over generations of human occupation in each of the village sites enriched the soil, affecting the vegetation growing near the villages. Stinging nettle was a common colonizer of these enriched soils near village sites in now–western Washington. Natives probably began to experiment with the plant, since it was close to hand, and they discovered it had several uses.[17]

Native peoples also used other resources immediately surrounding the villages, including downed branches, trees, sagebrush, and driftwood, which was used for firewood and tool construction. Whole old-growth cedar was laboriously cut in now–western Washington to make the cedar planks for longhouses and canoes, which were used for fishing, whaling, transportation, and shipping between villages and resource sites, and for trading with distant tribes.[18]

Trails connected each village to any number of resource sites, neighboring villages, or trade locations that were not accessible by canoe. Several groups traded across the Cascades, following trails through mountain passes. In what is now south-central Washington, the Klikitat people had an extensive trail network known as the Klikitat trail, which extended from present-day Vancouver, Washington, over the Cascades, to trail networks along the Columbia River and the Yakima River valley.[19]

Trails leading to a variety of resource sites fanned out around the villages. Starting in the spring, people throughout the region traveled to gather food and materials as these resources came into season. Native peoples spread across the land, fishing, gathering plant products, and hunting at locations their ancestors had discovered generations before. At each site, people made shelters using light, easily transportable tule and cattail mats, or cedar planks from the main longhouse.[20]

A myriad of plant and animal resources abounded and the harvest season usually began with the spring salmon runs. Salmon played a significant role in the cultures both east and west of the Cascades. Five salmon species and one anadromous trout species migrated up rivers and streams by the millions each year, providing a major source of food. In eastern regions, most Native peoples gathered in large groups along the Columbia River and its major tributaries to catch the spring run of chinook salmon that arrived by the millions. The groups favored places on the river where the salmon were concentrated, which occurred where there were natural barriers and rapids that forced the salmon to follow the easiest routes. Men would stand on wooden platforms built atop rocky basalt crags, reaching out over the water to catch the salmon with large dip nets and spears. Nearby,

SALMON FISHERY ON CHICKELIS RIVER.

An 1841 engraving of a salmon fishery on the Chickelis (Chehalis) River illustrates the use of a fishing weir. The structures hindered the passage of fish, allowing men to spear or net them from platforms along the weir. (Courtesy Manuscripts, Special Collections, University Archives, University of Washington Libraries, NA 3991)

the women and children would process the fish and hang them to dry on wooden racks. Fishing was limited each day by a salmon chief who would call for the end of fishing. The people believed that greedily catching more than necessary would be offensive to the salmon, causing them not to return.[21] The precautions seem to have paid off, as there is no archaeological record of serious salmon depletion before the twentieth century.

West of the Cascades, coastal peoples used several techniques, including varying forms of nets and weirs, to catch salmon by the tens of thousands. Archaeologists estimate that in the Pysht, Hoko, and Clallam watersheds, along the northern border of the Olympic Peninsula, Native peoples' annual average catch was nearly 45,000 salmon.[22] The nets, woven of stinging nettle fiber or twisted cedar bark, were set partway across rivers and streams to snag the salmon as they swam upstream. Weirs, lines of cedar posts driven into the riverbed across all or part of the river's width, operated as fences forcing the salmon through small openings, or created calm eddies in which salmon could rest. Men stood on wooden platforms along the weirs with dip nets or spears to catch the salmon slowed by the obstructions.[23]

In addition to salmon, the coastal Natives accessed a myriad of other marine resources, reaping the benefits of villages located near river estuaries. Clams, mussels, other shellfish, water plants, waterfowl, crabs, and occasional seals were just some of the resources accessible in the estuaries alone. In open waters, men hunted seals, whales, and porpoises and fished for herring, cod, rockfish, smelt, and other species, typically during spring, and then returned to salmon fishing during the large fall runs.[24]

Amid the springtime fishing flurry, bright green shoots peeked through the soil all over the state. Many of these sprouting plants provided a significant portion of Native peoples' dietary, medicinal, and implement needs. People were quite active in insuring the continued abundance of the plants they utilized, and to encourage continued yield of such plants, they harvested selectively, replanted immature roots, spread seeds, fertilized, and set fires.

These practices were common from tidal marshes along the coast, to meadows in the eastern mountains. In tidal marshes, where freshwater streams and rivers flow into saltwater coves, people tended rhizome gardens of at least endemic springbank clover and Pacific silverweed. They would clear the area of rocks, mark "property lines," weed out undesirable species, and fertilize the ground with nutrient-rich marine detritus. Harvesters left portions of the desirable specimens in the ground to insure a continued yield of healthy plants. Gathering the roots with digging sticks aerated the soil, which also encouraged rhizome growth. Depending on the intensity and frequency of human management, continual weeding and replanting led to monoculture plots after several generations.[25]

Similar selective harvesting methods helped shape both eastern and western prairies. The prairies of now-western Washington were flat, grassy plains that contrasted noticeably with the rolling, conifer-covered majority of the Puget Lowlands. From the Canadian border to the Cowlitz River basin, prairies dotted the landscape. Plant species found in the prairies included camas, bracken fern, stinging nettle, native blackberry, thimbleberry, oak, and a variety of grasses. Natives used many of these plants for a variety of dietary, medicinal, and tool-crafting needs, which presumably led to the desire to enhance production, or at least insure continued production of these plants. Puget Lowland groups used techniques of selective harvest similar to the coastal rhizome gardeners, and they added a new element—fire. Fire fertilized the soil and served as a weeding device by discouraging encroachment of competitive species. Most of the prairie plants were unharmed by fire because the returning bulbs or rhizomes were underground in the autumn burning season. Many prairie species actually thrive following disturbances such as fire or soil disruption.[26]

The use of fire and selective harvest to encourage desired resources was not limited to western regions or to prairies. East of the Cascades, people burned annually, selectively harvested, and spread seeds to enhance existing patches of camas, bitterroot, cous, Canby's lomatium, Indian carrot, and tule to increase production. Subalpine berry fields throughout the state also received fire treatment approximately every four to five years. [27]

Controlled burning also helped keep trails clear, kept forest underbrush to a minimum, fostered growth of deer and elk forage, and directly facilitated hunting. In the Okanogan Highlands especially, the Spokan people burned the underbrush to maintain an open forest, which eased travel and stalking of game. Certain species, like red-stemmed ceanothus, thrived following fire and attracted deer and elk in the eastern forests. Similarly, in western regions, fall burning stimulated new growth of grasses and browsing plants around the edges of the prairies, which provided food for deer and elk through the winter. Game hunters also used fire as a hunting tool. The hunters set fires around their prey in such a way that the fire drove the herd to a predetermined location where awaiting men shot the desired amount of game with their bows and arrows. Other hunting methods including game drives, deadfalls, and snares, along with basic stalking, were utilized to hunt a number of terrestrial mammals, including bears, rabbits, beavers, raccoons, and mountain sheep. Deer and elk were often the focus of fire surrounds, although they were also hunted using the other techniques. [28]

Whether fires were for hunting, clearing underbrush, or encouraging food plants, Native peoples took special precautions.[29] Fires were intentionally set in fall or spring so the rains would moisten the ground enough to prevent high intensity burns. In south-central Washington, the Natives burned the prairies from the edges inward to avoid catching the surrounding forest on fire. In the Okanogan Highlands a fire chief made all the burning decisions.

These management practices—fire and cultivation—affected the species dynamic of the prairies, forests, tidal marshes, and subalpine meadows by encouraging certain species while inhibiting others. The actions of the Native people "basically involved shifts in the proportions of native flora and fauna."[30] The prairies might have succumbed to the encroaching forest without the indigenous use of fire, leaving an almost completely tree-covered expanse from the Cascades west. Instead, the prairies were maintained, and species thriving in the ecosystem reached higher populations than they may have otherwise. For instance, deer are not well adapted to the mature western hemlock forests; they thrive on the early successional species in recently disturbed forests. Consequently, populations of deer—and their predators, wolves—most likely increased due to Native practices. Similarly in ponderosa forests, burning to keep the forest open benefited deer as well as people. Historian Richard White summarizes Native

American landscape alterations well, saying that "Through observation and tradition, Indians altered natural communities to fit their needs without, in the process, destroying the ability of those communities to sustain the cultures that had created them."[31]

The Native American landscape varied in degrees of human impact, from the permanently occupied village sites to uncharted mountain peaks. Wildness abounded in their landscape because much of the land was only visited seasonally. Even in the villages, the most humanized aspects of the Native American landscape, native plants and animals, and many other aspects of wildness existed. The Native peoples of Washington were able to continually adapt and create a relative balance with the land for 10,000 years without making drastic large-scale changes. Yet within the 500 years following Columbus's first steps in America, this landscape would come under the influence of a new force of change.

ENTER EUROPEANS

Beginning in the sixteenth century, a new wave of humans migrated into the Pacific Northwest. These new migrants entered present-day Washington with a unique and often domineering sense of place, and they began altering the region immediately upon their arrival. With European exploration and settlement, towns sprang up, forests were cut, estuaries diked and filled, grassland plowed, and shrub-steppe trampled. Most of this change culminated within the most recent 150 years, making humans one of the most dramatic forces changing Washington's mosaic.

The first Europeans to the region were explorers. Sailing up the coast by ship, they rarely ventured inland, although their imprints remain into the present. They renamed many of the region's landmarks, replacing Native sentiments with their own. Captain George Vancouver of England and his crew renamed many of the mountains and Puget Sound itself, while Captain Robert Grey renamed the Columbia River after the ship he used to sail past its mouth. These early visitors also began changing the region in ways that were more tangible. On the ships and within their own bodies Europeans harbored a variety of exotic pathogens. Since Native peoples had no previous exposure to such diseases, the pathogens spread rapidly. As early as 1775, the first smallpox epidemic decimated the Northwest's Native populations. Another epidemic occurred in 1801, so by the time Lewis and Clark reached the Columbia in 1805, Native numbers had already decreased to approximately one-half of historic totals.[32]

European explorers also initiated their own version of economic development. In 1778, English explorer Captain Cook journeyed to the Pacific Northwest, where he and his crew traded clothes, gunpowder, and utensils with the local peoples in exchange for furs. On their return trip to England, Cook's crew (Cook himself died in Hawaii) stopped in China and sold their recently received pelts. Finding that the furs demanded a high price, Cook's crew unknowingly began the fur trade.[33]

By the nineteenth century, the United States and England had become the last dominant countries claiming the territory encompassing Washington, and the two nations raced to develop the region's fur industry. Initially, three primary companies trapped in the region's river valleys and forests: the Pacific Fur Company based in Fort Astoria, and England's North West and Hudson's Bay Companies. During the War of 1812, Fort Astoria sold out to the North West Company after receiving word that the English had sent a warship to occupy the trading post. Then in 1821, the North West Company merged with Hudson Bay, effectively beginning what would be a twenty-one-year monopoly of the Pacific Northwest's fur trade.[34]

Desiring to continue its trading monopoly within the region, especially against the United States, Hudson's Bay began to actually wipe out the fur trade. George Simpson, an employee of Hudson's Bay, wrote, "We have convincing proof that the country is a rich preserve of Beaver and which for political reasons we should endeavor to exterminate immediately."[35] In cases such as this, not only were Euro-Americans transforming the region, they were nearly eliminating parts of it. The numbers of economically desirable species, including beaver, mink, and otter, decreased dramatically and the effects of such a change are still visible today. Fewer beavers meant fewer ponds, less woody debris, and simpler riverine systems, which altered the landscape and affected dependent species such as salmon.[36]

Meanwhile, the Hudson's Bay Company diversified its activities. Hudson's Bay's chief factor, Dr. John McLoughlin, believed that the company's future rested in agriculture. As a result, stockholders created the Puget Sound Agricultural Company. The group's two largest posts were on the Cowlitz and Nisqually plains, located in the southern portion of Puget Sound, near their respective rivers. As described by historian Robert Bunting, the Cowlitz was "an arable, level, undulating prairie of camas, flowers and course grasses."[37] By 1841, the company had turned up to 700 acres of the Cowlitz's camas, flowers, and course grasses into cropland.

When first settled by the company, the Nisqually plain was a 30-square-mile area between the Cascade Mountains and Puget Sound to the east and west and the Puyallup and Nisqually Rivers to the north and south. It was a patchwork of grasses, flowers, and 10- to 40-foot-high terraces intermixed with open, parklike groves of trees. With the company came cattle, and at the same time the Cowlitz was cultivated, Hudson's Bay converted much of the Nisqually plain into rangeland for 4,000 to 7,000 cattle.[38]

The Hudson's Bay Company's monopoly on Euro-American transformation did not last much longer. In 1846, the area comprising present-day Washington, Oregon, and Idaho became a territory of the United States. Consequently, Hudson's Bay and the Puget Sound Agricultural Companies shut down operations, and the alteration of Washington's mosaic fell upon the United States. Up until this point, relative to what would happen in future years, little of the territory's landscape had changed from the condition that Euro-American explorers had first encountered. But when the area became a U.S. territory, settlers arrived in droves.

The first areas settled were the same plains that the Hudson's Bay Company had occupied. Homesteaders built their homes where the open woods and prairies met, trying to ensure an adequate supply of wood while providing enough open land for pasture and crop fields. After thirty years of occupation, homesteaders were already witnessing the consequences of their settlement. In 1871, settler Francis Victor stated, "Twenty years of grain-raising, without manuring, has been wearing out the oldest land instead of improving it." Likewise, an Olympia newspaper reported, "The natural grasses are destroyed by being tramped for years."[39] Many Americans believed that unproductive grassland resulted not from their activities but from the "inferior" native grasses. To mitigate this "problem," agriculturalists imported eastern grasses, such as timothy, clover, and Kentucky bluegrass, which have all but completely outcompeted native grasses across the state.

As homesteaders continued to expand their agricultural activities, they started pushing into wetlands, estuaries, and other aquatic systems. Since many places within the western territory had subsoil composed primarily of glacial till, they were only moderately cultivable, if at all. River valleys, where periodic floods replenished the soil with nutrient-rich silt, however, were well suited for America's homesteaders. At least they were when settlers drained wetlands and estuaries and channelized rivers. By the 1880s, agriculturalists had converted nearly 30,000 acres of Puget Sound marshland to agriculture. Euro-Americans were slowly transforming Washington's waterways into commodities. Where once climate, geology, and, to a lesser degree, biology were the primary forces molding water courses, Euro-Americans shaped rivers to fit perceptions of what the landscape should be.

Many of these activities would happen throughout the territory, but settlement and development of eastern areas was slower than it was west of the Cascades. Communities developed along the Columbia River but rarely far beyond The Dalles. One reason was simply a lack of emphasis on eastern Washington Territory. England's success with Hudson's Bay

attracted attention westward and people speculated that the western portion of the territory was superior, an unfortunate assessment that some adhere
to even today. In addition, the eastern region was closed to settlement until
1858 due to conflicts with Native Americans. During this time, most activity within the eastern portion of the territory concentrated around temporary mining communities.

Once the government lifted the settlement ban, homesteaders steadily
moved into the Columbia Basin. The three most favored destinations for
the first years of settlement were The Dalles on the Columbia, Walla Walla,
and the Yakima Valley. The Columbia Basin provided many opportunities
for homesteaders. In 1847, settler Absalom Harden wrote in reference to
the Grande Ronde valley of Oregon, "the valley is very rich and fertile and
would produce grain in abundance if tilled up."[40] Yet few wagon trains moved
into eastern Washington Territory until prospectors discovered gold in the
1860s. Then settlers flocked to the region to stake their claims, hoping to
secure their fortunes. This created conflict with some Native tribes, as many
of the claims and mining camps were on their reservation lands. Indian
agents tried to protect Native American rights but eventually gave in to
the settlers and began issuing licenses.

Early mining's greatest impacts had little to do with mining itself but
with the other activities it encouraged. Within the 10-year period between
1860 and 1870, Washington Territory's population more than doubled, with
growth concentrated in the south-central and southeastern parts of the region. Population growth included the miners themselves, as well as other
merchants and agriculturalists. Miners demanded food, and stockmen and
farmers were happy to provide.

Stockmen grazed cattle on the open range in increasing numbers. In
1872, the *Settlers Guide to Oregon and Washington* noted, "There is probably
no branch of legitimate business in the world, requiring so little capital
and so little skill of technical knowledge, which pays such large and certain profits, as cattle-raising in eastern Washington."[41] The increasing cattle
herds disturbed much of the native shrub-steppe and grasslands, an ecosystem that had evolved mostly in the absence of large herbivores. Doing
what they do best, stock herds grazed grasses, trampled sage lands, and
turned waterways into mud holes.

This early ranching boom did decline, however, when the gold rush
went bust in the 1870s. When ranching declined, settlers increasingly relied on farming grains to develop the region. By the end of 1862, three
gristmills were already grinding the region's wheat into flour, and by the
1870s, Americans had turned 649,000 acres of land, primarily in the
Columbia Basin, into rows of crops.[42] Increasing settlement continued to

encourage agricultural practices and the groundwork was laid for the vast alteration of Washington's shrub-steppe.

"Improving" Washington for agricultural production was not as simple as just running cattle or plowing plains. It also meant removing species that settlers saw as a hindrance to progress. After Native Americans, large predators were the figureheads of the wild, uncivilized side of Washington. To bring order to chaos, hunters killed thousands of wolves, grizzly bears, cougars, and a host of other species. Federally sponsored programs offered bounties for kills, and soon many of the region's large predators became little more than mounted heads on cabin walls. As early as 1878, just thirty years after Washington became a U.S. territory, Daniel Waldo, a settler near present day Salem, Oregon, admitted he had "not heard a big wolf howl in 20 years."[43]

Not all Euro-American activity revolved solely around agriculture, particularly in the vicinity of the Cascades. When first settled, forests covered between one-half to two-thirds of the region, from the dense, mist-enshrouded stands of the west to the parklike, dry forests of the east. Early settlers filled their diaries and journals with passages describing the forests that would help dub Washington the Evergreen State. Telling about the area around the Willapa River, pioneer William Keil said, "the soil is covered three or four feet . . . [with] decaying tree trunks, moss, parasitic plants and underbrush so that it is impossible for man or beast to penetrate the forest . . . . Such forests are found throughout the whole territory and all the prairies are surrounded by such forests."[44]

These vast forests would eventually support one of Washington's largest industries. In fact, logging was an economic activity even before American settlers arrived in the region. The first shipment of logs was in 1833 when the Hudson's Bay Company sent 50,000 board feet of lumber to China.[45] Yet, during initial development timber harvests were limited. Loggers had the laborious job of cutting down gigantic trees by hand and then transporting them to a mill. The first feasible logging under such circumstances was highly selective. Loggers cut trees less than a mile away from either the mill or a floatable water source, such as the Puget Sound.

As a result, the total amount of land logged by the turn of the twentieth century comprised only a fraction of Washington's forest. The transportation and milling of logs was often more destructive than logging itself. One common mode of transportation used a splash dam, which created a pool of water that would hold the logs behind the dam. When the pool was sufficiently full loggers would release the gates, sending cubic yards of water and logs crashing down the river channel. This practice often wreaked havoc along riverbanks, tearing up the shore and decimating

A splash dam holds logs on the Chenois Creek in Grays Harbor in 1905. Logged trees were collected behind the dams before being released to travel downstream in a surge of water and wood. (Courtesy Manuscripts, Special Collections, University Archives, University of Washington Libraries, UW166)

wildlife habitat. Another common practice of mills was to dump their waste, including sawdust and woodchips, right into the river. In 1852, natural-historian James Swan observed "great quantities of drift-logs, boards, chips, and sawdust, with which the whole water around us was covered."[46]

🐻 INDUSTRIAL REVOLUTION AND THE RAILROADS

The 1880s brought statehood (in 1889) and the Industrial Revolution to Washington. Industrialization was indeed a revolutionary advancement in Americans' ability to alter their surroundings. In 1883 and again in 1893, two transcontinental railroads, the Northern Pacific and Great Northern, connected their rails through Washington. As they passed through, they turned cities such as Spokane and Seattle into the economic organizers for their respective regions.[47] From these organizing points, a system of more localized railroads spread across the region, forming a circulatory system of economic veins within an increasingly humanized landscape. As these railroads spread, they connected once remote settlements to the rest of the country and even the world. Responding to the demands of new, distant markets, Washington's resource industries expanded.

In agricultural lands, construction of railroads combined with federal irrigation funding and reclamation to change Washington in ways that dwarfed the previous forty years of development. People believed the government should have a key role in developing the Pacific Northwest and demanded support. For example, many settlers saw eastern Washington as a "bunchgrass waste" that required irrigation to make it productive. In 1917, the county agriculturist for the present-day Tri-Cities area claimed that "there is no other body of land in the Northwest where the per acre yield of those food products so much needed at this time, would be as great as here."[48]

The federal government responded and the amount of both irrigated and reclaimed land increased.[49] Between 1860 and 1920, irrigated land grew by more than one hundred times, from 475 to 529,899 acres. By 1935, Washingtonians reclaimed between 1 and 2 million additional acres of land. In 1880, 484,000 acres of Washington were in agricultural production. Only ten years later, that acreage stampeded to a total of 1,820,000 acres, and by 1930 agriculturalists converted and simplified well over 13 million acres of land—once grasslands, wetlands, estuaries, and valleys—to produce grains, fruits, vegetables, and livestock. This "arid waste," which had actually been a complex and diverse set of ecosystems, was transformed through a process understood at the time as development and progress, and the result was the rapid spread of monoculture fields.

Cattlemen also ran their stock over the shrub-steppe and dryland forests, trampling and browsing the native vegetation, literally removing riparian areas and changing species composition. The combination of heavy grazing and forestry practices began to significantly alter many eastside forests, particularly the Blue Mountains. When first settled, the forests were open, parklike stands of ponderosa pine up to 5 feet in diameter. Due to grazing, forestry, and fire suppression, the stand density increased and changed in composition to diseased lodgepole pine, Douglas fir, and true fir.

Agriculture was not the only activity encouraged by advances in transportation capabilities. Before the 1880s, logging was small scale and selective, so even by the turn of the twentieth century, an estimated 70 percent of Washington's forests were still old growth.[50] That changed with the development of railroad logging, the steam donkey, and highline skidding. Railroads made transporting logs easier and moved logging beyond the mills and waterways. Steam donkeys and highline skidding allowed loggers to fell trees that were both farther away from the transportation line and on terrain that was once unharvestable. In 1902, one eyewitness recounted how the steam donkey drew logs "up through the forest, threshing and beating and groaning, tearing up small trees and plowing great furrows in the earth."[51] That same year, U.S. Geological Survey maps indicated that loggers had cleared trees up to 2 miles from all floatable streams.[52] By 1909,

The steam donkey, shown here in Grays Harbor, allowed crews to log trees that were previously unattainable. (Courtesy Manuscripts, Special Collections, University Archives, University of Washington Libraries, UW10568)

Washington led the country in timber production.[53]

The construction of railroads also led to the checkerboard pattern of timberland ownership that characterizes the logging industry. Federal law granted railroads the lands needed to construct their tracks. These railroad companies then sold much of this land to timber companies. For example, the Northern Pacific Railroad sold 900,000 acres of Washington timberland to Frederick Weyerhaeuser in 1899. As a result, most of the region's timberland became controlled by large corporations by means of land transfers whose legality has been questioned in some cases.[54]

As both agriculture and logging expanded, so did their employment base, increasing the population of the state. Naturally, these people needed places to live, and the resulting towns and expanding cities made their own mark on Washington's mosaic. Few forces of human change are as dramatic as those produced by urban development. The best-known example is the development of the Puget Lowlands. When first settled, the surrounding terrain dictated how towns developed. As towns became more urbanized, people started directly shaping the land around them. In Tacoma, the townsfolk filled parts of Commencement Bay, turning it into a shipping and industrial district. Further north, Seattle residents cleared blocks of property by using pressurized water to literally blow surrounding hills into the bay. Then they would clear the land of springs and streams by burying them underground, replacing the original landscape with their own cover of tiles and bricks. The alterations of forestry and agriculture were more extensive, but those created by urban development were more intensive.

By the 1930s, Washington had passed through its first two frontier stages—settlement and initial industrial development. The impact on Washington was evident in nearly every part of the state. Agriculture converted and simplified land, logging cleared parts of the forest, and urban development completely altered the land's characteristics. Yet, at the end of these two periods most of Washington remained similar to its condition when settled by the first Euro-Americans. Every type of old-growth forest still existed and even dominated much of the landscape, and large areas of shrub-steppe were still intact. Euro-American culture had not tamed the entire "wild" Washington described by the first explorers and settlers.

WORLD WAR II AND THE AUTOMOBILE

With the advent of World War II, that began to change. The war increased demands on natural resources, putting greater strain on forests and fields, while the ability to extract, produce, and transport those resources likewise amplified. Global economic ties also increased as many of Washington's natural resources were shipped overseas. As these markets expanded, timber companies cleared more forest, cattle trampled additional shrub-steppe, farmers increasingly turned grasslands inside out, and dams obstructed more rivers. Interconnected with these transformations was the increasing use of the combustion engine. Although developed years before, residents had not widely used the combustion engine within Washington until after World War II. Once employed, it had much the same effect as the railroad—except the impacts were exponentially greater.

When put into a tractor, the combustion engine allowed farmers to cultivate more cropland in less time. When running a grain truck, more of those crops could be transported to market. As a result, farmland initially expanded, in both total land and land per individual farm. The stereotypical "Mom and Pop" family farms built by the homesteaders started turning into larger businesses. In 1954, 17.6 million acres of Washington were farmland, 778,000 of which were irrigated. By 1991, though only 15.7 million acres (roughly 35 percent of the state) remained in farm production (just 2 million acres more than in 1930), farms had spread well beyond the rivers, either plowing under or trampling the native mosaic.[55]

Often related to agriculture through irrigation projects, dam construction became increasingly prevalent at midcentury.[56] Although practiced before, it was around and after World War II that dam building peaked. Started in the 1930s, both the Grande Coulee and Bonneville dams were completed and operational by 1951. With the inundation behind Grand Coulee, Kettle Falls, once an important Native American fishing site, became little more than a submerged memory. By 1957, four more dams were barricading the state's largest river, and in 1989, eleven dams spanned the width of the once "mighty Columbia." Where there had existed tumbling rapids, cascading gorges, and meandering riverways, there now exist a series of holding ponds for electricity, irrigation, and recreation. The Columbia was not the only river to meet such a fate. There are currently 1,022 dams barricading rivers all across the state.[57]

If agricultural enterprises benefited from the combustion engine, so did logging. Timber industries capitalized on the ability to build logging roads deep into the forest and use trucks to haul out their harvest. Timber companies started cutting down previously inaccessible stands. Besides logging trucks, logging industries developed another use for the gas-powered engine. Before the chainsaw, loggers had to fell trees first with axes and then the cross-cut saw, a long arduous process that limited the number of trees that could be cut. Actually developed in the 1920s but highly used in later years, the chainsaw made felling trees dramatically faster, and it became ever more economical to clear all the trees from entire stands. Logging companies pushed farther into the forest, clear-cutting hundreds of acres at a time and then replanting them in monocultures—if replanting them at all.

Before World War II, almost all logging occurred on private lands. The public forestlands, largely controlled by the U.S. Forest Service (USFS), were held to conserve timber resources. After the war, the USFS began to change its practices. Pressured by industries and the desire to meet their demands, the USFS started acting much more like those same businesses they contracted with. They sold timber and allowed cutting of public forests far beyond a "sustainable yield," the legally mandated limit. By 1953, out of roughly 24 million acres of forest left in Washington (5.8 million of which was still old growth), nearly 20 million acres—almost half the state—were designated as public and private commercial timberlands.[58] Timber harvests grew to historic highs in the 1970s and '80s to harvests of 5 to 7 billion board feet annually.[59] Logging had breached the towering walls of

The area surrounding Lake Sammamish, east of Seattle near the city of Redmond, has seen development typical of the increasingly urbanized Puget Lowlands. In 1965 (above), roads and buildings were intermixed with patches of forestland. By 1998 (below), housing developments had filled in most of the blank spots on the map. (Source: Washington State Department of Natural Resources)

most Washington forests and the leftover polygonal clear-cuts gave rise to legions of second-growth monoculture stands. A patchwork quilt of greens and browns, stitched together by an abundance of logging roads, blanketed most of Washington's forests.

One of the final and possibly most sweeping effects of the combustion engine was its role in urbanization. With the private automobile, personal mobility greatly increased. People could still visit and work in the city while living at increasing distances. Cities such as Seattle, Tacoma, Spokane, and the Tri-Cities began to decentralize, sprawling out and pushing the rural/urban fringe farther away. In 1950, Washington contained 2.4 million people, all consuming land and resources. By the turn of the twenty-first century more than 6 million people called Washington home and the resulting increase in land use for urban development began covering the state's once diverse mosaic with concrete. By 1989, nearly 1.6 million acres of Washington, or 5 percent of the state, were classified as developed land (urban and transportation), most of which were concentrated in the Puget Sound area.[60] All across the state, but particularly within the Puget Lowlands, cities spread, converting forests, wetlands, estuaries, and farms alike into housing developments, shopping malls, and parking lots.

IF LEWIS AND CLARK RETURNED

Within the last 150 years, humans have changed Washington in unprecedented ways. If Lewis and Clark were to traverse the state today, their journal entries would be irreconcilable with their original observations. The vast wildness that they encountered is now fragmented, including the rivers by which they navigated. In their original travels, they continually faced daunting whitewater. Today a series of dams restrain the rapids. Where they once saw immeasurable expanses of Palouse grassland, only 1 percent now remains. Of the original 10.5 million acres of shrub-steppe, over half is monoculture cropland, and much of the rest is rangeland. The predominately unbroken blanket of forest is now a patchwork of clear-cuts and young stands. Only 3 percent of western and 15 percent of eastern Washington's old-growth forests remain. The huge congregations of waterfowl Lewis and Clark witnessed have diminished with the loss of 30 percent of Washington's wetlands and 70 percent of its estuaries.[61]

This is a bleak litany, but Washington's landscape is not static. For hundreds of millions of years, the movements of the earth have molded its form, and life has altered its surface. For thousands of years, people inhabited the lands that Lewis and Clark explored. Yet, only in the last two hundred years have human-induced changes been increasingly rapid and wide-reaching. The geologic processes of the past will continue into the future: mountains will rise, present volcanoes will give way to new chains, and the Pacific Ocean will shrink with the slow movement of the earth; species will advance and retreat, bringing their own modifications to the land. Among these changes will be those wrought by humans. But we have the ability to direct the changes we make, an ability evidenced by the efforts of some citizens to step away from the pattern of extensive alteration and to instead set lands aside from the forces of human change.

CHAPTER 3

Current Protected Areas and Geographical Assessment

◆ *Lana Byal and Shawn Olson* ◆

Thanks to a strong citizen movement, there are many protected areas in Washington. There are also many areas that remain in need of protection. For activists to expand current protections, they must be familiar with what can, at first, seem to be a confusing assortment of protective designations.

This chapter aims to make the convoluted world of protected areas more accessible, usable, and meaningful for those who may be working to save the wild places they love. We introduce government agencies that manage our protected lands and provide descriptions of our federal and state protected areas. We also use an international system of protected-area classifications to categorize Washington's protected areas according to the way they are managed. We chose this system in order to demonstrate the various levels of protection offered by each designation, facilitating an assessment of each category's ability to protect and maintain wildness.

Being aware of the extent to which existing protected areas may or may not perpetuate the state's wild character is important when conserving wildlands, because problems such as insufficient size, fragmentation, invasive species, fire suppression, and inappropriate management can threaten wildness even within areas that have been officially set aside for protection. These challenges to the existence of wildness and biological diversity must be met through such things as expansion of current protected area systems, better management of protected areas, and the employment of land-use zoning, land trusts, conservation easements, and growth management. Together, all of these are tools used by wildlands conservationists throughout the state, as illustrated in the stories told throughout this book.

 ## GOVERNMENT LAND MANAGEMENT AGENCIES

An understanding of the different types of public land designations first requires a rudimentary knowledge of the agencies that manage them.[1] The largest holdings of public land in Washington are administered either by the federal government or by the state. Smaller but important parks are managed by local government agencies at the county and municipal levels. At both the state and federal levels, there are several agencies that administer our public lands. These agencies are our public servants, charged by lawmakers with specific responsibilities for taking care of the lands that all citizens own, collectively, and that our children receive as their natural heritage, to be held in common forever.

Federal Agencies

The principal federal agencies that manage public lands containing conventional protected areas are the U.S. Forest Service, the National Park Service, the U.S. Fish and Wildlife Service, and the Bureau of Land Management. (For locations of most of the land systems and protective designations described in this and later chapters, see the map of wild and roadless lands in Washington, in the color insert.) In subsequent chapters (see chapters 10, 13, and 14), we will see that the U.S. Department of Energy (DOE) and the military are also important for wildlands preservation because these agencies are in charge of large landholdings in Washington where human use has been restricted for many years. For example, the DOE administers the 375,000-acre Hanford Nuclear Site, and the U.S. military manages the 320,000-acre Yakima Training Center. Each of these sites is bigger than Mount Rainier National Park, which contains 256,000 acres.

Under the U.S. Department of Agriculture, the U.S. Forest Service (USFS) administers the national forests. When the agency was created at the turn of the twentieth century, one of its main purposes was to protect watersheds from the massive erosion caused by ill-regulated logging practices of the time. Forest Service management has considerably broadened since then to reflect its "multiple use" mandate, allowing for outdoor recreation, timber production, livestock grazing, mining, watershed protection, wilderness preservation, and maintenance of biological diversity. There are eight national forests in Washington: the Olympic, Gifford Pinchot, Wenatchee, Mount Baker–Snoqualmie, Okanogan, Colville, Idaho Panhandle, and Umatilla National Forests.

The National Park Service was established in 1916 under the U.S. Department of the Interior to administer the new National Park System. The Park Service manages some of the most spectacular and well-known of our nation's landscapes in order to preserve their natural, historic, and wildlife features and to provide enjoyment for present and future generations. There are three national parks in Washington: Olympic, Mount Rainier, and North Cascades National Parks.

The U.S. Fish and Wildlife Service (FWS) was formed in 1939, though its roots extend back to 1871, when the U.S. Commission on Fish and Fisheries was established. The FWS along with the National Marine Fisheries Service works with other agencies to minimize impacts on endangered species and their habitats. Under the Department of the Interior, the FWS administers the National Wildlife Refuge System. There are twenty national wildlife refuges in Washington.

The Bureau of Land Management (BLM) was created in 1946 when the former General Land Office and Grazing Service merged under the Department of the Interior. The agency's purpose is to manage the public lands that were left after homesteading, prospecting, and the creation of national forests, parks, wildlife refuges, tribal reservations, land grants for schools and railroads, defense installations, dams, reservoirs, and other public land uses. These "leftover" lands are called the National Resource Lands, and are managed by the BLM according to parameters set by the 1976 Federal Land Policy and Management Act. Most BLM lands in Washington lie in small fragments scattered across the eastern side of the state.

State Agencies

There are three main agencies that manage lands belonging to the citizens of Washington State. The Washington Department of Natural Resources (DNR), formed by the state legislature in 1957, manages more than 5 million acres of public forests, farms, commercial properties, and underwater lands in Washington in order to regulate the use of state resources. A large portion of the land managed by the DNR is used to support public institutions like schools and prisons through revenue generated from timber sales and grazing permits and put into "trust funds."

The Washington Department of Fish and Wildlife (DFW) manages the state's wildlife and fishing resources. The agency's goal is to provide habitat for viable populations of fish and wildlife. The DFW manages many wildlife areas throughout the state, regulating hunting, fishing, and recreation on these lands.

The Washington State Parks and Recreation Commission (SPRC), established in 1913, is responsible for acquiring and operating recreational, cultural, and historical sites in the state park system. There are currently 125 state parks in Washington.

DECIPHERING THE LINES: PROTECTED AREA CATEGORIES

There are many types of protected areas in Washington, and each designation offers a different level of protection depending on its management goals and administrative policies. For the novice, these different designations can be confusing and difficult to differentiate. A basic understanding of each type and the level of protection each offers results in a set of powerful tools for citizens seeking wildlands preservation.

These tools, however, should be chosen wisely, with knowledge of all types of land designations and their respective management practices in mind. Large, glorified areas like national parks are the most well-known of protected areas and possibly the first that come to mind. For over a century, national parks around the country have been celebrated as the ultimate means of preserving our nation's "crown jewels." Though national parks do offer a high level of land protection, wilderness designation actually provides a higher level of protection through stricter management codes, especially when a wilderness area is designated within a national park. Highly protective designations may not always be achievable, however, due to challenging social and political conditions, and in these cases less restrictive designations may be considered.

To make it easier to understand and compare the wide variety of protected area designations in the world, a universal system for ranking protected areas was devised by the World Conservation Union, or IUCN (so called because it was once the International Union for the Conservation of Nature). The IUCN is a network that not only includes more than eight hundred nongovernmental organizations and approximately one hundred government agencies, but also includes more than seventy member nations and has been granted official Observer status in the United Nations General Assembly. The beauty of the IUCN system is that it places multitudes of different protected area designations within just six categories, ranked according to their management practices in order to show a gradation of human impact.[2]

Category I is the most restrictive and it includes strict nature reserves (*Category Ia*) and wilderness areas (*Category Ib*). The former applies to areas managed mainly to protect ecosystems and landscape features for scientific research and monitoring, whereas wilderness areas are established for a broader set of users while maintaining a generally undeveloped character. *Categories II* and *III* are national parks and national monuments, respectively. Both are similar to wilderness areas in many ways but they allow more human use and impact. The remaining categories are habitat/species management areas (*Category IV*), protected landscapes/seascapes (*Category V*), and managed resource protected areas (*Category VI*). Land-use classifications falling within these categories allow progressively more management intervention in order to achieve specific goals, including at least some resource extraction. The discussion below briefly presents each type of protected area in Washington, following this IUCN order.

Research natural areas (RNAs), Category Ia. RNAs are ostensibly to be permanently protected and maintained in their natural condition, seeming to match the strict nature reserve of IUCN Category Ia, but in practice, they are not the most secure type of protected area. The Research Natural Areas Program was established by the federal government to protect diversity of species and ecosystems, to preserve gene pools of both common and rare species, and to provide educational and research opportunities. In Washington, fifty-four RNAs have been established, totaling 141,771 acres. Twenty-seven of them lie within national forests (30,726 acres), ten within national parks (20,355 acres), eleven in national wildlife refuges (77,925 acres), five in U.S. Army lands (12,745 acres), and one in Bureau of Land Management lands (20 acres).[3]

Wildlands experts say that RNAs have not, in fact, been designed as what the IUCN would consider a strict nature reserve. They point out that RNAs in Washington are largely unrecognized even by federal land managers. RNA policies generally allow hunting, trapping, fishing, and roads, and they often impose no added restrictions on recreation use or mining beyond any restrictions that preexisted RNA designation. Moreover, the RNA classification may be modified or removed by the administering agency, if it so desires, potentially jeopardizing the long-term protection of these areas as ecological baselines for research and education.[4] Nevertheless, for areas that are too small to qualify for significant protection through a designation such as wilderness, RNA classification can be a useful tool for conservationists if they are committed to following through to see that protective management policies are established subsequent to RNA designation.

Natural area preserves (NAPs), Category Ia. NAPs were first established in 1972 by the state legislature as a result of scientists' and citizens' ecological concerns. This is the most protective of state-level designations in Washington. NAPs are designated for the protection of priority species and ecosystems, as described in the State of Washington Natural Heritage Plan. Use of NAPs is generally limited to scientific and educational endeavors. Minimal human intervention is preferred when and if possible to allow natural processes to dominate the landscape. However, most of the NAPs designated to date have been small and are subject to the same sorts of problems that prevent the federal government's RNA's from truly qualifying as strict nature reserves. Ultimately, like many protected areas, the quality of their protection is determined by each area's individual management plan.

NAP designation requires documentation of the presence and viability of priority species and/or ecosystems within the proposed site, approval by the state's Natural Heritage Advisory Council, a public hearing regarding the proposed boundary, and approval by the commissioner of public lands. NAPs can be on private or public lands; however, private lands are added to the NAP system only if there is a willing seller. Forty-seven NAPs are managed by the Washington Department of Natural Resources, comprising 28,478 of the total 32,462 acres of NAPs in the state. The remainder are managed by the State Parks and Recreation Commission (five areas totaling 2,084 acres), and the Washington Department of Fish and Wildlife (six areas totaling 1,900 acres).[5]

National wilderness areas, Category Ib. National wilderness areas may be designated on federal lands of at least 5,000 acres or, if smaller, they must be of a size that allows them to be preserved and used without damaging their wilderness qualities. This is the most protective of large, public land designations in Washington, and the state has thirty such areas, totaling 4.3 million acres. Wilderness areas are designated by Congress, and they provide an extra layer of protection within existing federal land designations. They can be administered by any of the following agencies: the Forest Service, Park Service, U.S. Fish and Wildlife Service, or the Bureau of Land Management.

The 1964 Wilderness Act defines wilderness as "an area where the earth and its community of life are untrammeled by man, where man himself is a visitor who does not remain." Wilderness areas are generally designated in places that were not previously impacted by intensive human activities such as logging or road building, though these criteria have changed in recent years, as evidenced by the second-growth forests included in the Wild Sky Wilderness legislation (see chapter 10). Wilderness areas are established when a proposal is made and a bill is passed by Congress and signed by the president.

Wilderness areas, which nationally compose the National Wilderness Preservation System (NWPS), are generally off-limits to roads, motorized vehicles or equipment, resource extraction, structures and installations, and other "non-conforming" uses. Livestock grazing, hunting, and fishing are allowed in wilderness areas, except for those designated within national parks, where such activities are prohibited even without a wilderness designation.

National parks, Category II. National parks are managed to preserve areas of outstanding natural, historical, and recreational resources. They are established when a proposal is made, and a bill passed by Congress and signed by the president. Washington's national parks are Olympic, Mount Rainier, and North Cascades. National parks offer a fairly high level of land

and wildlife protection, limiting road building and prohibiting hunting. However, the Park Service allows the construction of access roads and park facilities such as visitor centers and lodges, and visitors may drive their vehicles within boundaries on established roads. Many conservationists worry that our nation's national parks are being "loved to death," receiving 290 million visitors annually. Mount Rainier visitation for the year 2002 was 1.3 million people and Olympic National Park received 3.6 million people.[6] Still, national parks are intended to be among the most restrictive of protected areas.

National monuments, Category III. National monuments are created to preserve areas of rare scientific and historical features. Monuments may be designated by presidential proclamation under the Antiquities Act, in order to quickly protect a unique area due to immediate threats. They can also be created by an act of Congress. Both methods of monument designation have been implemented in Washington. National monuments are managed by the federal agency responsible for the land where they are established. The Forest Service manages one of the national monuments in Washington State, Mount St. Helens National Volcanic Monument, and the U.S. Fish and Wildlife Service manages the other, the Hanford Reach National Monument. National monuments are intended to provide recreational, educational, and research opportunities. They usually include facilities like campgrounds, roads, parking lots, and research stations, and allow many types of recreational activities, including the use of motorized recreational vehicles.

National marine sanctuaries, Category III. These sanctuaries are a different type of protected area. They are administered by the National Oceanic and Atmospheric Administration (NOAA) within the U.S. Department of Commerce. They can be designated administratively by the secretary of commerce, or legislatively, through an act of Congress. They only include the underwater marine territory within our nation's coastal areas and in the Great Lakes. These areas are managed to maintain their natural beauty and biological diversity, and to protect marine resources through education and scientific research. There are thirteen national marine sanctuaries in the United States, and one of them is in Washington, the Olympic Coast National Marine Sanctuary, adjacent to Olympic National Park on the western coast of the Olympic Peninsula. Fishing and shell-fishing are among allowed activities, and several Native American tribes on the Olympic coast collect sustainable amounts of these and other natural products, such as kelp, in keeping within the guidelines of the National Marine Sanctuary Program.

National wildlife refuges, Category IV. National wildlife refuges are areas of land and water administered by the U.S. Fish and Wildlife Service for the conservation, management, and restoration of fish, wildlife, plants, and habitats. They are established when a proposal is made, and a bill is passed by Congress and signed by the president. In the twenty-one refuges throughout the state, the FWS actively promotes recreational and educational uses, especially hunting, fishing, and trapping. Many of our refuges were purchased with funds raised through federal taxes on hunting licenses. The FWS also maintains nature trails, wildlife observation towers and boardwalks, educational and interpretive facilities, and auto tour routes. Wildlife refuges are also open to livestock grazing.

State wildlife areas, Category IV. More than seventy wildlife areas managed by the Washington Department of Fish and Wildlife are to conserve and regulate the habitat of fish and wildlife. Recreation is heavily promoted within wildlife areas, which allow fishing, hunting, and nonconsumptive recreational opportunities while still sustaining fish and wildlife populations. Educational and interpretive programs are conducted regularly within wildlife areas, as well as community recreation and wildlife viewing areas.

Natural resource conservation areas (NRCAs), Category IV. Twenty-five NRCAs have been established by the state to protect areas that have ecological, scenic, and recreational value. They contain small areas of land intended to protect exceptional native ecosystems, threatened and endangered habitats, and sensitive plants and animals. Unlike NAPs, NRCAs allow low-impact public recreation. However, they are mainly utilized with conservation and educational goals in mind.

National recreation areas (NRAs), Category V. NRAs in Washington are managed by the Park Service (though in general, NRAs can be managed by any of the four federal land management agencies) to provide recreational opportunities and the protection of natural, scenic, and historic areas. They are established when a proposal is made, and a bill is passed by Congress and signed by the president. NRAs allow hunting and use of motorized recreational vehicles such as trail bikes, snowmobiles, and motorboats. Two of the three NRAs in Washington are centered on human-made reservoirs and lakes. Because they allow hunting and motorized vehicle use, NRAs have served legislators looking for ways to forge compromises in passing controversial national park bills. When Congress created the North Cascades National Park Service Complex, the area included two NRAs, allowing various uses that would have been prohibited in a national park.

State parks, Category V. State parks are administered by the State Parks and Recreation Commission with public recreation as the primary objective. They are designated by the commission when funding allows acquisition of park land. State parks usually offer fully developed auto and recreational vehicle facilities and allow all types of recreation, from paragliding to snowmobiling to jet skiing. There are 125 state parks in Washington. Many are near major highways and serve as popular tourist destinations and automobile rest points.

Wild and scenic rivers, Category V. Wild and scenic rivers are protected tracts of free-flowing rivers with remarkable scenic, recreational, geologic, fish and wildlife, historic, or cultural values. The 1968 Wild and Scenic Rivers Act established this system, which can be administered by the Forest Service, Park Service, U.S. Fish and Wildlife Service, or the Bureau of Land Management. Wild and scenic rivers are established much in the same way as wilderness areas are. Rivers are surveyed, undergo an agency review and recommendation process, and are then put before Congress to be passed as an act and signed by the president. River management plans are drawn on a multi-agency basis, involving state and local agencies, with one agency taking the lead (usually the Forest Service). Agencies and local communities identify the unique values of a river, such as recreation, salmon, and water quality, and then a management plan is written that reflects objectives based on specified values. There are three classifications under this system that give general guidelines as to how the different wild and scenic rivers are managed:

Wild river areas are free-flowing rivers or river segments that are unpolluted and usually accessible only by trail, with shorelines that are essentially primitive and undeveloped.

Scenic river areas are free-flowing rivers or river segments with generally primitive and undeveloped shorelines. Logging and farming are permitted as long as they do not diminish the river's natural character.

Recreational river areas have easy accessibility to the river by road and are meant for recreational purposes. They may have experienced diversion or damming in the past.

Though the wild and scenic designation does not prevent logging or mining along rivers on federal land, it does prevent the construction of dams and additional developments. The Wild and Scenic Rivers System is a tool that is vastly underutilized in Washington; our state has only has three river stretches so designated (on the Klickitat, the White Salmon, and the Skagit), while our neighboring state, Oregon, has forty-eight.

State scenic rivers, Category V. The Washington State Scenic Rivers program provides a different form of protection than the National Wild and Scenic River System. Washington's program emphasizes the cooperative management of rivers by landowners, recreational users, and state and local governments. Its goals are to promote the participation of local governments in river conservation, to settle conflicts between landowners and recreational users, and to provide public river-access points and litter disposal facilities. Publicly owned or leased property along Washington's scenic rivers is administered by the State Parks and Recreation Commission. The state is authorized to purchase land or easements in the river corridor to protect scenic integrity, fish and wildlife habitat, and historical and recreational sites. The Federal Energy Regulatory Commission (FERC), which is responsible for licensing hydroelectric projects, is required by federal law to take into account the river's scenic designation before issuing a license for projects along the river. However, scenic designation does not prohibit FERC from issuing licenses to build dams, it does not prohibit government agencies from making "improvements" along river corridors, and it does not restrict the management practices of federal agencies such as the USFS and the BLM. In addition, private landowners are not required to sell sections of their land, they are not subject to additional land-use regulations, and they do not have to adhere to the management plan for the scenic river. There are two scenic rivers in the system—a portion of the Skykomish River (including sections of two of its tributaries) and a part of the Little Spokane River.

Marine protected areas (MPAs), Category VI. MPAs are areas of underwater and shoreline habitat managed to conserve marine resources. They serve as refuges for all types of species and marine ecosystems and are protected from overfishing and other major human disturbances. In many cases, MPAs are heavily utilized for recreation, such as scuba diving and sightseeing, and the relationship between tourism and ecosystem health is a delicate balance. There are several types of MPAs, including marine protected refuges, marine conservation areas, marine reserves, and intertidal reserves. Depending on the designation, MPAs can be managed by a variety of government and even private-sector entities. Because there are terrestrial protected areas in Washington with marine components, such as coastal wildlife areas and wildlife refuges, an adequate inventory of all MPAs in the state remains to be done.

 ## ADMINISTRATIVELY ESTABLISHED AREAS IN CONTENTION

Legislative protection is the strongest form of land protection because, just as it takes an act of Congress or of a state legislature to create, it requires the same to undo. Agencies in the executive branch of government, such as the Forest Service, can protect areas without undergoing the lengthy, complicated, legislative process, but such protection is not written into law and, therefore, may be more easily dismantled with shifts in the political climate. Both the Northwest Forest Plan and the Roadless Area Conservation Rule are important cases in Washington of administrative protection whose future is uncertain because of ongoing political debates.

The Northwest Forest Plan

All national forests in Washington from the Olympic Peninsula to the eastern slopes of the Cascades are managed under the Northwest Forest Plan (NWFP). In 1994, President Clinton implemented the plan in response to the "timber wars" of the late 1980s and early 1990s. During those years, conflicts escalated between environmentalists and federal agencies because the government was not maintaining the viability of old-growth-dependent species like the northern spotted owl, which it was required to do by the National Forest Management Act. The resulting NWFP was an attempt to solve many problems at once by implementing a program for ecosystems that crossed administrative boundaries, especially affecting management plans of the Forest Service and the Bureau of Land Management. The NWFP was to provide for both maintenance of biological diversity and sustainable timber production. The plan requires the Forest Service and the BLM to protect all old-growth-dependent species; because there is not much known about many of these species, a "survey and manage" provision requires surveys to be conducted for rare or endangered species prior to any management activities, primarily timber harvesting.

The NWFP designated areas for commercial harvest, but it also established reserves that contain older trees, including areas that were once logged and are to be restored to old-growth conditions over time. A system of late-successional reserves was designed to encompass well-distributed pieces of forestland managed to protect and restore old-growth forests and to provide and improve habitat for the species that depend on them. However, since many of these areas are so young that they are unsuitable as habitat for old-growth-dependent species, management practices such as thinning through selective cutting are permitted until forests reach eighty years of age, even though the benefits of such cutting for old-growth forest development remain uncertain. Adaptive management areas are units established for testing forestry techniques in order to develop late-successional forest characteristics, while integrating commercial timber harvesting for economic purposes. The plan's Aquatic Conservation Strategy established riparian reserves to maintain watershed ecosystems and aquatic functions and to restore habitat for threatened aquatic species such as salmon. Finally, matrix lands are where the majority of commercial timber harvesting occurs, including the continued logging of old-growth forests. The late-successional reserves and riparian reserves can be classified under IUCN Category IV because they are continually subject to active management and human intervention.

Legal challenges have been made to some of the NWFP's provisions. As a result of two timber industry lawsuits, the government was mandated to review protections for the northern spotted owl and marbled murrelet under the Endangered Species Act. In 2003, additional lawsuits challenged restrictions on cutting old growth, causing federal officials to propose eliminating the survey and manage requirements and weakening the Aquatic Conservation Strategy. Because Congress did not establish the plan, it can be weakened through local and regional agency planning processes. Concerned citizens should stay informed, letting their voices be heard in regard to these challenges and their potential environmental impacts.

The Roadless Area Conservation Rule

A large percentage of national forest and other public land in Washington remains without roads, mostly because of inaccessible and rugged terrain, low timber values, or environmental concerns. The future management of these roadless areas is a topic of interest to both environmental and commercial factions, for they are the last of the large areas of undeveloped, unprotected wilderness.

Contention over roadless areas goes back many years. The Forest Service began to assess roadless areas that could potentially be put into wilderness designation in 1967, with the Roadless Area Review and Evaluation (RARE). The resulting report only recommended a small amount of land for wilderness designation. Many conservationists found major faults in the RARE report's adequacy and thoroughness and, through several lawsuits, caused the Forest Service to reinventory its roadless areas in what came to be known as RARE II, which was conducted from 1977 to 1979. The resulting report was also found to be incomplete, and orders for a RARE III were in the making, but eventually the entire RARE process faded away and was regarded as a failed attempt.

National forest roadless areas did not again receive nationwide agency consideration until after issues of the 1994 Northwest Forest Plan were settled. Focus returned in October of 1999, when President Clinton asked the Forest Service to begin an open public process to discuss the future of roadless areas within national forests, halting all new road construction until a national management plan was established. The resulting Roadless Area Conservation Rule, also called the Clinton Roadless Rule, was established in January of 2001. The Roadless Rule prohibits the construction of roads on 58.5 million acres of national forestlands currently inventoried by the Forest Service as roadless. However, logging is still permitted if timber can be transported by other means. The Roadless Rule also requires the Forest Service to survey roadless areas of 5000 acres that were left out of the original RARE process.

Though the areas protected under the Roadless Rule represent a victory for wildlands preservation, their future is uncertain. Soon after President George W. Bush took office in 2001, he began announcing his administration's plans to amend the rule and to allow gas and logging companies more influence in managing roadless areas at the local level. Again, because the rule is not written into law, it can be easily reversed. In 2002 and again in

Table 3.1. IUCN Categories Applied to Washington's Protected Areas

IUCN CATEGORY	WASHINGTON PROTECTED AREAS	MANAGING AGENCY IN WASHINGTON*
Category Ia: Strict nature reserve (managed mainly for science)	Research natural areas (RNAs), in design but not in practice	BLM, FWS, NPS, US Army, USFS
	Natural area preserves (NAPs), in design but not in practice	DFW, DNR under the Natural Areas Program, SPRC
Category Ib: Wilderness area (managed mainly for wilderness protection)	National wilderness areas	BLM, FWS, NPS, USFS
Category II: National park (managed mainly for ecosystem protection and recreation)	National parks	NPS
Category III: National monument (managed mainly for conservation of specific natural features)	National monuments	BLM, FWS, NPS, USFS
	National marine sanctuaries	NOAA
Category IV: Habitat/species management area (managed mainly for conservation through management intervention)	National wildlife refuges	FWS
	State wildlife areas	DFW
	Natural resource conservation areas (NRCAs)	DNR under the Natural Areas Program
	Northwest Forest Plan (NWFP) designations: Late-successional reserves, Riparian reserves	BLM, USFS
	Inventoried roadless areas protected under the Roadless Area Conservation Rule (as of 2003)	USFS
Category V: Protected landscape/seascape (managed mainly for conservation and recreation)	National recreation areas (NRAs)	NPS
	Federal Wild and Scenic rivers	BLM, FWS, NPS, USFS
	State Scenic rivers	SPRC
	State parks	SPRC
Category VI: Managed resource protected area (managed mainly for the sustainable use of natural ecosystems)	Marine protected areas (MPAs)	NOAA
	Adaptive management areas (under the NWFP)	USFS

Alphabetical key to agencies: BLM (Bureau of Land Management), DFW (Washington Department of Fish and Wildlife), DNR (Washington Department of Natural Resources), FWS (U.S. Fish and Wildlife Service), NOAA (National Oceanic and Atmospheric Administration), NPS (National Park Service), SPRC (State Parks and Recreation Commission), USFS (U.S. Forest Service)

2003, Congress considered legislation that would turn the Roadless Rule into law. Fluctuations in roadless-area management will most likely continue in the future and are an important reminder that areas protected by administrative regulations are far from permanent.

 ## ASSESSING WASHINGTON'S WILDNESS: WHAT IS PROTECTED AND WHAT IS THREATENED?

Protected places are important for the maintenance in perpetuity of vital ecological relationships and processes that sustain life. The protection of mountains, forests, wildlife, arid lands, rivers, wetlands, and coastal areas provides cleaner air and water, rich soil, crucial habitat, and opportunities for recreation and spiritual connection with the natural world. Just like the human body, the natural world requires balance, connection, nutrients, water, rest, and harmony. And, just like the human body, the wild can only withstand so much abuse before becoming ill or incapable of functioning as it once did. Over time, Washington's natural body has been torn into pieces with uneven protection, leaving much of it fragmented and in critical condition. As a result, it is uncertain whether Washington's protected areas are capable of adequately safeguarding wild populations and processes.

Conservation biology is a tool used to assess how protected areas are functioning, ecologically. It can help us better protect the natural world if we use it to studying the dynamics of diversity, scarcity, and extinction of nature's wild components. It allows the application of research strategies in order to better preserve wildlands and their characteristics, helping to contribute scientific legitimacy and rationale to the greater movement for the perpetuation of the variety of life and its processes, including living organisms, the genetic differences among them, the communities and ecosystems where they occur, and the evolutionary and ecological processes that keep them functioning—in a word, biodiversity.

There are three criteria derived from conservation biology that are particularly useful for assessing the adequacy of Washington's protected areas and their ability to maintain biological diversity:

1. **Viable populations.** Sufficient numbers of individuals of every species are essential to the perpetuation of life's complex web of interactions and interdependencies. This criterion focuses on specific species threatened by human practices and calls attention to habitat needs and susceptibility to extinction.

2. **Ecological and evolutionary processes.** These are important to consider because species evolve in relationship to their environments. Patterns and processes of disturbance, nutrient cycling, and interactions between species shape the ecosystems we know today.

3. **Representation.** A broad spectrum of natural communities should be represented in a network of protected areas. This provides greater success in protecting individual and threatened species because it focuses on entire ecosystems and the habitats they depend upon.

With these criteria in mind, we ask the question: Are the existing protected areas in Washington adequate for maintaining wild, biologically diverse ecosystems? The evidence demonstrates that Washington's protected areas are at risk.

Viable Populations

Fragmentation is one of the largest threats to populations of wild species. Unprotected private and public property separate Washington's protected areas, making them less effective. The subdivision of habitats into smaller and smaller units of land not only reduces the total acreage available to native species, but also creates severe impacts like "edge effects," which occur when the biological effects of logging, road building, livestock grazing, agriculture, and other practices that border protected areas penetrate the outermost boundaries of protected wildlands. For example, in forested protected areas, edge effects can penetrate up to 1000 feet into the forest interior.[7] Old-growth forest interiors are generally cool due to the thick, insulating forest canopy, but when bordered by roads or clear-cuts, they are not buffered from strong winds or sun, causing greater variation in temperature and disrupting interior populations that rely on a cooler environment. Other effects of fragmentation include increased nest parasitism, invasion by nonnative species, and increased risk of disease.

Inadequate reserve size and lack of connectivity between reserves especially threatens populations that require a large range, such as lynx, fishers, gray wolves, and grizzlies. The inability or reluctance of species to travel between fragments can cause poor reproductive success. Isolated populations experience genetic and reproductive problems, often inhibiting a species' ability to breed with individuals from other populations. This eventually leads to islands of unhealthy, overly inbred species or species not mating at all, therefore causing local extinction within fragments. Starvation is another threat for a population or an individual if it happens to get trapped in a fragment that is too small for survival.

Species and populations that are most threatened by human activities do not always find hospitable conditions in protected areas. The Wilderness Act allows the continuation of some practices that were established prior to an area's inclusion in the National Wilderness Preservation System. For example, Forest Service, U.S. Fish and Wildlife Service, and Bureau of Land Management wilderness areas are open to livestock. Grazing is extremely prevalent in eastern Washington, especially in the shrub-steppe areas and the eastern dry forests, where livestock trample mixed riparian and shrub-steppe areas, endangering native species. Livestock graze on the east side of the Pasayten Wilderness in fragile, high-elevation meadows within the Okanogan National Forest. Sod grasses introduced for livestock invade protected lands, such as state wildlife areas, national wildlife refuges, and wilderness areas, driving out endemic flora, such as bluebunch wheatgrass.

If a plant community is harmed by incompatible practices on protected lands, the animals associated with the plants are disturbed as well. Areas in the shrub-steppe with deep and loamy soils have been mostly transformed for agricultural purposes. This has dramatically altered the distribution of sagebrush, which does best in deep, rich soils. Plant and animal communities associated with sagebrush, such as native grasses, birds, rabbits, rodents, and insects, are transformed as a result. For example, Washington's endemic pygmy rabbit is nearly extinct. This small rabbit species requires deep soils for burrowing and depends upon sagebrush for winter forage, along with the associated native bunchgrasses, when available. Pygmy rabbits are the prey of weasels, coyotes, bobcats, and raptors, playing an essential role in the food chain.

Ecological and Evolutionary Processes

Threats to ecological processes are exemplified by the history of fire suppression. Ponderosa pine forests that regularly experience low-intensity forest fires characterize parts of eastern Washington. These fires shape forest communities. Many wildlife species are not only adapted to this fire regime, but also depend upon it for survival. When fires are suppressed over time, woody fuel accumulates so that, when a fire occurs, the results are catastrophic. The high fuel load creates the opportunity for flames to reach tree crowns and, when exacerbated by wind, the fire spreads easily from tree to tree. The intensity of the fire can be so great that it kills the majority, if not all, of the adult trees. Severe temperatures from intense fires can also sterilize the soil, which makes it difficult for species that usually recolonize after fire because there are virtually no nutrients, microbes, or fungus available to assist in the growth of native plants. In addition, large disturbances of this kind can cause local extinction, where a population disappears for a period of time until it is reestablished by subsequent colonizers from adjacent habitats. The isolation of many of our protected lands makes it difficult for species to disperse or recolonize after such disturbances.

To ameliorate this dilemma of fire suppression and to reestablish important fire regimes, various protected areas, such as natural area preserves, are implementing management programs that mimic natural fire regimes. Restoring and maintaining regular patterns of fire can assist in conserving endangered species and in maintaining diversity.

Representation

Fragmentation, incompatible human activities, inadequate reserve size, and lack of connectivity threaten the continued existence of viable populations and ecological processes. Additionally, protected areas are unevenly represented across the state, resulting in inadequate or no protection for important ecosystems. One of the central goals of conservation is to include a broad spectrum of communities in a network of protected areas. This approach is more successful in protecting biological diversity because it focuses on entire ecosystems, habitats, and assemblages of species rather than on single species.

Washington's protected areas are located in three vegetative provinces, although not every province is represented equally. The alpine province is found near and above tree line, extending from the subalpine zone where herbaceous plants, low shrubs, and few tree species exist to the alpine areas where glaciers, permanent snowfields, and rocks dominate. The forest province includes diverse species of trees and plants occurring at various elevations and in different forest types. The shrub-steppe province consists of two zones, the steppe zone, characterized by native grasslands with bluebunch wheatgrass and Idaho fescue, and the shrub-steppe zone, characterized by sagebrush and accompanying grass species. Washington lies predominantly within the forest and shrub-steppe provinces.[8]

When looking at the map of Washington's protected areas (see the color insert), striking gaps in protected areas are obvious. Geographically, protection is disproportionately aggregated in the western portion of the state; thus crucial ecosystems located in the east are extremely underrepresented by Washington's most protective land designations. Washington's national parks and wilderness areas certainly protect some of the most breathtaking and visually stunning mountains, forests, and waterways in the state. However, the majority of these protected areas are in the alpine province, which does not adequately represent Washington's dominant ecosystems located in the forest and shrub-steppe provinces. Instead, they protect rugged, ice-covered mountain peaks, like those of the Cascades. A prime example is the cherished North Cascades National Park Service Complex, which is largely alpine rock and ice, found at high elevation. Ice and deep snowpack create conditions that limit the availability of hospitable habitat for many plants and animals.

When we think of protected areas, we should not forget Washington's wild waters. Waterways are the veins and arteries of the land. Riparian areas provide connective corridors for a variety of wildlife, along with supplying the fish we eat, scenic beauty, recreational opportunity and, most importantly, clean drinking water. Washington's rivers delight the hearts of poets, like Washington author Tim McNulty, who wrote the book

Washington's Wild Rivers to call attention to the need for their protection.[9] Washington's rivers are also essential to former governor Dan Evans, who expresses that his "lifelong love affair with Washington's wilderness includes our rivers, for they are the creator, lifeline, and channels of access for those who hike our ridges and climb our peaks . . . . We still have an opportunity to preserve stretches of our rivers that flow free and unspoiled . . . if we fail to preserve them now, we lose that privilege forever."[10]

Washington is rich in rivers, but deficient in terms of their permanent protection. There are more than eighty rivers eligible for Wild and Scenic designation across the entire state. The National Wild and Scenic Rivers System is one of the most promising and broad forms of permanent river protection, yet one of the most underutilized designations in the state. Only three segments of rivers are included in the Wild and Scenic Rivers System. These are portions of the Skagit River in the northwest corner of the state and segments of the Klickitat and White Salmon Rivers, which are two short tributaries of the Columbia along Washington's southern border.

Over the years, many of Washington's rivers have undergone a number of studies to determine their eligibility for Wild and Scenic status. In 1980 and 1982, the Park Service prepared a "Nationwide River Inventory" that listed the rivers that appeared eligible for Wild and Scenic designation. From 1985 until 1986, the Bonneville Power Administration and the State of Washington conducted a study that documented the value of each section of river for fish, wildlife, recreation, historical and cultural values, and natural features. The seven national forests, between the years of 1986 and 1988, released draft plans for managing forests, each with a section on eligibility and classification of rivers that were under consideration for Wild and Scenic designation. To date, no designations have materialized from any of these studies and planning processes.

UNFINISHED BUSINESS

Since the passage of the 1984 act that established over 1 million acres of national forest wilderness in Washington and the 1988 act that designated over 1.7 million acres of wilderness in the state's national parks, no new Washington wilderness proposal has made it past Congress. In fact, wilderness areas account for only 9.4 percent of the state, out of a 45.9-million-acre land base.[11] Millions of acres of roadless public lands await permanent protective status in Washington State. Additionally, private landowners have the power to safeguard biological diversity by placing their lands in protective designations, such as land trusts and conservation easements.

Cores, corridors, and buffers are methods of connecting these areas, providing wildlife with the opportunity to travel from site to site without being exposed to developed areas and highways. Cores are areas such as national parks and wilderness areas, and corridors are designated swaths of land that radiate out from these central pieces of land, creating linkages between them. Buffers are areas that soften the ecologically shocking effects of incompatible practices. They create and maintain wild space in developed or resource extractive areas, such as organic farms or forests managed for sustainable uses in areas abutting protected areas.

The remaining roadless areas possess Washington's biological richness, where a variety of rare species and ecosystems are highly concentrated. In an effort to identify Washington's remaining roadless areas, the Pacific Biodiversity Institute carried out an intensive inventory and mapping project of the state's public and private lands. In 1998, a project report was released, and the results of the study revealed that 39 percent of Washington State is in an unroaded condition. Public lands represent the majority of this percentage, but significant roadless acreage exists on private lands as well (see the color insert map).

The national forests alone contain more than 3 million acres of roadless areas in Washington that qualify for protection under the National Wilderness Preservation System. Many of these are areas that should have been included in the 1984 designations of Washington wilderness areas. The Pacific Biodiversity Institute criticizes the Forest Service for overlooking at least 860,000 acres of roadless areas during the RARE process. They state in their 1998 report that "[h]ad the Forest Service conducted an adequate inventory of roadless lands in earlier attempts, these extensive wildlands would have been considered for wilderness designation during several rounds of Wilderness legislation."[12] For example, the institute inventoried 348,045 acres of roadless areas adjacent to the Salmo-Priest Wilderness in the Colville National Forest, concluding that when the lines were drawn for the wilderness designation, these areas were excluded because they included trees of high timber value. These roadless areas are protected only through administrative regulations, like the Roadless Area Conservation Rule, leaving them vulnerable to the political and environmental agendas of changing presidential administrations.

The current system of protected areas in Washington is inadequate for maintaining viable populations, ecological processes, and full ecological representation of wild Washington. Wildness must be protected in big, interconnected networks that embrace the full variety of species, waterways, and wildlands in the state. The protected areas we have today are essential, and enormous effort has gone into making them a reality, as the accounts in Part II of this book will demonstrate. But the existing protected areas are only the first steps if Washington's wildness is to be effectively defended in perpetuity, and increased citizen participation will be key in making that happen.

CHAPTER 4

Surfing the Tides of Change: Understanding the Shifts of Washington's Social Landscape

◆ *Caitlin Houser and Travis Keron* ◆

Former governor and wilderness proponent Dan Evans once made an analogy that compared political timing to surfing: to catch the wave of a historic moment and ride it through, you must neither try to get aboard too soon, for fear the wave will crush you, nor wait too long and miss the ride completely. If you catch the wave at just the right moment in history, you can stand up and surf all the way to shore. Looking back at the wave of social and environmental activism that Dan Evans himself caught as governor of Washington during the late 1960s and early 1970s, his sense of timing is clearly demonstrated. The social climate was changing in response to the contentious political climate and many people actively voiced their growing concern for social and environmental issues. Named in a University of Michigan study as one of the ten outstanding governors of the twentieth century, Dan Evans saw to the priorities of his constituents during an age of civil unrest and was able to give an unprecedented degree of attention to protecting the environment.

The social climate is again changing nationwide, and the changes occurring within Washington State may help define the course of the local conservation movement in coming years. These changes involve the transformation of land, lifestyle, and livelihood, but they all essentially revolve around people. People brought about changes, people are affected by changes, and people are ultimately in control of them. These changes carry with them significant implications for the survival of Washington's wild places—wild places that can be more effectively protected through understanding and responding to shifting economic, social, and geographic trends. In order to fully grasp the present status and the future possibilities of the conservation movement in Washington State—and to have a chance at catching the wave that is currently swelling—it is important to be familiar with not only the region's physical geography but also its current human geography.

Washington, like much of the world, is undergoing a transition as it adjusts to the growth of the global economy. This, coupled with Washington's position as one of the fastest growing states in the country, has stimulated unusually expeditious social and economic changes. In the past few decades especially, the state's population has boomed; and the U.S. Census Bureau estimates that, from 1995 to 2025, Washington's population will continue to grow by nearly 2.4 million people, with migration accounting for just more than half of the increase (931,000 immigrants coming from other states in the country and 394,000 immigrants from other countries).[1]

This is a dynamic time in history. The sweeping relocation of people to Washington and the evolution of the region's economy, culture, and style of living mirror changes that have occurred in many places worldwide, and Washington can be viewed as a microcosm of global change: the region has become largely reliant on the international economy instead of its indigenous resources at the same time that the service sector is growing and manufacturing and resource extraction are shrinking; rural countryside is transforming into parking lots, strip malls, and housing for commuting exurbanites; and life in general feels different than it used to for people whose landscapes and livelihoods have been transformed by these rapid changes. For some residents, these changes in the landscape are sure signs of progress. But the consequences of modern living are a mixed blessing, as many people witness the wooded hills explored in childhood disappear, replaced by new stretches of freeway or homogenous, residential cul-de-sacs.

As conservationists have watched the natural environment diminish, they have worked hard for the protection of what remains. But taking a proactive, rather than reactive, approach is possible if we sharpen our awareness of changing social trends and anticipate their implications for wildlands preservation. Just as these changes were set in motion by the actions of people, we as citizens can meet the challenges that result by using insight into the trends as a tool. Washington's geographic trends are closely interrelated and difficult to simplify, but to facilitate the navigation of the state's socioeconomic landscape, we have mapped out four categories of change: new settlement patterns, the postfrontier economy, racial and ethnic diversification, and dramatic shifts in civic engagement.

 NEW SETTLEMENT PATTERNS

Since the advent of industrialization in the mid-nineteenth century, vast numbers of people have left rural areas for opportunities in cities, creating high-density urban areas.[2] As personal mobility increased, especially with escalating use of the automobile after World War II, people spread beyond the city center. They began moving into small towns and the surrounding countryside, turning rural areas into commuter communities; thus began the process of suburbanization. Large "vertical" cities spread out across the landscape, and midsize "horizontal" cities grew.[3] Yet, a majority of the country's rural hinterlands were still losing population even into the 1970s. As some people moved away from city centers, others from rural communities moved toward cities like Seattle, which represented one quarter of the region's total populace. As a result, cities started decentralizing, or spreading away from some focal point (in this case, the city center), but metropolitan areas still grew in both population and development.

Beginning in the 1980s and '90s, this trend dramatically changed. Decentralization drastically increased as people began repopulating rural areas. Between 1990 and 1994, 75 percent of the country's rural places grew almost twice as fast as urban areas.[4] From 1990 to 1995, places in Washington with populations of 2500 or fewer grew by 16.5 percent, while size classes of 500,000 or more grew by just over 3 percent.[5] Even some of the most remote counties in northeastern Washington, including Ferry, Stevens, and Pend Oreille Counties, have been growing in recent years.[6] As one of the fastest growing states in America, Washington's growth rate is concentrated in or near rural areas.

The fact that most of Washington's nonmetropolitan counties are growing, however, does not mean that all small, remote communities are growing. Many individual towns are still losing population. There are many reasons for this, including failing resource economies, few amenities, and extreme isolation, each of which reinforces the others. Furthermore, population decrease in some towns is concentrated within the middle class, who leave to find jobs elsewhere. While the middle class leave, the poor cannot afford to move and the rich often buy new homes in these areas, turning the towns into "rural playgrounds" for the upper class.[7] Washington's southeastern counties, including Garfield and Columbia, are examples of areas where some rural towns are still dwindling despite the resurgence of rural repopulation.

Nevertheless, most counties in Washington are gaining population overall.

Contrary to popular belief, those moving to nonmetropolitan parts of Washington are members of all ages, not just retirees. Young, educated, and affluent people are among the largest groups moving to rural areas. They are looking for what they believe to be a better quality of life. They are not concerned solely with economic factors, but look more for environmental quality in surrounding areas and a comfortable pace of life, and they are willing to accept lower wages to live where they are comfortable. This is the concept of a "second paycheck." People are willing to give up the higher wages of cities to live where the surrounding landscape and community provide even greater benefits, such as lower crime rates, less congestion, safer environment for children, and greater access to the wild.

These new rural residents believe they will find such qualities in their adopted areas, particularly in those locations that are close to protected landscapes. In Washington, some of the highest growth has been within counties that contain wilderness areas or national parks, while most places with few amenities are growing slower, if not decreasing. In the 1980s and early 1990s, wilderness counties grew nearly twice as fast as other nonmetropolitan counties all over the West, including Washington.[8] According to Gundars Rudzitis, a professor of geography at the University of Idaho, 53 percent of people he surveyed in "wilderness counties" throughout the West said that wilderness was a central aspect in determining whether they would live in an area.[9]

 ## THE POSTFRONTIER ECONOMY

Even though the Census Bureau determined that America's settlement frontier closed in 1890, it was not until the last decades of the twentieth century that Washington's frontier economy began to be displaced by other sectors. Only now, when much of the West is transitioning into a postindustrial, technological landscape, resource extraction is no longer the dominant economic force in Washington. The fastest growing activities throughout much of Washington are in the high technology, information, and service sectors. Washington's economy is experiencing a complete and inevitable overhaul.

There are many reasons for this transition, some residing in history and all tied to national and global forces. One such reason is interconnected with Washington's demographic shifts. Dispersing populations, increased mobility, and technological infrastructure have all allowed both employment and service industries to decentralize.[10] As people move, services move with them. Once, businesses were limited in locale by physical and economic constraints, such as lack of transportation and distance to markets. Increased information technologies and infrastructure, however, are allowing many businesses to locate wherever they desire. High technology and service industries are moving into rural areas to take advantage of local benefits. Rural areas can provide both quantity and quality of space for expanding firms. They afford lower rent, taxes, and wages. At the same time, rural communities provide a higher quality of life which attracts skilled labor.[11]

In contrast to the decentralization of service industries, resource extraction and related manufacturing industries, including timber industries and their mills, have historically had a tendency to centralize. First, they tended to congregate near cities to take advantage of developed infrastructure and the urban workforce. With the advantages provided by cities, these industries were able to force many smaller, rural-based companies out of business. As a result, a smaller number of large corporations began to dominate resource extraction. Concurrently, corporations began to mechanize, becoming less dependent on the surrounding workforce. In the last three decades, and particularly during the 1980s recession, industries in Washington and throughout the industrialized world decreased production costs by replacing workers with machines in the factories, mills, and fields.[12]

Eastern Washington provides one example of the effects of centralization. Martha Henderson Tubesing, a professor of geography at The Evergreen State College, has called parts of eastern Washington an "abandoned landscape."[13] Family farmers are leaving as agribusiness grows. In Washington, the number of farms decreased between 1987 and 1997 from nearly 34,000 to 29,000, while average land per farm increased from 480 acres to 523 acres.[14] Agricultural production in eastern Washington is centralizing around a smaller number of large firms, leaving a depopulated landscape.

Another reason for the transition to a postindustrial condition is the increasing complexity of the world economy.[15] Washington's extractive industries have always been linked to distant markets. One of the reasons nineteenth-century railroad workers built transcontinental tracks through Washington was to connect eastern Washington's wheat fields to China. As the world economy becomes more complex and interconnected, Washington's economy shifts accordingly. Resource extraction develops or expands in other countries, creating greater competition for Washington's industries. As a result, many of the large, corporate industries based in the West have themselves moved operations out of the United States in order to lower the cost of resources, labor, and other business expenses. Not only does this result in increased competition for remaining firms, but it also "exports" jobs, striking a double blow to Washington's rural industries. Most of Washington's rural-based industries cannot compete and have shut down.

At the writing of this book, one such example is taking place in Republic, Washington, where the local timber mill is in danger of shutting down. The primary reason for the mill's plight, as explained by Thomas Power, chair of the University of Montana's Department of Economics, is an excess supply of logs and wood products.[16] Part of this excess supply has come from imported Canadian lumber, which has gutted prices. This trend is not limited to Washington. Mills all across the country are shutting down, as they cannot compete with foreign industries cutting trees from neighboring Canada or from more distant countries like Brazil.

While the economy restructures, business activities shift.[17] Between 1988 and 1998, Washington lost 7,300 jobs in the forest products industry, once the most important source of employment in the state. At the same time, the state's workforce gained 726,000 jobs in other sectors. Within every region of Washington and nearly every county, more jobs were created during that ten-year period than were lost. In most counties, the fastest growing industries among those new jobs were in the service sectors.[18] Resource extraction industries are declining, while other industries, particularly non-goods-producing sectors, grew by an increasing margin.

As Washington's resource economy is transitioning, many rural communities are changing. In the most extreme cases, towns are losing employment and population faster than communities can restore them. This occurs in communities that are isolated from larger towns and are still chiefly dependent on export-based resource economies. People are forced to find different occupations, and some move as their livelihoods in logging, agriculture, or mining become less available.

Nevertheless, most rural counties and even towns are not suffering as much as once anticipated. On multiple occasions, economists and politicians have predicted the outright economic collapse of rural areas when resource extraction diminishes. This has not happened. As stated earlier, more jobs have actually been created than lost, but instead of traditional resource extraction, the newly created jobs are in service sectors. One major source of these service industries is self-employed entrepreneurs. Many small-town residents are creating their own employment to take the place of jobs lost in resource extraction. Beginning in the 1990s, the number of entrepreneurs throughout America's rural areas actually began to grow faster than in the cities.[19] However, as new economic ventures blossom, many rural residents feel that the transition is negative and that their towns are decaying. For more than a decade, they have seen their traditional economic activities shut down while they and their neighbors lose their jobs. At the same time, new jobs have moved into town, but they seem to be lower paying and of lower quality. This has created a disparity between "good" jobs in resource extraction and "lousy" jobs in the other activities.

While average income has decreased throughout much of nonmetropolitan

Washington, there is little evidence that this is solely because of new ser-vice-sector employment. Average pay has decreased in all economic sec-tors within rural Washington, including both service and resource extraction industries.[20] Reverting to primary dependence on resource industries would not decrease the gap in average pay and income. In fact, in 2001 the aver-age self-employed rural entrepreneur in America, many of whom were based in the service sector, had a higher income than other rural employees.[21] Furthermore, unemployment in rural areas is no higher today than it was during peak timber harvests of the 1980s.[22] While some towns are in se-vere economic distress, most are not. Instead, residents' distress results in part from losing a cherished and age-old way of life.

As resource industries suffer and rural communities lose a way of life, the people impacted look for a reason for their plight. Regardless of the boom-and-bust cycles that have always characterized the globally integrated resource-extraction industries, these rural residents understandably try to find a more tangible reason. Unfortunately, this causes industry and rural communities to repeatedly blame environmental groups and government land-protection policies. While it is true that there are fewer trees avail-able for harvest and less land available for cultivation, this decline in ob-tainable resources is not significant enough to create declining resource economies. The problem lies in global connections. Worldwide, timber and agriculture have excess production capacity, meaning that the supply of natural resources and agricultural products is so high worldwide that lo-cal production becomes unprofitable. Consequently, the first businesses to shut down under such circumstances are the small, inefficient compa-nies competing in a global setting. And most of these businesses are un-fortunately located in our rural communities. As Thomas Power and Gundars Rudzitis have both said, placing blame on environmental groups and gov-ernment land protection is little more than scapegoating.[23]

Repeated fluctuations in resource extraction industries have sent ru-ral residents through a whirlwind of economic twists and turns. In response to vast global trends, Washington is experiencing another twist—a com-plete reorganization of its economic structure. As a postindustrial, tech-nological economy, Washington is increasingly important to interconnected global markets. Instead of being a producer of natural resources, Wash-ington is becoming a producer and merchant of technology, information, and services. Peter Daniels, a University of Birmingham professor, and William Lever, a University of Glasgow professor, have said that the growing importance of the U.S. West Coast as a "nexus of global interaction and trade" means that its major cities, including Seattle, may one day surpass New York as global financial centers.[24]

NEW SETTLEMENT PATTERNS AND THE POSTFRONTIER ECONOMY: IMPLICATIONS FOR WILDNESS

As the political and economic landscape of Washington changes, so do the implications for the state's wildness. The changing demographics and transitioning economy within the state are swaying public opinion about how to manage Washington's diverse landscapes. Statewide, a greater number of people favor preservation of Washington's natural heritage over resource extraction.

It is often said that most rural communities desire commodity uses of public land over protection. This is no longer so. In a one-hundred-county survey of Idaho, Montana, Washington, and Oregon, Gundars Rudzitis found that the majority of people believed that federal lands should be managed for watershed and environmental protection, while only 16 percent believed that managing for timber harvests was most important. When choosing between "protective or commodity-based management strategies," 76 percent of the people surveyed chose protection. While many people feel that management for resource extraction is important, most feel that protection is imperative. As Rudzitis summarizes, "Clearly, even in the conservative West, the majority favor protecting public lands first, then allowing some tree harvesting and grazing within that overall protective strategy."[25]

Today, there is no longer a clear distinction between the priorities of the so-called urban environmentalist and rural utilitarian. When choosing between protection versus consumption, poll results fluctuate by no more than ten percentage points between urban and rural residents. In fact, 57 percent of all Washingtonians consider themselves environmentalists.[26] More people across the state, whether in rural towns or in cities, are becoming concerned with environmental protection. This trend will likely continue into the future and can prove advantageous to perceptive individuals or groups that capitalize on this opportunity. Now more than ever, people can bring large, diverse groups of concerned citizens together to find and work toward a common goal.

Amid these positive outlooks, however, the shifts in urban/rural demographics and the changing economy can potentially be a double-edged-sword for wilderness. While more people move into rural communities for wilderness characteristics, these new residents may also bring more development. It is easy to forget that all urbanized areas were once rural towns that were desirable locations to move to. Regarding rural areas on a global scale, Martin Phillips, a lecturer in human geography at the University of Leicester, states, "Recent rural in-migrants seek to prevent further development within their backyards even though they themselves may be living in a recent development."[27] Many migrating citizens desire the quality of life afforded by rural areas while still demanding some of the benefits that urban services and opportunities provide. Essentially, people want to live within a rural setting while still enjoying an urban lifestyle.

As a result, urban amenities frequently follow populations into rural areas, which increases pressure to develop the land. Between 1970 and 1990, developed land within the Pacific Northwest grew over seven times faster than the area's population.[28] Paradoxically, as more people want Washington's landscapes protected, their demand for a better quality of life consumes more of it through one of the most destructive land uses humans have contrived. While pointing to a picture of the Seattle metropolis, Larry Mason, a timber mill owner from Forks, Washington, said, "There's the biggest clearcut in the state. The difference is, they don't plant their clearcut back. They pave over it."[29]

Lastly, when fighting for more protected wildness within Washington, it would be folly to think only about this one state. As the state's economy connects to the rest of the world, so does its wildness. Stopping the consumption of Washington's landscapes could, depending on economic and political conditions, unknowingly create problems elsewhere. Washington's transition to nongoods production does not mean that natural resource demand is decreasing; it only means that supply is coming from elsewhere, including wild places in other countries.

Between 1969 and 1990, the number of multinational firms originating from just the world's fourteen leading industrial countries increased by about 30 percent.[30] Many of those firms, including some of Washington's resource extraction industries, have moved to newly developing countries. Consequently, since the 1980s, imports into developed nations like the United States have increasingly been coming from developing or newly industrializing countries.[31] These imports include many of the same natural resources producible here, but instead they come from countries with weaker environmental and labor standards. As long as there is a strong demand for commodity resources, someone will supply them.

Furthermore, if overseas production is made economically attractive to corporations through incentives such as government subsidies, those corporations may enter foreign wild places. For example, within the last thirty years, multinational corporations have replaced thousands of acres of Chile's ancient forests with exotic pine plantations.[32] The issue of protecting wild landscapes does not end by simply addressing threats to wildlands in a localized area. The United States is one of the biggest consumers of natural resources, and protecting the wild places where those resources are extracted involves addressing the basic issues of consumption, on both local and national levels.

RACIAL AND ETHNIC DIVERSIFICATION

Our cultural norms and ideologies are constantly challenged and altered by the ever-changing political climate, the diversification of economies and populations, and any number of forces that arise in a growing and changing nation. Washington State, not only because of its rapidly changing economy and burgeoning population, but also because of multicultural influences, has an unusually high potential for shifts in perspective.

Seattle, as the largest city in the state and a thriving seaport, center of commerce, and cultural hub, is a good example of the diversity that is growing throughout the state. Consumers in the city have a multitude of products from other parts of the world from which to choose. They can window-shop for Chinese herbal remedies and Guatemalan clothes, dine on Vietnamese, Ethiopian, or Indian cuisine, or lose themselves in a medley of exotic sights, smells, and sounds. Washington residents can attend tribal pow wows and other public ceremonial activities, or they can participate in African-American-inspired historical celebrations, such as Juneteenth or the Martin Luther King, Jr. birthday holidays.

As the populations of ethnic and racial minority groups are increasing, the region is becoming more diverse. Washington's geographic position along, and its economic ties to, the Pacific Rim have contributed to it becoming a major migratory destination for Asians and Pacific Islanders, whose population in Washington grew by 64 percent between 1990 and 2000. Other minority populations grew as well, at rates far exceeding that of the white population, which grew by only 12 percent during the same decade.[33] It is estimated that in the near future these populations will have a far greater influence in Washington's predominately white society than they currently do. Non-Hispanic whites are expected to represent 76 percent of Washington's population in 2025, as compared to 85 percent in 1995. The proportion of Hispanic peoples in the state population (Hispanic peoples can be of any race) is expected to rise to more than 10 percent by 2025, compared to just more than 5 percent in 1995.[34]

Although the majority of elected governmental officials is currently white, political involvement and power have increased among minority racial/ethnic populations as they become a larger segment of the general population. Not only are more members of minority racial/ethnic populations voting but the degree of participation in political lobbying organizations, political coalitions, campaigning and running for office has also increased.[35]

Strong trends related to politics are observable in specific racial and ethnic groups, pointing toward a positive future in strengthening the voice of minority opinions. The trends in the U.S. Hispanic population, for instance, indicate an increased ability to influence politics in coming years. In this group, the percentage of citizens who are ineligible to vote due to naturalization laws is quite high (40 percent of the U.S. Hispanic population), and an unusually large proportion of the population is composed of youth. In upcoming generations, the number of eligible voters will increase as more children are born to Hispanic couples within the United States, and young Hispanics could eventually experience a boom in political involvement, according to studies showing that political participation increases with age. The Asian population provides another example of increasing political power. As candidates for political office, Asians have been more successful at gaining the vote of constituencies of other backgrounds than any other minority racial/ethnic group, and the number of elected Asian American officials is rising. In fact, a second-generation Chinese American, Gary Locke, was serving his second term as governor of Washington during the writing of this book.

RACIAL AND ETHNIC DIVERSIFICATION: IMPLICATIONS FOR WILDNESS

As students and authors, we spoke personally with dozens of activists and organizations in order to thoroughly understand the ins and outs of the movement to protect wildlands. We traveled all over the state, meeting with organizations that use an array of tactics and that range from tiny community-based groups to well-funded international organizations. On a sage-covered bluff overlooking the Columbia River, we ate a picnic lunch with Bob Wilson, a founder of the initially three-person grassroots group Save The Reach. We spent an afternoon speaking to executives of the Nature Conservancy in the well-appointed meeting rooms of a Seattle skyscraper. We were privy to invaluable information from all walks of life, and we were fortunate to hear their impressions of the movement and their concerns for the future.

After a few months of speaking to these groups, an interesting pattern emerged—almost every face we saw was white. We were perplexed to find this in such a progressive and forward-looking movement. The predominantly white make-up of conservation organizations was acknowledged to be a problem by most everyone, but usually only after we asked about it specifically. This recognition seemed to be a skeleton in the movement's collective closet, and the people we spoke to were regretful but ultimately at a loss about how to address the issue. Spokespeople for small and large conservation and preservation organizations all over the state were all bothered by this, but by their own admission, no one seemed to be doing anything very effective about it.

The growth of diverse segments of Washington's population opens new doors of opportunity for the largely white movement to expand its numbers. It also suggests a chance for the movement to increase the involvement of presently underrepresented minority populations. People in all ethnic and racial groups recognize the value of wild places and agree they should be protected. For instance, the results of the federal government's National Survey on Recreation and the Environment show that while 69 percent of the general population favors the designation of more federal land as wilderness in their own state, an even larger proportion of Hispanic-origin respondents (75 percent) supports more local wilderness.[36] As the population of Washington changes, so can the movement to protect Washington's wild places, by broadening its agenda to be more inclusive and welcoming to potential allies throughout the increasingly diverse citizenry.

The people involved in the movement commonly began their love affair with wild places after having had firsthand experiences with it; an obvious correlation exists between experiencing a wild place and being compelled to act on its behalf. It seems that a logical first step in diversifying the movement could be to explore what factors influence wildlands visitation among the minority populations, enabling preservation recruiters to respond creatively and effectively. The information available about this issue is very limited, but studies on related topics can be useful in helping us understand why the representation of people from racial/ethnic minority populations on wildlands trails is not proportionate to the ratio of these populations in society at large.

Recent studies of national park visitation by people of racial/ethnic minority populations identify several possible constraints to wildlands visitation. One such constraint is racist attitudes that still pervade our society. African-Americans in particular have disclosed that national parks are commonly seen as "white space," in other words, places that are culturally exclusive to white people. Some people from racial/ethnic minority populations have actually described being "stared at, stared down, and eventually stared out of [national parks]."[37] Some studies reviewed by Megan Brokaw, a scholar of minority representation in national parks, suggest that "a cultural history of dependence on the land in the face of rural poverty, spanning from slavery to modern life in the rural South has led to a negative cultural view of 'the woods' among African Americans."[38] But while negative cultural views were acknowledged in these studies, some subjects who enjoyed and felt comfortable in wild places attributed this outlook to positive personal experiences on trips with organizations such as the YMCA or other prior exposure.

Another potential constraint to wildlands visitation by racial/ethnic minority populations is lack of transportation. Data from the 1995 Nationwide Personal Transportation Survey show that about 78 percent of trips taken by poor people involve driving or riding in private vehicles, while private vehicle use accounts for about 91 percent of trips taken by people who are not poor (by U.S. Census Bureau standards).[39] Poverty rates for Blacks, Hispanics, and Native Americans are disproportionately high compared to the poverty rates of whites, leading to the deduction that large segments of people from these minority groups have less access to cars and therefore less access to wildlands. The concentration of people of racial/ethnic minority background in urban areas (with the exception of Native Americans) is considerably higher than in rural areas, which are closer to wildland destinations.[40]

Brokaw writes that "Lack of transportation as a constraint may help to explain why wildland areas . . . on the urban-rural interface often have a higher diversity in their visitation than do remote national parks."[41] Wild places on the fringe of the Puget Sound metropolis offer nature opportunities in convenient proximity to the city. The Issaquah Alps, for instance, provide a wilderness experience less than 15 miles away from downtown Seattle, and the Issaquah Alps Trails Club leads free hikes in addition to providing a shuttle from downtown Issaquah (which is accessible by bus) to the trailheads.

Even after the problems of racism, transportation, and accessibility have been addressed, wildlands visitation is contingent upon access to information. A study conducted by the National Park Service showed that for those who visit national parks, information about the parks is most commonly obtained via word of mouth.[42] This fact could partially explain low levels of visitation among some populations if the wild areas are not commonly talked about.

Finally, another determinant of wildlands visitation is differing preferences for outdoor recreation. One study cited by Brokaw found that white respondents ranked hiking and nature walking as their primary reason for visiting wildland areas, saying that escapism (the desire to get out of the city or neighborhood) was another motivation. In contrast, Hispanics tend to regard escapism as a very low priority, and a majority of African-Americans in the suburban Puget Sound area were found to prefer picnicking and barbecuing to other forms of outdoor recreation.[43]

No matter what the reason for the differences in wildlands visitation rates between different ethnic and racial groups, much work can be done to help more people have better access to and become more comfortable with wild places, as a way to build the ranks of wildlands advocates in an increasingly diverse state.

SHIFTS IN CIVIC ENGAGEMENT

In addition to the more obvious economic and demographic changes occurring in the human geography of Washington State and the rest of the country, less palpable changes in community life and civic involvement in the past several decades also carry significant implications for the success of social and political movements, and consequently, for the movement to protect wildlands in Washington. Changing patterns of civic engagement have resulted in the disintegration of social structures and our sense of community, the effects of which have contributed to the erosion of vital grassroots networking and organizing. In 2000, Robert D. Putnam, professor of public policy at Harvard and president of the American Political Science Association, published an influential book, *Bowling Alone: The Collapse and Revival of American Community*.[44] The trends we identify in civic engagement and their consequent effects on grassroots organizing are mostly drawn from this vast collection and interpretation of data.

With the possible exception of the Great Depression, America generally saw an upward trend in civic participation during the first half or so of the twentieth century. Involvement in politics, philanthropy, church, and even in community groups and social events, such as bowling leagues and reading groups, proliferated during this time. This trend peaked around the heyday of political activism in the 1960s, after which involvement declined at remarkable and seemingly inexplicable rates.

Monthly surveys conducted by the Roper survey organization between 1973 and 1994 show that the frequency of virtually every form of community involvement fell steadily, including in important vehicles of democracy such as petition signing and running for office. The number of those assuming leadership roles in any local club or organization plummeted by 50 percent between 1973 and 1994, and the average number of club meetings attended each year by Americans fell from twelve in 1975–76 to five in 1999.[45] Other changes were evident as well; even informal socializing decreased drastically from about 65 percent of Americans who socialized daily in 1965 to 39 percent in 1995.[46]

Putnam pinpoints the causes of this unsettling phenomenon as revolving around several factors. He estimates that trends of greater mobility and suburban sprawl account for 10 percent of the problem, and that the pressures of time and money contribute no more than 10 percent to civic disengagement. He asserts that the effect of electronic entertainment, namely television, is responsible for roughly another 25 percent of the decline, and most importantly, he blames generational change—"the slow, steady, and ineluctable replacement of the long civic generation by their less involved children and grandchildren"[47]— for perhaps half of the waning participation in civic activities.

It may be true that a relatively small proportion of the decline can be attributed to sprawl, but this factor is particularly significant in Washington State, given the rapid spread of suburban development. Putnam asserts that more time necessarily spent in cars, more social homogeneity, and less community "boundedness" has affected civic involvement. As the incidence of suburbanization increased, so did the separation of workplace, residence, and areas of commerce, resulting in greater dependence on cars and more hours spent driving. The upshot of this increased reliance on driving was the development of a car-loving culture. A survey conducted in 1997 revealed that 45 percent of all drivers—and 61 percent of drivers aged eighteen to twenty-four—agree that "driving is my time to think and enjoy being alone."[48]

Kenneth T. Jackson, a leading historian of the American suburb, summarizes the relationship between suburbia, cars, and deteriorating social ties: "[A] major casualty of America's drive-in culture is the weakened 'sense of community' which prevails in most metropolitan areas. I refer to a tendency for social life to become 'privatized,' and to a reduced feeling of concern and responsibility among families for their neighbors and among suburbanites in general for residents of the inner city." What Jackson describes is a paradigmatic shift, wherein focus on collective needs has been superseded by a culture that is more concerned with individual needs. But, as Jackson contends, "The real shift is the way in which our lives are now centered inside the house, rather than on the neighborhood or community. With increased use of automobiles, the life of the sidewalk and the front yard has largely disappeared, and the social intercourse that used to be the main characteristic of urban life has vanished....There are few places as desolate and lonely as a suburban street on a hot afternoon."[49] Although Putnam admits that his approximations are in no way precise and are not to be taken as the absolute truth, his best guess is that "each additional ten minutes in daily commuting time cuts involvement in community affairs by 10 percent."[50]

In addition to their affinity for their cars, another characteristic of suburban residents that contributes to the atrophy of civic society is the homogeneous nature of these communities. In contrast to the classic American city, where people of varying ethnicities and classes lived not necessarily in the same neighborhoods but at least in adjacent ones, people of similar race, class, education, and lifestyle sorted themselves into segregated regions of suburbia. Political scientist Eric Oliver has found that lower levels of political involvement correlate directly with the prevalence of social homogeneity in a community: "By creating communities of homogeneous political interests, suburbanization reduces the local conflicts that engage and draw the citizenry into the public realm."[51] By Putnam's estimation, "the residents of large metropolitan areas incur a 'sprawl civic penalty' of roughly 20 percent on most measures of community involvement."[52]

That people are more likely in recent years to frequently change neighborhoods also plays a crucial role in suburbia's injurious effects on civic involvement. Putnam makes an analogy between plants and the nomadic tendencies of Americans, noting that "frequent repotting disrupts root systems."[53] In other words, residential stability is strongly connected to rates of civic involvement. "Recent arrivals in any community are less likely to vote, less likely to have supportive networks of friends and neighbors, and less likely to belong to civic organizations," Putnam maintains.[54] Given the influx of people to the state and to its suburbs, Washington in particular could witness the connection between the changing composition of its neighborhoods and a decline in community activity.

Putnam discusses the pressures of time and money, estimating that they account for perhaps 10 percent of the deterioration in civic participation, but the connection is less definitive or easily understood. It can simply be said that financial anxiety, busy-ness, and the pressures associated with the increase of two-career families all contribute in some way to the fall of civic society.

With the introduction of the television in the 1950s came possibly the most sudden and rapid shifts in lifestyle and choice of leisure activity that America has seen to this day. In 1950, less than 10 percent of homes contained television sets, but nine years later 90 percent of American families owned TVs. By 1995 we spent 50 percent more time watching television than in the 1950s, absorbing almost 40 percent of America's free time and a sixth of the average day. Television viewing is especially on the rise among young people. In 1970, 6 percent of sixth graders had a TV in their bedrooms, but by 1999 this number had grown to an alarming 77 percent.[55] Putnam alleges that "A major commitment to television viewing—such as most of us have come to have—is incompatible with a major commitment to community life."[56]

A wide range of studies suggests that the rise of TV did not simply coincide with the decline of civic society, but rather that it helped cause the decline. In the 1970s, a group of researchers studied three isolated but similar communities in northern Canada. The major difference between the three towns was that one community, dubbed "Notel" by the researchers, did not have television reception due to its location in a valley, whereas "Unitel" and "Multitel" did. TV was then introduced to Notel, and the results were striking: "Before Notel had television, residents . . . attended a greater variety of club and other meetings than did residents of both Unitel and Multitel, who

did not differ. There was a significant decline in Notel following the introduction of television, but no change in either Unitel or Multitel."[57]

It is important to note that generalizations about the ills of television
viewing do not necessarily pertain to every American, nor are they meant
to imply that everyone who watches TV is less involved in socializing and
various civic responsibilities. TV news viewing is positively associated with
civic involvement and Americans who watch television selectively (turning the TV on to watch a specific program), rather than habitually (turning on the TV regardless of what's on), are 23 percent more active in
grassroots organizations and 33 percent more likely to attend public meetings
than other Americans of the same demographic makeup.[58] But television's
detrimental effects on American society continue to gain momentum with
each generation. Putnam asserts that "Nothing—not low education, not full-
time work, not long commutes in urban agglomerations, not poverty or financial distress—is more broadly associated with civic disengagement and
social disconnection than is dependence on television for entertainment."[59]

A connection between increased television viewing and generational
differences in civic involvement is difficult to establish. The historically
civic generation that was born between 1910 and 1940 did grow up without the influence of television, but there were surely many other factors
that contributed to the differing levels of involvement between generations.
This older generation reached its zenith in the 1960s, precisely when involvement in civic society climaxed and began to drop. It was not a decrease
in activity among the older generation that accounted for this decline. For
indeterminate reasons, the following generations failed to pick up where
their elders began leaving off.

Contrary to common belief, the Baby Boom generation (born between
1946 and 1964) was the first to show serious declines in social, political,
and community involvement. Although more educated, Boomers know less
about politics, are less likely to vote, "contribute less, and in general avoid
their civic duties" more than previous generations.[60] The Boomer generation, the first to be introduced to television at a young age, had by age
sixteen watched more than one and a half years' worth of television, or
more than 10,000 hours. But other factors are thought to have contributed to the generational difference, such as the disillusioning effects of
the Kennedy and King assassinations, the Vietnam War, and Watergate.

Generation X (born between 1965 and 1980), while more commonly
branded as apathetic, is actually the second generation exhibiting the decay
of civic participation (albeit X-ers are significantly less engaged than their
Boomer parents). Trends in this age group point to even less engagement
in politics, community, and so forth, though individualistic tendencies were

inherited from the previous generation. Generation X grew up during a competitive time that focused on private rather than public or collective needs, and X-ers have not been involved in politics to a degree comparable even to that of their Boomer predecessors in the 1960s and 70s. The Baby Boomer generation, although possessing individualistic ideologies, stood up for the causes they believed in and were engaged in politics and activism as young adults.

 ## SHIFTS IN CIVIC ENGAGEMENT: IMPLICATIONS FOR WILDNESS

Although most trends appear disheartening, a few flickers of encouragement can be derived from shifts in civic society. For instance, though patterns of television viewing are unlikely to be reversed any time soon, studies show that watching TV is surprisingly unsatisfying.[61] It ranks as about as pleasurable as housework and much less enjoyable than all other leisure activities; even work proves more enjoyable than watching television. Watching television is directly related to depression, loneliness, and plenty of free time, and while kids spend more time watching TV now than ever, rates of depression, obesity, loneliness, and suicide among children are also growing.[62] Whether watching television is a cause or a symptom is debatable; nevertheless television viewing is associated with social isolation.

As wilderness advocates far and wide already know, visiting a wild place can be an emotionally and spiritually rewarding experience, and many involved in the movement learned to love these places during outings with the Boy Scouts and other such groups. If the movement recognized the untapped potential for future activists among the current generation of unsatisfied children and developed similar strategies for exposing youth to wild places, the voices speaking out on behalf of precious wild places could multiply and resonate well into the future.

Although for the past several decades civic participation in almost every form has declined with each succeeding generation, one countervailing trend has made itself apparent. Within the past ten years, the amount of volunteering and community service performed by young people has actually risen substantially. In 1989, 62 percent of college freshmen had volunteered during their last year of high school, but by 1998 the number had climbed to 74 percent.[63]

While newly amended school requirements may account for much of the increase, the fact remains that adults who volunteered as youth are twice as likely as those who did not to volunteer in later years. The survival of the citizen movement for Washington's wildlands depends on the continued existence of the dogged volunteers who willfully commit themselves to the cause regardless of pay. It is a matter of finding the next generation of prospective activists, infusing them with a love of wildness, and providing them with avenues of involvement through any means possible, whether it is accomplished by sponsoring field trips, recruiting at schools, promoting environmental education, or even pushing for more coverage of environmental campaigns on television. The targeted demographic should be those who will carry an appreciation of wildness into the future with fresh energy and perspectives, instead of being limited to those who have already made their contributions.

Generation X and the millennial generation (born after 1980) may be more reticent in politics and civic life than their parents were, but their environmental and humanitarian values are strong. In November of 1999, more than 40,000 protestors took to the streets of Seattle to demonstrate against the World Trade Organization's undermining of human rights standards and its careless environmental practices. Many young people participated in the rally, perhaps experiencing for the first time the true power of grassroots action. Today's controversies may give rise to a new age of activism, perhaps someday paralleling the surge of political involvement that escalated in the 1960s and '70s. Young people, although perhaps lacking the political savvy of yesterday's generation, have grown up with environmental values taught in school and at home and feel as strongly about our fleeting wild areas as their 1960s contemporaries did.

In fact, results released in 1998 from the "largest and most comprehensive study on teen leadership," conducted by Roper Starch Worldwide show that it is presumptuous to assume that values of the newest generation of teens mirror those of the blasé Generation X.[64] Millennials, the children of Baby Boomers, make up the largest generation of youth ever. They are also known as echo boomers for their inherited tendencies of individualism and cynicism, but this generation is distinguished by their independence and sense of responsibility. When asked which groups will make the most positive changes for society in the future, the majority of teens cited themselves, and nearly half cited environmental groups. Interestingly, echo boomers tend to embrace traditional values and morals and emphasize the importance of home, family life, community, and education.

So are kids today actually as lackadaisical and self-absorbed as they are sometimes made out to be? The answer is no. Millenials care deeply about the environment and consider it a priority for the future. If more attention is given to recruiting young people into the movement, the makings for a legacy of fresh, insightful, and determined wildlands advocates already exist.

A NEW WAVE

Members of the historically civic-minded generation, after building up a legion of wilderness supporters in the years after World War II, saw the fruits of their labor in the 1964 Wilderness Act, which created of the National Wilderness Preservation System (see chapter 3 for a discussion of protected-area designations). Washington's wild places had been hit hard in the spree of devastation that took hold of the developing state during the prosperous 1950s, moving onlookers to take action. In the meantime a new war was mounting, and many citizens were ill at ease. As the social impacts of the Vietnam War era rocked the nation, a commonly felt sense of disquietude ignited and fueled the surge of environmental and social activism that hit the United States in the 1960s and '70s.

The publication of Rachel Carson's *Silent Spring* in 1962 brought environmental issues to the forefront of America's attention, and young activists representing various progressive movements diversified their objectives and joined the environmental movement. The time was right to push for environmental gains as citizens grew more concerned with the loss of their wild countryside, and for many, the need to protect our natural heritage struck an even deeper chord during the age of volatile global and national affairs.

During the years of Dan Evans's governorship (1965–77), a wave of political activism gathered momentum, creating a suitable climate for the environmental movement to press forward with success. Riding this environmentally fortuitous tide, the movement to protect wild areas attracted a new generation of activists. As shown in part 2 of this book, those citizens persuaded Congress, in the years from 1968 to 1988, to designate more than 3.5 million acres of wilderness areas, more than 83 percent of the wilderness areas in Washington State at the time this book was written (the remainder was designated by the 1964 Wilderness Act itself).

Today a new wave is swelling, propelled by the currents of change now blowing into Washington's landscapes. Changes in Washington's economic, social, and political environments are swaying public opinion about the value of wildness and increasing potential support for the conservation movement. Taking all of these factors into account, the latest wave of political opportunity will soon be cresting and ready to break—now is the time for those involved in the movement to stand up on the board and surf it in to shore.

PART II

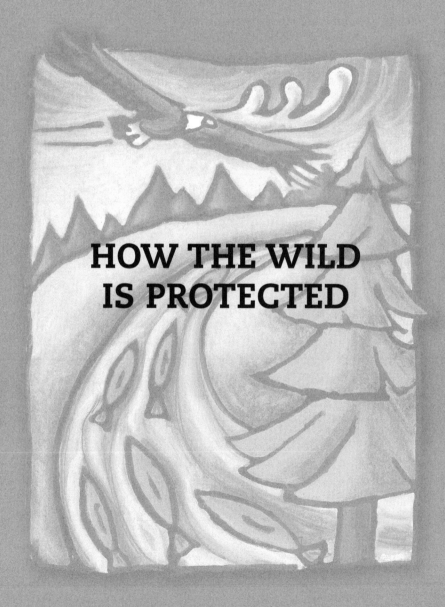

HOW THE WILD
IS PROTECTED

CHAPTER 5

Entering the Political Wilderness:
An Overview of Citizen Action

◆ *Benjamin Shaine* ◆

In the afternoon, I walk from my house in the city of Port Townsend, down through the Fort Worden State Park gate and onto the beach. Wildness surrounds me on this corner of the Olympic Peninsula, at the edge of the Puget Sound metropolis. Oyster catchers squawk, poking red beaks between rocks smoothed by winter waves, finding mussels and clams. An otter rolls from a boulder into the surf, scared by an eagle passing overhead. The eagle lands on a wind-beaten spruce, in forest growing atop the bluffs that isolate the beach from sight and sound of town. Crows pester the eagle, then divert to pick up snails exposed by the low tide, flying to drop them on the rocks to break their shells, dropping to eat them.

I pull twigs from a black deposit exposed in the bluff. They are the remains of willows that grew here in the outwash of glaciers 200,000 years ago, crushed flat as popsicle sticks under the weight of a hundred feet of overlaying gravel and sand, brittle now, turning into coal. Hunching over to shelter a match from the wind, I set it alight. It burns. Wildness connects me to the deep past.

At night the wildness penetrates my dreams. From our bed we hear coyotes yelping in the state park woods, where a forest regenerates to engulf abandoned artillery emplacements. Last month, the park staff posted signs, warning of cougars: don't let children wander alone. Last year, my wife Marci found a partly-eaten deer under an overhanging branch, from which the cat apparently dropped. At our breakfast table, we watch deer grazing on the lawn. We drape netting over the maples and lilacs in the yard, protecting them from the deer.

These deer, coyotes, and cougar move along strands of wildlands that link the town with the forests and mountains, often on a corridor of critical habitat being acquired by our local land trust organization. From the beach I can see ancient forests lying between the snow-covered ridges of the Dungeness and the Graywolf Valleys, within the Buckhorn Wilderness Area and Olympic National Park, where logging is not allowed. Private and state property in the foreground foothills is still being clear-cut in wide swaths, but behind them national forest lands logged or burned in the last century regrow within reserves established by the federal Northwest Forest Plan.

Looking east over the water to Whidbey Island, I see marshes, lagoons, and farmed prairies, maintained for 10,000 years by the Salish people and their predecessors. Now in Ebey's Landing National Historical Reserve, a trust board of local, state, and federal representatives works with private landowners, collaboratively trying to protect the place from subdivision and development. Mount Baker's volcanic cone rises behind Whidbey, and beyond Baker the white teeth of the North Cascades, their peaks and some of the surrounding forest within the boundaries of federal wilderness areas and North Cascades National Park, where their wildness is largely protected.

Even as the metropolitan region sprawls with close to 4 million people (and growing fast), this scene demonstrates hope for retaining wild nature in Washington. We find this hope not only in the region's great complex of established wilderness preserves and their potential additions, but also in dams considered for removal to restore salmon runs, in regrowing forests, and perhaps even, eventually, in recovery of grizzly bear populations and reintroduction of wolves. East, in the expanses of the Columbia Basin and Washington's part of the Rocky Mountains, current still flows through a portion of the region's greatest river, vestiges of its shrub-steppe and forest ecosystems remain, and visions build for restoring the web of habitat that once spanned millions of acres.

The action of committed, organized citizens was essential in designating each and every one of these protected places and in creating all of these wildland regeneration efforts. Without their continuing dedication, the wildness of these special places would erode. The second part of our book tells the story of how this citizens' movement for wild Washington came to be, what it has accomplished, what remains to be done, and how, working together, individuals can participate in this process. Our method is personal and historical: we tell stories of the people who combined their efforts to change the laws and rules governing wildlands in this state.

Our approach is also analytic, evaluating these stories in their social, economic, ecological, and political contexts. We explore the movement, looking at its perceptions, premises, underlying values, methods, strategies, goals and objectives, and models of political action. We seek to understand its strengths and weaknesses, in order to make encouraging suggestions for its future. We hope our work provides a map of the terrain useful to those participating in the movement or interacting with it, and to those who are not yet involved, but would like to be.

Co-author Ellen Trescott worked with Evergreen State College student Rachel Corrie for a year in Mount Rainier National Park. Ellen writes of a day their crew worked at Cougar Creek campground:

> *The site lies on an old volcanic ash deposit that restricts vegetation growth due to lack of important nutrients. We watched that day as trees were cut, to make room for concrete pads to hold dumpsters. Some tried in vain to count rings on the trees, only 8 inches in diameter, that had weathered many centuries in their destined yet adverse environment.*
>
> *Driving home that day, Rachel probed our friend and supervisor about the need for such destruction, about the sensitivity and rare condition of the plant communities there. When she received acknowledgement of her concerns, yet admittance that they would never be brought to bear on the project, she began to cry, silently . . . . She embodied a natural instinct, which she felt was her duty, to defend the priorities of life against a shifting and often nameless destruction.*[1]

Rachel's commitment to life led her to speak out for the Washington wilderness and, in ways she saw as similar, for peace and justice in other arenas. Early in 2003, Rachel went to the Middle East, hoping to protect people from violence. On March 16, at the age of 23, she died while trying to stop a military bulldozer from destroying a family's home. In the midst of complexity, uncertainty, distrust, and fear on all sides, Rachel stood her ground. As she wrote the year before about her caring for her home in Washington State, "I look at this place now and I just want to do right by it."[2]

When I reflect on the efforts of the many people dedicated to maintaining hope that the life-giving beauties of wild nature will continue for future generations, I remember Rachel's priorities. These people have committed themselves to action. With every such commitment comes risk: risk of failure, of error, of embarrassment, of harm to ourselves, of producing results contrary to those intended. It brings the temptations of arrogance and egotism, and with them the possibility of resentment, conflict, and bitterness, if events do not unfold exactly as we wish (and they never do). Activism is scary. And yet action brings the possibility that the path to seemingly inevitable destruction will be reversed, and it creates the prospect for regeneration.

The authors of this book remember Rachel as we make our own commitment, encouraging the activist life through our writing.

Rachel Corrie (center) with Ellen Trescott (left) and another volunteer in Mount Rainier National Park while working for the Washington Conservation Corps in 1999 (Photo by Molly Larkin; reprinted by permission)

🌲 DEFINING KEY TERMS

Activism to protect Washington wildness comes in many forms, which evolve as situations change. This chapter describes a variety of types of activism, as a guide for understanding and evaluating the strategies and tactics described in the chapters that follow. Each of these types of activism has achievements, limits, and consequences. And each can be found in the diversity of the Washington wildlands protection movement.

We tell stories in this book about people acting together to influence choices made about the future of wildlands. These decisions are mostly made by society, and often by governments, so citizens working to influence these choices are engaged in politics. The people involved are acting in their role as public citizens, rather than as isolated individuals. In Washington, all citizens potentially have some access to this rough-and-tumble public arena; thus it is a democratic politics. And the wildlands that citizens seek to protect and restore are a shared heritage. As a whole, these lands cannot be preserved by individual efforts, and the stake that activists have in the matter is not defined by their ownership of private-property tracts. Wildlands are thus a wealth held in common, part of our commonwealth.

Examining these concepts, I draw in part on the work of Harry Boyte, co-director of the Center for Democracy and Citizenship at the University of Minnesota, who has devoted himself to chronicling citizens' efforts to empower themselves in their communities across the United States.[3]

Politics

A common theme in the stories told to us by citizen activists is the participants' confidence that their involvement in policy issues can make a positive difference. Holding this view does not imply that outcomes are necessarily always influenced by our actions, or that money and entrenched interests might not rule, regardless of any efforts. But we find that confidence is in itself empowering, much as the contrary perception disempowers. Even if they enter the political sphere without experience and training, people who believe that the system can bend for them often find that it does.

American wildlands protection is premised on the fact that our political system can be responsive to organized, citizen interest-group pressure, especially when core interests of the biggest economic players are not at stake (which, fortunately, they seldom are in Washington wildness issues today), or if a group succeeds in defining their concerns as consistent with those interests.

Boyte defines politics in this positive way: "The politics of serious democracy is the give and take, messy, everyday public work through which citizens set about dealing with the problems of our common existence. Politics is the way people become citizens . . . . "[4] He quotes Baltimore activist organizer Gerald Taylor as saying "politics is really the discussion and action of creating community."[5]

The stories told in the coming chapters reveal that, despite limits and inequities, the U.S. political system sometimes does allow people, neither wealthy nor ensconced in high corporate or government positions, to touch the levers of power, changing the course of events. Telling these stories is in itself empowering. By contrast, the discrediting of political activity disables us as citizens. When we bow out of the political arena, decisions are left in the hands of those inside who still play the game, and the democratic process is jeopardized.

The question remains whether the incremental steps possible in our political system, such as wilderness area designation, forest plan implementation, land trust creation, endangered species listings, and land-use regulation, will suffice to protect and regenerate the natural wild. What happens may depend on demographic and economic patterns and on resulting concentrations of political power much greater than a citizens' movement can muster. This question underlies some of the debate over strategy and tactics we evaluate in chapter 10.

Citizenship

Boyte defines three types of citizenship: "Three main conceptions of the meaning and activity of citizenship have arisen in our history . . . . Citizens have been understood as: 1. rights-bearing members of a political system who choose their leaders, ideally those of virtue and talent, through elections; 2. caring members of a moral community who share common values and feel common responsibilities towards each other; and 3. agents of public work who address common civic tasks and create common things."[6] All three of these kinds of citizenship play a role in the movement for the natural wild, and all contribute to it in different ways.

Citizens of the first type vote, but otherwise mostly stay apart from the political process. They may write letters to government officials, but generally leave the action to their representatives and to the organizations to which they donate money. We will see in subsequent chapters how such relatively passive citizenship plays a role in an increasingly professionalized wilderness preservation movement and has always been important in legislative campaigns. But for the most part, citizens who define themselves in this way are not at the table when decisions are made about processes they care about and about specific wild places. The maneuvering, negotiating, and strategizing that makes a difference happens without them.

In the second category, citizenship is a private activity that takes place outside of government and the business economy, and includes doing volunteer service in churches, clubs, and nonadvocacy organizations. Citizens working in this arena are not direct players in the political realm. By assertively defining appropriate action this way, some recent U.S. administrations have attempted to exclude direct participation in public lands policy, and much more, from the American vocabulary of citizenship. On the positive side, working within this concept of citizenship, land trusts make significant contributions to wildlands protection and regeneration without rocking the political boat.

Boyte's third category is the citizen who considers him or herself a full player in the decision-making game, a public citizen who has the right and responsibility to be part of the governing process, not leaving this work to elected officials or experts. Such citizens consider themselves active builders of their society. Boyte points out, "When we help to build something, we experience it as ours. We gain authority and confidence to act, and a deep stake in governance."[7]

The distinction between paid and unpaid work fades in this definition of citizenship. As they engage in the detailed work of politics, professionals and volunteers may collaborate in informal networks across organizational lines. What they share as citizens is a view of their efforts as important not just to themselves, or their family and friends, but to a larger community of which they are a part and whose future their work empowers them to influence. Caring for a forest, beach, or city park can be such public work.

Democracy

Historically, Americans have been characterized by their brash confidence in their right and ability to participate in public decisions, an unwillingness to defer to bureaucrats and elected officials, and an insistence on being part of events at every step. British political scientist Bernard Crick points out that Plato was skeptical of such brashness. Although the term "democracy" is of Greek origin, literally meaning "rule by the people," Plato thought it implied "rule by the rabble."[8] In fact, democratic politics often does resemble a poorly officiated football match, with more than two teams playing at once on an uneven playing field strewn with rocks and logs. The citizen activist takes this situation as a given and plays the game anyway, hopefully with skill and poise. As Winston Churchill said, "democracy is the worst form of government except all those other forms that have been tried . . . . "[9]

The right and responsibility of the people to rule, of governing by political debate between citizens, goes back to ancient Greek and Roman conceptions of what it means to be human. Crick writes about how "both Roman paganism and later Protestantism had in common a view of man as an active individual, a maker and shaper of things, not just a law-abiding well-behaved acceptor of and a subject to a traditional order." In fact, he says, the Romans "stressed the duty of all who were citizens to participate actively in public life . . . . "[10] Democratic citizen activism is deeply embedded in Euro-American culture.

In a democracy everyone can play the game, but clearly, not everybody has the training to understand the intricacies of modern ecological science, natural resource management, land-use planning, and the like. So inevitably there is a tension in democracy, between the many who exercise their right to rule and the few whose credentials confirm their scientific, technical, and managerial expertise. As you read the following chapters, note how powerful it has been for citizen activists to move into the territory claimed by the experts, often outdoing them in their own specialized areas, with significant results.

Commonwealth

The politics of wildlands protection requires organizing to mobilize groups of people, usually those who care about particular places. So it is fundamentally a community, rather than individual, activity.

Though sensitive writers point out that we can find wildness in our backyards, both the experience of vast natural spaces and the continuation of ecological processes require more land than we can possess individually. Most remaining wilderness in Washington is government held. And even those wildlands in private hands gain value from the larger habitat and landscape of which they are a part. As we attempt to allow regeneration of additional wild places, we find that nature's web penetrates across the landscape, disregarding jurisdictional and ownership boundaries. Beyond the practical necessity to treat the wild as a matter of common instead of individual concern, those of us who value the wild usually see it as the heritage of all life, rather than the property of a few. It is our common wealth.

In American history, as Boyte says, people have used the term "commonwealth" to describe our shared participation both in democratic governance and in caring for the place where we live: "The word suggested an ideal: a commonwealth was a self-governing community of equals concerned about the general welfare—a republican or democratic government, where citizens remained active throughout the year, not simply on Election Day. And commonwealth brought to mind the touchstone, or common foundation, of public life—the basic resources and public goods of a community over which citizens assumed responsibility and authority."[11]

Though the movement for the natural wild most often works incrementally through the existing political and economic system to achieve piecemeal results, powerful notions at its core have the potential to challenge a selfish and cynical approach and thus enable it to support an empowered, positive sense of politics and public life. [12]

 ## APPROACHES TO LEADERSHIP

The following chapters feature the stories of leaders, but they are also about people working together. In her great work on the human condition, Hannah Arendt writes about how this relationship between individual and group effort is inherent in our notion of "action." She points out that Greek and Latin each have two altogether different words for "to act," one meaning to set in motion and to lead, and the other to achieve, to finish, and to bear. "It seems," she says, "as though each action were divided into two parts, the beginning made by a single person and the achievement in which many join by 'bearing' and 'finishing' the enterprise . . . . "[13] As we examine various activist strategies, it is worth looking for the relationships they embody between individual leadership and group collaboration, noting the consequences both for the people engaged and for the land.

This book focuses on the essential role played by citizen activists who volunteer their time and energy to advocate for wildlands protection. The many people who join together in this effort are often called the "grassroots" of the political movement. Working over more than half a century, well-organized efforts to mobilize the grassroots across the state have succeeded in convincing Congress to pass wilderness legislation and, to a lesser extent, in altering federal agency policies. Community grassroots groups raise money to purchase threatened habitat and recreation areas and to influence local government's land-development decisions.

We will see in coming chapters how this volunteer, grassroots citizens movement has professionalized over time. As membership and budgets grew, larger groups hired administrators to manage what became internal bureaucracies. When lobbying efforts became more sophisticated, some groups added professional lobbyists and publicists to push for legislation. As legal options and environmental laws increased in complexity, some groups brought on lawyers full-time. When science-based support for complex policy decisions became more important, other organizations specialized in data collection and analysis by technically trained staff.

Looking at Pacific Northwest forest issues in their book on environmental conflict, Steven Daniels and Gregg Walker write about what they call "the fundamental paradox" in American public-policy creation. "Citizens demand technically sound decisions, but as situations become more complex, fewer people have the technical background needed to either meaningfully contribute to, or critique, the decisions. By the same token, these complex situations often touch people's lives in fundamental ways."[14]

All the way back to Plato and the Greeks, grassroots politics—empowering the many—has been in tension with control by the expert few. Defining the relative roles of citizen volunteers and professional activists has become a critical question for the Washington wildlands protection movement, as both the movement itself and the issues it addresses have increased in complexity.

APPROACHES TO CONFLICT

There are many ways to be an activist working to preserve and regenerate wild places. Each activist strategy has its consequences, both for the people who engage in it and for the land. Each reflects the personalities and preconceptions of the people involved, as well as the situation in which they find themselves. As Dante says, "in every action what is primarily intended by the doer . . . is the disclosure of his own image . . . . "[15] When we look carefully at the types of activism within the Washington wildlands protection movement, we gain insight into the motivations and goals of its diverse groups. We see what enables each of them to be effective, and what limits that effectiveness; and we see where they make a unique contribution, and where their vision is blind.

When people work to protect wild Washington, they tell themselves a story explaining what they are doing and why. Based on the facts as they perceive them and their previous life experience, this story helps them understand what is happening and how they should behave. They may consider themselves as soldiers in a battle, performers in a play, or dancers on a stage. They may seek heroic victory, conquest, simple survival, conflict resolution through cooperation with those holding other views, or a variety of other solutions. They may see humans as managers, needed to re-create the wilderness, or as meddlers, who should keep off of wild terrain and out of the way of natural processes. The way people understand their situation—the metaphors they use to describe it—makes a big difference in their choices of action. As we read about the history of the movement in the following chapters, we can look for the causes and consequences of metaphor choices. We can be curious about what might happen if people used alternative metaphors when they made decisions on goals, strategies, and tactics.

Wildlands protection today encounters new challenges and opportunities that are calling forth additional metaphors, in addition to those used in the past. Some ancient forest activists, for example, say they find themselves in a "paradigm shift"[16] resulting from changed attitudes in rural communities and among field-level agency personnel, in which former naysayers are becoming more supportive of ecosystem protection, thereby increasing the potential for various sorts of new alliances and collaborations.

Another motivation for new stories and new metaphors is the changing character of the lands available for preservation. Scattered, sometimes small tracts as well as both existing and potential corridors are getting increased attention for their ecological and recreational values.[17] These places are less amenable to the boundary drawing and territorial defense strategies traditionally employed in legislative campaigns to designate wilderness areas. Desire to restore wildlands that have been altered by fire suppression or clear-cutting leads some activists to endorse some road building and selective logging in these areas as part of their strategy. Such intervention contradicts common premises of wilderness area preservation. These say that people should not try to manage nature in wild places. Supporters of such active management are challenged to come up with alternative descriptions of wildness and of wildlands protection that do not embody these contradictions.

Looking at some of the roles played by participants in Washington wildlands controversies can help us understand various types of activism.

Politics as War

Though graciously poetic inside and anything but embattled, the cover of Michael Frome's book about wildlands preservation bears the title, *Battle for the Wilderness*.[18] Whoever chose this title was reflecting the deep and pervasive use of the war metaphor in our politics.

I had the good fortune to begin my career in wilderness preservation activism as an intern with Brock Evans, the respected and successful Seattle-based field organizer for the Sierra Club and Federation of Western Outdoor Clubs in the 1960s. Now working in Washington, D.C., Evans recently wrote a bulletin to friends describing the current federal administration as the "Forces of Darkness," urging citizens to carry on against this evil in the tradition of the battles for designation of North Cascades National Park and national forest wilderness areas during his years in the state:

> *These successful struggles to protect our beautiful land are
> among the greatest and least-told stories of our times. We must
> remember them now, because it is in these stories—which are
> almost always a tale of small bands of plain ordinary citizens,*

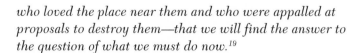

who loved the place near them and who were appalled at
proposals to destroy them—that we will find the answer to
the question of what we must do now.[19]

His terms are similar to those that a revolutionary guerrilla organizer
might use:

It was these ordinary folks who decided to take action and fight
for the places they loved who are the whole reason we enjoy
those places now. Rarely did they have any money or support
from the political powers that be when they began. Armed only
with the passion of their own hearts, they just set out—and
won . . . . After ten years of struggle and gathering massive
public support, over 2 million acres of wilderness and forests
in Washington's North Cascades had permanent protection,
safe forever.

Wildlands preservation is like defense of country, derived from our innate
territoriality:

Draw a Line around it. There is a magic and a power to stir
human hearts when we draw a line around a place we know
and love. It gives that place weight and heft—identity, perhaps
stirring something very old and "territorial" inside the human-
race memories of each of us.

We strive for victory:

I think most of us agree that what we are facing—and not just in
the environment either—IS a struggle between Good and Evil,
insofar as so many values we cherish in this country are at risk . . .
I know that we all will do everything in our power to stand up
and fight back now against those who would destroy all the
things we value and love about our country. These are scary
times, maybe: but we don't scare easy, do we, dear comrades?
And we will never quit, will we? We will prevail.

In his reference to good and evil and use of metaphor, Evans's approach
to political action is similar to that of many of his opponents. As he points
out, in using this approach the movement has been strikingly successful
in creating 220 million acres of legislatively protected wilderness in the
United States, most of it before 1985, in straightforward campaigns for places
with lines drawn around them. When we use the battle metaphor, we live
with it—the camaraderie and the conflict, the potential for victory and for loss.

Minimizing Conflict

Often in reaction to the embattled character of political struggles, people and groups attempt to substitute harmony for controversy, emphasizing alternatives to conflict in one of several forms. An activist whose priority is conflict reduction can assume the role of neutral bridge builder, helping participants find mutually satisfactory solutions. This sort of intervenor in the political scene can be an arbiter, equalizer, and healer.[20] Elected officials seeking to defuse conflicts in their districts may try to become mediators, rather than take an advocacy position that attracts opposition. And there are many professional mediators skilled in bringing parties together to seek consensus solutions. We do not usually see wildlands protection groups taking a mediating role, but they often may be asked to participate in mediated processes.

While outside facilitation can be very useful in some situations, emphasis on partnership and cooperation does not always consider the power relations between groups participating in the controversy. What happens if some stakeholders are not visible or not represented, or if wealth and power are inequitably held by a few? And how is a decision reached on issues for which the disagreement is rooted in basic value differences, not amenable to win-win solutions?

Consensus building can also be used as a tool to manipulate less savvy participants, revealing that exploitation of power imbalances can persist despite claims to the contrary. If real, underlying differences are ignored, a superficially cooperative partnership process may yield control to those who remain politically active and to bureaucracies that are intertwined with and dependent upon them. Compromise will be weighted in favor of the powerful. In comparison, acceptance of ongoing conflict may retain more opportunities for the citizen participation and democratic governance that has been key to protection of the natural wild in Washington.

For example, government agencies have a choice about how to conduct legally required public meetings about pending controversial decisions. Conventional proceedings, at which people testify and debate with staff and the audience, enable citizens to build a formal record, which can be difficult for the agency to ignore. At such proceedings, I have seen new coalitions between contending citizen groups form as participants discover common interests in the course of listening to each other (and perhaps seeing the agency as a common adversary). Unfortunately, the soapbox these forums provide also often encourages strong rhetoric and escalates tensions.

To avoid these sorts of engagement, some agencies, including the U.S. Forest Service, can depoliticize these public meetings by conducting them as "open houses." Instead of providing for healthy expression of disagreement and discovery of common ground (to which the agency must respond), in such sessions the staff chats informally with citizens. This removes opportunities for direct interaction between contesting interests. Much as at a cocktail party, group expression is replaced by individual conversation.

The Role of Science

Another way to avoid contention is to take the stance that policy decisions can be made rationally by scientific and technical experts, who have the knowledge to make the right choices. But, given its internal debates and varied emphases, expert science can be used to support a variety of policies, depending on the studies you choose to look at and the assumptions on which they are based. The resolution between them often rests in a choice between values, not facts, and thus is political.

For example, industrial logging forestry, ecological management, and hands-off wildlands regeneration all can be supported by science. A few decades ago, well-publicized science advocated rapid clear-cutting of big trees and the establishment of young plantations. Now, technically trained agency managers focus on restoring old-growth forests to protect species dependent on this ecosystem from extinction. To some extent, science has advanced during this period. But the biggest difference is in society's changing goals for the forest, with priority switching from wood fiber production to ecosystem diversity and ancient forest protection. As activist and poet Tim McNulty pointed out to *Defending Wild Washington* authors as we looked out over clear-cuts on the Quilcene River in the Olympics, a sustained grassroots, legislative, administrative, and legal campaign was the driving force behind changes in public forest policy, rather than any scientific justification.[21]

Side-Stepping Contention

Some organizations avoid contention on issues, choosing to focus on goals amenable to nonconfrontational methods. Elliott Marks, Nature Conservancy vice president in Seattle, explains, for example, that his group is always looking for "win-win" solutions and emphasizing "the art of compromise" to accomplish what otherwise would not be possible.[22]

Using their research program to identify ecosystem protection priorities and publicizing the results, the Nature Conservancy can, within limits, influence both private landowners and government policy. Raising money to buy land and development rights from willing sellers, the group achieves protection of private wildlands often not attainable through legislation, regulation, and overt lobbying. Without engaging in tussles over contentious public policies, their results are limited to what scientific information and cooperative discussion can achieve, and to what their money can buy and what landowners will sell.

Finding Peace within Politics

Acknowledging both the problems with depoliticized harmony and the difficulty of achieving consensus on contested issues, a working group at the Harvard Negotiation Project writes about coping with conflict, rather than eliminating it. [23] William Ury, director of the Global Negotiation Project at the Harvard Law School writes, "Getting along does not mean harmony, after all, but rather a great cooperative struggle to resolve our differences with a minimum of harmful strife. Getting along is not the absence of conflict, but the strenuous processing of conflicting needs and interests."[24] The crux of the matter is somehow being able to acknowledge difficult differences, neither looking away from them nor letting them reach destructive levels.

Some psychological models, particularly those developed in the Buddhist tradition, demonstrate how we can easily become emotionally fixated on our differences, dysfunctionally escalating anger and conflict. [25] But Boyte views anger as able to reveal underlying problems in society and does not simply call for its reduction, believing that this could obscure issues and reduce the potential for citizen political empowerment: "The etymological roots of anger, from the Old Norse word *angr*, suggest grief—the sense that grows from separation, deep loss, failure to attain fundamental goals . . . . The question is whether anger can be disciplined and directed in a constructive, positive fashion or whether it becomes 'rage,' leading to violence, disruption, and social disintegration."[26]

As you read the interviews in the following chapters, note how grief at the loss of wild nature can be central to activists' commitment to their cause. Similarly, grief and fear can be at the core of the hostile reaction motivating many members of anti-wilderness "wise use" groups, insecure about their own and their community's future.

If succumbing to grief and anger is one danger, the opposite is also true. Those who recognize the devastating problems that escalating rage creates around the world today can quite reasonably decide not to participate in activities that exacerbate such feelings. So out of that fear, they stay away from political activism. "The strenuous processing of conflicting needs and interests" is indeed difficult and dangerous work. Evidence shows, however, that it can be done, without generating bitterness and rage. For the individual, a key can be finding the time and making the effort to calm personal emotions and develop understanding of other peoples' views.[27]

Both individuals and groups face the challenge of finding ways to engage with controversy, while neither backing off from the issues nor feeding anger. The Japanese martial art of Aikido provides a metaphor for this kind of activism. The Aikido practitioner stays aware of the position and

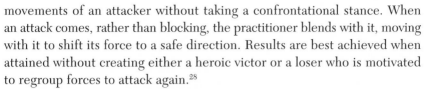

movements of an attacker without taking a confrontational stance. When an attack comes, rather than blocking, the practitioner blends with it, moving with it to shift its force to a safe direction. Results are best achieved when attained without creating either a heroic victor or a loser who is motivated to regroup forces to attack again.[28]

The Nature Conservancy's Elliott Marks reflects this principle when he asks, "How can we achieve outcomes in which we win what we want without making the other side feel like it lost?"[29] Aikido concepts can be applied not only in the noncontentious strategies employed by Marks's organization, but also in the midst of the most vigorous legislative and legal campaigns.

Collaborative Processes

In the face of today's increasingly difficult and partisan environmental disputes, professionals are developing new methods for bringing opposing parties together in ways that decrease the heat of the controversy. Like "politics," "collaboration" is a complex idea, with both positive and negative connotations. No one wants to be identified as a collaborator with an enemy, but collaboration with colleagues is valued, especially if it brings useful results.

If a process ignores real disagreements and inequities in political power, citizen activists would be rightly suspicious of that collaboration. But such duplicitous circumstances are not always the case. In their book on environmental conflict, Steven Daniels and Gregg Walker list five assumptions underlying the process of "collaborative learning" that they advocate.[30] Taking some liberties to simplify them, I summarize these as follows:

1. Conflict is inevitable.
2. Conflict is irresolvable, but manageable.
3. Truly vexing situations are often complex.
4. Good collaborative processes are learning opportunities for everybody.
5. The best way to improve decisions in complex situations is to consider decision making as a learning process.

I would add another:
6. Conflicts embody power relationships between the participants that cannot be ignored.

Instead of (or in addition to) legislative battles and court cases, collaborative projects usually involve bringing representatives of contending interests together in workshops, often facilitated by professional mediators. President Clinton and his Forest Service chief, Jack Ward Thomas, initiated a major experiment of this sort, bringing together managers, scientists, and competing interest groups in an attempt to resolve disputes over logging and forest preservation in what have been called the "Northwest timber wars." In the wake of that effort, Dr. Thomas concluded that "ordinary citizens can help solve problems that affect their lives [including] even relatively complex problems of natural resource management. However, they must be truly engaged in the process. They must learn from one another about the issues, and they must gain the skills necessary to fully participate in democratic governance."[31] Later chapters of this book evaluate the Northwest Forest Plan adopted by the Clinton administration, noting what the plan has achieved and how it imperfectly reflects the collaborative process.

EVALUATING ACTIVIST STRATEGIES

With an understanding of both political processes and the issues at stake in wildlands protection, we can establish criteria for evaluating activist strategies employed by the movement. These criteria include, of course, whether an organizational effort is successful in preserving or regenerating wildness in a specific place. Beyond that immediate goal, it also makes sense to address the larger question of whether the campaign contributes to the long-term strength of the movement, to the commitment of its members, and to the health of its constituent groups. Further, we can ask how the strategy alters the situation in which activists are working: How are other groups, including opponents, affected? As a result, how are they likely to change their behavior in the future and with what consequences? And, who gains in power, who loses, and with what outcome?

If, as we've discussed, politics is the creation of community, we can also ask, does the strategy in fact build trust, communication and mutual support between participants in the movement? Granted that the harmony of consensus may not be possible or even desirable, does the strategy promote methods of dealing with conflict between contending groups that are nondestructive to those involved and that minimize escalation of anger and fear, especially in ways that avoid harm to other issues and relationships?

On the personal level, does participating in the strategy contribute to a person's happiness, sense of fulfillment, and his or her ability to be a positive influence on other people involved? If, as is always possible, the strategy fails utterly to protect wildlands, will the participants be able to reflect afterward and, regardless of outcome, conclude that they, their family and neighbors, and the world are better off because of the action they chose to take?

We can reflect on these criteria as we read the stories in the following chapters.

ENTERING THE POLITICAL WILDERNESS

In its complexity, the politics of citizen action mimics the natural wild: those seeking to preserve and regenerate wildlands find themselves in a political scene that can be viewed from a variety of perspectives, that opens an array of options, and that calls for a diversity of goals, strategies, and tactics, depending on the specific, evolving situation. Thus perhaps the metaphor most useful for the activist is the "political wilderness." So we would expect that the adaptability and flexibility useful in wilderness life should be applicable to citizen action in the political sphere, and one would hope that wildlands activists would be well suited to this mode of operation.

Activists try to assemble a coherent program of wildlands protection within a political system that is messy and only intermittently responsive. Much as natural wildness is to be pieced together from scattered and incomplete parts, which must be combined and regenerated into a functioning whole, the political process is a piecing together of interest groups, opportunities, strategies, and tactics. As such, a good term for describing the citizen activist would be *bricoleur*. Educator and musician Steven Nachmanovitch explains that *bricolage* is a French word meaning "making do with the material at hand; a bricoleur is a kind of jack-of-all trades or handyman who can fix anything. In popular movies, the power of bricolage is symbolized by the resourceful hero who saves the world with a Swiss army knife and a couple of clever tricks . . . . The artistic attitude, which always involves a healthy attitude of bricolage, frees us to see the possibilities before us; then we can take an ordinary instrument and make it extraordinary."[32]

Washington's citizen activists are at their best when they remember that they are citizens of the wilderness. Reading the following chapters, we can appreciate their journeys into the political wilds and their efforts at improvising resourceful ways to defend wild Washington against seemingly impossible odds. And we can evaluate the citizen activists with an eye to natural wild processes: To what extent are activists' perceptions and actions responsive to the complex, unpredictable, mysterious political world in which they find themselves? Do they evolve and adapt well, and what enables them to survive and flourish?

CHAPTER 6

Climbers to Conservationists: Early Organizations in Washington's Wilderness Movement

◆ *Shawn Olson* ◆

What we call the wilderness movement today in Washington is built from a long lineage of spirited people who became citizen activists. Industrial activities, primarily logging, and other encroaching developments that wreaked drastic change upon the landscape have propelled citizens to act to protect their public lands since the late nineteenth century. A current map of Washington's protected wildlands reveals the fruit of their labor (see map in the color insert).

Conservation began in Washington with the formation of alpine clubs in the early twentieth century, when members witnessed the heavy devastation wrought by industry on lands they hiked and climbed in and became active in proposing areas for protection. As logging and road building progressively cut through forest and mountain wilderness—especially after the two world wars demanded full mobilization of the nation's natural resources—a building wilderness movement sprouted citizen conservation organizations that worked on specific issues in different regions around the state. Until the passage of the 1964 Wilderness Act, the tools activists had were primarily limited to designations as national park lands. Even so, before and after the act, it was the voluntary, self-informed, and highly dedicated work of citizen conservationists that secured the future of many wilderness places around our state.

The movement that built through the twentieth century was one that evolved and adapted according to the different obstacles that arose. National events such as World War II, which increased timber harvest in the national forests, as well as more localized situations like the early 1960s proposal for a dam on the last free-flowing section of the Columbia River, moved citizens to act on behalf of the wildlands they cared about. And they did this as volunteers, without compensation for long hours spent working to secure the wild places we appreciate today. Until the early 1960s, before large wilderness groups had the funding to employ professional advocates and scientists, all citizen conservationists in Washington were volunteers, organizing and learning together how best to achieve their goals. Even as the 1970s rolled around and the wilderness movement in Washington and around the country experienced a vast diversification, volunteer citizen groups around the state retained their vital role as guardians of the wild.

To learn the stories of these early conservationists, and to understand how their efforts established not just the essential lines on the map, but laid the foundations for a persistent, impassioned wilderness movement in Washington, is an invaluable endeavor, especially for today's wildlands activist. It is also an enjoyable one, rich with a human history that highlights the value of maintaining hope even when faced with the most daunting tasks. In this chapter, we will come to know the character of these early conservationists, watching as their tactics and motivations evolve from the early twentieth century to the 1970s; and we will come to understand that behind each of Washington's protected wildlands boundaries are stories laden with spirit, telling of dedicated citizen groups that organized to preserve the places they knew should not be destroyed. More important than lines drawn on a map, it is this spirit of innovation and perseverance that is the legacy of these early citizen conservationists.

WASHINGTON'S FIRST: MOUNT RAINIER NATIONAL PARK

In the late 1800s, a curious migration began. Before then, only Native Americans gathering berries and a few rugged prospectors had wandered the high flanks and glaciers of Washington's volcanic peaks. However, as settlement established itself in the Northwest, men and women with a love for the outdoors began to turn from frontier exploration to outdoor recreation, and many began to pursue the summits of the region's icy mountains. Out of a growing curiosity and fondness for Mount Baker, in 1868 Englishman Edmund Coleman succeeded in climbing to its top, the peak's first recorded ascent. Two years later, in 1870, Hazard Stevens and Philemon Van Trump officially recorded their climb to the summit of Mount Rainier. Southeast of Rainier, future founding member of the American Alpine Club C. E. Rusk made the first ascent of Mount Adams in 1891. Glacier Peak, Mount Olympus, and Mount St. Helens garnered attention as well, and soon Washington's six most prominent summits became the frequent destinations of early adventurers.

As access to the mountains improved, especially with the expansion of railroads in the 1880s and an increasingly widespread network of prospecting and logging roads, the trip from city to mountain peak became less difficult and less time consuming. Mount Baker historian John C. Miles writes: "The days of epic trips to the mountain, when approach equaled the climb for adventure and difficulty, were rapidly fading. The mountain was opening, and what would become the 'epidemic of mountaineering' was about to begin."[1]

Stories and photographs that these early mountaineers brought back to their friends and families created a growing interest in what would become the sport of mountaineering. Both men and women participated in these early mountain-climbing escapades. In 1890, Fay Fuller was the first woman to climb Mount Rainier, and during the 1891 La Conner Party expedition, artist Sue Nevin stood on the summit of Mount Baker. "By the late 1890s enough people had stood atop Rainier and brought back impressions that the entire populace felt an acquaintance with the big white mountain on the horizon," Ruth Kirk writes in *Sunrise to Paradise*. "Even a camera had gone to the top."[2]

By the end of the century, enthusiasm for climbing and hiking had swept the western states, popularizing spectacular landscapes like Mount Rainier and California's Yosemite throughout the country. Soon, the federal government responded by setting aside certain natural areas as "parks" to protect them from encroaching civilization and to provide recreational outlets. In 1872 the first "Nation's Park," or national park, was created "for the benefit and enjoyment of the people."[3] Seeing this government protection, nature lovers witnessing the advance of civilization into the wilderness realized they could influence the protection of places they valued. In Washington, a few local scientists and mountaineers had climbed, studied, and become fascinated with the geology and history of Mount Rainier. When talk began about the possibility for a national park, they and others with personal ties to the mountain supported the idea. A coalition of outdoor clubs from around the country, led by the young Sierra Club of San Francisco and the Appalachian Mountain Club of Boston, wrote a letter to Congress in 1894 stating the reasons that a park should be established.

They were not the only ones in favor of the idea. The Northern Pacific Railroad Company was one of the park's main advocates. When the transcontinental railroad was completed in 1884, the company immediately advertised the natural and scenic attributes of the mountain to the wealthy in New England who could afford the long trip west. A national park on Mount Rainier was certain to attract many, and the new rails were the quickest way to get there.

The Northern Pacific Railroad also supported the national park because it entailed lucrative land trades. The railroad had been given parts of Mount Rainier's high alpine meadows, lava flows, and glacier fields through the Railroad Land Grant of 1864 and thought most of it useless. A land exchange to create a national park meant that the railroad would receive lower-elevation, more profitable forestland elsewhere in Washington that could be sold for a pretty sum to timber companies.

The chambers of commerce and newspaper editors in Seattle, Tacoma, and smaller towns nearby also supported the park for the boost its tourists would bring to local economies. Senators and congressmen, seeing a potential park as a cause benefiting the people of Washington, introduced legislation, and Congress designated Mount Rainier National Park in 1899.

The campaign was successful mostly because of endorsement from the railroad and other businessmen. However, the park became a symbol and source of pride for residents of Washington, and the lines that were drawn separating wilderness from development were the first in the state. With this, an idea stirred among those witnessing the decline of wilderness elsewhere, and a realm of possibility was opened unto nature lovers across the state.

EARLY ETHICS: THE ALPINE CLUBS

Toward the end of the nineteenth century, alpine clubs formed along the West Coast as part of mountaineering's increasing popularity. Influenced by the Sierra Club of California, the Mazamas was established on the summit of Mount Hood in Oregon in 1894. Women made up one-third of its first slate of officers. Early members resolved to "explore mountains, to disseminate authoritative and scientific information concerning them, and to encourage the preservation of forests and other features of mountain scenery in their natural beauty."[4] Though the club was based in Oregon, members took frequent trips to Washington and helped bring the sport of mountaineering to adventurous Washingtonians.

The Mazamas influenced the creation of many other alpine clubs in the Northwest. The first club to form in Washington was conceived of during a Mazamas trip to Mount Baker in the summer of 1906, which was attended by climbers from the Puget Sound area who visualized a similar club in their own region. The idea took off; the Mountaineers was formed in Seattle with 151 charter members and University of Washington geologist Dr. Henry Landes as president.

From the start, the Mountaineers proclaimed its mission as being "to render a public service in the battle to preserve our natural scenery from wanton destruction."[5] Along with engaging in the club's other climbing and social activities, individual Mountaineers like Asahel Curtis, Edward Allen, George Wright, and Irving Clark worked to realize this goal. George Wright, a wealthy Seattle lawyer, was responsible for the first successful effort to rescue parts of the Olympics from large-scale logging. Earlier, in 1904, legislation to establish an Elk National Park had been introduced in response to the massacre of elk herds that once roamed the peninsula, but it failed because of logging interests. In 1909, with the Mountaineers behind him, Wright convinced U.S. Representative William E. Humphrey to propose a national park in the Olympics. Though the bill failed, Wright persistently urged Humphrey to lobby President Theodore Roosevelt in favor of the Olympics, despite uproar from the logging and mining sectors. Two days before he left office, President Roosevelt created a 750,000-acre Mount Olympus National Monument.

The Mountaineers helped encourage a budding conservationist community in Washington. Members with specific interests and outside connections frequently broke off to form their own organizations. Mountaineers members formed a Northwest chapter of the Audubon Society in 1907, and in 1914 the Mountaineers created a legislative committee to work specifically on conservation issues.

Primarily, the Mountaineers was a club dedicated to climbing mountains. The club made frequent outings, inviting anyone interested to attempt the snowy summits of Washington's peaks. Photos from these early days portray hordes of fifty to two hundred wool-clad climbers, ascending in single file up the dangerous slope of a crevasse-laden glacier. They carried primitive ice tools called alpenstocks, went unroped, and endured all the hardships of mountaineering alleviated by later technology. Despite these difficulties, the popularity of mountaineering in Washington only grew.

Catching the spirit of adventure, outdoor clubs formed across the state. Though first and foremost recreational groups, they continually brought new citizens to the wild, exposing them to the increased logging and new roads biting into the wilderness, which in turn motivated these budding

A procession of mountaineers ascending Mount Baker in 1908 (Courtesy Whatcom Museum of History and Art)

outdoor enthusiasts to protect their local landscapes. In Bellingham, a local realtor named Charles Easton, who got his start with the Mazamas, helped found the Mount Baker Club in 1911. The club instigated local pride in Mount Baker and soon made the first proposal for a Mount Baker National Park. In Seattle, the Washington Alpine Club organized in 1916, holding classes and outings into nearby wilderness lands and promoting stewardship and enjoyment of the outdoors. On the Olympic Peninsula, a small group of thirty-six formed the Olympians in 1920 and organized frequent hiking trips into the Olympic Mountains.

On the eastern side of the state, women from a local library formed the Spokane Walking Club in 1915. The club held several hikes each month and grew in popularity. The name was eventually changed to the Spokane Mountaineers (no relation to the Seattle-based club) when the group was incorporated in 1935 "with the tradition of developing an outdoor fellowship and responsibility for preserving wilderness values of the Inland

Northwest."[6] Pioneer American mountaineer C. E. Rusk influenced the formation of the Cascadians in Yakima in 1920. Rusk had been one of the founding members of the prestigious American Alpine Club in 1902, and he later moved to Lake Chelan, bringing with him enthusiasm and expertise in mountaineering. With Rusk as their first president, the first 104 members of the Cascadians popularized hiking and snow sports around Yakima throughout the 1920s. In its first decade, the club became involved in conservation and worked with the Forest Service to designate 90 acres of public forestland as a camping and picnic ground.

The popularity of outdoor recreation and climbing fostered around Washington by these clubs also meant that a growing number of people were venturing into the wilderness. Because of this, many outdoor clubs began to advocate for more roads and trails into the state's pristine areas. Though he subscribed to the Mountaineers' mission of preserving natural scenery, first Mountaineers president Henry Landes clearly outlined his goal to make "our spots of supremest beauty accessible to the largest number of mountain lovers." As Jim Kjeldsen, a historian of the Mountaineers, writes, "The Mountaineers tried to balance its stake in conservation with its desire for greater accessibility to the mountains."[7]

This paradox was not unique to the Mountaineers. Budding outdoor clubs across the state were responsible for popularizing and developing the wilderness. In many cases, the promotion of outdoor recreation and increased access to wilderness areas was linked to regional growth and the encouragement of tourism for economic reasons.

 ## GROWTH AND THE DEVELOPMENT OF WILDERNESS: 1916–1929

When legislation was passed to establish the National Park Service in 1916, its proponent and director, Stephen Mather, embarked on a nationwide search for worthy landscapes to designate as additions to his new park system. To citizens and outdoor clubs in Washington, this meant the chance that natural areas they loved and lived with could win national acclaim and protection. Several groups around the state wrote proposals for areas they thought should be turned into national parks. Many of these proposals came from those with business interests who saw the economic potential a nearby national park would bring. In 1919, residents and business owners in Spokane supported a national park in the Cascades, and between 1919 and 1921, three bills were written for the establishment of a Yakima National Park farther south in the range. In Bellingham, the Mount Baker Club continued to work on its proposal for a Mount Baker National Park. In the late 1920s, the Mountaineers board pushed for a Glacier Peak National Park, and later, a group of Mountaineers from the Everett branch organized themselves into the Glacier Peak Association to work toward a park in the White Chuck Valley and on Glacier Peak. In the Olympics, local and national groups had been working for a national park ever since they realized that the boundaries of the designated national monument would not hold against an insatiable onslaught of timber companies.

With heavy promotion from the National Park Service, and with World War I cutting off tourism in Europe, national parks around the country became popular destinations for vacationing Americans. In 1916, Henry Ford perfected the assembly line and mass production of cheaper Model Ts, bringing swarms to the national parks. Soaring annual visitation numbers, and a steady stream of automobiles that created a growing demand for pavement and roadside facilities, caused the Park Service to render large-scale "improvements" to the wilderness in places like Mount Rainier National Park. To Washington State citizens who believed the mission of the national parks was "to conserve the scenery and natural and historic objects and the wildlife therein," it seemed the Park Service was more focused on accommodating tourists than preserving the landscape.[8]

Citizens' concern grew as this trend spread throughout other domains of public land. With the advent of the motor tourist and the development of the "recreational vehicle," state and county planners built auto camp and picnic facilities along roadways throughout Washington. A multitude of state parks were created, many at the prompting of conservationists like Mountaineers member Robert Moran, who donated his property on Orcas Island to the state for a public park. By the mid-1920s, Washington harbored seven state parks, soon adding over a dozen new destinations that catered to motorists, while over one half of the states in the union had none. Conservationists saw these places become increasingly developed and littered, and watched as rural landscapes around Washington fell under an advancing front of pavement, billboards, accommodations, and wheels.

The national forests, too, underwent developments, and the Forest Service began in the 1920s to encourage tourism by improving and extending roads deeper into the wilderness. With the threat of an expanding park system and the transfer of national forest land into national parks, the Forest Service tried to prove it was managing its forests for the benefit of the people. The agency erected roadside camps, built trails and shelters, distributed maps, and stocked lakes for fishing. Cooperating with state highway planners, the Forest Service constructed a Mount Baker Highway from the western lowland valleys to Heather Meadows and pushed for an "around-the-mountain highway" on both Baker and Rainier.

Cars crowd Stevens Pass along U.S. Highway 2 at the crest of the Cascades in June 1929. (Courtesy Manuscripts, Special Collections, University Archives, University of Washington Libraries, Pickett 3908)

Observing the fate of the "loved to death" national parks and the trampled campgrounds of state parks, conservationists sought alternative means of wilderness protection. They took particular notice when, in 1924, the Forest Service established the world's first designated wilderness area, the Gila Wilderness Area in New Mexico. Five years later, under the vision of forester Aldo Leopold, a new Forest Service regulation, called the L-20 Regulation, provided a way to set aside natural areas, experimental forests and ranges, and "primitive areas," to preserve the wild character of certain lands. Mountaineers member Irving Clark, who had been questioning the Forest Service for several years about its plans for undeveloped land in the Cascades, was among the first in Washington to realize the potential implications of these new rules for administratively preserving wilderness in the Cascades. Pressuring the Forest Service about implementing the regulation, however, he still received only vague answers informing him that certain areas such as Glacier Peak and Lake Chelan were under study.

Some urban conservationists focused on wilderness closer to hand. Booming urban centers like Seattle and Tacoma were host to a network of garden clubs, and members became enthusiastic about preserving remnants of wildflowers and birds within their cities. Another organization, the Washington State Conservation Society formed in 1926 and focused mainly on the aesthetics of preservation in urban areas, especially along highways (though its bylaws did hold provisions for reforestation projects outside of cities).

RECREATION AND STEWARDSHIP DURING THE GREAT DEPRESSION

Local climbing and outdoor clubs in Washington did not suffer the effects of the Depression felt by the rest of the country. More than ever, people took to the hills and the woods for relaxation and challenge. The Mountaineers' membership heightened with the introduction of its Basic Climbing course, and several new organizations and outing clubs formed during the 1930s, many of which embodied conservation values. In 1932, the Federation of Western Outdoor Clubs was established to unify clubs across the western states in "mutual service and for the promotion of the proper use, enjoyment, and protection of America's scenic wilderness and outdoor recreation potentials."[9] In 1937, a group of Seattle Boy Scouts, forbidden by the organization to partake in the dangers of mountain climbing, broke off to form the Ptarmigans, based out of Vancouver, Washington. In Yakima, the Cascadians remained as active as ever, growing and accelerating the exploration of the eastern slope.

Though the 1930s was a decade made for outdoor recreation, the Depression bankrupted logging, mining, and road building companies, leaving hikers and climbers to enjoy the wilderness in relative peace. Perhaps that is why prominent conservation groups like the Mountaineers took a temporary leave from wilderness preservation efforts. It was individuals, not organizations, who carried the conservation flag through the Depression.

During one of the nation's major conservation controversies—the creation of a national park on the Olympic Peninsula—Mountaineer Irving Clark again employed his vision and authority to help the effort succeed. A leader of the Democratic Party in Washington State, Clark persuaded the state's congressmen to introduce legislation for an Olympic National

Park. Other individuals from around Washington were also involved in establishing the park. Arthur Vollmer of Port Angeles, a retired army officer, rallied local support against logging on the peninsula. Irving Brant, a Northwest novelist, also played a key role. Surprisingly, much of the advocacy came from the East. Mrs. Rosalie Edge, a wealthy New Yorker with many connections in the government, directed a group of twelve eastern scientists and formed the Emergency Conservation Council, which was very active in turning the nation's attention to the Olympic mountains. In 1938, after a long struggle, Olympic National Park was finally created, due also in large part to the conservationist leanings of President Franklin Roosevelt.

 ## WILDERNESS PROTECTION AS LAW: AN IDEA STIRS

During the 1930s, competition between the Forest Service and the Park Service increased. Each agency rallied to bolster the amount of land under its jurisdiction and subsequently entered a fierce "who-can-best-protect-wilderness debate."[10] Urged on by wilderness advocates, this debate resulted in the passage of wilderness regulations within each agency. In reaction to Forest Service claims that the parks were being overdeveloped, the Park Service drafted a generic national park wilderness protection bill, which was introduced in Congress in 1939. It did not pass.

In the same year, the Forest Service, to show that it was the best guardian of wilderness, adopted a new set of wilderness regulations. These so-called U-Regulations superceded the earlier L-20 Regulations, mandating a higher level of wilderness protection, with logging and road building excluded. New "wilderness" areas of at least 100,000 acres in size could be established, and "wild" areas of 5,000 to 100,000 acres could also be created. Existing primitive areas were to be managed just like the wilderness areas. The biggest difference between the L-20 Regulations and the U-Regulations was that wilderness decisions were made at a higher level within the agency and could not be as easily reversed. Wilderness and primitive areas could only be changed by the secretary of agriculture, although the chief of the Forest Service could tamper with wild areas after public review.

Wilderness advocate Robert Marshall, in his position as head of the Forest Service's Division of Recreation and Lands, was instrumental in drafting these new regulations. Marshall had joined the Forest Service in 1925. A staunch believer in wilderness and a follower of John Muir, Marshall reshaped Forest Service wilderness policies. He also recognized the need for "outside agitation" and in 1935 helped found the Wilderness Society, a national organization, to generate support outside the Forest Service for wilderness preservation.

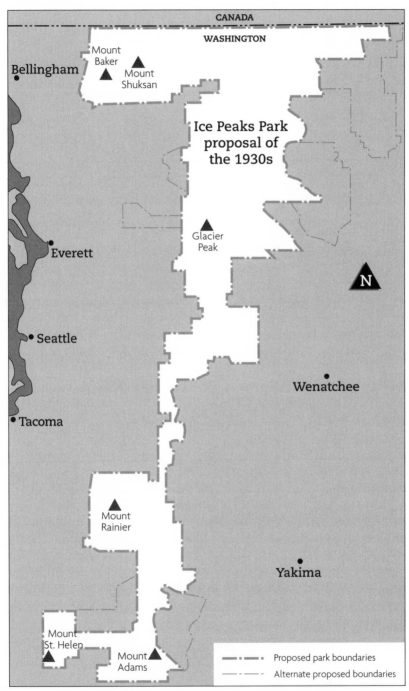

CANADA

WASHINGTON

Mount
Baker

Bellingham

Mount
Shuksan

Ice Peaks Park
proposal of
the 1930s

Glacier
Peak

Everett

N

Seattle

Wenatchee

Tacoma

Mount
Rainier

Yakima

Mount
St. Helen

Mount
Adams

- · - · - Proposed park boundaries

- · — · - Alternate proposed boundaries

Map 6.1. The Ice Peaks proposal of 1937 would have designated a "super park" encompassing the Cascades all the way from the Canadian border to Oregon. (Source: National Park Service)

Marshall's influence was greatly felt in the Northwest. In 1935 he proposed a 794,440-acre Glacier Peak Wilderness Area in the North Cascades. His proposal was supported by Forest Service chief Ferdinand Silcox and was on its way to becoming official when Marshall died suddenly at the end of 1939. A month later Chief Silcox also died. Ultimately, the Forest Service established a Glacier Peak Limited Area in honor of Marshall and Silcox, though its size was substantially reduced to 325,000 acres by the Pacific Northwest regional forester.

The North Cascades had also received attention from Interior Secretary Harold Ickes, who oversaw Park Service activities. In 1937, Ickes initiated a study for a potential Ice Peaks Park to encompass the entire Cascade Range, including its five volcanic peaks, St. Helens, Adams, Rainier, Glacier Peak, and Baker (see map 6.1). The idea was bold; such a "super park" had never before been proposed. Nonetheless, the study committee's report concluded that the range was "unquestionably of national park caliber" and that "[e]stablishment of this area as one superb park is an inspiring project to fire the imagination."[11] However, opposition to Ice Peaks was strong. The Forest Service, still sore from the land it had lost in the establishment of Olympic National Park, conducted several of its own wilderness studies for sections of the range under park study to defeat or at least delay the proposal. The timber industry also fought the park, pointing out that interspersed pockets of development within the range made it unworthy of national park status. Opponents locked horns for several years, and eventually the super park idea faded as World War II approached.

Though the Glacier Peak Limited Area that was established was small, and though none of the Forest Service administrative designations provided permanent protection from development, the creation of these areas strengthened an important idea in preservationist circles: as advocates stewed over the concept of wilderness preservation, they began working on a piece of legislation that would protect wilderness forever.

WILDERNESS AND WORLD WAR II

Times of war have always had serious consequences for the integrity of wilderness, and World War II was no exception. Demand for natural resources, especially timber and metals, surged during the war, increasing pressures on wildlands. The coinciding perfection of the chainsaw also contributed to increased cut levels. Secretary Ickes issued a nationwide decree that called for full use of the nation's resources, including those that lay within national parks if need be. On the Olympic Peninsula, large stands

WWII poster "Behind the eagle stand the forests" (Courtesy National Archives, NWDNS-44-PA-478)

of Sitka spruce were harvested for use in airplane production from land that was designated for later addition to Olympic National Park. A bill introduced in 1943, backed by strong commercial interests, aimed to actually reduce the park's size and "unlock," in modern industry parlance, valuable stands of timber. A similar bill followed in 1947. Mining also occurred within the park's boundaries, as well as in Yosemite, Death Valley, and Mount McKinley National Parks. The Forest Service heightened its program of road building and timber sales and, despite the newly proclaimed U-Regulations, began limited cutting within established Forest Service wilderness areas.[12]

The impacts of war on the land did not go unnoticed. Though traditional conservation clubs in Washington remained mostly inactive throughout the 1940s, there were exceptions, and a few national organizations like the Audubon Society established statewide local chapters. For the most part, the Mountaineers club was absent from conservation issues, contributing to the war effort by providing lookouts to man fire towers in the mountains and to watch for Japanese submarines along the coastline. Again, the biggest efforts came from individuals. Local residents John Osseward, Richard Brooks, and Irving Clark were the only three voices that contested the first bill (1943) to reduce Olympic National Park. Mountaineer Arthur Winder, who was the lone wolf in the club's conservation efforts throughout the 1940s, issued a call for action at the end of the decade, asking "Will we be too late? . . . Complacency is not a virtue for preservationists."[13] But it was not until the war was over and the country had somewhat recovered that his plea was answered.

 ## THE PEOPLE WAKE UP!

The war's end did not lessen the strain on the land and the demand for natural resources, but quite the opposite. A booming post-war economy and resurgence in home building required massive amounts of wood, and the forests of Washington were hit full force. Weyerhauser and other powerful timber companies introduced intensive management practices like clear-cutting, stepping up operations to satiate a hungry market. The resulting swaths of brown, naked earth became increasingly visible to the public eye; motorists driving down highways, urban residents looking to distant hills, and especially the throngs of hikers and climbers, all felt shock and dismay upon seeing their first clear-cut. Eyes were opened, and a restless feeling stirred within the hearts of those for whom the diminishing wilderness held irreplaceable meaning.

In *The Idea of Wilderness*, Max Oelschlaeger writes, "the economic boom after World War II led to an enormous escalation in demand for wilderness resources to provide recreational outlets for increasingly well-to-do middle and upper classes."[14] Indeed, massive growth along the urban coast of Washington brought newcomers to the area with careers that allowed them free time to explore nearby natural wonders, and a broadening base of wilderness constituents was born. The newfound energy stirring in Washington got a chance to test its wings when the second bill aiming to reduce the size of Olympic National Park (1947) came up for a public hearing. Richard Leonard, secretary of the Sierra Club, suggested to local activists who opposed the reduction that they form a consolidated group dedicated to saving the park. The next year, Olympic Park Associates was created.

The group had its work cut out for it. The timber industry had its eyes on the dense forests within Olympic National Park and continued through the 1950s to put heavy pressure on the government and the Park Service to open sections of the park for cutting. In 1951, the Park Service compromised and allowed for what it conceived to be a small-scale program of salvage logging within park boundaries. The program gave timber companies the chance to remove dead or downed trees, which at that time were not considered important to the ecosystem. However, observers soon found that companies were not just taking salvage logs, but were cutting live trees, some as large as 10 feet in diameter.

In September 1956, Patrick Goldsworthy, member of the Joint Committee on Salvage Logging, examines a 9-foot-diameter stump felled between 1953 and 1955 near La Poel Campground in Olympic National Park. A 180-foot section of the Douglas fir was removed between the stump and crown. (Photo by Phil Zalesky; courtesy Manuscripts, Special Collections, University Archives, University of Washington Libraries, University of Washington Libraries, UW23037)

The atrocity was discovered in 1956 by a seasonal ranger, Paul Shepard, who was also the executive secretary of the Garden Clubs of America. He and two other seasonal rangers, Bill Brockman and Carsten Lien, both Mountaineers, decided to inform Olympic Park Associates, who then alerted major conservation groups in the area. The Joint Committee on Salvage Logging in Olympic National Park was immediately formed to investigate the situation and included representatives from major conservation groups in the area such as the Audubon Society, the Mountaineers, the new chapter of the Sierra Club, and the Federation of Western Outdoor Clubs. Committee members set out to witness and photograph the damage. Carsten Lien discovered that the scandal had been authorized at the highest level by the park's superintendent Fred J. Overly himself. Within park boundaries, the committee photographed several large stumps, which they then used to convince the Park Service regional director to go see the devastation for himself. Dismayed by what he learned, he immediately took steps to end the program and Superintendent Overly was transferred to the Great Smoky Mountains National Park.

Around Washington, increased awareness in the 1950s moved many citizens to speak up for wilderness preservation and outdoor clubs around the state began to realize the need for action. A 1950s annual publication of the Cascadians club in Yakima portrays these sentiments: "[T]he emergence of Conservation as one of the major interests of all mountaineering clubs can be no surprise to any student of ancient Oriental wisdom. 'Mandarin who like sauerkraut had better spray his cabbage . . . . ' We like and we use the natural scene. We'll have to fight now for the continuing opportunity."[15] When the Sierra Club began hosting wilderness conferences in San Francisco at the beginning of the 1950s, Washington outdoor clubs sent delegates to strategize with activists from around the country and to learn how to launch a wilderness campaign in their own region.

Around the country, support built for a national wilderness bill. Such a bill would enable citizens to propose large tracts of undeveloped land for permanent protection by Congress. In Washington, conservationists were concerned about increasing timber sales in the North Cascades, and with hopes for the passage of the wilderness bill, they began organizing.

🌲 TURNING POINT: THE NORTH CASCADES CAMPAIGN

In 1951, the Forest Service began to study a plan to reclassify the Glacier Peak Limited Area as a wilderness area. Though logging wasn't allowed within the established limited area, the most valuable of the forested areas had been left out of the boundaries drawn in 1940, and conservationists began to push for more wilderness. In the 1950s the Forest Service adopted a rhetoric that emphasized "multiple use" of the national forests, using founder Gifford Pinchot's old line, "the greatest good for the greatest number." Under this language, Forest Service officers tried to incorporate an array of interests—commercial, economic, recreational, scenic, ecological, and so on—that represented the "greatest number" of constituents. This meant that the agency was not overly eager to jump into an expansive wilderness designation that would "lock up" timber resources from other users.

When the Forest Service began its study, activists recognized that it was time to act. During the 1953 Federation of Western Outdoor Clubs convention in Oregon, Washington member Polly Dyer suggested that the organization focus efforts on the Glacier Peak area. The following year, the Federation adopted an official resolution to work on the matter, and in 1955 the group formally asked the Forest Service to create a wilderness area corresponding to Robert Marshall's original 1935 proposal. Also in 1955, Mountaineers members took Forest Service representatives on a series of field trips around Glacier Peak with the intention of studying boundaries together. Mountaineers Polly Dyer and Phil and Laura Zalesky were dismayed when they heard the Forest Service's plans for a wilderness boundary that skirted along at 3,500 feet in elevation and excluded the lower valleys containing rich, old-growth forests.

In the summer of 1955, the Zaleskys and Dyer made a trip to the eastern side of the Glacier Peak region, deciding that they should become familiar with the area they were attempting to protect. At the time, few conservationists living west of the Cascades knew much of the range's eastern slopes. After backpacking for a few days, the group had a fortuitous meeting with a local woman named Jane McConnell, who they met by chance in a Stehekin restaurant. Jane introduced the westsiders to her husband, Grant McConnell; Jane and Grant had lived in the area many years and were bent on protecting it, but also knew the obstacles. Grant advised that it would take a dedicated, single-purpose organization to secure protection of Glacier Peak and the North Cascades.

In 1957, the Forest Service came up with a proposal for the Glacier Peak area that included 434,000 acres of wilderness (little more than half of the original Marshall proposal) and omitted three key valleys—the Suiattle, White Chuck, and Agnes—that were heavily forested and low in elevation. This gravely concerned conservationists, and a month later a coalition of northwest groups held a meeting in the Mazamas clubhouse in Portland, Oregon. With McConnell's advice in mind, the Mountaineers invited all northwestern member clubs of the Federation of Western Outdoor Clubs to attend the meeting. Herbert Stone, the regional forester, also attended and presented the Forest Service's proposal for the Glacier Peak region.

Out of this meeting, the North Cascades Conservation Council (NCCC) was born, solely dedicated "[t]o secure the support of the people and the government in the protection and preservation of scenic, scientific, wildlife, wilderness, and outdoor recreational resource values in the North Cascades."[16]

NCCC executive officers were primarily westside affiliates and many of them were Mountaineers, with Phil Zalesky as president, Patrick Goldsworthy as vice president, and Polly Dyer as secretary. Board members, however, represented many parts of the North Cascades, including members from Lake Chelan, Spokane, White Pass, Manson, and Cashmere. Several members of the Cascadians also joined the NCCC board. Several resolutions were made and included decisions to oppose the current proposal for a trans-Cascade highway, to advocate deferring Forest Service developments in key areas, to support an end to mining on Miner's Ridge, and especially, to "work for wilderness area protection for the Glacier Peak area and to explore the possibilities for protection of the Stehekin Valley."[17]

In 1958, however, the NCCC and other conservationists were also thinking about another approach. Rather than struggle with the Forest Service over wilderness designation boundaries, a national park could be proposed in Congress with leverage from conservation advocates and public support. Many conservationists were opposed to a national park in the North Cascades because of Park Service policies. The Park Service had, in the early 1960s, instigated "Mission 66," a plan to expand tourism in the national parks. Many conservationists cited recent troubling developments within the Park Service, pointing out that mining and even some tree cutting had been allowed within Mount Rainier National Park. Others were worried that a major campaign for a national park would draw energy away from the national campaign to pass a wilderness bill. The Mazamas outright opposed a national park because they believed the timing was poor and that it was politically infeasible. Most skepticism towards the national park idea came simply because conservationists did not trust the Park Service.

The question was, which agency—the Forest Service or the Park Service—could best protect the North Cascades? David Simons, a student at the University of California, Berkeley, and a National Merit Scholar, greatly influenced the debate. As an intern under Sierra Club wilderness activist David Brower, Simons made a study comparing Forest Service wilderness and national parks. The national wilderness legislation had not yet passed, and Simons pointed out that land, especially the lower forested areas with profitable trees, would not survive long under a Forest Service wilderness designation. He argued that the Park Service would guarantee permanent protection for the North Cascades and finally persuaded the majority of conservationists to support a national park proposal.

The final wilderness proposal that the Forest Service put out in 1959 confirmed this decision. By 1960, all the major groups around the Northwest, as well as national groups like the Sierra Club and the Wilderness Society, were focused on promoting a national park. Conservationists concentrated on increasing awareness and selling the park idea to the public, funneling the new wave of urban interest in wilderness into the campaign. In this regard, the North Cascades had one disadvantage. Unlike the Olympics or Mount Rainier, mountains in the northern part of the range were not highly visible from the major cities and highways in Washington. Seeking urban sympathies, conservationists created a parade of brochures, pamphlets, and articles on the region that highlighted the threats and called for support. Influential groups with large, broad memberships, like the Wilderness Society and the Sierra Club, published articles in their newsletters and organized outings to the area. David Brower made a film, *Wilderness Alps of Stehekin,* which was shown around the country. Brower also designed "exhibit-format" books with large, glossy photos and compelling text. In 1964 the Mountaineers published such a book, called *The North Cascades,* and distributed it widely. The Sierra Club put out *Wild Cascades: Forgotten Parkland*, with a forward by Justice William O. Douglas, and gave each member of Congress a copy.

Hiking guidebooks also became a tool widely used by Northwest conservationists to draw the interest of the public outdoors. The first of these, *100 Hikes in Western Washington* written by Harvey Manning, sold 15,000 copies after one year in print. In 1960, the Mountaineers produced *Mountaineering: The Freedom of the Hills,* the club's first complete mountaineering textbook, incorporating a philosophy of wilderness preservation in the text.

The North Cascades Conservation Council proposed a 1.2-million-acre national park around the Glacier Peak region. It was based on David Simons' earlier research, and also included an area called the Chelan National Mountain Recreation Area that would allow hunting. The recreation area was strategically included to gain support from the hunters who made up a large percentage of the voter base and were traditional opponents of national parks. Conservationists also grappled with economic issues. Undertaking original research, the NCCC justified the park on many levels, predicting that a national park would generate a tourist industry with enough jobs to replace those lost in the timber industry.

In 1960, the Forest Service approved final boundaries for a Glacier Peak Wilderness, to be managed under the U-Regulations, increasing the acreage slightly from the 1959 proposal in hopes of curtailing the campaign for a national park. The agency continued to log and build roads around the North Cascades, and many forests were lost.

NCCC approached Republican congressman Thomas Pelly for support and he became a reliable ally, helping to secure a moratorium on logging and road building in the region proposed for a park. In 1961 and 1962, he helped pass legislation creating a study team to explore the matter, and in 1963 a North Cascades Study Team was appointed that included representatives from the Department of Agriculture, the Department of the Interior, and the Bureau of Outdoor Recreation. The team was meant to be a joint effort between the Forest Service and the Park Service, whose tensions had heated up over recent years. The study area included the broad expanse of the Cascade Range in Washington, and an eventual proposal for a national park and wilderness areas was reached after two and a half years.

In 1964, conservationists around the country celebrated the passage of the Wilderness Act. The act created a National Wilderness Preservation System by which citizens could propose to Congress large tracts of land to be permanently protected as wilderness. In Washington, three areas were added to this system—Goat Rocks Wilderness Area, Mount Adams Wilderness Area, and Glacier Peak Wilderness Area. The Glacier Peak area encompassed some of the land that the NCCC and other groups sought to protect, and the wilderness designation was thus a victory, but it did not slow conservationists' push for a national park. It instead made the going rougher, since opponents of the national park pointed out that huge portions of the region were already set aside in the Glacier Peak Wilderness Area.

To pass park legislation, the NCCC knew they needed a political champion. Congressman Thomas Pelly took their proposal to Senator Warren G. Magnuson, who referred him to Senator Henry M. Jackson. Jackson was the chair of the Senate Committee on Interior and Insular Affairs and thus had a potentially significant influence on the issue. When he was approached for support, he replied, "I can't give you a national park. But if you get up a big enough parade, I'll step out front and lead it on."[18] Jackson agreed to sponsor legislation for a park, but meanwhile he was promoting a North Cascades Highway that would cut from east to west directly through the range.

In 1967, Jackson introduced a national park bill and it was passed by the House and Senate and was signed into law by President Lyndon B. Johnson in 1968. The resulting North Cascades National Park was a significant victory, though conservationists were also disappointed because it was only one-half the size of their proposal. The park was accompanied by Ross Lake and Lake Chelan National Recreation Areas and, in all, accounted for the protection of almost 671,000 acres of land.

The North Cascades campaign brought two very important elements to the wilderness movement in Washington. One, it represented a crack in the long-standing authority over wilderness decisions that the Forest Service had enjoyed for many decades. The establishment of a park in the North Cascades signified a loss for the agency—resulting in a land transfer of almost 700,000 acres of land—and indicated the new power that citizens had to stand up to the agency. Second, the campaign unified conservationists in Washington, generating strategies and organization that brought the wilderness movement to a new level of sophistication.

 ## CONSERVATION ON THE COLUMBIA

In eastern Washington, local citizens began to speak out against development on a pristine segment of the Columbia River. In the early 1960s, the Army Corps of Engineers introduced a plan to dam the last free-flowing stretch of the Columbia River, in an area known as the Hanford Reach. For years fisherman had come to the Reach for its pristine conditions and isolation, and when three local fishermen learned of the dam proposal, they immediately began forming a coalition designed to protect the river.

The proposed Ben Franklin Dam was intended to power a network of cranes that would lift barges upriver, providing yet another transport channel and electricity generator along the Columbia. The first conservationist to discover this plan was local fisherman Richard Steele who worked for the Department of Energy at the Hanford Nuclear Site. Steele had spent many years fishing in the Hanford Reach, and knew the land well. He and other local fishermen soon formed the Columbia River Conservation League (CRCL) to combat the dam. The CRCL was a diverse coalition of several member organizations, including the Lower Columbia Audubon Society, Kodiak Bowhunters, Fishing Rod and Gun Club, Mid-Columbia Archeological Society, Sierra Club, Steelheaders, and others. Each member group had its own motives for saving the Reach, and together they created a powerful front of local voices that won the support of the community.

Employing an array of strategies, the CRCL set to work. Because they had many volunteers with scientific and economic backgrounds, the group was able to produce hard facts proving that the dam should not be built. Many studied the damage the dam would render to this pristine and last wild area of the Columbia, citing the natural and historic values of the Reach. The presence of salmon spawning grounds and waterfowl nesting areas was an important aspect of the area, and at one point the CRCL used an argument resting on the existence of several rare plant species to keep the Corps temporarily out. Some coalition members made economic arguments, pointing out that the dam was estimated to cost $14 million, in addition to a then-staggering 4.58 percent interest rate. They also completed studies showing that the power produced would only be sufficient to load one barge per day, making the economic benefits of the dam questionable.

Other CRCL volunteers took pains to inform the public and rally support. They offered frequent tours of the Reach, open to anyone interested, explaining its rich and essential biological function and the looming threat. Volunteers especially targeted public officials. In addition to the group's rich stock of educated and dedicated volunteers, the aspect that made the CRCL most effective was that its volunteers were all motivated by reasons other than personal gain. As Richard Steele recalls, "One of the things that gave us more validity was that during the entire campaign, none of us had one thing to gain from this for ourselves, monetarily. And the other people who were against saving the Reach were all doing it for economic reasons."[19]

Because of the CRCL, the Corps' proposal became highly controversial, and when it was included in a 1971 House bill, the dam proposal was defeated. Additional proposals were made for the Hanford Reach throughout the 1970s and 1980s, including a proposal to dredge the Reach for a navigation channel upriver, and the CRCL continued to fight to protect the river's wild character. For the time being, the Reach had been saved by the dedication of the local citizens that knew it.

SUCCESS FROM SCRATCH: THE ALPINE LAKES

The establishment of the North Cascades National Park and the successful opposition to the Ben Franklin Dam proved that dedicated citizens could make real changes. With this confidence, and with the powerful tool they had acquired in the passage of the 1964 Wilderness Act, conservationists turned to regions that remained unprotected.

An area known as the Alpine Lakes was one of the largest tracts of undeveloped wilderness at the time and the obvious candidate. It was also one of the most daunting. The area was to have been included in the earlier study done by the North Cascades Study Team, but was abandoned because of complexities and disputes over timber versus recreational values. Composed of a mixed checkerboard pattern of public and private land, the region spanned five congressional districts and two national forests, and included land on either side of the Cascades. It was an area heavily used by the public for recreation, and its location, directly east of Seattle and close to eastern Washington centers like Wenatchee and Yakima, attracted many hikers and hunters. In 1945, the Forest Service had designated part of the region as the Alpine Lakes Limited Area, an administrative classification that offered no permanent protection. As increased timber cutting and road building in the 1950s and early 1960s began to encroach on the Alpine Lakes, conservationists realized the need to act.

In the 1960s, large-scale wilderness organizations began to employ professional wilderness advocates to generate campaigns in strategic regions around the country. Brock Evans was one of these advocates, filling the position of northwest representative of the Sierra Club and Federation of Western Outdoor Clubs. He realized that the Alpine Lakes needed a local, specific group of dedicated people to work for its protection, and so began discussions with interested people. Evans found Ben Hayes, who was then the administrator of the Department of Biochemistry in the School of Medicine at the University of Washington, and who was involved in the Sierra Club and matters of public land use. Members of the Yakima River Conservancy also became interested, as did other members of the Puget branch of the Sierra Club. Soon, the Alpine Lakes Protection Society (ALPS) was formed and was officially incorporated in 1968.

ALPS consisted entirely of volunteers who were dedicated to the Alpine Lakes. None had prior experience in conservation or knew the specifics of designating wilderness. "We were as ignorant as hell . . . we were set adrift and didn't know anything," first president Ben Hayes recalls.[20] However, each had skills they brought to the cause. David Knibb was a bright young lawyer with formal training as a forester in an area adjacent to the Alpine Lakes. Ben Hayes had a master's degree in retailing and an aptitude for politics and organizing. Bill Beyers, an economic geography professor from the University of Washington, developed a system to measure the impact the proposed wilderness area would have on employment. Henry Steinhart, an architect, generated the first topographical maps of the conservationists' proposed wilderness area. There were also many teachers involved: Hal and Gloria Lindstrom and Jeb and Gloria Baldi in Ellensburg, and Bill and Janice Asplund in Wenatchee, whose advocacy skills would prove invaluable.

As its first task, ALPS identified the need to raise awareness, and its members developed a wide variety of effective strategies to do this. They realized right away that it was important to include members from both eastern and western Washington; the activists knew politicians would be more supportive if they believed the issue affected the state's majority. Initially, ALPS set up three chapters—in Seattle, Ellensburg, and Wenatchee—and kept the group's permanent address and bank account in eastern Washington to maintain a local face. They encouraged landowners, environmental groups, hunters and fishers, multiple-use advocates, hikers, ranchers, Forest Service officials, and even representatives from the timber industry to attend their annual open meetings and continuously sought to educate local communities. A large amount of energy was put into a newsletter, which was sent out to as many people as possible. They made presentations around the state and featured a slide show of dramatic Alpine Lakes scenery. They developed a hiking program and invited politicians to join them on a tour of the area. They took their issue to the media, held press conferences, learned how to lobby, did a study estimating timber volume within their proposed boundaries, monitored trends in outdoor recreation, and generated large amounts of public comment during Forest Service hearings.

In brainstorming a proposal for the Alpine Lakes, ALPS members knew they had to address issues that came from a range of opponents. The area was used by many off-road vehicle motorists, who opposed the creation of a wilderness area because it would preclude motorized use. The timber industry coveted the region's valuable old-growth forests, and companies pointed to the state's already relatively impressive tally of protected areas as sufficient. Any additions to protected areas, the industry argued, would result in widespread, devastating unemployment. The Forest Service was also opposed to a large wilderness designation. Especially territorial after its big loss in the North Cascades, the agency did not support a designation that would remove significant acreage of additional forests from future logging. Further complicating matters was a checkerboard pattern of public and private land ownership—the legacy of the railroad land grants of the previous century—that ran through the heart of the Alpine Lakes region and meant that one-fourth of the area consisted of private land. Convincing Congress to buy up the private land with tax dollars was a daunting task.

To meet the needs of the larger community, the plan that ALPS ultimately proposed addressed many of these issues. It consisted of a wilderness core, to be managed under the National Wilderness Preservation System, and was surrounded by a perimeter of "recreation management units" that would be managed as a national recreation area and allow motorized recreation and other nonwilderness activities.

These recreation units worried other conservation groups in Washington State, as the earlier battle in the North Cascades had resulted in the carving of two national recreational areas out of the North Cascades National Park. Groups like the Mountaineers, the North Cascades Conservation Council, and the local Sierra Club chapters made their own proposals. In fact, proposals were put up from many different groups. In the name of the Sierra Club, Brock Evans proposed a national park to establish a radical edge that would make other proposals look more reasonable. The Forest Service made its own proposal. The agency's study and recommendation was, however, very small. Even the timber industry made a proposal, the first wilderness ever proposed by timber interests, of 223,580 acres. It was a strategic move intended to splinter support for ALPS by appearing reasonable and to provide a moderate choice for legislators.

As the NCCC did in the campaign for the North Cascades National Park, ALPS knew they needed a political champion. Surveying the scene, they sought out Congressman Lloyd Meeds, a Democrat with environmental sympathies whose district encompassed most of the west side of the Alpine Lakes region. Though he was taking a very large risk on a controversial issue, Meeds agreed to introduce and sponsor the bill, and ALPS member Dave Knibb took charge of the frequent, critical negotiations between ALPS and Meeds's staff. By 1973, four bills were introduced together into the House and Senate: that of ALPS, the larger conservation organizations' plan, the Forest Service proposal, and the timber industry plan.

Soon after, conservation groups around Washington finally realized that they needed to unify their voices in order to successfully pass a bill, and so the issue became primarily a struggle between a united front of conservationists and the timber industry. The industry rallied its support from rural workers and labor interests, contending that wilderness designations in the Northwest negatively impacted employment and local economies. The conservationists countered by pointing out that the majority of recent employment drops in the timber industry were due to log exports to Japan and increased automation.

The Alpine Lakes legislative process brought sophistication and a complex variety of strategies to both the conservationists and the timber industry. While members of ALPS and other groups solicited a broader base of supporters and employed innovative tactics like mapping original data of the area and reaching out to nontraditional allies, the timber industry also utilized new approaches and strengthened an already powerful lobby.

The bill that finally passed the House and the Senate in 1976 was a victory for conservationists, including much more land than the small area proposed by the powerful timber lobbies. Though it did not include a national recreation area—dropping the additional designation was Congressman Meeds's eventual concession to getting the measure through—ALPS and other groups celebrated what they had achieved.

The final step required Republican president Gerald Ford to sign the bill. An important supporter throughout the process, Washington governor Dan Evans (also a Republican) interrupted a vacation in Europe to personally lobby the president in favor of the Alpine Lakes bill. For a ten-minute meeting with President Ford, Evans brought along a friend's copy of the Mountaineers' large-format book, *The Alpine Lakes*. The president, delighted by the photos, took forty-five minutes to browse through and comment on the book. Whether or not the book itself was enough to influence the president, on July 12, 1976, facing a recommendation for a veto by the Department of Agriculture and the Office of Management and Budget, Ford signed the bill creating an Alpine Lakes Wilderness Area.

The story of the Alpine Lakes is a prime example of what can be done by dedicated, informed, and persistent citizens of a democratic society. In

1977, the Environmental Protection Agency honored ALPS with an award that described the group as a model for citizen activism. The high level of commitment and expertise of ALPS volunteers enabled the group to effect real change and to preserve a place they cared about deeply.[21]

 AN ERA TO REMEMBER

After the 1964 wilderness designations and the North Cascades National Park Service Complex had been established, wilderness opponents considerably strengthened their political lobby and the power they had to oppose further designations. Conservationists realized that strategies centered primarily on legislation, which had won them previous victories like the North Cascades, were no longer strong enough to accomplish all of their goals. Many politicians, too, felt that after the 1964 Wilderness Act and the 1968 North Cascades Act, enough of Washington's land was locked away in protective designations. Subsequently, conservationists had to seek ever-new approaches for wildlands protection.

This branching out paralleled a national shift in wilderness activism. Events such as the release of Rachael Carson's 1962 *Silent Spring* caused tidal waves of public and political awareness and concern for the environment, incorporating a broader range of issues such as clean air and water. With the nationwide introduction of Earth Day in 1970, wilderness activism began a symbolic transformation from a conservation movement that sought to protect isolated areas of wilderness to being part of an environmental movement with broader concerns about ecosystem health. Science played an increasingly important role as well. By the early 1970s, a growing concern among scientists and the public for ecosystem health and the diminution of certain plant and animal species led to the 1973 Endangered Species Act and other land mandates based on scientific reasoning.

These national shifts penetrated the wilderness movement in Washington. A conservation network that had been previously unified in the push for the North Cascades and the first wilderness designations began to fracture, as new groups, many of them large-scale, moved in with diverse motivations and strategies. The era of small, dedicated groups of local citizens, strategizing together in each other's houses well into the night over how to save the land they loved, gradually made room for the coming wave of well-funded organizations with paid, professional staff and office space.

Still, local groups continued to work in their own way for wilderness protection around the state. On the Olympic Peninsula, pressure for the construction of a highway down the West Coast spurred Supreme Court Justice William O. Douglas to lead a hike along the coast (officially sponsored by the Wilderness Society and the Federation of Western Outdoor

Clubs but brainstormed by board members of the Olympic Park Associates), bringing media attention to the issue. After a second hike was held in 1964, also led by Justice Douglas, the Olympic Park Associates and its allies sought out permanent protection for the remaining 7 miles of unprotected coast. In 1976 they succeeded in getting the area added to Olympic National Park.

In the North Cascades, the North Cascades Conservation Council partnered with a citizens group in Canada to counter Seattle City Light's plan to raise Ross Dam, which would have flooded the Big Beaver Valley in the park complex and the Canadian Skagit Valley. Together, the NCCC and the Canadian ROSS (Run Out Skagit Spoilers) Committee engineered an agreement with Seattle City Light that kept the dam as it was and the valleys unspoiled. In the Columbia Basin, volunteers of the Columbia River Conservation League continued to fight off proposals for damming the Hanford Reach.

Though the coming of larger organizations and broader environmental issues in the 1970s signaled the debut of a new era for activists of Washington's wilderness movement, there were many groups that continued to employ the same type of volunteerism and perseverance that had carried conservationists before them to victory. It seems undeniably important to draw on the dedication of these and previous conservationists because they embody the true spirit of the wilderness movement. Starting with the wilderness activism of early-twentieth-century alpine clubs and continuing through the progressive blossoming of conservation organizations after World War II, the genuine dedication of an active citizenry has safeguarded the future of our wildlands.

CHAPTER 7

Pathfinders in the Political Wilderness

♦ *Glenn Burkhart and Lin Skavdahl* ♦

The Washington wilderness movement began with small groups of citizens dedicated to protecting wildlands. Working together, these determined and courageous individuals became the resolute pathfinders of wilderness politics. Today many of these advocates are still active wildlands stewards. They continue to monitor areas with protected status while supporting efforts for restoration and new designations. What inspired them to become involved in the movement and what keeps them going? These and other questions were posed in oral history interviews with various leaders.[1] Their stories are gifts that provide the inspiration, insights, and leadership tools needed to lead the wilderness movement into a successful future. Woven within their accomplishments are stories and strategies for those who are already active as well as for those poised to take up the preservation of wildness.

 POLLY DYER[2]

The name Polly Dyer is synonymous with Washington wildlands protection. She is a founding member of the first northwest chapter of the Sierra Club, the North Cascades Conservation Council, and Olympic Park Associates. For twenty years she worked for the University of Washington's Institute for Environmental Studies (now called Program on the Environment) where she developed conferences and programs on a variety of environmental topics such as wetlands and nuclear waste. Every bit as involved with conservation issues today as in the past, Polly continues to serve in leadership positions in many of the organizations she helped establish.

A few weeks shy of her eighty-third birthday, on a drizzly January afternoon, having driven from Seattle to Olympia, Polly sat in an Evergreen classroom and told her story. Her childhood memories are packed with outdoor adventures. Her father grew up in White Fish Bay, on the shores of Lake Superior, where she remembers visits that included hayrides at her grandparents' farm and explorations in the neighboring woods and in the Au Sable Dunes: "We loved wandering through those dunes and walking in the woods. Years later I realized they were probably virgin forests." Throughout most of Polly's childhood she and her family spent a portion of the summer on the eastern shore of Chesapeake Bay. "It wasn't wilderness, but it was outdoors. You might say the water was wild though. We had stinging sea nettles."

As a child Polly saw a great deal of the United States. "My dad was an engineer in the Coast Guard which meant we transferred every so often. We moved from Honolulu to Seattle, to New York City, to New London, Connecticut, to Philadelphia, back to Connecticut, to Baltimore. I had five years in Baltimore, all of my high school education at one place." Polly was eleven when the family moved to Connecticut the second time, where they stayed in a boarding house until they could find a permanent home. There was not much room for everyone so she was sent off to Girl Scout camp. This was her first adventure away from the family and she loved sleeping out under the stars. She recalls, "There wasn't too much wild, but Cassiopeia was out and the counselors showed us different things in nature."

In 1940, as the United States was coming out of the Great Depression, Polly moved with her family to the Alaska Territory. She recalls the circumstances: "You couldn't leave a nineteen year old on the streets of New York, especially one who didn't know how to find a job. So I ended up in Ketchikan, Alaska." Her first Alaskan hike was 3 miles to the top of three-thousand-foot Deer Mountain. "Back in those days the girls on the East Coast didn't know about pants. The girls on the West Coast had jeans when they went out, but I was hiking in skirts way back then." She recalls soaking up the immenseness of the scene: "When I went up that mountain and looked out beyond, I didn't have the word for wilderness, but [I had] an Edna St. Vincent Millay poem our English teacher had us memorize, 'God's World.' There's a line I kept repeating in my mind, 'Here such a passion is as stretcheth me apart.' That's the way I felt that day."

A few years later Polly met her future husband, John Dyer, on that same mountaintop. He was skiing the mountain without the benefit of a lift, having lugged his cross-country skis to the top. Polly remembers he wore a Sierra Club rock-climbing pin on his hat. It turns out that John was quite a climber, having made several first ascents on his own and one with Sierra Club activist David Brower. "That meeting on the mountain, Johnny says he knew I was a conservationist because I buried my orange peel in the snow." The week after they met, they had their first date, a bushwhacking hike around Perseverance Lake. Polly remembers, "In a few months we were married. I started reading Johnny's Sierra Club annuals, which were not fancy like they are now. That's where I started getting my education." One of the articles she read described the threat of logging on the Olympic Peninsula in the Bogachiel. Later, she would be instrumental in efforts to protect that very area.

At the time of their marriage in 1945, John was a chemical engineer managing a plant in Ketchikan that extracted vitamin A from fish liver and viscera, a wartime necessity. Once vitamin A had been synthesized, John saw his job coming to an end. He and Polly decided to embark on an adventure: "John had a 16-foot skiff with a ten horsepower outboard motor. He quit his job and we cruised southeast Alaska for a couple of months, ending up with almost a month in Glacier Bay. Before we went north, Johnny made sure I read John Muir's accounts in his *Travels in Alaska,* which is basically that same route. Years later (we were gone by then), I wrote a statement [in favor of wilderness designation] for the area. That was my first testimony, and it was actually read at a hearing by someone else."

In 1950, Polly and John moved to Washington State after a brief stay in California, where Polly had involved herself with the Bay Area chapter of the Sierra Club. "We lived in Auburn, so we did a lot of hiking in the Carbon River area and got to know Mount Rainier." They also explored the Olympic Peninsula. Polly remembers one of their first hikes there: "It was Christmas Eve; we often went hiking on Christmas Eve. We hiked up the Elwha in the rain. When we got to the ranger station there was all sorts of horse manure. We didn't like it, so we backpacked out and camped by Lillian Creek. The moon came out and was shining through every drop of water hanging from the needles on the trees. It reminded me of childhood fairytales."

Polly and John promptly joined the Mountaineers. Polly says of the meetings, "I got roped into it because of my shorthand." They also became affiliated with the Federation of Western Outdoor Clubs (FWOC) and then urged the Mountaineers to adopt the FWOC's preservation resolutions. In 1953 David Brower visited the Dyers and asked them to organize a Northwest chapter of the Sierra Club. Polly recalls, "The Goldsworthys [see Patrick Goldsworthy interview this chapter] and the Dyers got busy. At that time the Sierra Club had about 150 other members in Oregon and Washington and one in Idaho. Johnny worked on the bylaws and suggested we include British Columbia and Alberta as well as Alaska. That started us off."

Efforts to remove forests from Olympic National Park led to Polly's tremendous involvement in preserving the wildness of the Olympic Peninsula, which continues to this day. Representatives of the Mountaineers and Olympic Park Associates met with Governor Langlie in 1953. Polly remembers, "I was a footloose and fancy-free housewife and I just tagged along. It was the first time I was in a meeting of that kind. The governor told Art [Winder] and John [Osseward] he'd just appointed the Olympic National Park Review Committee. Well, the review committee was stacked of course. The whole idea was to get another recommendation to remove the trees and forest from Olympic National Park."

The threesome returned to the Mountaineers office, housed at that time above a Seattle landmark known as the Green Apple Pie. There they crafted a letter to Governor Langlie voicing their opinion that the review committee should have broader representation. The governor responded by appointing five more people, including the president of the Mountaineers. "The president of the Mountaineers couldn't get away from his job so he asked me to sit in on the first meeting. Emily Haag [representing Seattle Audubon Society] had a lot of parliamentary experience. The first thing she said at that meeting was that she hoped the agreement, should there not be a consensus of opinion, would have a place for a minority report. That's a very important point . . . . By default I became a member of the committee. That was a major education . . . I learned to speak out. I used to be considered shy, but no more."

The Mountaineers organized a letter-writing campaign in which more than three hundred letters were submitted in favor of retaining the park. Largely due to this campaign and the minority report Polly had learned was so important, the review committee could not recommend removal of any acreage from the national park.

Once Polly became involved in the conservation movement, she did not hesitate to continue even though it was not an easy task. Polly and John lived in the budding community of Auburn prior to a community transit system. They owned one automobile, which John took to work each day. In order to attend a multitude of meetings, Polly had to take the one Greyhound bus leaving Auburn early each morning, not to return until late in the evening. Finally, when it was affordable, Polly purchased a Volkswagen Beetle that made the commute much easier. She recalls her earliest experiences: "I started going to meetings and reading as much as I could. I'd go to those forestry meetings and when I think back on it, I might have been the only woman in the room unless there was a secretary, but I didn't hesitate to get up and ask a question. It didn't occur to me that I became visible that way. I think that's maybe why I became better known among industry people."

Polly recounted a story concerning her part in the wording of the 1964 Wilderness Act. She remembers, "Zahnie [Howard Zahniser, then executive director of the Wilderness Society] visited us in Auburn in 1956 just after announcing at the Northwest Wilderness Conference in Portland that Senator Humphrey had introduced the wilderness bill in Congress. Zahnie asked what we were concerned about and I brought up the threat of a proposed road along the Olympic coastal strip. Apparently, in our discussion I used the word 'untrammeled.' I heard later from Doug Scott that Zahnie [who drafted the wilderness bill] had been told untrammeled was an archaic word that nobody used anymore, but that on the train going home, Zahnie wrote a letter saying it couldn't be archaic because Polly Dyer used it to describe the Olympic Coast. The word stayed. Maybe it goes back to that good English teacher I had in high school."

Polly's college education finally began in 1961 when John was transferred to Boston: "I was accepted by Cal [University of California, Berkeley] before we moved to the Northwest, but John got a job in Seattle, so I never got to Cal. When John was in Boston, I started at Harvard's evening school. I suddenly had no responsibilities, except I was on the Sierra Club Board of Directors, but they could only afford to bring me out [to California] to two meetings a year. I was a temporary, then permanent secretary for Educational Services, Inc. They wrote textbooks for African schools and I ended up typing and editing them. During the summer of 1963 they asked me to go with them to Africa. When I left, I knew John would be transferred soon, so I asked at Harvard if my thirty-one credits would be transferable to another school. The woman, all full of herself said, 'Harvard credits are accepted everywhere.' I was just going to evening school. That was the beginning of my college education when suddenly I wasn't active in the conservation movement for a while. But we did organize a New England Chapter of the Sierra Club."

Polly Dyer at a meeting of the Federation of Western Outdoor Clubs at Camp Parsons on the Olympic Peninsula in 1960 (Photo by David Brower; courtesy Polly Dyer)

Polly returned to Seattle from her assignment in Africa, but not before visiting Athens. "I wanted to see where I considered the seat of democracy began, so I went to Athens, to the Acropolis. When I got to my hotel, there was a letter, not from my husband, but from Harvey Manning [see interview this chapter] saying, 'You've got to get back here. We need to have another wilderness conference.'"

Looking back on strategies that worked, Polly remembers the road threat along the Olympic coastline. Howard Zahniser asked Supreme Court Justice William O. Douglas to lead a hike along the coast to show support for keeping it wild. Polly recalls, "The Wilderness Society sent out invitations and I did the nitty-gritty organizing. We invited the pro-road people, but only one would go and at the last minute, he ducked out. The press was along and said,

Polly Dyer outside of her home in Seattle, year unknown (Photographer unknown; courtesy Polly Dyer)

'This is just a put up job. Where's your opposition?' We started at Cape Alava and hiked three days. When we came out at Rialto Beach a pro-road person was there with signs, 'Bird Watchers Go Home.' He made our story. Had he not done that, the press would not have believed us. We always felt that hike really turned it around."

Polly has cut back a bit on her responsibilities in recent years: "I've been chair of the Mountaineers Conservation Committee a couple of times. I've finally taken myself off of the committee with the proviso that I can come back whenever I want. I'll keep an eye out. If they don't cover the Olympics, North Cascades, and Alaska, I'll come back." Looking to the future Polly says, "Remember, if you think you've won, you've lost. We must recruit more people and build the lay public's interest and education." She reminds us that nothing is permanent. If we are to keep our public lands wild, we must continue to promote preservation. Given this advice, it came as no surprise when she described a new organization forming to support the Olympic Coast National Marine Sanctuary and that she had agreed to preside as its president.

HARVEY MANNING[3]

Harvey Manning is one of the most passionate environmental activists and prolific environmental authors in the Pacific Northwest. The outspoken advocate for Washington's wilderness has nearly seventy titles to his credit, and after more than forty years of activism Harvey continues to defend Washington's wilderness. Writing has been the most influential medium for his preservation work. Read any of his forewords in the famous *100 Hikes* series and one can admire his spirited debates concerning the treatment of our wildlands. His 1984 book, *Washington Wilderness: The Unfinished Work,* outlined many of the pieces left out of the 1964 Wilderness Act. Several of the areas described in that book were included in the 1984 Washington State Wilderness Act, but many others were overlooked again; therefore, Harvey's work continues.

Harvey Manning first spoke to us at the replica of the old Burke and Gilman railway stationmaster's house in Issaquah, Washington. It serves as the Issaquah Trail Center, gateway to the Issaquah Alps—an area Harvey helped to protect. Later we interviewed him at his home in Bellevue where Harvey, his wife Betty, and their daughter Penny live on Cougar Mountain. Their small cabin rests humbly among the sword ferns and salal, shaded under a thick canopy of hemlock and cedars. Harvey is often described as a bit of a cantankerous curmudgeon at times, but his candid wit and genuine intellect can be infectious and charming.

As a young boy growing up in western Washington during the late 1920s and early 1930s Harvey experienced what he calls the "edge wilderness" during camping trips with his family. His first memories of wildness take him back to early fishing trips in the Cascades. "The fishing was across the White River in Huckleberry Creek," Harvey recalls. "My dad and uncles would put on their hip waders and wade the White River, which is no cinch, and get to the good fishing over in Huckleberry Creek and then come back in the afternoon with creels full of trout which my mother and my aunts would fry up and we would eat on the spot, never take anything home; you'd eat it right there in the woods. Our folks would let us sleep outside the tent, so we'd huddle up together in our blankets out in the mysterious night and look up at the stars." This early memory would lay the foundation for much of Harvey's future connections to the land.

On a hike up the Quilcene drainage to the high alpine meadows and sprawling vistas of Marmot Pass, Harvey found what he describes as "the deep wilderness." "At the age of thirteen, in the scouts, I went to Camp Parsons over on the Olympic Peninsula and was introduced to wilderness. I would save up my Parson stamps; every week I would come to a scout meeting and buy a twenty-five-cent stamp. By the summer of '38 I had enough

Harvey Manning sitting on a ridge below Spire Point in the North Cascades, with Glacier Peak in the background, July 5, 1952 (Photo by Tom Miller; reprinted by permission.)

saved up for a week at Camp Parsons. I went on what they called the Three Rivers Hike, three days in what is now the Buckhorn Wilderness Area."

Prior to this trip Harvey's only experience with mountain passes included highways and small stores stocked with treats. The older kids on the trip were telling the younger ones, including Harvey, to remember their money to buy ice cream at the top. But Harvey's hopes for cold treats soon faded as he fell deeply in love with the wild landscapes that were spread out before him. "I got to Marmot Pass and there were no roads, we were 9 miles from the nearest road. I remember walking up there in the sunset from where we were camped at Camp Mystery, walking a mile up to the pass, and I looked out . . . my god, I'm looking at wilderness," Harvey exclaimed, "I'm in wilderness. Until that time I had been reading the normal adventure stories, I thought wilderness was in The Darkest Africa, The Roof of the World. That was my discovery that wilderness was right here where I lived. I saved up my money and went back to Parsons two more summers."

Over the years Harvey would take more hikes into the wilderness, and with every trip he grew more and more passionate about the landscape. In 1948, Harvey began to notice the logging roads encroaching into the wilderness areas that he visited. On his approaches to Glacier Peak he took note of extensive logging in the White Chuck Valley. Harvey began to realize that the wildlands he loved were becoming more and more threatened.

"I grew up in logging country, my family were all in the timber industry, and as much as I appreciated the nonlogged areas, Olympic National Park and Mount Rainer National Park, I didn't even think about setting aside other areas. I regretted the fact that they were logging . . . but it was logging and that's what we do here."

"I remember one time another guy and I were on the Ptarmigan traverse. We got to a peak above White Rock Lake. I sat on that peak and gazed north into a wilderness of peaks farther than I could see, looked east toward Lake Chelan and wilderness there as far as I could see, south to Dome peak and beyond as far as I could see, then I looked west and through the summertime haze the forest down below the peaks were brown. Why were they brown? I realized they weren't forests at all, they were clear-cuts! I was in the middle of a roaring wilderness and I could see a clear-cut. So that's when I became 'the irate birdwatcher.'"

"The activism to which I was led was derived mainly from the Sierra Club, through Johnny and Polly Dyer [see interview this chapter], and later David Brower. When they came up from [California] where they had been active, John and I started climbing together. They would talk about what they were doing in California. These crazy Californians, they think you can fight the steam roller. I didn't worry about the wilderness because there was lots of wilderness in the North Cascades . . . I wasn't interested in conservation, it was kind of a freakish thing."

"Somebody then brought me a Forest Service map showing the logging plans for the Quilcene Valley. I thought, 'My God they can't do that!' I got very upset by what they were doing in the Quilcene; then I got upset at everything they were doing."

"I had joined the North Cascades Conservation Council [NCCC][4] in 1957. I didn't immediately become active because I was in the middle of developing *Mountaineering: The Freedom of the Hills*. But when I became an activist in 1961, in the NCCC, I didn't know anything; I hardly knew the difference between the Forest Service and the Park Service, but I had a lot of good teachers—David Brower, Grant McConnell. After all it took better than fifty years to get Olympic National Park, and each generation had to make its contribution. I felt that, I'm not going to let the bastards get away with it without a yell."

Later, Harvey began to criticize the Forest Service's appetite for timber and its hierarchy of bureaucrats. "The closer you get to D.C. the worse it gets . . . they're obedient to the dogmas of Gifford Pinchot—'the greatest good for the greatest number in the long run.' What the hell does that mean? That was multiple use; of course we called it multiple abuse. It was like throwing all the cats in the same bag and letting them fight it out. The Forest Service was all gung-ho engineers building roads and the driving force of the service was to clear out all the ancient timber and replace it with young second growth."

Harvey recalls the contentious issues surrounding the North Cascades in the 1960s. "There never would have been a North Cascades National Park had the Forest Service followed in the path of [wilderness advocate]

Bob Marshall. Our park movement was based on the multiple-use failures of the Forest Service. There was a faction of the NCCC who wanted to give up on the Forest Service and go to the national park movement. [However] there were plenty of people with gripes against the National Park Service. Phil Zalesky served as a summer ranger and knew the rotten things that the Park Service did. There was a really intense debate in the NCCC . . . whether to stick with the Forest Service and try to reform them, or give up on them and go to the Park Service. A decision was made to go with the Park Service."

Harvey's fervent love of the land also emerged during his campaign to save Cougar Mountain. In 1943, while sitting atop Parrington Hall at the University of Washington looking east, Harvey marveled at the submissive peaks that he would later name the Issaquah Alps, and Cougar Mountain was among them. Harvey and Betty moved to Cougar Mountain in 1952, and twenty-four years later his concerns for the Cascades and Olympics—"the wilderness without"—turned to his own backyard—"the wilderness within." From spring to fall of 1976 he walked 1,000 miles on Cougar, Squak, Tiger, Taylor, and Rattlesnake Mountains. He wrote about the footpaths he traveled in the first volume of *Footsore: Walks and Hikes around Puget Sound,* describing the area's "geographical oddity" as "a finger of mountains reaching 20 miles out from the Cascade front and poking Puget Sound City right in the eye."[5]

Manning foresaw the trickle of trucks crossing the new floating bridge over Lake Washington, escalating to a torrent of traffic. By the late seventies he knew something had to be done. In 1977, Manning and others staged the infamous "Wilderness on the Metro 210," a public awareness stunt that spurred more than one hundred pairs of boots off the bus and onto the trail.

In February 1979, Harvey typed up a one-page flyer summarizing the potential of Cougar Mountain. He mailed fifty copies to environmental organizations, community leaders, newspaper editors, and public officials. Sensitive to the implications of advocating for a park per se, Harvey's flyer called for a "Great Big Green and Quiet Place."

Issaquah city councilor Tim O'Brian sponsored Harvey and his core group of hikers to lead a series of spring hikes for Issaquah Parks, using public transportation. The Metro (or bus) hike was then repeated as a "Public Officials' Awareness Hike" in the spring of 1979. O'Brian invited fellow members of the Puget Sound Governmental Council. Informal conversation during this hike led to a discussion of forming a citizen organization that could cosponsor hikes with Issaquah Parks while simultaneously engaging in politics, an activity impermissible for city staff.

One month later, while sitting on the summit of Long View Peak, Harvey and his group of enthusiastic hikers organized the Issaquah Alps Trails Club. Soon after, the *Issaquah Alpiner* began publication, carrying a weekly schedule of year-round hikes and walks and an action program to save the trail country. Simultaneously, the club intensified a drumbeat of public information and agitation—articles and interviews in newspapers and on television, talks to environmental groups and pieces for their newsletters and magazines, and tailored hikes for their members.[6]

On May 21, 1985, King County executive Randy Revelle formally

Harvey Manning in August 1998 on Whidbey Island (Photo by Tom Miller; reprinted by permission.)

dedicated the Cougar Mountain Regional Wildland Park, and proclaimed that day as Harvey Manning Day throughout King County. Since that day the park has grown from 1,560 to 3,000 acres and is the largest regional wildland park in the country. Harvey says that it isn't finished yet.

Harvey's vision reflects a belief that we don't have to go far to experience wildness. "We call this [the Burke and Gilman stationmaster's house] trailhead center. Our trail system starts from here and goes up all the mountains; therefore it's possible to take the bus here and hike the Issaquah Alps."

Harvey is optimistic about the future of our wildlands. "In my judgment, America is about to undergo a revival; rather, a resurgence of the movement symbolized by the Wilderness Act and Earth Day. The stimulus will come from within—from a recognition that there is such a thing as the Good, such a thing as the Bad, and that the definitions are not economic and they are not hedonistic. The era of anthropocentrism has ended, the pendulum must swing toward biocentrism."[7]

PATRICK GOLDSWORTHY[8]

Patrick Goldsworthy is an honorary vice president of the Sierra Club, a lifetime achievement award bestowed upon the club's most notable long-time volunteers. He served as president of the North Cascades Conservation Council (NCCC) through many campaigns and continues his involvement today as that organization's chairperson.

Patrick's sixty-plus years as an advocate for wildlands preservation may have started in the 1930s when, as an eleven-year-old, he and his neighborhood pal set out on an adventure from their Berkeley home. The boys packed knapsacks with canned foods and hopped on the trolley to the ferry dock; they crossed the bay from Oakland to San Francisco in one ferry and took another from San Francisco across the opening of the bay where the Golden Gate Bridge stands today; then they boarded a northbound train to the far reaches of Marin County where they backpacked on the northern side of Mount Tamalpais. "We figured it all out. We knew where the ferries were because we'd been on those before, but we didn't know what we were going to get into beyond the bay. The countryside was very rural and undeveloped and remote. We stayed out about a week building campfires each night and cooking by wood fire."

From that time on Patrick was intrigued by the notion of getting out of Berkeley. For most of his youth, his family didn't own an automobile. They bicycled, walked, and rode the streetcar. He remembers wondering, "How do you get out of Berkeley? The Packard dealer lived a few doors down from us and I always wondered how they got to their cabin near Lake Tahoe." Patrick was still living at home and a student at the University of

California, Berkeley, when his father bought the family their first car. "That's when I found out [how to get into the mountains]."

A colleague of Patrick's father owned a cabin on the shore of Lake Tahoe and invited the Goldsworthys up for the summer. Patrick's father drove the family to Tahoe at the beginning of the summer and picked them up at the end. "We stayed on the back lot in a tent. The three of us, my younger sister, my mother, and I would be up there all summer long." It was during one of these summers that a photographer in a neighboring cabin, Cedric Wright, asked Patrick to accompany him on a backpacking trip, what the Sierra Club called a High Trip, in Yosemite. Wright was getting on in years and needed someone to carry his photography equipment on the backcountry outings. Patrick says, "I became Cedric's sherpa. That's where I met [Sierra Club activist] Dave Brower. He was the assistant leader."

Patrick went on to assist the Sierra Club in numerous backcountry trips, which consisted of 100 to 150 people, mules, baggage, stoves and food supplies, evening campfires, and huge garbage pits dug each day, filled up, and covered over. "I hate to think of those things," Patrick says, "What they did then, you don't do anymore." Patrick remembers the campfire programs: "David Brower would say, 'We are out here enjoying this country and I'm glad you're here, but this isn't the end of the story. You have an obligation now to help defend and protect this country and I want you to follow up.' He had a wonderful way of talking. He became an inspiration to me."

Patrick eventually became Brower's assistant until World War II took him to the Pacific Islands where he served as an Army Air Force meteorologist. After the war, he resumed his involvement in the Sierra Club. In 1956 he led a Sierra Club High Trip into the North Cascades. "We went up White Pass, near Glacier Peak. [The then Wilderness Society executive director] Howard Zahniser was there along with Dave Brower and all his family. I remember Howard Zahniser standing on a ridge, looking out and saying, 'I've never seen such wonderful scenery: mountain ranges one after another just like ocean waves.' He was very impressed."

Patrick finished graduate school at Berkeley, earning a doctorate in biochemistry. Early on he realized his field of study could easily take him into a career with a major oil company, but he wanted to do work that he considered helpful. When the time came to choose between an oil company job in Texas and a teaching job in Washington State, Patrick chose teaching. "I realized by going into teaching, I wouldn't make as much money, but I'd grown up in an academic family with my father a professor of mathematics at the University of California, Berkeley, and that was fine with me." He took a job at the University of Washington Medical School, where his assignment was divided between the Departments of Medicine and Biochemistry. "Being in conservation had a wonderful effect. I met people in departments on the campus that I had no connection with because they had conservation interests and they heard about mine."

When Patrick arrived in Washington the first hiking tip he received was about the North Cascades. "People said, 'Why don't you drive up to the end of the road and walk up to Cascade Pass?' On the way I went by numerous logging operations that left an impression on me. When I finally got up to Cascade Pass I was very impressed with that country. The whole trip gave me a feeling of the mountain range and the development moving into it." Patrick remembers friends telling him that when they were children, forests had covered the land from Seattle east to the trees of the foothills. "This made me feel that perhaps we could stop some of the development." Patrick joined the Mountaineers and was one of the original founders of the North Cascades Conservation Council. He worked to secure protection of the Glacier Peak area years before the 1964 Wilderness Act made it a wilderness area. "That didn't go far enough, so the North Cascades National Park was another thought and we went with that. With time, more areas have been added."

Looking back on his involvement in wilderness preservation, Patrick says the fruitful campaigns were made up of scores of advocates at all levels from newsletter collators to members of the Washington congressional delegation. "I've always felt, and I think I'm right on this, that the way to win success is to get support, to get individuals involved. Early on in the North Cascades Conservation Council we had work parties where we'd put newsletters together. Out of that came some people who continued on and put a lot of effort into our other causes. It's my conviction that you don't do something alone. You have to get support."

He also believes that compromise is a necessary element of political success. He refers to the creation of the North Cascades National Park Service Complex. "During an intermission at a public hearing, [Senator] Henry Jackson came to me and said, 'Pat, I want this park and I'm sure we are going to get it, but we are going to have to make some compromises.'" Jackson was referring to the hunting interests that were eventually accommodated by designating the Lake Chelan National Recreation Area contiguous to the park and administered by the National Park Service. Patrick says, "Some people would argue that you never compromise. You go for 100 percent of what you want and maybe you win and maybe you don't, but I believe you have to be realistic and I agreed with him [Jackson]. He told me if we could demonstrate support for the park, he would go full blast for it. We collected thousands of signatures on petitions and got so many people testifying at the Seattle hearings that they had to set up two simultaneous hearing rooms to accommodate everybody and it went on for two or three days. The battle went on and on, but we finally got a

North Cascades National Park and two national recreation areas [all part of the North Cascades National Park Service Complex]. It's different than we envisioned and it doesn't include Glacier Peak Wilderness, but it does include a lot of other important areas."

A highlight among the park campaign strategies was the production of *Wilderness Alps of Stehekin,* a Sierra Club documentary film that generated enormous support for the park. "I saw the original footage of this movie and thought what a jumbled thing it is, but I was amazed how Dave Brower could take this footage, cut it up, add his voice, and put it back together. Out of what seemed like a jumbled mess came a wonderful tool, which helped people not just regionally, but nationally, get to know the area." Patrick and others, like Polly Dyer (see interview this chapter), showed the film in hundreds of presentations at churches, chamber of commerce meetings, schools, and service clubs. "I am still amazed at how many people wrote asking to see that movie," he says.

Shortly after the park was established in 1968, Patrick was invited to join Harvey Manning (see interview this chapter) and two additional advocates on what became annual backpacking trips in the North Cascades. On one such trip he remembers, "We went up Little Beaver Valley and down Big Beaver Valley. We came through tremendous forests of great cedar trees in the Big Beaver Valley." They were hiking in the Ross Lake National Recreation Area, one of the compromises Senator Jackson referred to in his conversation with Patrick before the final passage of the park legislation. Jackson had agreed to make this section of the proposal a recreation area in order to secure support from Seattle City Light, the utility that already had three dams within the originally proposed park boundaries. The utility's plans to raise Ross Dam could not be accomplished if it were within a national park, however they could continue with their project if the area were designated a national recreation area. The addition would flood a large portion of Big Beaver Valley. Patrick says, "When the four of us went through the cedar forests and saw what was going to happen there, it was devastating. So we started an opposition to Seattle City Light's plans for raising Ross Dam. The original Ross Dam was a loss because none of us were around. We didn't know about the Upper Skagit. That's a shame. It's like Hetch Hetchy in Yosemite. It's a whole valley gone."

Patrick and the North Cascades Conservation Council formulated their campaign around the newly established park. "Our argument was, 'We have a new park. Are we going to flood it by raising a dam?' We argued before the Seattle City Council, in public hearings, and in British Columbia." NCCC joined with citizens in Canada who did not want more of their Skagit Valley wilderness flooded by the proposed expansion of Ross Lake. Patrick recalls his first conversation with a Canadian advocate: "I told him we wanted

Patrick Goldsworthy at Harts Pass in July 1999 (Photo by Charlie Raines; reprinted by permission.)

to fight the raising of the dam and he said, 'That's good news. We thought you Yankees wanted that dam. If you guys are organized against it, we'll get together and organize against it.'" NCCC led the American opposition while the Canadians formed ROSS, short for Run Out the Skagit Spoilers. Their simultaneous protests eventually produced a treaty that permanently prevented any additions to Ross Dam in exchange for a British Columbia agreement making available the amount of electricity Seattle City Light would have generated with the expansion.

The treaty also called for the establishment of the Skagit Environmental Endowment Commission (SEEC), a committee made up of four Americans and four Canadians empowered to designate funding for projects that protect and preserve wilderness and recreational features of the upper Skagit area both in the United States and in British Columbia. In 1984 Patrick became the Seattle mayor's first appointee, a post he held for fifteen years. "There has always been a member of the NCCC on the commission. It is important to keep that perspective present." One of the most successful outcomes of the SEEC committee from Patrick's viewpoint was their convincing the British Columbian government to create the Skagit Valley

Provincial Park. "BC Forestry planned to log it right up to the border. Instead we have two parks protecting a big stretch of the Cascades and the Skagit River valley. That's a success a lot of people don't know about."

Another significant accomplishment in Patrick's memory took place in the 1970s within the Glacier Peak Wilderness Area. He recalls the story: "Kennecott Copper Corporation had a patented claim on a big section of land not far from Image Lake. They announced plans to establish an open pit mining operation right there in the wilderness area, which would include building a road and hauling in mining equipment." David Brower had an idea to advertise the company's plans to the public. Patrick helped with a little research in the astronomy department. "I asked an astronomy associate at the University of Washington if an open pit mine of the size being planned could be seen from the moon. He said probably not with the naked eye, but you could with a pair of binoculars." Next, full-page ads appeared in a number of newspapers depicting a mining operation beside a pristine mountain landscape with the caption "An open pit mine you can see from the moon!" Patrick says, "We didn't use the astronomer's name, but we used the modified quote. It was printed in I don't know how many newspapers. The mining industry fired back saying that it wasn't accurate, but in the meantime, it stirred up a lot of people. We raised a tremendous fuss and finally Kennecott decided to abandon their plans. I think if we hadn't raised the question to the public, Kennecott might have gone ahead with the mine."

Along with the triumphs, Patrick acknowledges disappointments, some involving interactions between environmentalists themselves. Patrick served on the national board of the Sierra Club during the conflict between the board and its executive director, David Brower. "One board member said, 'Dave, if you continue to spend our money like this I'm going to sue you.' That really shattered me. Here was a group of top brass people of the Sierra Club fighting among themselves. I found the experience very disturbing."

With an eye on the future Patrick believes it is essential to monitor government agencies in their administration of public lands. "NCCC is constantly in the minds of national park and national forest administrators. They send us proposals and environmental assessments. We are in a position of giving input and this is important. You have to keep watching the agencies."

Patrick is concerned with recreational use of wildlands. "People are loving the place to death. I was never a hunter or a fisherman. I just go into the mountains to enjoy being there, but lots of people go into the mountains for other reasons. The off-road vehicle people and the motorcyclists are very disturbing. The volume and the categories of use are becoming more of a problem and these [recreational] conflicts are going to get worse."

Looking to the past, Patrick remembers his friend and fellow activist John Osseward pointing out that diligent citizens who keep the history of events are in a position to provide a perspective not readily available to newly appointed agency personnel. "We are in touch with a past that administrators are not. We can have an impact on those who manage our public lands."

Patrick believes one key to his sixty-some years as a wilderness advocate is passion. "I get mailings from all over the country regarding many conservation issues. My personal philosophy is that I can't be effective if I try to get involved in everything. I should concentrate on what moves me the most, and for me that's the Cascades."

KAREN FANT[9]

Karen Fant is the co-founder of the Washington Wilderness Coalition. Currently, she devotes a great deal of energy to the passage of the Wild Sky Wilderness bill (see chapter 10) and to defending the Arctic National Wildlife Refuge from oil exploitation. She serves on the steering committees of both the Wild Washington Campaign and the Alaska Coalition of Washington.

Karen spent her childhood in Bakersfield, California, at the southernmost portion of the Great Central Valley, with the foothills of the Sierra Nevada rising to the east. When she was nine, her parents decided she and her younger brother were old enough to join them on pack trips into the high Sierra. The family hiked into a base camp, with mules carrying food and camping equipment. Later, she graduated to traveling pack trips, where new camps were set up every night and the family stayed out for two weeks at a time. Walking along trails that kissed the stars at more than 10,000 feet, she remembers being awed by the grandeur surrounding her. "I was totally enamored with being in the mountains. The Sierra is high, rocky, and very wild. It was exhilarating . . . something I was immediately drawn to." The high country got into her blood and when she was seventeen she got a job as an assistant cook with the very pack trip outfitter that had ferried her family on their many backcountry trips. She spent five summers working in the Sierra and later, with then-husband Ron Yarnell's wilderness guide company, assisted and led many trips in Alaska, Mexico, and Nepal. "I've been in vast beautiful places repeatedly and it continues to be an important part of my life."

Family trips into the backcountry of the Sierra Nevada introduced Karen to the wilderness, but her parents didn't teach activism. "It was not an environmental household that I grew up in. Although the outdoors was important to us, as we went on fishing and hiking trips, my family was in business and was politically conservative in a conservative part of the state." However, once Karen was hooked on wild places, she joined the Wilderness

Karen Fant on Gokyo Ri with Mount Everest in the background (Photo by Ron Yarnell; courtesy Karen Fant)

Society. "I wanted to see nice pictures of mountains. I didn't read the stuff at first. I just wanted to see the photographs, but of course the Wilderness Society magazine is full of articles and you get drawn into all of it."

After high school, Karen enrolled at the University of California, Santa Cruz, studying earth sciences. In her senior year she took a wilderness issues course from Ben Shaine (one of this book's co-authors), who encouraged students to put into practice some of the concepts they learned in class.

Ben told her about his experiences in Seattle working with the Northwest regional office of the Sierra Club and encouraged her to move to that Northwest city. In the summer of 1971, Karen headed north. "I decided I was going to go up to Washington State and become an environmentalist."

Her first stop was at the home of Patrick and Jane Goldsworthy (see the Patrick Goldsworthy interview this chapter) to pick up a car Ben had left there on his way to Alaska. Karen recalls, "They asked me to stay for dinner. Then Jane asked if I had a place to stay. The arrangements someone at the Sierra Club had made for me weren't working out, so I said, 'I'd be more than happy to spend a couple of nights here until I get settled.' I guess I made myself useful enough to the household because they asked me to stay. I spent that summer and the following summer helping out around the house . . . in the meantime, I was being introduced to the environmental community through Pat Goldsworthy and their friends, Polly and Johnny Dyer [see the Polly Dyer interview this chapter], Phil and Laura Zalesky, and Joe and Margaret Miller. I was working as a volunteer for Brock Evans in the Sierra Club office and learning the history of the North Cascades fights. All this fed into a growing awareness about the importance of the environment."

She worked with Patrick Goldsworthy and the North Cascades Conservation Council researching issues related to Seattle City Light's final addition to Ross Dam. Another project involved the proposed Alpine Lakes Wilderness Area. As part of the rationale to protect it, Brock Evans wanted Karen to prove that the most extensive grove of the largest ponderosa pines grew in the Coulter Creek portion of the proposal. "Coming from [the University of California,] Santa Cruz, I was still in my pseudo-scientific mode where we were doing stand exams in areas, measuring heights, and looking at ground cover. Unfortunately that was my first loss because Coulter Creek was logged despite the fact that I had amassed all of this information."

This loss taught Karen a lesson she never forgot. "I came away with a much stronger understanding that the key was to organize people. No longer was I trying to pretend I was a scientist. I'm not saying it isn't important to have scientists providing data and information, but I realized, at that point, what I needed to do was organize."

After two summers in Seattle, Karen made a permanent move to the Northwest. She recalls making the decision to be a professional environmentalist: "It just seemed to me to be the next step. My degree was in earth sciences. What was I going to do? There was the USGS [the U.S. Geological Survey], there were mining companies and oil companies, and there was teaching. I made an abrupt change at that point. I'd taken Ben's class and I felt there were some things calling me to do environmental work, whereas being a mining geologist simply wasn't going to happen."

She began by working for the Sierra Club at the Northwest regional office. "My first real project was with Dick Fiddler writing the Sierra Club response to RARE I, the Forest Service's first Roadless Area Review and Evaluation. I ran around all over eastern Washington talking to a lot of people and gathering information. I did a lot of reviewing of environmental impact statements [EISes] and writing comments. The National Environmental Policy Act had just passed, the Forest Service was doing unit plans, and their EISes were very thin in those days."

In the late 1970s the Forest Service undertook the second nationwide Roadless Area Review and Evaluation (RARE II) to address the flaws of RARE I. Karen believes a new wave of activism rose up in Washington State as a result of these Forest Service recommendations. "We had the EIS and we had a map. There was a lot of wild country that was not protected that people in the state cared about." Drawing on her earlier realization that organizing is the key to protecting wildlands, Karen and fellow environmental activist Ken Gersten envisioned an organization that would help people across the state either strengthen existing groups or establish new ones with the specific focus of protecting wilderness in each area. "In 1979 Ken and I, plus several others who became our board members, started the Washington Wilderness Coalition. We looked at a map, looked at all of the places where there weren't groups and went about setting them up. Because I had a car and Ken didn't, I had eastern Washington and Ken had the western part of the state. The whole thing was to help form groups and to help them put together information on maps, make proposals, and also provide the political expertise and assistance on how to deal with their members of Congress."

Before visiting a community, Karen created lists of names drawn from Sierra Club and Wilderness Society mailing lists. "Once we had a contact in a community, we would talk with them about who else they knew [from the lists] and we'd help connect folks." She remembers talking with an individual who had no idea one of his acquaintances was a fellow member of the Sierra Club or the Wilderness Society. "In small communities people don't talk about their particular views on things because your neighbors or the people at the grocery store may not share your perspective."

Karen credits [legendary Northwest environmental and social justice activist] Hazel Wolf with giving her organizing tips. "If you get the right number of people together, you know there's going to be someone who will take on a leadership role. I was constantly on the scout for who was participating and would ask if we could have the next meeting at their house. Usually they'd say yes. Find the spark plug in the community and things happen around that. You have to have someone who will keep things moving."

The Washington Wilderness Coalition continued to provide support and information to local groups, while the individual groups evaluated boundaries and developed their own wilderness proposals. "Once an organization has an identity with a name, post office box, and letterhead," Karen says, "it takes on its own life, and we could remove ourselves and continue setting up other groups in other parts of the state. We would continue the care and feeding of each organization, but we didn't need to be in the center of what they were doing."

In this fashion Karen helped establish or bolster groups throughout eastern Washington. "In my circuit I worked with groups in Walla Walla, Spokane, Colville, Republic, the Methow Valley and Yakima, and with individuals in Wenatchee and Ellensburg; and I was over in the Tri-Cities several times." The results of Karen and Ken's labors and the work of the many groups throughout the state are reflected in the 1984 Washington State Wilderness Act. Karen is philosophical about the outcome, acknowledging both joys and disappointments. "Anything dealing with Congress is a compromise. While we had major victories—we established nineteen new wilderness areas and expanded four existing ones—a lot of areas were left out, even where we fought very hard."

In Karen's view, the 1984 act provided the movement with plenty of work left to do. "We had places all over the state where lines were drawn, but they were not our lines, not the proposals we'd walked in with. The '84 act protected a million acres of land, but our proposal was two and a half million acres out of the then identified three and a half million roadless acres. It wasn't perfect. I don't think we will ever be finished. We will continue to work on these issues as long as there is wild land left in the country."

Looking to the future, Karen says, "We need to continue doing the sorts of things we've been doing, and I think organizing is key to any success. We have to work in communities, find people who care about areas, and integrate them into what's going on." She believes we must address the balance between professionals and volunteers. As organizations create more professional staff positions, Karen sees a need to also develop volunteer outreach. Groups need to simultaneously foster programs that get volunteers out on the land as well as teach them the strategies of advocacy. Organizations also need to accommodate their volunteer forces. For example, she says, "If you have all of your meetings during weekdays, you are going to cut out your volunteers unless they are giving up days of pay. You can't have that go on too much and have a very effective organization."

In addition, Karen sees a need for more diversity within the wilderness movement. "Hazel Wolf was quite an advocate of diversity. She used to ask me, 'Why are you working on wilderness when all of these urban issues need to be addressed?' She worked with a more diverse group of people because of the urban setting. Issues of diversity were discussed quite a bit at the last North American wilderness conference [2002]. There were some difficult conversations, and we will have more in the future, because there hasn't been as much outreach as there could be. I think we will see more diversity with younger people. Kids growing up now are exposed much more to environmental issues than when I was growing up."

Karen is definitely someone who puts her ideas to work. As long as there is a Karen Fant, there will be nearly around-the-clock organizing: leaving the interview, she headed to the Sierra Club office to oversee the volunteer phone bank she had set up to rally support for a Snake River dam removal study.

TIM MCNULTY[10]

Tim McNulty stands on the back porch of his Lost Mountain home on the northeast side of the Olympic Peninsula. Raising a hand he gestures, "To the east is the Graywolf drainage, those peaks farther south are in the Buckhorn Wilderness, and to the west is Mount Angeles." Tim is engrossed in the lands he has devoted his life to protecting. His dedication to their wildness is apparent in nearly every sentence he speaks. He is currently the president of Olympic Park Associates (OPA), an organization dedicated to protecting Olympic National Park and the surrounding national forests.

Tim grew up in Connecticut's Quinnipiac Valley during the 1950s and '60s, in a noisy Irish-Catholic family with three sisters and a brother. Of that time he says, "I was always drawn to the wild outskirts of town, the undeveloped areas, a several-thousand-acre city park with a lake, trails, and some cliffs. My grandfather had a farm at the edge of town. It was pretty wild behind his place. I spent a lot of time roaming . . . it was perhaps partly an escape from what was going on at home, which was always a lot of everything, but also just a great sense of adventure for me to be out in the wilds."

Later, joining the Boy Scouts gave his explorations a focus. "All these things I had a natural curiosity about were given some kind of a blessing and sanction from society, from my elders. So I really leapt into that." During his scouting years Tim's father introduced him to Jim Berry, the head of the city parks department, who lived in a stone house at the edge of the woods and who also happened to be the merit-badge counselor. "I developed a relationship with him and he taught me about birds, small mammals in the area, about habitat, forests, cavities and snags and nesting sites. He was my first wildlands mentor."

Another strong childhood influence was reading: "I became a devotee of Mark Twain. I thought it my ill fortune that I wasn't born in 1840 on the Mississippi River. The wildness and power of the river seeped into my bones and even though there was no big river near my home, I always responded to rivers when I was around them."

Tim began reading and writing poetry in college and was introduced to contemporary poets like Theodore Roethke, whose writing included Pacific Northwest landscapes, and Gary Snyder, who wrote about wilderness experiences. Tim says, "I got it in my mind that I wanted to come west. I wanted to see this big wild country. I had this yearning for another landscape, another level of experience." So during a summer break, Tim joined friends for a trip out to the Colorado Rockies. From there he hitchhiked to Big Sur and up the Oregon coast and into Washington, camping and hiking in the Olympics and Cascades while visiting the landscapes of the writers who had lured him there.

That fall, because of the Vietnam war, the draft, and a girlfriend, Tim went back to Boston to complete his undergraduate degree. "From that point on," he says, "I had made up my mind. I wanted to see more of this wild country and steep myself in a wild landscape and see where my writing would take me." The following spring, after earning his degree, packing up a few books, and giving away most of his things, Tim headed west, spending close to a year hitchhiking and backpacking through the Sierra, Cascades, and Olympics. It was a time of soul searching, of figuring out who he was apart from the academic setting in which he had been living. He was also searching for a home. "Of all the places I saw, it was the Olympic Peninsula that was the most biologically rich, the wildest, the most beautiful, and from what I understood at the time, pretty well protected. There was no question. This was the place I wanted to settle."

During his first winter on the Olympic Peninsula in 1972, his friend David Shedd offered Tim the use of an 8-by-10-foot cabin with the understanding that when Tim was ready to move on, he would dismantle the structure and return the area to its natural state. The cabin sat atop an 80-foot cliff north of Cape Alava on the Olympic coast. In Tim's words, the setting was "remote, rugged, storm-bound, and cliff-carved oceanfront . . . everything I'd been dreaming of, the blend between Thoreau, Han Shan, and Robinson Crusoe . . . with sea birds and mammals and incredible intertidal communities." Tim lived on the bluff for most of a year. "It was the experience that wedded me to this place."

From his cabin, he explored much of the west side of the Peninsula, getting to know the forests, the wildlife, the migratory patterns of the birds, and some of the Native people living there. It was a part of the coast that wasn't protected, and when he hiked back into the uplands, to the sources of coastal rivers and creeks, he saw the clear-cuts marching west. "That kicked me into environmental activism. I had fallen in love with this place. It was in my blood and I really cared for it. The fact was that people had been living there for thousands of years and here was this industrial juggernaut moving in. I got involved."

He began by joining photographer Steve Johnson in writing letters to anyone they thought might listen. Tim also wrote articles for environmental newsletters in an effort to draw attention to the place. Olympic Park Associates joined the fight to protect the Peninsula's wild, northwestern coast. "The momentum built suddenly," he says, "and within a few years the area was included in Olympic National Park. We were on a wave of success."

In the early 1970s, Tim moved back to Lake Leland on the east side of the peninsula. The entire economy of the region was dominated by the timber industry. "That's what was going on," Tim recalls. "That's who people listened to. It was the main agenda of every chamber of commerce, business, and social organization. I was looking at where I fit in." An opportunity came up to plant trees, and while it was not an ideal restoration project, Tim decided it was on the positive side of the equation so he took the job. "I needed to plug into this place in some way and there wasn't a big market for wilderness poetry back then."

The seasonal nature of tree planting gave Tim summers to explore all of the valleys and uplands of the peninsula's east side and he describes what he saw as "spectacular, forested valleys and subalpine uplands that were not protected in any way." Tree planting and hiking fed into Tim's winter occupation of staying home in his cabin to write (by kerosene lamp) letters, stories, poems, and essays in an attempt to get people to realize what they had and to urge them to help preserve their forests. "I saw all this road building and logging and knew if it were left up to the local economy, local elected officials, there would be no question where it would go."

On the political scene the first Forest Service Roadless Area Review and Evaluation (RARE I) had been challenged, and the second evaluation (RARE II) was expected but had not yet been authorized. According to Tim, the Forest Service administrators in the Olympic Peninsula districts realized they had a window of opportunity to exempt some areas from further study if they moved ahead with their planning process. Tim says, "Within several months we saw over 50,000 acres of some of the most richly forested, beautiful, dense westside rainforests just put right on the chopping block because nobody was paying attention."

"We knew the next round of planning was going to be on the east side of the peninsula in the Quilcene and Hoodsport districts. We mobilized." A small group of local citizens, mostly Tim's friends, formed an organization called Ohode. Tim explains, "*Ohode* is a Makah [Indian] word meaning 'all of us.' We interpreted that as the entire biotic community and our role would be as spokesmen for the entire living community." Ohode members used a combination of their intimate knowledge of the land and sound scientific research of ecosystems. Much of the data used by the group came from studies authorized by the Forest Service. "We pointed to the Forest Service's own research and presented that back to them to justify our claims and concerns. The group was a wonderful coming together of knowledge, ideals, energy, and political activism. Ohode was totally anarchic; no dues, no membership, no officers."

Ohode began working closely with Olympic Park Associates. "Our work became their work." Soon after, OPA appointed Tim as its delegate to the Forest Service Planning Committee for the Canal Front. This committee, with representation from a dozen other environmental organizations, put together a detailed wilderness proposal for the eastern Peninsula. "We paid close attention

Tim McNulty in August 2000 (Photo by Mary Morgan; courtesy Tim McNulty)

to winter elk range, salmon habitat, mid- and low-elevation forests, looking for a way to incorporate the lower-elevation ecosystems that were not represented in the park or any protected area." They were successful in getting several areas considered for further study, but many were overlooked.

Beginning in the 1980s, Tim's work centered around OPA's efforts to get eastside Olympic forests included in the 1984 Washington wilderness bill. In addition, he became a founding board member for the Washington Wilderness Coalition, where he enjoyed meeting with other rural advocates living in places they were passionate about protecting. He still worked in the woods, but now with Olympic Reforestation Cooperative, a group formed with some members of Ohode and other friends. They did plantings and precommercial thinning projects. Tim also worked for a small logging contractor using selective logging methods. "The opportunity gave me a handle on what it takes to do careful logging, the fact that it can be done and that it is difficult."

During one particularly complex planting contract, Polly Dyer (see interview this chapter) urged Tim to testify at a congressional hearing in Washington, D.C. Tim really wanted to go, but couldn't see how he could leave his crew in the middle of a large and demanding project. Nor could he afford to give up wages during the one time of year in which he was able to earn money. The crew found out about Tim's D.C. invitation and offered to keep him on the payroll while he made the trip east. "I don't know of any other forestry company that sponsored a wilderness activist to D.C. at that time. We may have made a little history. It was my first experience lobbying in D.C. Polly took me under her wing and brought me around to meet committee staffers down in the basements of various legislative buildings, which is where everything got done. It was a lot more fun than planting trees in the rain."

Tim worked especially hard to get the Graywolf drainage included in the 1984 Washington State Wilderness Act that created the Buckhorn Wilderness Area. The Forest Service recommended half of the valley for wilderness and the other half for logging. Congressman Al Swift, who represented the district, was in Tim's words, "not hot on wilderness even though he was being showered by letters and passionate pleas to save the Graywolf." Swift would agree to the Forest Service recommendation, but would go no further because of the many loggers and mills within his district. Olympic Park Associates shared with him figures showing the small amounts of timber in the area, but he would not budge. "This was so frustrating," Tim says. "It was many years into the campaign and the chips were down. Our ace in the hole was Senator Dan Evans. He had a passionate connection to the Olympics, but he was unfamiliar with the Graywolf." Nevertheless, Evans sent his aide, Joe Mentor, to the Peninsula to investigate. It was January 1983 and there was a lot of snow on the ground, but Tim agreed to take Joe as far up the mountain as Tim's '61 Volvo humpback would go. Logging trucks hauling timber out of the lowlands packed down the snow, allowing Tim and Joe to drive all the way up the valley to within a mile of the trailhead. "We hiked up the lower Graywolf Valley about 5 miles to Camp Tony. The sun was breaking through, cliffs were plastered with snow, the river was a deep blue, mossy rocks were covered with snow. I'd never seen the valley that beautiful. It was breathtaking, spectacular, and Joe was just blown away."

The next day Joe was scheduled to fly over the area with representatives from the Forest Service and the U.S. Fish and Wildlife Service, so Tim explained where to go to get a clear picture of how the drainages fit together and where logging had occurred. Early on the morning of the flight, Tim got a call from Joe requesting that Tim join the flight. Apparently neither the Forest Service, the Fish and Wildlife reps, nor the pilot knew the area Tim wanted Joe to see. After watching a rough landing on a frozen grass strip that was the Port Townsend airport, Tim climbed aboard and gave the group a tour of the northeastern Olympic National Forest, where Joe took photographs to share with Evans. "When the final decisions were made, the Graywolf was included. I think a lot of it had to do with Dan Evans's power of persuasion, and I'm sure that trip up the Graywolf was kind of the trump card for Dan and Joe getting total protection for that valley."

After the passage of the 1984 bill, Tim turned his energies to developing his writing into a feasible way of supporting himself. He hooked up with photographer Pat O'Hara, and the two collaborated on a number of books on national parks. The books were successful and launched Tim's wilderness writing career. During this time activists realized that the critical links in migration corridors outside wilderness designations were the river systems and that the next step in preservation should be a statewide campaign for Wild and Scenic River designations. The Mountaineers approached Tim and Pat to create a book about Washington's rivers, and in 1990 The Mountaineers Books published *Washington's Wild Rivers: The Unfinished Work,* a companion book to Harvey Manning and O'Hara's *Washington Wilderness: The Unfinished Work.* Tim remembers the story: "The book was to give a big push to the Wild and Scenic Rivers bill that Congressman Miller was to introduce right after the book came out, and we'd be on our way to another conservation victory." Instead, the old-growth forests came under even greater threats and the northern spotted owl was listed under the Endangered Species Act. The Mountaineers did have a big press release for the book, but as Tim recalls, "The northern spotted owl issue grew and grew and grew into a major crisis that occupied Congress and the White House for years. The river issue disappeared beneath it. It disappeared so well that it's never resurfaced again."

"Interestingly enough," Tim remarks, "Olympic National Park is just about to release its alternatives for its General Management Plan and that's one of the issues OPA is pushing, that the Park Service take a look at potential Wild and Scenic rivers." Tim and OPA believe the park is overdue for a revision of its plan. "My first public testimony was during their last review. I remember because I came in from Shi Shi to testify. It was November of 1973."

Tim spends a great deal of time and energy working with OPA on park and surrounding national forest issues. Echoing Polly Dyer, who he succeeded as president of OPA, Tim says, "You aren't done after the designations. It's a continual job . . . . We [OPA] keep a finger on the pulse of the ecosystem: salmon recovery, wolf restoration, river habitat, roadless areas, and recreation management are all issues we work on. We are taking on responsibilities and obligations regarding the ecosystem that are a little over our heads. But we work with national organizations that do have paid staff. They frequently defer to us on recommendations and approaches to issues, and we rely on them for their lobbying capabilities, access to large membership rosters, and the clout of their letterhead to agency officials."

Besides new wilderness designations, the main issue for OPA in the Olympic National Forest is the Forest Service Access and Travel initiative that calls for decommissioning more than 700 miles of old logging roads. "It is the biggest restoration project facing the forest, but at the existing pace of funding, it will take thirty or forty years. We have a great big opportunity here to help salmon streams and this abused land recover through that road restoration program. This forest is way out ahead of most in having gone through the process of looking at road systems through many ecological screens. We are trying to support them as much as we can."

Polly Dyer, Harvey Manning, Patrick Goldsworthy, Karen Fant, and Tim McNulty: these long-time wildlands advocates have experiences, needs, and values in common. As children and young adults, each experienced nature or wilderness in ways that profoundly influenced their adult lives, from exploring the woods and stargazing to backpacking into the wild; each also expresses a longing to continue their connections with the natural environment today. At some point in their lives an event or culmination of experiences tipped the scale and set them in motion as wilderness advocates. But no one acted in isolation. They either joined established organizations or helped launch new ones. Some did both. Working within organizations, they found energy, creativity, and strength as well as community.

Today these activists continue to devote enormous amounts of time and energy to the wildlands in Washington State. They agree that the integrity of our wilderness areas, no matter their current protection status, requires constant vigilance. They see a continuing need for groups to monitor government agencies and policies while constantly gathering new volunteers to become stewards of our wildlands.

▲ *This forest canopy is in Olympic National Park, about 95 percent of which was set aside by Congress as a designated wilderness area of 876,669 acres.* (Photo by Art Wolfe; reprinted by permission)

◄ *This scene typifies what was encountered in Washington's backcountry by an earlier generation of citizens who created the movement to defend what was left of wild Washington.* (Photo by Ira Spring; reprinted by permission)

▲ *In 2001, there was a clear boundary line between the Mount St. Helens National Volcanic Monument (right) and Weyerhaeuser timberlands reforested with Douglas fir in 1983 (left).* (Courtesy the Weyerhaeuser Company)

◄ *Recreational use of wild Washington requires careful attention to the maintenance of both environmental quality and recreational opportunities, making it a controversial topic among citizen conservationists.* (Photo by Ira Spring; reprinted by permission)

▲ Shrub-steppe on the Yakima Training Center has been spared from the ravages of grazing. (Photo by Steve Herman; reprinted by permission)

▲ A grazed location in the Sagebrush Flats Wildlife Area of southeastern Washington (Photo by Steve Herman; reprinted by permission)

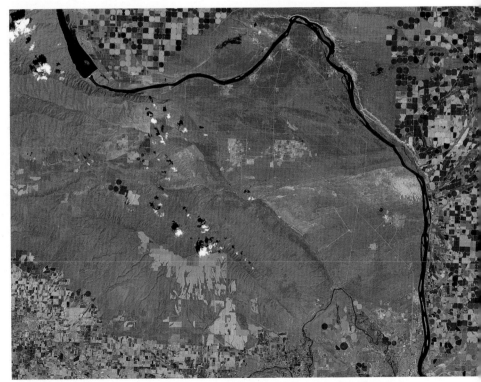

▲ In this Landsat 7 satellite image, the stretch of the Columbia River known as the Hanford Reach curves through a shrub-steppe environment untouched by the agricultural development that surrounds it. The Hanford Reach National Monument extends in a U shape around the Hanford Nuclear Site (in center of photo), following the bend in the Columbia before stretching southeast. (Photo by Ron Beck; source, USGS EROS Data Center, May 6, 2000)

Wild and Roadless Lands

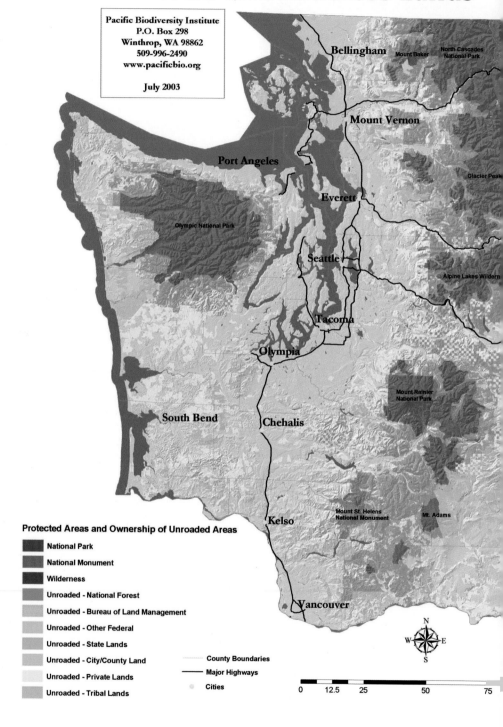

Pacific Biodiversity Institute
P.O. Box 298
Winthrop, WA 98862
509-996-2490
www.pacificbio.org

July 2003

Bellingham   Mount Baker   North Cascades
                             National Park

Mount Vernon

Port Angeles

Glacier Peak

Everett

Olympic National Park

Seattle

Alpine Lakes Wildern

Tacoma

Olympia

Mount Rainier
National Park

South Bend   Chehalis

Mount St. Helens   Mt. Adams
National Monument
Kelso

Vancouver

Protected Areas and Ownership of Unroaded Areas

- National Park
- National Monument
- Wilderness
- Unroaded - National Forest
- Unroaded - Bureau of Land Management
- Unroaded - Other Federal
- Unroaded - State Lands
- Unroaded - City/County Land
- Unroaded - Private Lands
- Unroaded - Tribal Lands

County Boundaries
Major Highways
Cities

N
W   E
S

0   12.5   25   50   75

in Washington State

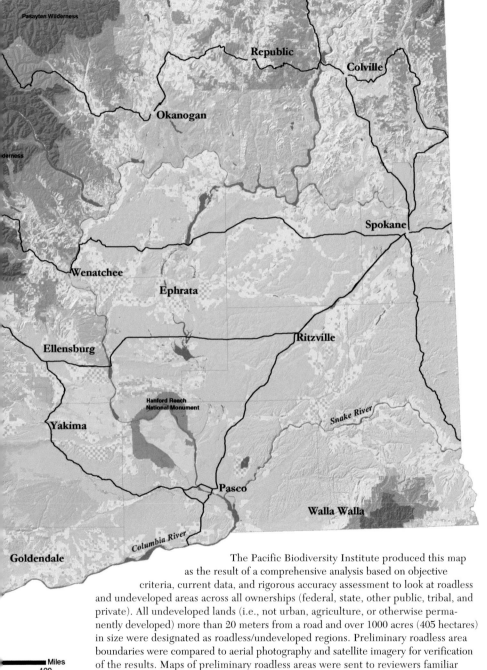

Pasayten Wilderness

Republic

Colville

Okanogan

derness

Spokane

Wenatchee

Ephrata

Ritzville

Ellensburg

Hanford Reach
National Monument

Snake River

Yakima

Pasco

Walla Walla

Columbia River

Goldendale

Miles
100

The Pacific Biodiversity Institute produced this map as the result of a comprehensive analysis based on objective criteria, current data, and rigorous accuracy assessment to look at roadless and undeveloped areas across all ownerships (federal, state, other public, tribal, and private). All undeveloped lands (i.e., not urban, agriculture, or otherwise permanently developed) more than 20 meters from a road and over 1000 acres (405 hectares) in size were designated as roadless/undeveloped regions. Preliminary roadless area boundaries were compared to aerial photography and satellite imagery for verification of the results. Maps of preliminary roadless areas were sent to reviewers familiar with a portion of the state, who then checked their accuracy in the field. Their comments and suggested changes were incorporated into the final roadless area designations shown here. Overall, unprotected roadless and substantially undeveloped lands were found to comprise approximately 27.1% of the state's land base.

◀ *The Northern Spotted Owl has been at the center of conservation politics since it was discovered to be dependent upon old-growth forest habitat.* (Photo by John and Karen Hollingsworth; reprinted by permission of the U.S. Fish and Wildlife Service)

Mount Rainier as seen from Mazama Ridge. This Cascade Range volcano, a classic landmark of Washington State, is the centerpiece of the state's first protected area, Mount Rainier National Park, which was established in 1899. (Photo by Ira Spring; reprinted by permission) ▼

CHAPTER 8

On the Trail from Wilderness to Wildness: The Movement Diversifies in the Late Twentieth Century

◆ *Melissa Carter and Tyler Winchell* ◆

After the 1964 Wilderness Act, Washington's conservationists sought to create more congressionally designated wilderness areas. This strategy culminated with the congressional passage of statewide wilderness bills in 1984 and 1988, which protected many critical wildlands. But citizens felt compelled to go even further, to safeguard areas that were not likely to receive wilderness designation in time to protect them from development pressures, fragmentation, or a wide variety of other problems. As recognized by Howard Zahniser (an early Wilderness Society executive director and principal author of the 1964 Wilderness Act), "the essential quality of the wilderness is wildness,"[1] and wildness exists in small and large pockets throughout Washington State. Consequently, in the final two decades of the twentieth century, the conservation movement broadened its visions and diversified its goals, tactics, and organizational styles, leading Washington's citizen conservationists along a trail from wilderness to wildness.

When the 1984 Washington State Wilderness Act became law, it designated 1.1 million acres of new national forest wilderness, to the delight of activists across the state. However, another intent of that legislation was to allow the Forest Service to proceed with the development of other roadless areas. This made it politically impractical for roughly fifteen years to return to Congress asking for more national forest wilderness designations to protect endangered ecosystems like ancient forests. As a result, conservationists began to utilize new tools, ranging from simple ideas such as gathering their own data about ancient-forest groves, to more direct action, like confronting bulldozers and occupying the canopies of ancient trees to stop logging. Activists' passions ran deep, because by 1990, only 15 percent of the Pacific Northwest's ancient forests remained, and they were largely unprotected.[2]

In this political environment, litigation soon bypassed legislation as an activist tool, culminating in a moratorium on timber sales from 1990 to 1994: a federal judge ruled that the government was obligated to reevaluate its forest management plans because of their effects on endemic and endangered wildlife. In response to the stalemate and at President Clinton's direction, the Forest Service adopted the Northwest Forest Plan, fashioned by foresters and ecologists from around the region. The plan drastically limited the timber cut from national forests, but it did not ban old-growth logging, and activists renewed forest action in 1995 when legislation sought to circumvent the plan's allotments. Other fights to save forests in this era spurred disagreement within activist circles, but also inspired partnerships with local, resource-based communities, showing that former opponents could work together for the future of wildlands preservation. Activists were also encouraged by Clinton's road-building ban in national forests, issued at the end of his term, but they knew action would be needed to make sure that it was upheld with the changing of the presidential guard.

In addition to engaging in intensive debates over forest management during this period, activists expanded their focus beyond national forest land. They advocated successfully for adding wilderness lands within Washington's national parks and sought local-level protections in the form of wildlife refuges and land trusts. Together with advocacy on the federal front, these events defined a multifaceted citizen movement at the end of the twentieth century.

GAINING WILDERNESS IN 1984

The Forest Service initiated the second Roadless Area Review and Evaluation (RARE II) in 1977 in order to create a sense of closure to the wilderness debate and "to resolve the issue of RARE in Washington,"[3] as Senator Jackson stated. The survey would both recommend some lands for wilderness designation and allow for more predictable timber sales on roadless lands no longer considered for preservation.

Rupert Cutler, formerly assistant executive director of the Wilderness

Society, was the undersecretary of agriculture in President Carter's administration, which allowed him to oversee the Forest Service's RARE II survey.
Washington's activists hoped that Cutler's oversight would bring a better
inventory of the roadless areas in Washington's national forests along with
substantial wilderness recommendations. However, Washington's timber
industry continued to work at keeping the roadless areas with valuable and/
or easily accessible timber out of consideration for wilderness designation.

The Forest Service inventoried 2.5 million acres as roadless in the
national forests of Washington State, of which only 269,000 acres were recommended for wilderness designation. The majority of these recommended
acres were located in high elevations, out of the commercial timber base—
what activists refer to as "rock and ice." Dissatisfied with these minimal
wilderness recommendations, motivated citizens decided to create their own
proposals. Activists wanted more than just mountaintops protected, they
wanted forests, watersheds, valleys, rivers, and fields protected as well.

Because there were still wildlands with insufficient or no local defenders,
wilderness activists Karen Fant and Ken Gersten started the Washington
Wilderness Coalition in 1979 to catalyze local communities and teach them
the ropes of wilderness politics. Fant traveled across eastern Washington
showing how to coordinate canvassing operations and getting local leaders on board for wilderness proposals.[4] (See Fant's interview in chapter 7
for more information on her activities at the time.)

The effort to create a coalition encouraged place-based groups across
the state, strengthening the momentum for wilderness designation. East
of the Cascades in the Kettle Mountain Range, a group called the Kettle
Range Conservation Group that began in 1976 to protect the region's forest joined the coalition's efforts. In the Columbia Basin, the Friends of
the Juniper Forest struggled against off-road-vehicle groups to protect ancient juniper forests and sand dunes. The Salmo-Priest Defense Fund cam-
paigned to keep the Selkirk Mountains of northeast Washington from
becoming logged. To the west, the Gifford Pinchot Alliance (now the Gifford
Pinchot Task Force) worked diligently to protect the low-elevation roadless
areas in the Gifford Pinchot National Forest, such as the Trapper Creek
and Indian Heaven roadless areas. The Olympic Park Associates collaborated with an organization called Wild Olympic Salmon in creating plans
to protect the rainforests that lie outside of the Olympic National Park,
such as those in the Colonel Bob roadless area southeast of the park.

The biggest question in activists' minds was how they were going to
protect all of these areas across the state. Because of efforts like Senator
Jesse Helm's (R-NC) proposed legislation to end wilderness designations
after those that resulted from the RARE II surveys, wilderness proposals
were scrutinized more closely in the early 1980s. The Sierra Club, which

had the greatest conservationist influence on wilderness issues in Washington, began pushing for an overall omnibus bill, which would include multiple areas throughout the state—an alternative strategy to advocating completely new legislation for each new wilderness area. This strategy had succeeded in Oregon in 1978 and so Washington activists were hopeful that an omnibus proposal would work for their state's wilderness areas as well.[5]

In 1983, Washington senators Henry Jackson and Slade Gorton—one a Democrat and the other a Republican—introduced in Congress what they dubbed "A Citizen's Wilderness Proposal," calling for protection of 1.6 million acres across Washington. There were hearings held in Spokane, Seattle, and Washington, D.C., but before Congress debated the bill, Senator Jackson died in September of that year. Congress did not address the bill until it reconvened in 1984.

The 1984 Washington wilderness bill became much larger than the previous version, calling for 2.1 million protected acres. The change was made because Jackson's successor was Republican Dan Evans, who Sierra Club's Charlie Raines believed "knew the value of the [wilderness] land" and would be more likely to defend a larger bill in Congress.[6] Evans was essential in merging Congressman Mike Lowry's (D-WA) separate wilderness bill containing rare, low-elevation land with the larger bill.

During the hearings, many activists in support of the proposal provided research findings. Activist and outdoor photographer Ira Spring presented an economic argument for the importance of wilderness recreation in the state's economy. Geology professors from Western Washington University prepared survey reports that disproved some claims about mineral potential in the proposed Mount Baker Wilderness.[7] Friends of the Juniper Forest offered to take college students and their faculty on tours of the proposed Juniper Dunes Wilderness to show them the ecological significance of the area. Many of the professors and students from the tours were impressed and so submitted written testimony in support of the bill. Each local group found a tactic to draw attention to its proposed wilderness.

The congressional delegation had its hands full. A dedicated group of activists had created an impressive wilderness proposal, but it included areas of virgin or second-growth timber that industry was counting on for future harvest in the national forests. And, although the timber industry presented the nearly unanimous position that no additional wilderness was necessary in the national forests, their opinion did not seem to be that of the majority in the state. Powerful timber companies like Boise Cascade and labor unions including the Western Council of Lumber, Production, and Industrial Workers lobbied the delegation to greatly minimize the amount of valuable timber that would be placed off-limits in wilderness areas.

The state's D.C. legislators did not agree about the size or location of future Washington wilderness areas. Senator Evans and Congressman Lowry worked to designate as much acreage as possible, which inevitably clashed with Congressman Tom Foley's (D-WA) original position of no eastern Washington wilderness areas. Congressman Sid Morrison (R-WA) proposed a compromise of high-elevation wilderness areas along the east side of the Cascades, containing less valuable timber reserves. Foley would accept a Salmo-Priest proposal (which was in his district), similar to a wildlife preserve the timber industry had proposed, in lieu of wilderness protection for the area. Evans took the delegation to Foley's office on March 9, 1984, in order to hammer out the bill's final language themselves. The ten delegates emerged five hours later with the bill that was ultimately passed on July 3, 1984, protecting, in a single legislative act, nearly one-fourth of all the lands that are now designated wilderness in Washington State.

This accomplishment was an historic event in the history of Washington wilderness preservation, but it did not come without a price. Not only were many of the conservationists' proposed wilderness areas left out, but the act included what was called "release language," which had important effects on how conservation history was to unfold thereafter in this state. The nationwide RARE II inventory had been created to identify roadless areas on national forests with the potential for wilderness designation, but it was also intended to establish a climate of predictability for timber sales in national forest roadless lands. The Forest Service knew that conservationists would hold the agency to its legal obligation to carefully evaluate the suitability of roadless areas for wilderness designation prior to selling timber or allowing road construction. Since this process could dramatically slow down the timber sale programs in national forests, wilderness bills passed in the mid-1980s included sections that "released" the Forest Service from the obligation to consider the wisdom of wilderness preservation before developing a roadless area. This release was to last until the revision of the existing forest management plans, which were revised every ten to fifteen years.

Among the areas that were taken out of the "citizens proposal" and subject to the release section of the Washington State Wilderness Act (section five) were the Kettle Range, the Okanogan Highlands, and the Dark Divide. The Kettle Range, in northeastern Washington (see chapter 14) became the one proposal that Congressman Foley would not accept because of commitments to the timber industry and labor. Congressman Morrison fought to remove the Okanogan Highlands wilderness in a political compromise, after his attempt to eliminate the Goat Rocks additions became unpopular in the state. The timber industry also targeted the Dark Divide in the Gifford Pinchot National Forest of southwestern Washington, ostensibly because the Forest Service's RARE II inventory had not identified it as a roadless area, even though it is one of the largest unprotected roadless areas in western Washington.[8]

The 1984 Washington State Wilderness Act did not end the wilderness debate as resource interests had hoped. Activists remained committed to seeking wilderness designations when each forest's management plan came up for revision. Nevertheless, Congress's temporary release of roadless areas made it politically impossible to seek another omnibus wilderness bill for national forest roadless areas in the state, forcing the movement to find other ways to protect Washington's wild areas after 1984.

MORE WILDERNESS, BUT MORE LOGGING

Although wilderness designation can permanently protect ancient forests, very few were included in the 1984 act. Timber interests had largely succeeded in keeping the wilderness boundaries at higher elevations through effective organizing of workers in many smaller timber towns, who feared the economic impacts of wilderness preservation in lands with commercially valuable timber. In reality, conservation policy played less of a role in the future of timber-dependent workers and towns than the dramatic changes in industry practices that occurred in the 1980s. The national economic downturn in the early 1980s caused more than half of the timber mills in Washington to either shut down or cut production.[9] In order to survive in the face of international competition, the industry exported many larger logs to overseas markets where they could be milled more cheaply and have a larger cash value. Many jobs became mechanized, requiring fewer people to complete the same job as in the past.

Yet, despite the recession, the 1980s saw the height of logging in Washington's national forests. In one year, an estimated 120,000 truckloads of timber came from the Gifford Pinchot National Forest alone.[10] By 1985, 900,000 acres, containing some of the Northwest's last large groves of ancient forest, had been clear-cut within inventoried roadless areas in Washington and Oregon (Forest Service Region 6).[11] Wilderness designation was not the solution for many of Washington's ancient forests because of the 1984 release language, the powerful political and financial influence of the timber industry, and the simple fact that not all such forests qualified for wilderness designation—they were either too small, contained roads, or did not qualify for other reasons. Consequently, forest activists began to look for new protective strategies. As it turned out, the emerging field of forest ecology empowered activists like never before, leading forest defenders to elevate science to a new position of prominence within the movement.

The Forest Service had long claimed that the best forest policy was to liquidate old growth as fast as possible to promote the rapid growth of young stands, accelerating the yield of wood fiber. Some of the money from timber sales was used to fund research for improving these future stands of valuable timber. But in 1981, one research report began to put the brakes on old-growth timber sales. *Ecological Characteristics of Old-Growth Douglas-Fir Forests,* a Forest Service publication by some of the Northwest's foremost experts on forest ecology, including Jerry Franklin, concluded that the ancient forest was a thriving ecosystem that was not yet fully understood.[12] The report recommended that the Forest Service maintain viable sections of this type of ecosystem until further research could conclude that forestry would be able to replicate an entire ancient forest, literally from the remnants of a clear-cut timber sale.

An ancient forest has yet to be created by professional foresters; only natural processes have created them. The best available science serves as a guideline, but there is a tremendous amount of guesswork involved. The ability to replicate an ancient forest is further complicated by the fact that there are different types of old-growth forests. In eastern Washington, pine and larch species create a mixture that defines that region's old growth. In the west, Douglas fir, western hemlock, and western red cedar are the mixed ancient forests that have received so much notoriety.

The Forest Service also financed the work of an Oregon biologist, Eric Forsman, who studied the northern spotted owl. Forsman's research established that the owl depended on old-growth forests. The owl became one of many species that the Forest Service and the U.S. Fish and Wildlife Service discovered were dependent on ancient forests. The marbled murrelet, Pacific salmon, and bald eagles were linked to old-growth forests as well. It was the spotted owl, however, that received the most public attention. Forsman's research revealed that the owl was more dependent on old-growth ecosystems in the western Cascades than previously thought: the owl needed 1,000 to 3,200 acres of continuous habitat. Other biologists like Harriet Allen observed that the owl needed even larger tracts of old growth in the Olympic Peninsula for habitat and food sources than in other forests. Old-growth clear-cuts substantially affected the owls' survival.[13] (See photograph in the color insert)

 ## THE "TIMBER WARS": SCIENCE, DIRECT ACTION, AND LITIGATION

The Forest Service chose the northern spotted owl as an indicator species to meet the stipulations of the National Forest Management Act (NFMA) that national forests "maintain viable populations of existing native . . . vertebrate species in the planning area."[14] The act requires the Forest Service to collect population data for certain sensitive and indicator species occurring in national forests. Sensitive species are those that are in decline; indicator species are chosen because they represent certain species types or habitat conditions. Information about indicator species enables the Forest Service to assess and predict the impacts of logging and other activities on the ecosystem generally.

Conservation organizations realized that they needed to understand forest ecology in order to use the NFMA to challenge Forest Service practices and so groups quickly integrated current scientific findings with citizen research of their own. At the suggestion of Brock Evans, then vice president of the National Audubon Society, Adopt-a-Forest programs were started by Audubon Society chapters in 1987 to educate citizens about forest ecology. Activists became better defenders of their local forests by counting trees, noting the location of old-growth species, observing the wildlife, and keeping track of species' locations and numbers. Local forest activists at times established working relations with the Forest Service district offices to better understand the environmental impact statements and the timber sale planning process. By gaining this knowledge, citizens empowered themselves to effectively challenge timber sales they believed violated statutes such as the NFMA.

Though the Adopt-a-Forest program helped, some activists thought it would not be enough to stop ancient-forest timber sales, and when Earth First! reached Washington in the early 1980s, these activists saw the group's direct action approach as a better alternative. Earth First! used nonviolent civil disobedience in order to stop projects or to bring attention to issues. For example, to draw the public's attention to the dramatic environmental impact dams have on Washington's rivers, a Port Angeles group of Earth First!ers, called the Elwha Liberation Front, "cracked" the Elwha Dam by scaling the structure and painting a 100-foot-long crack and the motto "Elwha Be Free" on the dam itself.[15]

At the same time as the campaign for the 1984 Washington State Wilderness Act, Earth First! began a campaign of tree spiking (hammering nails into trees) in national forests where timber sales were planned for inventoried roadless areas, including in Washington's Wenatchee National Forest.[16] Tree spiking is one form of ecological sabotage, or ecotage, and is also referred to as "monkey wrenching," a term taken from Edward Abbey's novels. Earth First! remained secretive about its use of ecotage from the first instances in 1980 until the Round River Rendezvous (Earth First!'s annual get-together) was held in the Kettle Range in 1988. For the first time, the radical organization openly acknowledged and endorsed the use of monkey wrenching through a series of seminars held in the Colville National Forest.[17] When trees are spiked, a timber company has to decide whether to finance the removal of such spikes in order to harvest the timber or to abandon a sale in order to avoid the high costs of removing the nails from trees. Spiking has the potential to seriously injure workers if chainsaw blades make contact with the nails in the trees. Earth First! activists used tree spiking as an economic deterrent for halting timber sales, but not as a tactic to hurt loggers. The saboteurs notified Forest Service rangers, informing them of the spiked areas in order to prevent the trees from being cut. The incident helped stop each of the timber sales with spiked trees, and helped to keep the areas roadless as well.

During the early Earth First! campaigns of sabotage, many participants also used a process called siltation. This involves pouring various chemicals into the transmissions of logging and/or road-building equipment and leaving the solution to fester for a few days. The saboteurs are generally able to escape detection, leaving a collection of useless equipment—and an intact forest. From the early 1980s through the mid-1990s, the Weyerhaeuser timber company has reported losing nearly $10 million of equipment to ecotage.[18] Timber industry analysts believe the figures could be a great deal higher because of incomplete reporting.

For most Earth First! activists, direct-action civil disobedience includes many ways of using one's body to try to halt logging operations, and this approach has remained a preferred tactic. Of all the direct-action tools, tree sitting was one of the most innovative techniques for protecting old-growth trees. During campaigns in Oregon in the 1980s, activists decided to halt logging of ancient forests by scaling trees and camping out in the canopies. Although tree sitting was an essential component of Earth First!'s actions in defending Oregon's ancient forests, it never gained as much momentum in Washington.

Despite fewer tree sits in Washington, Earth First! activists have been quite active here. One incident included 120 members of Earth First! descending upon the Okanogan National Forest supervisor's office to deface government property, banging on the walls and windows and disrupting the operations inside. Other actions included placing cow pies over the office's air vents, all to convey disapproval of grazing in the forest.[19] Earth First! activists in Aberdeen also blocked the entrance gate of Weyerhaeuser's local mill with their bodies in a chain-gang set up, trying to block trucks from entering the mill, and they were successful in doing so for at least a few days.

The actions carried out by Earth First! have been vehicles to convey important messages. Protests are driven by the activists' concern that the ancient forests of Washington may disappear through clear-cuts and that direct action is the only way to bring additional attention to the noncommercial value of the forests and their biological diversity. Earth First! activists have shown that they are dedicated, passionate activists for the preservation of ancient-forest ecosystems in Washington.

The plight of the spotted owl and the deteriorating condition of national forests were substantiated through scientific research, grassroots efforts, and direct action. Yet, the grassroots organizations could not obtain the political support to legislatively save ancient forests from being cut. Direct action did not offer a long-term solution either, thus a new approach was needed. At an environmental law conference at the University of Oregon in 1987, activist Andy Stahl suggested that the way to achieve protection of ancient forests was to impose it through the courts. Armed with recent scientific research, activists were prepared to challenge the Forest Service in court for neglecting to guarantee the survival of old-growth forest species.

The strategy worked and in 1989 U.S. District Court Judge William Dwyer issued a preliminary injunction on behalf of the Audubon Society's Seattle, Pilchuck, Portland, and Lane County (Oregon) chapters, the National Audubon Society, and the Oregon Natural Resource Council. The injunction halted logging until the Forest Service created a management plan, as required by the NFMA, to provide habitat for the northern spotted owl. The injunction polarized timber interests and conservationists. Loggers and their communities felt threatened and alienated at the close of the 1980s and early 1990s. The increasing instances of civil disobedience as well as ecotage set the tone of a battle. The issues that divided the sides centered on the issue of preserving jobs verses preserving nature—thus the logger verses the environmentalist. Each side of the debate used statistics to rally support for its side. The timber industry estimated that from 102,000 to 150,000 jobs would be lost, and old-growth advocates countered with estimates of 1,000 jobs lost.[20]

The timber wars were on. But the debate involved more than just numbers; citizens across Washington were visibly choosing sides. Signs painted in fluorescent orange dotted the timber community of Aberdeen, saying "This home supported by timber $$$." Soon, political candidates from the Olympic Peninsula identified themselves as pro-timber or anti-owl, as was the case with Forks resident and wife of a logger Ann Goose, during her 1990 campaign for the state house.

Robert Lee, a professor at the University of Washington's College of Forest Resources, has conducted extensive studies among Washington's loggers and has recounted the anguish felt by many of them during the logging injunctions. Sandra Hines, a writer for the university's Office of Information Services, described his views by saying, "It goes beyond differences of opinion about how much old growth is left and how much should be cut. The threat is against loggers themselves, as if they violate some natural law every time they fire up their chain saws."[21]

Unfortunately, increasing polarization resulted from a lack of outreach and understanding between the ancient-forest advocates and the industry workers. Many activists now believe, in hindsight, that if mutual issues had been addressed, such as reforming the international timber trade and resisting other industry changes, the conception that the ancient-forest campaign meant owls versus jobs would not have become as prevalent.

To lift the injunction, the Forest Service produced the Thomas Report in late 1990. It was supposed to create guidelines for legally harvesting timber, but it did not follow environmental rules under the NFMA, and the plaintiffs who filed the first lawsuit challenged the legality of the Forest Service plan again in May 1991. Judge Dwyer agreed with the conservation groups, forcing the Forest Service to complete an environmental impact statement that would adequately protect all old-growth-dependent species and not just the northern spotted owl. Dwyer said that he was convinced by testimony given in support of protecting the owl that the timber industry would be able to sustain itself for at least two years with existing timber reserves. He believed the Forest Service was quite capable of creating a plan to protect old growth, owls, and timber workers under NFMA regulations.[22] Until the Forest Service produced a plan that met with Dwyer's specifications, the injunction on timber sales remained. The requirement to address all old-growth-dependent species led to the creation of the Northwest Forest Plan.

 ## CREATING THE NORTHWEST FOREST PLAN

The stalemate that existed in the Northwest gained national attention, especially during the 1992 presidential campaign. As a candidate, Bill Clinton announced that, if elected, he would hold a conference to find a resolution. On April 1, 1993, President Clinton made good on his promise and held such a conference in Portland, Oregon, to address the gridlock over the management of Northwest forests. Armed FBI agents guarded the rooftops around the conference. Below the buildings, under a torrential downpour, citizens from all sides of the debate protested in the streets, holding banners and shouting their positions.

Inside, Northwest activists gave presentations while even more sat in the bleachers showing their support. The conference addressed Judge Dwyer's orders to create a management plan that protected all old-growth-dependent species. Although activists were brought to the table, Clinton sought to keep his promise to labor and industry to allow as much logging as possible while meeting environmental requirements.

After the forest conference, President Clinton instructed the Forest Ecosystem Management Assessment Team to create a plan within sixty days that was "scientifically sound, ecologically credible, and legally responsible."[23]

Although eight options were presented, the Clinton administration decided that none of them offered enough timber while still upholding the ecological requirements. Jerry Franklin, who had studied old-growth ecosystems in the early 1980s, was asked to develop alternatives. What became known as "Option 9" was modified by the administration and selected for implementation. This was an alternative that allowed for higher harvest along with ecological management that would comply with the law, thus enabling the court to lift the injunction. President Clinton had come through for labor in creating a plan that still allowed the logging of ancient forests.

Even so, the amount of national forest timber harvesting allowed by the plan was dramatically decreased, though controversy still exists regarding the amount of timber cutting projected by the plan. Activists who were deeply involved with the timber wars and the Portland Forest Conference, such as Pilchuck Audubon Society member Bonnie Phillips, recall hearing Clinton's interior secretary, Bruce Babbitt, announce that 1.1 billion board feet would be made available each year from federal lands covered by the plan. Industry representatives latched on to Babbitt's announcement as a promised minimum level of harvest and continually point out that the actual harvest levels have averaged only about 60 percent of that amount since 1994.[24]

In June 1994, Judge Dwyer lifted the injunction, stating that Option 9 was barely legal. Lawsuits followed, challenging the legality of the Northwest Forest Plan (NWFP), but it withstood every challenge. Logging was allowed to resume in the national forests, but it did return with a system addressing the health of species, habitats, and watersheds. Forest management zones were established, as described in chapter 3 of this book. These include late-successional reserves, which will be allowed to grow into ancient forests, providing habitat for old-growth-dependent species; adaptive management areas, which are designed to develop and test new forestry management approaches; riparian reserves, which are areas along all streams, wetlands, ponds, lakes, and unstable or potentially unstable areas, established to protect the health of the aquatic system and its dependent species; and matrix areas, where most timber is harvested, including old growth. In recent years, forest advocates have learned to embrace the plan, despite its shortcomings in protecting the environment. They now monitor forest management according to the plan and fight to keep it from being dismantled through administrative means.

PROTECTING WILDNESS IN ALL PLACES

Although the high-profile old-growth campaign was underway, conservationists continued to expand their focus in other directions as well, working to preserve wildness in different landscapes throughout the state. This included advocating wilderness designations within national parks, seeking out state and local protection of wildlands, and getting involved in planning for future growth and development.

As a central means of preservation, besides direct action and litigation, activists continued to advocate setting aside more land as protected areas. Increasing tourism and recreation in the national parks of Washington threatened to undermine the wild qualities activists had worked so hard to set aside. As early as 1975 both the Wilderness Society and the Sierra Club had begun planning for wilderness legislation within each of the state's national parks.[25] During the 1984 Washington wilderness bill campaign, the timber industry actually suggested wilderness designation for the parks instead of for national forests. Senator Dan Evans eventually became convinced that wilderness designation was needed for Washington's national parks to prevent further road building and increased mechanized recreation, and to preserve their wild qualities. The 1988 Washington Park Wilderness Act designated wilderness areas in more than 90 percent of Mount Rainier, Olympic, and North Cascades National Parks.[26] The combination of national park and wilderness designations provides the highest possible protection for these 1.7 million acres of Washington's wild Olympic and Cascade ranges.

Citizens also advocated for tools to preserve Washington State lands. Washington had been one of the first states to enact a natural heritage program in 1972 (championed and financially sponsored by the Nature Conservancy). This program provides for the acquisition of private lands to protect them as natural area preserves for scientific and educational purposes (see chapter 3). However, the heritage program did not address the issue of state lands with wilderness values. In 1987, Washington wilderness advocates within and outside of the Department of Natural Resources convinced the agency to sponsor legislation to create something approximating a state-level preservation system. Only a handful of state legislatures have passed legislation to preserve wilderness on state lands. In Washington, the result was the Natural Resource Conservation Area Program which, as discussed in chapter 3, falls short of the level of protection afforded by federal wilderness areas. Nevertheless, the program enables citizens to nominate lands for protection and to participate in the development of local management plans for each area.

There have always been important wildlands that lie outside of the public domain and which are in need of protection. For example, birdwatchers and researchers had, for years, witnessed hundreds of thousands of shorebirds land in the late spring in the tidal flats along Grays Harbor in southwestern Washington. These birds came from as far south as Argentina on their way to the Arctic Circle, their summer breeding ground. The Grays Harbor lands these birds visited were discovered to be one of four crucial stopover sites along the Pacific Flyway, but the lands remained unprotected. In 1988, in response to citizens' and scientists' initiatives, Senator Brock Adams (D-WA) secured the passage of Senate Bill 1979, which allowed the federal government to buy private and public lands to create a refuge. The lands were acquired ahead of schedule, and the Grays Harbor National Wildlife Refuge opened in 1990. Later, in 1996, the Grays Harbor Estuary, which is contained within the refuge, was designated a hemispheric reserve by the Western Hemisphere Shorebird Reserve Network as a site of international significance.

Another legislative initiative in Washington to protect lands from development was that of an organization called 1,000 Friends of Washington. In the late 1980s, this coalition of activists marshaled the public desire to manage growth in a vigorous campaign for the Growth Management Act. While the ancient-forest debate reached a fevered pitch in the western portion of the state, the effects of growth on open space was an issue for citizens across the state. As Washington's population continued to grow, many citizens were worried that increasing population would conflict with both the quality of life and the remaining wild areas. Eventually enacted by the state legislature in 1990, the Growth Management Act requires twenty-nine counties and 213 cities to set urban growth boundaries and adopt comprehensive plans addressing land use, shorelines, and rural areas, ensuring clean water and watershed planning (see the act's description in appendix A).

LOGGING WITHOUT LAWS: THE 1995 SALVAGE RIDER

When the 1994 Northwest Forest Plan enforced a dramatic reduction in the amount of timber available from national forests, the timber industry turned to Congress to increase harvest levels. In 1995, the American Forest Resource Council's Washington, D.C., lobbyist Mark Rey drafted legislative language that would increase national forest harvests in the name of forest "health," by salvaging trees that had been damaged or killed by insects and the extensive forest fires of 1994. The legislative proposal would allow the taking of not only dead or dying trees, but also those that had been scarred or singed. In addition, it mandated that the Forest Service carry out timber sales it had proposed in the Northwest since 1989 but that had been withdrawn because of environmental concerns or delayed by legal challenges. Such sales were to be protected against further litigation under the terms of the legislation.

The form chosen for this legislation was that of a rider, which is an amendment to an appropriations bill. Since riders do not have to be approved by a committee, they can more easily "ride" through Congress without being seriously challenged, especially when attached to urgent or essential legislation. This strategy worked well for the Salvage Rider, which was attached to what became the 1995 Emergency Supplemental Appropriations and Rescissions Act (Public Law 104-19). The bill's authors, Senator Slade Gorton (R-WA) and Representative Charles Taylor (R-NC), insisted that the Salvage Rider would be attached to any appropriations bill leaving Congress that year. President Clinton knew that he could not veto every one, given that appropriations ensure that the federal government has the funding to carry out day-to-day operations.

On the eve of this legislative move by the timber industry, many forest-protection groups that had fought long and hard for ancient forests before passage of the NWFP had lost their funding or moved on to other issues such as urban sprawl, thinking the crisis past. Upon discovering that the Salvage Rider would actually be passed, the ancient-forest movement was reenergized with both activism and renewed funding from major foundations. Activists across Washington began holding protests against the possibility of the rider, as well as flooding President Clinton's mailroom with thousands of calls, and even pieces of wood, encouraging him to use his veto power. Eventually, however, the president signed the bill on July 27, 1995, and the Salvage Rider went into effect immediately, to be terminated on December 31, 1996. Vice President Al Gore later admitted that allowing passage of the Salvage Rider of 1995 was "the worst mistake the Clinton administration made during its first term."[27]

With the release language of the 1984 Washington State Wilderness Act, Washington's conservation activists had needed to learn how to protect wild areas without wilderness designations in the mid- and late 1980s. Now, in the days after the 1995 Salvage Rider, they also had to protect some of the last wild and ancient forests without litigation. As a result, in late 1995, direct action came of age in Washington. Various factions of the movement came together in displays of civil disobedience that would help minimize the effect of the "logging without laws" rider, as conservationists called it.

In one unique display of solidarity, activists ranging from Earth First! to members of the Audubon Society, urged a member of the Washington congressional delegation to work to repeal the Salvage Rider. In January 1996, twenty-eight activists, dressed in formal business attire, entered the Tacoma office of Congressman Norm Dicks (D-WA), who had been supportive of the 1995 rider. They sat down in protest against the salvage sales occurring on the Olympic National Forest, which were in the congressman's district. The group announced that they intended to remain in his office until Dicks acknowledged his constituents' environmental concerns and promised to support repealing the rider. Fifteen protesters were arrested when they remained in the office past a deadline set by the Tacoma police. Shortly thereafter, Congressman Dicks, who had been absent during the demonstration, personally met with key leaders of the protest, who were able to impress upon him the seriousness of the threat to forests in his district.[28]

Civil disobedience continued in the forests of Washington as well. On September 2, 1996, *High Country News,* a newspaper covering environmental news of the West, reported that Washington "got an early taste of civil disobedience last winter when more than one hundred protesters were arrested at the Caraco Cat and Rocky Brook sales on the Olympic Peninsula."[29] The civil disobedience in Washington was unable to protect all of the forests marked for salvage sales, but it helped minimize the damage before the rider expired on December 31, 1996. Even after the rider expired, similar congressional moves to increase logging in the name of healthy forests have continued to emerge, requiring that conservationists remain on guard.

THE I-90 LAND EXCHANGE

As wildlands advocates developed a variety of campaigns over the years, with some activists specializing in forest protection and others in obtaining new wilderness areas, the movement generally gained strength through its diversity. Occasionally, though, one conservation approach worked at cross-purposes with another. In the late 1990s, efforts to obtain additional wilderness through a land exchange clashed with the need to preserve ancient forests. In the end, important lessons were learned and the forest protection movement became even more effective, as its community outreach efforts produced a powerful coalition of unlikely allies.

The protection of wild, public lands sometimes requires an exchange in land ownership, to consolidate public land where a checkerboard pattern of private lands frustrates management objectives. Many wilderness activists desired to expand the Alpine Lakes Wilderness Area in the Snoqualmie Pass area, along Interstate 90 (I-90). This longstanding goal of the Alpine Lakes Protection Society could be realized if private property owners in the vicinity would trade with the Forest Service for parcels of national forest lands elsewhere.

Thus, a new campaign began in 1995, promoting a land exchange between the Forest Service and the Plum Creek Timber Company, the second-largest timber company in Washington. Plum Creek stood to gain parcels of public old-growth forests, which it planned to log, while the cause of wilderness preservation was advanced by expanding the land that could someday be added to one of the most popular wilderness areas in the state. Plum Creek offered the Forest Service 8,808 acres adjacent to the Mount Baker–Snoqualmie National Forest and 53,576 acres adjacent to the Wenatchee National Forest. In exchange, the Forest Service offered Plum Creek parcels of the Gifford Pinchot National Forest on Watch Mountain near the community of Randle, and at Fossil Creek, located near Mount St. Helens. These two parcels made up one-third of the area and the highest timber volume per acre of the entire deal, containing trees that were more than 450 years old. Plum Creek Timber Company's land was primarily old railroad grants; much of it was previously logged and did not offer viable habitat for old-growth-dependent species.

The land exchange process allows for public participation, and exchanges must be in the public interest, according to the law. Thus, when the Forest Service announced it was working on details of a land exchange, activists awaited their chance to offer public comments and, if necessary, to challenge the legality of the exchange in the courts. Since a land exchange previous to the I-90 deal had been successfully challenged in court, Plum Creek decided to protect itself against similar court action by seeking to make the exchange using a congressional rider to an appropriations bill, which would authorize the exchange and insulate the timber company from legal challenges.

Activists differed in their opinions regarding the land exchange. The Sierra Club and the Alpine Lakes Protection Society publicly supported the rider. Others believed that the parcels in the Gifford Pinchot National Forest were wrongly sacrificed for possible additions to the popular Alpine Lakes Wilderness Area. The Wilderness Society and Northwest Ecosystem Alliance silently supported the exchange initially but later changed their position, publicly speaking against it. In the end, the rider passed, allowing the exchange and also protecting Plum Creek Timber Company.

One place that was directly affected by the exchange was Randle, which lies between steep mountain slopes in the Gifford Pinchot National Forest. Randle is a logging town going through a transition caused by decreased timber supplies. Its previous experience with Plum Creek was in the form of a landslide that leveled resident Elmer Day's house after the company logged an area nearby. Plum Creek did not take full responsibility for the landslide and thus did not entirely reimburse Day for his losses. The residents did not want a timber company to come in and log this area again.

Sarah Vekasi, an Evergreen State College student, took the initiative on her own to rally the community by going door-to-door, informing Randle residents that Plum Creek was planning to log Watch Mountain again. Although the I-90 exchange had already been authorized by Congress,

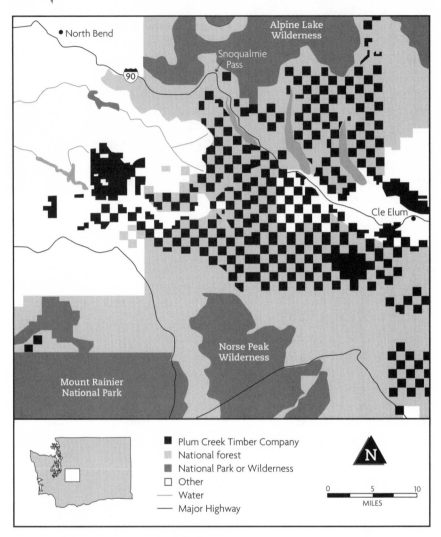

Map 8.1. Before and after: checkerboard land ownership in the I-90 corridor.
This map shows checkerboard land ownership before the land exchange.

citizens told Vekasi that they would still like to prevent the logging. That
was the beginning of a dynamic if unlikely alliance between activists from
outside the community and local residents.

Cascadia Defense Network, an organization known for tree sits, established a "tree village" in a stand of old growth on Watch Mountain. The
village consisted of platforms and cables linked from tree to tree, about
160-feet high. The tree sit garnered significant support in Randle. Community residents provided food for those in the trees, and some ventured
all the way up to the platforms. This even became the first ever legal tree

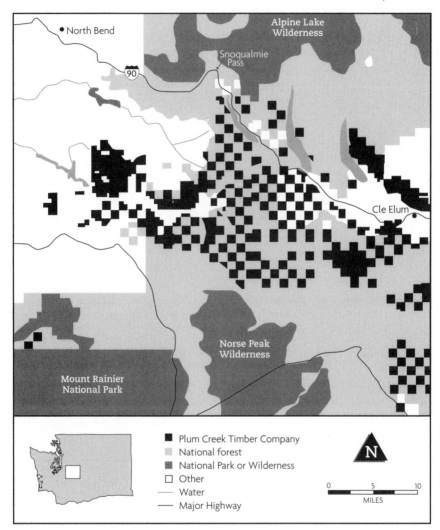

This map shows the new distribution of ownership after the exchange (note the consolidation of national forest lands adjacent to the Alpine Lakes Wilderness Area). (Courtesy the Wilderness Society Center for Landscape Analysis)

sit, when the Forest Service and the Cowlitz Tribe issued permits allowing the occupation of the trees.

Shortly after the tree sit began, Plum Creek discovered marbled murrelets on the Green River Watershed units it had gained in the exchange. This meant that Plum Creek would have to create a habitat conservation plan, as required by the Endangered Species Act, before that area could be logged. To avoid this, Plum Creek asked the Forest Service to offer another parcel or money in place of the land with the marbled murrelets. However, Plum Creek had to go back to Congress to remove the areas from the exchange lands. This allowed activists another day in Congress to influence the exchange process.

Activists from outside of Randle and residents themselves traveled together to Washington, D.C., to express their concerns. The trip, as participant Bonnie Phillips recalls, was successful. The coalition between rural residents of Randle and conservationists showed that this issue required congressional attention. Not only did they meet with key staff of the Washington congressional delegation but they also met with Sierra Club board members in Washington, D.C., and in San Francisco. That led the national Sierra Club to overrule its Cascade chapter, which still supported the exchange.

Litigation further complicated the issue. The Northwest Ecosystem Alliance, the Western Land Exchange Project, Seattle Audubon, the Gifford Pinchot Task Force, and the Pacific Crest Biodiversity Project (later renamed Biodiversity Northwest) filed an administrative appeal with the Forest Service, challenging the legality of the exchange. The appeal was unsuccessful and, moreover, Plum Creek responded by filing a lawsuit against the groups, claiming that this would expedite the process and prevent future litigation. The organizations being sued by Plum Creek described this tactic as a Strategic Lawsuit Against Public Participation (SLAPP), a corporate maneuver to deter citizens from using litigation. In the midst of this legal wrangling, Congress once again addressed the issue. An appropriations bill was passed containing a rider amending the I-90 exchange, but it only removed the marbled murrelet parcels.

Residents of Randle, activists participating in the tree sit, and the organizations involved in the litigation met with the Alpine Lakes Protection Society, the Sierra Club, and the Mountaineers to decide on a united course of action. They agreed to contact Plum Creek to discuss a settlement. After days of intense negotiations, a compromise was reached. Plum Creek agreed to drop the SLAPP lawsuit and to forgo acquisition of all of Watch Mountain and half of its parcels from Fossil Creek. The company gained a three-year option to purchase the remaining parts of Fossil Creek. As stated in the *Seattle Times,* "The compromise is a victory for Plum Creek, too: The deal comes with a promise from environmentalists to forgo any legal action over the land exchange or the company's access across public land to some of its property."[30]

Activists and local residents of Randle had found common ground in this controversy, whereas ten years earlier they may not have. They took a stand and won through direct action, community mobilization, public outreach, lobbying, and administrative appeals. Forming a diverse coalition and using a variety of tactics, citizens saved not just the old-growth forests of Watch Mountain, but they also protected and enhanced a sense of community empowerment.

 ## THE NEW WILDERNESS APPROACH

Almost two years after the implementation of the Northwest Forest Plan (but still two years before the troubles of the I-90 land exchange), some wilderness advocates in eastern Washington began to vocalize the need to begin national forest wilderness campaigns again in Washington State. The 1994 forest plan did not provide adequate protection for forests in the eastern part of the state because it only addressed federal lands within the range of the northern spotted owl, which does not extend to the state's eastern mountains. As a result, timber sales continued unabated on federal lands in eastern Washington. But it was at the very time when the NWFP began to be implemented in western Washington that the Forest Service had to once again consider wilderness preservation as an option on national forests all over the state before it could allow developments in roadless areas. (The 1984 Washington State Wilderness Act had "released" the Forest Service from this obligation until the forest plans were revised, which generally happens on a ten-year cycle.) Representatives from the Kettle Range Conservation Group of Republic, in the northeast corner of the state, reached out to wilderness advocates across Washington in hopes of creating a dialogue about how to approach wilderness at the close of the twentieth century and into the next.

The wilderness community was much different in 1996 than it was in 1984, however. Many of the place-based groups of the 1980s had faded away. The Greater Ecosystem Alliance (now the Northwest Ecosystem Alliance) and the Pacific Crest Biodiversity Project (which later became Biodiversity Northwest) were using scientific arguments to pursue large networks of protection across lands of different ownership instead of focusing on the establishment of isolated wilderness areas on parcels of national forests. Yet, through informal meetings, many of which were held around campfires in wilderness areas, a coalition was formed between fourteen groups. It was called the Wild Washington Campaign. Even the name of the coalition seemed to reflect the diversification of the movement within the past decade, since it implied that there is wildness outside of wilderness areas.

The Wild Washington Campaign was established to advance the agenda for defending wild Washington in the twenty-first century. But what would it look like? This coalition of wildlands professionals and volunteers agreed to pursue wilderness designation one place at a time instead of using the omnibus models of the 1984 and 1988 acts. Part of the reasoning for this approach was to avoid being forced to accept more release language in future wilderness bills. Campaign leaders also believed that place-based campaigns would bring statewide attention and political pressure to move wilderness legislation through Congress quicker than previous campaigns. Many of Wild Washington's place-based campaigns have been intentionally located within congressional districts where it expects the most support from the local member of Congress.

After creating a plan for involving the state's congressional delegation, the Wild Washington Campaign needed an even larger plan to galvanize public interest in wilderness designation, which as an issue had been on the sidelines for eight years. Fortunately, the Forest Service was about to launch a nationwide planning process that would revitalize the wilderness movement.[31] Forest Service Chief Mike Dombeck was working on a plan that could potentially erase the negative legacy of the agency's two Roadless Area Reviews and Evaluations. Dombeck convinced President Clinton in 1998 to allow the review of RARE II lands in order to either classify them as candidates for future road building and development or to protect them from alteration. Internally, the agency was suffering from a nearly $8.4 billion maintenance backlog in its 380,000-mile road network, and it was evaluating whether it was wise to expand that system. A roadless initiative could prevent further financial burdens associated with new roads by designating areas where their construction would be prohibited.

In Washington, the Washington Wilderness Coalition (WWC) made the Forest Service's new roadless area review its top priority for grassroots activism. The goal was to create a sizable number of public comments in Washington State that were in favor of the highest protection for the remaining roadless areas in the state. WWC built a broad coalition to support maximum roadless area protection, including fisherman, hunters, religious organizations, economists, members of the disabled community, and both Republican and Democratic public officials at the local, state, and federal levels. The coalition set up tables at public events and at outdoor recreation outfitters to get signatures on petitions and postcards and to generate letters of support to the Forest Service. It worked hard to encourage citizens to participate in the Forest Service's roadless area meetings around the state, and as a result over 1,200 people took part and an average of three-to-one spoke in favor of a strong roadless area protection policy, in both eastern and western Washington meetings. In the Seattle hearing, of the more than 400 people present, only two spoke against the roadless area conservation plan while 217 spoke in favor of a strong roadless area protection policy.[32]

The result of this outreach was a total of more than 60,000 responses to the Forest Service (the fourth largest amount from any state in the country) with more than 90 percent favoring the highest amount of protection for roadless areas in Washington's national forests. Nationwide, after holding more than six hundred public meetings and receiving an unprecedented 1.7 million official comments (five times more than had ever been received in any other government rulemaking process), the Forest Service found that more than 95 percent of the comments advocated protecting all remaining national forest roadless areas.

Despite this unprecedented expression of popular support, political advisors warned President Clinton not to introduce a sweeping conservation measure into a Congress dominated by Republicans who were out of sync with the bipartisan majority of the American people who favored protecting the remaining wild areas of public lands. So, Dombeck simply established a new Forest Service policy on January 5, 2001, called the Roadless Area Conservation Rule (also called the Clinton Roadless Rule). This policy decision committed the Forest Service to maintaining the roadless condition of all inventoried roadless areas in the nation, while leaving open all existing roads and guaranteeing access across roadless areas to state and private property. Approximately 58.5 million acres of the national forests (31 percent of the national forest system and 2 percent of all lands in the United States) would be off-limits to most commercial logging and road building. New roads could be built to fight fires or to protect the public from other natural disasters. Limited logging would be permitted to reduce the risk of wildfire, and existing oil and gas development would be allowed to continue. For Washington State, this meant that 1.3 million acres of national forest roadless areas would be administratively protected on an indefinite basis.

Right on the heels of the Roadless Rule, President George W. Bush was inaugurated and two separate lawsuits were introduced in the Ninth Circuit Court of Appeals and the Idaho Federal District Court. The Boise Cascade Corporation, a timber operation, and the governors of eight western states filed the lawsuits against the rule on the grounds that it violated provisions of the National Environmental Policy Act's (NEPA) public comment rules. The Department of Justice did not respond to requests from the federal courts to defend the government's own rule, and an Idaho District Court judge ruled that the plan's implementation had to be delayed. A coalition of wildlands and environmental organizations including the Wilderness Society and the Western Environmental Law Center successfully defended the rule in the federal courts. Unfortunately, neither the Bush administration nor the Forest Service seemed committed to supporting the rule at the time this book was prepared.

CONTINUING ON THE TRAIL

Wildlands conservation in Washington underwent historic changes in the last two decades of the twentieth century and the initial years of the twenty-first.

This period saw the most sweeping wilderness legislation in the state's history, the beginning of a new statewide wilderness campaign, and an unprecedented movement to protect all of the remaining roadless areas in the state's national forests. But this was also an historic period because it saw the development of a broader array of conservation goals and tactics that went beyond the traditional wilderness preservation agenda in response to new needs and opportunities.

The resulting diversification of the movement signaled the coming of age for wildness protection, not just in Washington State, but in the nation as a whole. For example, the accomplishments of the ancient-forest movement included major reforms in forest management. There has been a considerable reduction in the amount of old-growth timber being taken from Washington's national forests and two of them, the Olympic and Mount Baker–Snoqualmie National Forests, have developed plans that do not depend on the cutting of old growth, even though that would be allowed under the Northwest Forest Plan.[33] Activists using state and private land protection measures have set aside tens of thousands more acres of ecologically critical and publicly cherished wild areas. As situations changed, activists modified or created new tactics in order to further their cause of preserving and regenerating wildness in the state. Their sacrifices and accomplishments provide inspiration and important lessons for the next generation of activists to defend Washington's wildness.

CHAPTER 9

Leaders in Today's Movement

◆ *Katherine Jones and Lin Skavdahl* ◆

Washington State's conservation movement is made up of thousands of individuals in organizations throughout the state that are dedicated to the preservation and regeneration of wildlands. The driving forces behind these volunteers and organizations are their leaders. These frontrunners are executive directors, board presidents, activists speaking at public hearings, and advocates knocking on constituent's doors, all keeping preservation and regeneration issues in the public eye and motivating citizens to defend our wildlands.

Political action regarding public lands has become more complex. Increasing pressure on remaining wildlands, rising opportunities to restore previously logged forests and tainted watersheds, a growing number of organizations advocating land protection, and an ever-changing political climate propel current leaders into using a broader variety of strategies than their predecessors. Interviews with leaders in large and small organizations from across the state illustrated this, uncovering the ideals, experiences, and attributes that led these exemplary advocates to activism and recording their current goals and the methods for achieving them.

 ## SUSAN JANE BROWN[1]

As part of her work with the Gifford Pinchot Task Force, former executive director Susan Jane Brown analyzed every timber sale environmental assessment in the Gifford Pinchot National Forest. In addition she was involved in the monitoring of national forests east of the Cascade Crest in both Oregon and Washington.

Susan Jane lived in the varied landscapes of Texas, Colorado, and Indiana while she was growing up. "It was a shock to be living in Colorado Springs, at the foot of Pikes Peak and then going to Indiana which is flat, boring, and ugly." The family spent much of their time camping, hunting, and fishing. Susan Jane says a love and respect for nature were instilled in her from childhood, but she was not initially called to protect it. By the third grade she had settled on a law career with the goal of making money. During high school and later at Vanderbilt University, on debate teams, her interest was piqued by environmental topics. Later, she chose the Northwestern School of Law at Lewis and Clark College for its reputation in environmental law.

Lewis and Clark was an adjustment. She remembers, "At Vanderbilt I'd gone to school every single day for four years in heels and a skirt. Going to Lewis and Clark was a bit different. A lot of people go to class barefoot." Shortly after arriving at Lewis and Clark, she acquainted herself with the Northwest Environmental Defense Center (NEDC), a student-run organization where second- and third-year students teach first-year students environmental law statutes and how to apply them to projects involving litigation. She explains, "These are practical skills that law school doesn't actually teach until the third year, if at all."

A few weeks into the first term, Susan Jane joined the NEDC group focusing on public lands issues on a field trip to the Detroit Ranger District in the Willamette National Forest. Prior to this, she had no experience with Northwest forests other than a six-week bicycling trip around Puget Sound and the San Juan Islands where, she recalls, "I had my first encounter with a logging truck. I got run off the road." During the weekend field trip, Susan Jane learned that the Detroit Ranger District had, at one time, produced millions of board feet of timber per year until an advocacy group managed to stop the logging. Her recollection of hiking there is vivid: "I saw my first old-growth tree. I saw my first old-growth forest. I also saw my first old-growth timber sale and my first clear-cut, which struck me immediately as incredibly wrong. At that point I thought, well, corporate law isn't going to be an option."

Susan Jane returned from the trip and immediately began volunteering at the NEDC. She describes her first case: "A second-year law student said, 'Here's an EIS [environmental impact statement] that just came in. Why don't you read it and write an administrative appeal?' I said, 'I've been in law school for a total of four weeks and I have no idea what to do.'" He handed her a three-volume document and told her to read it and tell him what was wrong with it. "I knew how to do that, given I'd been in debate for eight years and that sort of critical analysis was relatively easy for me." The second-year student showed her the statutes that applied to the EIS and she wrote the administrative appeal for a postfire salvage proposal. "I couldn't believe the government was allowing the type of degradation that was being proposed . . . all kinds of sediment washing into the creeks, soil impacts were going to be tremendous, and wildlife was going to be impacted, and yet they were still proposing to do all of this logging. That was morally offensive."

Susan Jane found a footnote in the EIS describing a sediment monitoring project the Forest Service had tried to do, but she explained, "The monitoring boxes had been buried under six feet of sediment. I didn't think that was okay, so I highlighted that in the appeal." The NEDC filed the appeal on behalf of the Blue Mountains Biodiversity Project, but it was denied and logging began. The groups retained an attorney who agreed to take the case, but they lost in district court. By the time the court of appeals heard the case, reversed the district court's decision, and stopped the cutting, much of the forest had been logged. Still Susan Jane was encouraged. "My favorite part is that the court picked up on our little statement

Susan Jane Brown on The Evergreen State College campus, January 22, 2003 (Photo by Lin Skavdahl)

about the sediment boxes buried under six feet of sediment and said, 'There's a problem here.' That case set the standard for postfire salvage logging in the Northwest." Susan Jane was hooked on environmental law.

In 1998 the NEDC received a flood of environmental assessments for timber sales from the Gifford Pinchot National Forest. Susan Jane mapped out the locations of each of the proposals. "There were about twenty-six timber sales. Altogether that would have logged a huge corridor of old-growth timber from the north end to the south end of the forest, about sixty million board feet in a single year." She filed administrative appeals on all twenty-six sales. "Over time, my appeals got longer and longer and they ended up being sixty pages with four hundred pages of attachments explaining why these timber sales were illegal . . . . I was unruly . . . . I was really angry that this was going on and I wasn't cutting the Forest Service any slack at all." As a result of the appeals and a declining timber market, the ancient forest stands on the Gifford Pinchot Forest have not been logged since 1997. "That brings me a great deal of joy because all of those sales were classic old growth; I'm talking five-hundred-year-old, big, fat trees."

In 1999 Susan Jane joined the board of directors of the Gifford Pinchot Task Force. A year later, the task force decided to hire an executive director. After a six-month search didn't produce any candidates, some of the board members asked Susan Jane if she would do it. "I said, well, okay. I'd never been an executive director before. I'd never had a real job. I had to figure out how to do it, and it's been an interesting process along the way. For example, there are probably a sum total of three executive directors that are women in the forest protection movement in the Northwest. It doesn't really bother me, but it gets very tiring and wearisome dealing with male colleagues with huge egos when you are a woman with strong opinions."

Susan Jane described the Gifford Pinchot Task Force as a group focused on rural organizing, forest protection, and restoration. Communities within the Gifford Pinchot have gone from being completely dependent on logging to no logging at all. It has been a difficult transition, with increased unemployment, domestic violence, and substance abuse. Susan Jane said, "That's not right either. It's important for us to go from an organization that is fighting the Forest Service at every turn to getting them to do something that is more sustainable." The task force does not advocate eliminating all logging from public lands. According to Susan Jane, "All along we've been trying to tell the Forest Service that if it doesn't log mature and old-growth forests, it won't be in the same controversial spot as when it tries to log big old trees."

The task force is also working to convey that message to the communities. "We aren't going to support the logging of big old trees, but we're not anti–rural community. They have a legitimate right to make their liveli-hood off of the forest, but it probably won't be the way it used to be. Com-munity members know that. They just want something that's predictable and sustainable."

"My view has changed," she said. "I've gone from, 'you can't log any-thing' to having a deeper understanding of ecology and civic culture. There are areas where management can occur. You can thin young managed stands and provide a sustainable flow of timber volume. There's a livelihood to be made there."

The idea of working with rural communities evolved with the Watch Mountain campaign in 1999, which protested a land exchange between the Forest Service and the Plum Creek Timber Company (see "The I-90 Land Exchange" in chapter 8). Susan Jane says, "We approached the folks of Randle and said, 'Do you know this big corporation is going to come in and clear-cut the land behind your house?' Folks asked, 'What can we do? How can we work together?' That's a shift in tactics. It's very slow. It takes a lot of trust building, but it's very satisfying to see that transition. Last summer we did a rural canvass where we didn't ask for money; we wanted to talk with people. We fully expected to be run off of porches with shot-guns, but it didn't happen. People were very open about talking about res-toration of forests and thinning. They realize there's not a lot of old-growth forest left and it's precious."

Susan Jane sees progress. For example, she visited with a mill owner every few months. "We are trying. He doesn't agree with us, but he re-spects what we are doing, that we are talking to people. That wouldn't have happened five or six years ago." She also sees a shift in the Forest Ser-vice. "The agency seems committed to shifting their focus from contro-versial logging to restoration. It will take time, but we're starting to see projects that were inconceivable just a few years ago. It's a promising start."

Susan Jane believes the battle over the westside forests is drawing to a close. "It's definitely not over, especially in the [George W.] Bush ad-ministration, but the mentality is changing within the Forest Service and that's the key. It's happening on the westside of the Cascades, but not the eastside. I fear for the eastside." She isn't counting on positive changes coming out of Congress either. "There's no legislation out there to pro-tect old growth. I don't see any getting passed or even introduced." She is committed to using administrative means even in the current political cli-mate. "I'm a minority voice in that opinion, but it has worked on the GP [Gifford Pinchot] so, coupled with rural organizing, I think that's what we will continue to do."

From Susan Jane's point of view, the futures of the old-growth and wil-derness movements are dependent upon broad community support. "We need the local folks on our side. Rural organizing is really important. We need to be much more open to the fact that it takes a long time." She worries that activists get tired and are tempted to settle for something less because they want it to be over. "This is a long-haul endeavor. We aren't going to protect the forest overnight."

"My view is, you come in and set some goals for yourself and your organization. You get as close to those goals as you can, and then you move on. I don't want to do this work forever. That's a very rare view and I think that's a problem because you don't have a fresh influx of ideas and new blood." For example, Susan Jane cited the initial reaction to rural organizing. "When the task force really started to get into rural organizing it was looked at as a huge waste of time. The view, 'How 'bout if we try it? You never know?' was met with a huge amount of resistance. It got nasty and it got personal. When people come into the movement and see that sort of behavior, why would they want to add their voices? That behavior needs to change. It drives good people away from the movement. For the touchy-feely reputation the environmental movement has, we're really not. We kind of eat our young. If we want to sustain ourselves and get things accomplished, we need to work together, not fight our friends. That's a fundamental thing we've got to change if we are to protect the land that we love."

Susan Jane is a courageous and articulate spokesperson for the preservation of wildlands. She skillfully litigates on behalf of national forests throughout Washington State, but perhaps an even more powerful contribution is her modeling of collaborative efforts between forest advocates, rural communities, and government agencies.

In keeping with her philosophy, six months after our interview, Susan Jane resigned as the executive director of the Gifford Pinchot Task Force to serve as the staff attorney for the Pacific Environmental Advocacy Center. "Having met all of my goals for the organization [the task force] and the [Gifford Pinchot] forest, I have decided it is time for me to move on to find other venues in which to cause trouble."[2]

 ## GEORGIANA KAUTZ[3]

Georgiana Kautz, the Natural Resource Manager for the Nisqually Indian Tribe, approaches the concept of wildlands and what should be done with them from a unique perspective. She speaks about herself in the context of the tribe as a whole. Her personal stories are linked to the history and experience of the Nisqually people and her goals are for the future of the people as well as the future of the land. On the reservation and in the traditional areas of the Nisqually people, environmental protection is an issue

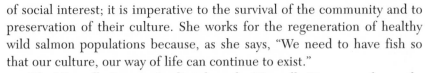

of social interest; it is imperative to the survival of the community and to preservation of their culture. She works for the regeneration of healthy wild salmon populations because, as she says, "We need to have fish so that our culture, our way of life can continue to exist."

The Nisqually Reservation lies along the Nisqually River near the southern tip of Puget Sound. In 1917, Pierce County illegally condemned and seized tribal lands on the east side of the river for integration into the 60,000-acre Fort Lewis military installation.[4] The tribe was relocated to the west side and was encouraged by the government to become farmers. However, "There are so many rocks that you couldn't even bury the dead," says Georgiana. "So we did not become farmers because we were fishermen, gatherers, hunters." Georgiana's father, George McCloud, was born on the condemned land. He was part of the generation of Nisqually people that moved to the west bank of the river. Georgiana is part of the first generation to grow up there.

In 1941, Georgiana Rose Kautz was born in an Indian hospital in Everett, Washington. Her mother had to travel 80 miles to the nearest medical facility that would provide assistance to Native women. Their family of thirteen lived in a two-room house on the Nisqually Reservation. Until 1969, the family did not have running water or electricity in their home, as these amenities had not yet been made available to people living on the reservation. Because of the difficulties of life on the reservation, many families chose to leave. "Most of the people had left the reservation except my parents and a few other people." The Nisqually consider this process to be an intentional attempt at termination—cultural and social death of their way of life through assimilation, driving people off the reservation, and separating the tribe. Despite the fact that "they took us to the brink of termination . . . the Nisqually people had a mission and that was to survive the United States government and to keep being what we were and that was Nisqually Indian people."

Georgiana grew up watching her mother and father and draws a lot of motivation from them. Her mother was very active in tribal governance, serving on the tribal council and working hard to improve life on the reservation. She was also involved in the salmon harvest, carrying fish for miles from where they were caught to their home. Georgiana recognizes all the struggles that her parents endured and has a deep respect for all that they accomplished; they were instrumental in directing her life choices. Pregnancy and the prospect of starting a family took Georgiana out of high school before graduation. She soon joined her husband in the boats catching salmon. "I became a fisherman because it was my right."

This was the time of the Nisqually fish wars, when to fish was to openly defy state law. The 1854 and 1855 treaties insured that tribal members would

Georgiana Kautz in front of the Nisqually Tribal Department of Natural Resources (Photographer unknown; courtesy Georgiana Kautz)

be allowed to fish in their "usual and accustomed grounds and stations."[5] However, increased development of the Puget Sound region throughout the early twentieth century had decimated wild salmon runs, leading the state to restrict harvest on specific salmon-bearing streams. Many of the restricted rivers were on Indian fishing grounds. Throughout the 1950s, '60s, and '70s tribal members fought for their right to fish. They staged "fish-ins" in their "usual and accustomed" fishing areas to gain national attention. State authorities responded with surveillance planes, speedboats, and numerous arrests.[6] Georgiana's husband, Neugen Kautz, was among those arrested. He spent thirty days in jail simply for being a fisherman who was exercising his treaty right to fish. The one-sidedness of the struggle was apparent. Georgiana remembers the nature of the interactions between the tribe and the authorities, "We would build these barriers and when the state came down [dressed in full riot gear, armed with tear gas and police batons], we would get behind logs and throw rocks at them because that is all we had. My husband would get arrested and there would be huge battles all along the rivers over Native Americans exercising their right to fish, being able to do the things that we have done for hundreds of years." The wars were settled in court with the 1974 decision by Judge George Boldt, validating the Nisquallys' treaty right to 50 percent of the harvestable salmon and guaranteeing their right to fish as their treaty stated when signed in 1855.

Georgiana attended night school to get her high-school diploma, and then she attended a vocational school and college, graduating from The Evergreen State College in 1972 with an emphasis in Native American studies. She spent some time on the tribal council, and she was chairperson of the Nisqually Tribe for a while, always working to improve the social, cultural, and economic opportunities on the reservation. In 1991 the tribe offered her the position of fish manager, which she accepted. Her position was later renamed "natural resource manager." She now has a much broader scope of issues to deal with, including hunting-and-gathering rights in addition to her work on salmon and shellfish issues. She holds positions on both the Northwest Indian Fisheries Commission and the Tacoma City Light Board.

The fish wars may be over, but there is always something to fight for. Georgiana holds on to the emotion that drove actions on the riverbanks and works with the same passion everyday. "Today, as a natural resource manager, I still have to go out and defend our treaty rights. It is in a different arena but it is still the same. I am still out there trying to protect the treaty rights of the Nisqually Tribe."

Treaty rights apply to all traditional areas within the Nisqually watershed, not just to reservation lands. But the tribe's mission extends beyond treaty rights; they are trying to encourage healthy and sustainable land practices throughout the watershed. Therefore in dealing with issues of hunting, fishing, and gathering, Georgiana has to work with many landowners as well as management agencies between Mount Rainier and the Puget Sound. She works with farmers, with Fort Lewis, Mount Rainier National Park, Nisqually Wildlife Refuge, the cities of Olympia and Tacoma, and Pierce and Thurston Counties. "As co-managers, we strive for cooperation and solutions," she says.

Not all of these agencies are as enthusiastic about collaboration as are the Nisqually, however. In dealing with Washington State, Governor Locke has been invited several times to visit the reservation and talk about issues, but he has been unable to fit it into his schedule. Georgiana says, "It's just something that we have to live with." The tribe also intends to continue what has been a cooperative relationship with the Park Service, even though the Nisqually peoples' right to gather medicinal plants in Mount

Rainier National Park has been challenged by the nonprofit organization Public Employees for Environmental Responsibility. Georgiana says that the Nisqually feel strongly that they will continue their close relationship with the park despite such pressures. In dealing with the U.S. Army, even though tanks have run through a "protected" gathering site in a camas prairie in Fort Lewis, the tribe is working together with the military under an on-going agreement to protect natural resources on military land. Finally, continued development in the Nisqually Basin is shrinking elk meadows and the habitat loss is affecting everyone's resources. "As co-managers," says Georgiana, "we learn to set realistic goals" to resolve problems and protect habitats and the environment.

The Nisqually Tribe continues to buy land. Georgiana says, "We buy land to create infrastructure for our people and for protection of all natural resources." Georgiana does not separate issues involving the land and issues involving the tribe. "All things are connected to the well-being of our community." A 410-acre farm at the mouth of the river was bought to restore salmon habitat. The tribe acquired the private farmland, removed the dikes that were keeping the Puget Sound salt water out of the fields, and allowed the wild flora and fauna to return naturally while the channels that protect juvenile salmon are regenerating. Other lands are being purchased to build infrastructure and to provide a land base for the tribe.

Environmental and cultural restoration is not aimed at attaining an historical condition; it is about reestablishing processes. "It is the past, it is the present, it is the future of how we will exist. Our way of life is very much alive and grows stronger [in] tradition and culture. This is the circle of life. All things are connected." Georgiana is committed to the future of the Nisqually people and expresses the deep sense of place that informs her decisions in life. "This is where I was born, this is where I was raised, this is where I want to die, this is where I want to always be, as our ancestors before us . . . I will be here forever . . . it's kind of like a salmon that has an imprint and knows where to go back to, and in the end the salmon will die and create life."

MITCH FRIEDMAN[7]

In his shared corner office, Mitch Friedman, the executive director of the Northwest Ecosystem Alliance (NWEA), talked about his experiences and strategies for land protection in Washington. His walls speak to his passions—they are decorated with posters of beautiful landscapes, pictures of him and his daughters, and an enlarged photo of the old-growth Douglas-fir log that he took all over the United States in 1989 during the spotted owl controversy.

Mitch Friedman is the outspoken, passionate activist that William Dietrich wrote about as the subject of "The Environmentalist" chapter in *The Final Forest*.[8] He stands out as a prominent voice for the old-growth campaign (see chapter 8) and is recognized by many for his progressive, innovative ideas on community organizing.

Mitch says he does not know where he gets his passion. Of his childhood in suburban Chicago he says, "I spent a lot more time throwing tennis balls against the garage door than playing out in the wood lot," but "for some reason, I had a very strong connection to nature . . . . I was always probably more interested in wildlife than in people."

His vision of an unaltered, pristine landscape was illustrated on his bedroom corkboard as a child. "I had made a collage of all these postcards of the West that I had gotten and if there was a powerline or a road or anything I painted over it with green magic marker so the whole thing was just forest and wildlands, a romantic image of unhumanized nature."

"What motivates me about protecting nature, it's a view of justice I guess, of biocentrism. I've always viewed it as unjust that you have this world with all of its rich and ancient evolutionary designs and people trying to direct it. It has been analogous in my mind to damming a river . . . . Evolution is about self-expression, about adaptation and it's just amazing to me."

Mitch took these passions with him to Montana State University, where he studied wildlife management, but he soon realized that management was not what he was most interested in. He left Montana and later finished at the University of Washington (UW) with a degree in zoology. "Spring quarter of my first year there, there was a flyer up in the hall, 'Earth First! Meeting' and I said 'What's that?' and a classmate said, 'Oh that's a radical environmental thing, we should go to that.' I went to the meeting that night and it was the first Earth First! meeting in Washington. A fellow who had been involved in the forest protests in southern Oregon had come back to school at UW and had needed people to drink with, so he called a meeting. I had already read Aldo Leopold and Ed Abbey . . . and it was natural for me. I had fantasized about a group like this. I made some commitments that night."

"I was lucky, the ancient-forest issue was just coming to Washington . . . . I found myself in school in the crucible of forest conservation, the Northwest forest wars. I was having fun, going from protest to protest, again I was lucky, I was there at the right time."

Mitch's first act of civil disobedience with Earth First! was to participate in the tree sits in the Millennium Grove in Oregon opposing the cutting of old-growth timber. After that he participated in actions all over the Pacific Northwest. He was arrested several times in defense of forests and grizzly bears. He organized the first protest for the spotted owl in the Wenatchee National Forest in 1986.

During the late 1980s and early 1990s, Mitch's perspective began to shift away from the direct action and civil disobedience of Earth First!. Mitch stirred up the Earth First! community with a speech he delivered at a forest conference that later ran in the Earth First! journal about "civil disobedience as a tactic not culture," which he also calls, "Lies Earth First! Told Me."

"Within Earth First! we did a lot of talking about how to get arrested, not a lot of talk about why to get arrested. We would ask, 'Is this a media stunt or is it a moral stand?' 'Do we expect these trees that we're dangling from to be saved?' But no one was really talking about how you define success . . . . I was tired of getting arrested with the same hippies and it seemed to me that the movement was stagnating. If I was getting arrested with the same hippies, it meant that I wasn't getting arrested with the little old lady or the handicapped person or people from diverse ethnicities or ever more people. In short, I sensed that the movement was in a different age."

Mitch did not leave Earth First! quietly. He said good-bye with a feat of guerilla theater that is used today as an example of how to shock and enlighten the national public concerning environmental matters: the Ancient Forest Rescue Expedition of 1989. "I took a giant log on a semi truck and drove it around the country." This tour drew on the aspects of Earth First! that appealed most to Mitch, the shock factor and the theatrical presentation. But Mitch added a new idea that was brewing in his head. "This is what I wanted to do, this is why I left Earth First!, I wanted to popularize, I wanted to go to the heartland, I wanted to go to the swing congressional districts and the media markets, to the people who needed to see the big trees to experience what we were talking about." The Rescue Expedition conducted a total of four tours with the tree, visiting forty-two states along the way.

As a biologist and an activist, Mitch was interested in incorporating science into conservation. He recognized that the need to protect biodiversity in old-growth forests was playing an important role in the debate. Science was the emerging political powerhouse. Science could provide logical, concrete biological reasons to protect land. Driven by this new wave of potential, Mitch formed the Greater Ecosystem Alliance (GEA) in 1989 (which would later become NWEA). GEA was established to integrate concepts of conservation biology into advocacy and land management. It envisioned a "scale of ecosystem large enough to encompass viable populations of even big mammals . . . . It seemed to be a cutting-edge topic at the time and I wanted to export it from Yellowstone to here, and nobody was really working

Mitch Friedman backpacking in the Olympics in 2003 (Photographer unknown; courtesy Mitch Friedman)

on grizzly-bear conservation at the time," continues Mitch. "So, I wanted to take those themes of bringing science into advocacy particularly at the landscape scale, the greater ecosystem, along with working on ancient forests and grizzly-bear conservation in the North Cascades."

As times changed, the direction of GEA changed to match. "America is a place of trends and of fashion, not just of clothes but also of ideas." Just as every fad does, science gave way to a new phase. "When Gingrich took over in the '94 election, we had a few scientists on staff here, and decided to put them in the back room. We still needed them to say where we wanted to get to on the beach, but it was obvious that another wave was coming. So we hired community organizers . . . . We hired a guy as conservation director who did things like organize with the commercial fisherman over the Endangered Species Act and organized with the medical community over the medicinal benefits of biodiversity."

The next wave to come in was an economic one. "I started realizing what a powerful tool economics is. It is a measure of preferences of the American public." After meeting some of the important natural resource economists of the time, like Daniel Hagen, Thomas Power, and Ed Whitelaw, Mitch learned that his former ideas about the ability of economists to direct policy were not true. "Politics is no more informed by sound economics than it is by sound natural science."

In the summer of 1995, wildfires raged in central Washington. Thunder Mountain in the Okanogan National Forest was the site of a fire, and the Forest Service decided to sell the burned trees. Because of the 1995 Salvage Rider (see chapter 8), environmental organizations could not appeal Forest Service timber sales at that time even though the environmental impacts of this sale would be high and the timber value was very low. During a telephone call about Thunder Mountain, a NWEA staff biologist complained that due to the poor timber market, the trees would sell to anyone who was even willing to bid on the job. Mitch coolly responded, "Oh, yeah, someone will bid on it, we will." It was a spontaneous decision made in the midst of the conversation that spawned a revolutionary idea. In the end, the timber sale was awarded to a company that logged the trees, but NWEA's tactic garnered favorable national publicity and new Republican congressional support in the fight against money-losing public timber sales. It also increased public awareness of the need to repeal the Salvage Rider.

In 1996, Mitch continued to ride this economic wave with a landmark campaign to protect wild state lands in the Loomis Forest, close to federal lands of Thunder Mountain and the Pasayten Wilderness. The Department of Natural Resources (DNR) interprets state law as dictating the management of its trust lands for timber production in order to raise money for public school construction. In 1996, the DNR released an eighty-year landscape plan, which included plans to build more than 100 miles of road and to log virtually all the roadless areas of the Loomis Forest even though, like on Thunder Mountain, environmental impacts would have been high and timber value low. NWEA, Friends of the Loomis Forest, and others sued under the Endangered Species Act, arguing that the plan would lead to the "take" (death) of protected grizzly bears. The judge directed the parties into mediation, out of which the DNR and NWEA agreed on a settlement in which NWEA had the opportunity to raise the money to protect the land. NWEA organized a massive fundraising campaign and raised a total of $18 million in just over a year. Mitch's skillful strategizing was key to making it possible. The Loomis was protected much faster through an economic approach than it would have been through a political one. "On a philosophical level that solution was anything but pure, that land should have been saved in its own right according to my views of economics and our state constitution. I saw an opportunity; we could save the Loomis, and gain some strength in the process. We could use the Loomis as a springboard to educate people about the conservation value of forests and the

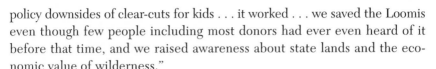

policy downsides of clear-cuts for kids . . . it worked . . . we saved the Loomis even though few people including most donors had ever even heard of it before that time, and we raised awareness about state lands and the economic value of wilderness."

Mitch is very community-minded in his thinking and returns often to consideration of average Americans and how they can be included in this process. "Seventy to eighty percent of Americans share my values for nature. People are informed to varying degrees as to what the trade-offs are or what it means to protect nature, but most ways that you find to phrase the question you find that the values that conservationists hold dear are really commonly held. So it is a mistake to antagonize the public to adopt strategies that are us versus them, in terms of the public being the 'them,' and those realizations inform my activism today. Those are the basis for how the Northwest Ecosystem Alliance runs campaigns."

According to Mitch, the only way that the goals of the conservation movement will be met is through "broad and committed participation and creative strategies that are both visionary and not offensive, alienating, or excluding. In other words, we have to be visionary but not too out of touch, idealistic but not ideologues, firm but not rigid. Sometimes this means pragmatism, such as making uncomfortable alliances with conservatives, timber interests, or whoever we might share objectives with on specific issues." It is this flexibility, creativity, and unwillingness to buy into the good versus evil approach to conservation that has allowed Mitch and NWEA to be so successful in their various campaigns.

Mitch considers himself both a visionary and a pragmatist at once. He questions strategies that promise too much and deliver nothing as much as he questions strategies that progress in tiny increments, never adding up to a solution. "The key," he says, "is to bridge increments and the vision. People are inspired and movements gain strength by making significant, positive steps toward a lofty vision. That is the groove we must search for, building hope and optimism as we achieve success. The world won't be saved all at once by a few solitary champions. If it is to be saved at all, it will be by a hopeful, inspired, and inclusive movement that is oriented toward solutions."

BOB WILSON[9]

The attributes that set Bob Wilson apart are his energy and boldness. He thoroughly enjoys himself while engaged in the fight to protect the places he loves. He makes the process of conservation fun, accepting the twisting nature of politics and opposition as part of the game. Bob was one of the primary activists involved in the campaign to protect the Hanford Reach,

Bob Wilson (center) shaking hands with Bruce Babbitt (right) during the former secretary of the interior's visit to the future Hanford Reach National Monument, one month before it was designated (Photographer unknown; courtesy Bob Wilson)

the last free-flowing, nontidal stretch of the Columbia River (see chapter 14 for the full story). He is strictly a volunteer activist for Save the Reach. Because he is not a paid representative of an organization, Bob is not bound to uphold organizational ideals and therefore has the freedom of expression afforded only to a volunteer.

He draws on a deep connection to the environment, one he has sustained since he took his first step on wild earth. One summer in the 1950s, while living in Berkeley, California, the Wilson family carried baby Bob into Yosemite Valley where they spent their summers; his mother erected a chicken-wire enclosure, and in this space he took his first steps. "I learned to walk in Yosemite Valley," he states proudly. "My parents liked to get us out in the country as much as they could."

Hunting was an activity that encouraged Bob to spend time outside as a kid. "Like most guys at that time, I was an avid duck hunter. But even then I never cared if I ever shot anything. In fact, shooting things was kind of a pain 'cause then you had to deal with it. But just being out there in the cold and slopping around in the swamp had an attraction to me."

It was evident when he began college in 1975 in North Carolina that he was going to engage in an environmental discipline. He originally wanted to study wildlife biology but was assured that he'd never secure a job in that field, so he chose forest management. "The curriculum was strictly economics, road building, all industrially oriented; there was not one course that was about conservation, ecology, or any plant growth that wasn't fiber production. It was all about growing trees and cutting them down."

His degree in forest management naturally led to a position with the Forest Service, which brought him to Washington State. He moved around the state for a couple of years working in temporary positions in Forks, Twisp, and the Gifford Pinchot National Forest. "That was in the heyday of logging. I was caught up in the thrill of the whole thing. My job was to lay clear-cuts, but even then I felt like I was destroying what I really loved. . . . I was out there before the trees were cut. I was out there when it was really gorgeous. Then, toward the end of my three or four years in the Forest Service, I started going back out to the areas that I had laid out and that were cut and saw what happened and thought, 'Man, this can't be right.'"

He left the Forest Service and moved around for several years. While in California he attended part-time classes at UCLA and finally left Los Angeles with a degree in waste management, headed again for the fair state of Washington. "I knew the whole time I was away that I wanted to be in the Northwest working on environmental work."

Bob got a job with the Department of Ecology in 1993 and eventually became the senior compliance inspector of the clean-up efforts on the Hanford Nuclear Site in central Washington. However, his homecoming was not to the Washington he had left ten years prior. "When I got back, the Cascade Crest had been cut, the Olympic Peninsula was devastated. I remember driving down the Peninsula in the mid '70s, going down Highway 101 through Forks; it was a cathedral of 250-foot-tall trees, just an amazing place. I went back, and it was leveled as far as the eye could see. The devastation was overwhelming and I knew that this wasn't right. That really got me going, 'Okay, I've got to become active; I've got to do something to stop it.'"

"By that time, I had given up hunting. I liked hunting but I didn't like killing things. I liked to fish. I liked to hike way down to the bottom of the canyon, to the hard-to-get-to places. When I came back to the Northwest, I found that even the hard-to-get-to places were full of people. It was amazing just how much population pressure had pushed into the woods and to the canyons. You couldn't get away from people. That was another flag to me that there's too much impact on the forests."

Upon arrival in the Tri-Cities he learned of the Hanford Reach and the fact that it was the only free-flowing inland stretch of the Columbia River. He sought out the local conservation group, Save the Reach, and met Rick Leaumont and Mike Lilga during one of their routine meetings at the Richland Library. "I walked in and I introduced myself and I said, 'Hey, I want to do something to help you guys preserve this place, I think it's great.' Rick Leaumont actually broke down and almost cried at meeting somebody in the Tri-Cities who actually showed enough interest and wanted to devote time to help."

It was obvious that Bob was signing on to a fight in a community that had not yet been motivated to action over these concerns. Support for Save the Reach was limited primarily to the three or four people in the organization. In 1992, when Bob first joined the group, probably no one on the Tri-City streets could have told him how to get to the Hanford Reach. Within about two years they had a newsletter going out to 1,500 people, and they had media coverage. They had established the Hanford Reach as one of the region's top issues.

The greatest obstacle Save the Reach had to overcome on the road to protection was an environmentally unfriendly local government. Farming and ranching interests control the politics in the region. Instead of sitting down at the outset and working out a plan with the county commissioners or Congressman Doc Hastings, Bob Wilson and Save the Reach had to adopt slightly more aggressive tactics in order to bring their issue to the public conscience.

One instance involved former speaker of the house Newt Gingrich. Hastings invited Gingrich to take a tour of the Reach to support a bill that Hastings had cooked up to take the Reach away from the federal government and turn it over to county control. Save the Reach requested, and was denied, a short meeting with the speaker so that they might present their side of the argument. Organizers of the event were very obstructionist, guarding details of the event and preventing environmentalists from participating. Determined to attend, Save the Reach engineered a way in. "We found out where he [Gingrich] was coming in from the boat tour on the Reach with Hastings, so we got there a half hour early . . . . The Secret Service guys were there so we had to not be too obvious, but we got pretty close to where the boat was coming in. There were three of us and we unrolled this huge banner saying 'Save the Reach.' Of course they had TV cameras there. So we were right there saying 'save the reach' when Gingrich and Doc get off the boat." While the scene at the docking site was unfolding, other Save the Reachers were sneaking up to the podium where Gingrich was going to speak and plastering Save the Reach bumper stickers across the front. There was not enough time to peel the stickers off, so when Gingrich stepped up to speak about Doc's bill to give the Reach to the county, he was framed on TV screens throughout the state with the blue and white Save the Reach stickers.

There were several county meetings in which citizens would come together to discuss local issues. These were the places to find out what the locals were planning for the river. Bob would infiltrate, learn, and report

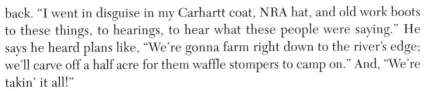

back. "I went in disguise in my Carhartt coat, NRA hat, and old work boots to these things, to hearings, to hear what these people were saying." He says he heard plans like, "We're gonna farm right down to the river's edge; we'll carve off a half acre for them waffle stompers to camp on." And, "We're takin' it all!"

"About half way through, I'd stand up and say, 'Well, I got a different idea, I think we ought to make it a Wild and Scenic River. I think we should protect it.'" He was not exactly voicing a majority sentiment. On a couple of occasions he met with unfriendly responses—angry farmers—but he did meet some who agreed with protection. These younger guys told Bob, "'We really agree with you, man. This place is great, we live here because we love it but we can't get up in front of this crowd and say anything like that. We'd be run out on a rail.' . . . I've found it to be the case in a lot of environmental stuff, you've got more friends there than you really think you do."

"When you get involved in these big environmental things, you find you have really strange allies, and one of them was the Department of Energy here at Hanford . . . . They saw an opportunity through making this a park or wild and scenic river to get rid of this land. So someone from the [DOE] national office in D.C. said 'Hey, we should make it a national monument.'" The paperwork started rolling in and administrative officials contacted Save the Reach to take care of all the requirements: "I was at work one day, and I get a call. This guy says 'Can I meet with you for lunch?' I said, 'Okay, but who in the hell are you?' 'I am Al Gore's advance team organizer. Al Gore is going to come out here next week to announce the Reach as a designated national monument.' The next week, Al Gore came out and announced the monument." After seven years of working on an issue that had been fought for since the 1960s, the national monument was designated only three months after the idea was mentioned in Washington, D.C. "It happened so fast, I couldn't believe it." When an opportunity like this comes up, "you got to be ready to do whatever it takes to take it over the line."

Bob describes his role within the group as the "barking dog." He is willing to stand up and say the hard things. He is the one that many of their opponents aim their anger at, "the bad guy." Perhaps filling this role is what finally brought Save the Reach to the attention of the Tri-Cities. "Somebody needs to get up there and raise hell . . . sometimes you have to get up there and yell in these peoples' faces." As well as speaking out at public forums, this barking dog put his comments in writing. Other members of Save the Reach praise Bob's ability to speak out through the medium of the newspaper. Throughout his time with Save the Reach, local papers were inundated with letters to the editor that Bob himself wrote and those he elicited from their supporters. In this way, politicians could not plead ignorance to public opinion.

Sustained connection to the outdoors and to the shrub-steppe environment is very important to Bob. He hikes and goes backpacking whenever he gets the chance. He quotes Edward Abbey's advice to frazzled environmentalists, "Spend half your time out battling the bastards, but spend the other half out there enjoying the places you're trying to save."

"So that's what I try to do," says Bob. "God help me, I enjoyed every minute of it."

DR. JOHN OSBORN[10]

Dr. John Osborn is a tireless advocate for preservation and restoration of the inland Pacific Northwest. He has chaired the conservation committee of the Northern Rockies Chapter of the Sierra Club for the past seventeen years and founded the Spokane Resident Physicians Action League known today as the Lands Council, which under his leadership developed a forest-watch program that became a model for forest-watch groups across the country. He also co-authored *Railroads and Clearcuts: Legacy of Congress's 1864 Northern Pacific Railroad Land Grant,* calling attention to the misuse of the checkerboard lands across the west.[11]

John credits his parents with nurturing his connection to the land and instilling a sense of commitment to its preservation. His family invested much of their time hiking the North Cascades and exploring the mountains of southern Idaho. "When I was in junior high my mother took me to Sun Valley to a public hearing. The issue was the future of the White Cloud Mountains in the Sawtooth country of central Idaho. There was a massive molybdenum mine proposed for the base of Castle Peak. Eventually the Sawtooths were protected as part of the national wilderness system, but the White Cloud Mountains still today are not fully protected."

In college John worked as a firefighter for the Forest Service, piquing his curiosity about the agency's fire policy. This eventually led John to spend an extra year in college in order to write a book about the subject. "I was fascinated by the evolution of fire policy. When I tried to write the history of the policy, one issue led to another so the book covered far more than just the evolution of fire policy in the U.S., but also included a history of the wilderness system and the national forest system."

John went on to medical school at the University of Washington and did an internship at the Spokane Veterans Hospital. Because he specialized in Third World medicine, John originally intended to spend just a short time in Spokane. "I was practicing medicine at a mission hospital in west Kenya; it was late at night and one of my patients had just died. I stood on the porch struggling with my future. I came to the conclusion that the good I could accomplish in conservation in the Pacific Northwest would be greater than or equal to the good I could do in a Third World hospital."

A short time later John returned to Spokane, accepting a staff position at the Veterans Administration Hospital. One day while completing his rounds, he looked up at a patient's television to see a logging truck convoy encircling a college campus in Coeur d'Alene in protest of proposed wilderness. John telephoned the local chapter of the Sierra Club and attended his first meeting. It was November 1983 and the chapter was focused on the passage of what was to become the 1984 Washington State Wilderness Act. John recalls, "I asked, 'Who is working on Idaho wilderness?' and there was no answer. The painful realization sunk in that, at least in Spokane, there was tremendous organizing that needed to be done."

John talked with fellow doctors, physical therapists, nurses, and other hospital workers and together they organized the Spokane Resident Physicians Action League, which became the Inland Empire Public Lands Council and today is called the Lands Council. Their immediate objective was wilderness designation for an area in northern Idaho called the Mallard Larkin. John eloquently describes its beauty, but beauty did not motivate his commitment to its preservation. He explains, "The value of the Mallard Larkin is especially clear when you look at its surroundings. Devastation surrounds the Mallard Larkin. The forests have been massively clear-cut and thousands of logging roads bulldozed into it. The Mallard Larkin is an island of wilderness in a sea of clear-cuts."

John's organization collected 350 letters in support of wilderness designation, which he delivered when he testified at a Washington, D.C., congressional hearing. He summarizes the events: "What took place on Capitol Hill in the summer of '84 was a high stakes political poker game." The Idaho bill was plagued by an unsupportive state senator, a series of meetings in which conservation organizations and timber interests could not come to agreement, and eventually House and Senate representation that could not come together. "Eventually no Idaho wilderness designations were proposed. Sixteen million acres in the Northern Rockies of Montana and Idaho were left unprotected."

This set the stage for John's next undertaking, the review of national forest planning documents. John believes one needs a historical context to understand forest planning. "We were the last of the timber frontiers. Always in this country's history there was another stand of virgin forest just on the other side of the ridge. So it was in New England, the Midwest, and so it seemed in the Pacific Northwest. What became clear to the public in the 1980s, and was clear to scientists years earlier, was that on the other side of the ridge isn't another great stand of virgin forest. On the other side of the ridge is the Pacific Ocean." In John's view, corporations, having over-cut their own lands, placed tremendous pressure on the Forest

Service to provide them with harvestable forests. The lack of available private lands affected communities as well. "Timber-dependent communities were in a similar bind because they were increasingly dependent on a flow of logs from national forests. Unlike corporations who can transfer capital around the globe in a split second, communities cannot move."

John's initial research on the Mallard Larkin led to his conclusion that, "The Forest Service had plundered the forests to produce high volumes of timber at unsustainable levels." This realization propelled him into action: "When I completed the reviews of these eight-pound documents, I located a Sierra Club publication called *The Practical Guide to Media* and called my first news conference."

John felt a responsibility to the Inland Northwest communities. "I worked with environmental groups, hunting and fishing groups, outdoor recreation groups, home owners and tribal members." In addition, John sought out religious leaders. "I see these issues [preservation of national forests] as fundamentally moral issues. Religious leadership in the Pacific Northwest has an opportunity and a responsibility to help others understand that the decisions made [about the forests] are moral issues."

Forest plans all over the Northwest needed reviewing. The postal service regularly deposited volumes on John's front porch. He and other activists divided the work, identified volunteers, and asked people to take leadership roles in their communities. "It was a desperate time and we were desperate to find individuals to look after the land." John was the primary author of the first appealed forest plan on the Colville National Forest in northeastern Washington. "These forests would have been devastated were it not for individuals there who put together teams of volunteers to review the various forest plans. They found extensive assessments of stream damage. The Forest Service didn't use science, they used ocular assessment, which means they just went out and looked at the streams. They had a predetermined goal. They based their forest plan around a timber target."

The Colville National Forest came to national prominence during the development of the westside old-growth controversies in the early 1990s. "The Colville forests were being ravaged so we asked Tom Foley to push the Clinton administration to include the east side in his upcoming forest summit [that resulted in the 1994 Northwest Forest Plan]." In the midst of this debate John thought it essential for Congressman Foley to see the Colville National Forest. "We knew if he could just see the extent of the clear-cutting, he'd be supportive." They arranged for LightHawk, a nonprofit organization that donates planes and volunteer pilots for environmental causes, to fly Foley over the area. John recalls, "Just as we boarded, Foley remarked that he had trained himself to fall asleep on airplanes." Sure enough, up in the air and over the Colville, Foley fell asleep. John and

Dr. John Osborn poses before a clear-cut made by the Plum Creek Timber Company in the Mallard Larkin area of the Idaho Panhandle National Forest. (Photo by Paul Chesley; courtesy John Osborn.)

the others all realized the strain and pressure Foley was under and that he must be exhausted. "Still," says John, "this was our only opportunity to show him the Colville. Barry [Rosenberg, a volunteer,] sat next to Foley. When he fell asleep Barry said, 'He's asleep. What'll I do?' I said, 'Wake him up.' Barry said, 'He's the speaker of the house.' I said, 'Wake him up.' Barry did and Foley saw the Colville." The east side didn't get included in the forest summit, but John remembers that Foley criticized the Clinton plan for providing inadequate protection.

At the same time, the Lands Council ran a huge publicity campaign using billboards, buses, and yard signs depicting a photograph of a clear-cut overlaid with the caption "Clearcut Shame." John remembers, "We went door to door in Spokane with hundreds of volunteers. They put up well over a thousand yard signs. Once I was putting up signs in a neighborhood and a guy drove by, slammed on his breaks and yelled, 'Are you the yard sign guy?' I thought, everyone has been so positive, but this was it. This guy is going to give me hell. I said, 'Yes,' and he said, 'Can you get me one?' Those signs disappeared, but not for a long time. I saw some still around years later."

While John and other advocates reviewed forest plans, national forest timber sales continued. Frequently these sales needed to be challenged. John says, "They represented considerable watershed and habitat devastation." In early 1986, overwhelmed by the daunting task, John and a colleague decided to organize a citizen watch to oversee Forest Service decisions. The Reed Foundation donated money to the Inland Empire Public Lands Council, and John gathered a diverse representation of community leaders for a board of directors. "With an idea, a little money, and a board of directors, the forest-watch program was [born]." John asked Barry Rosenberg to oversee the program. "Barry was a hero of a very dark time. He started appealing timber sales and went out to small communities and taught other volunteers how to review timber sale documents. He figured out how to successfully challenge the Forest Service."

John is explicit about relaying the philosophy behind the forest-watch program. "The goal was to build some solid relationships with Forest Service officials and to involve the public, not to appeal every timber sale." The volunteers did establish some good relationships with Forest Service personnel and often they found problems with the timber sale proposals. "In many cases the documentation was deceptive and contained gaping holes. Barry would file an appeal and he would win. This was a huge turning point. Timber cuts dropped dramatically. On the Colville the drop was from 80 million board feet per year to 15 million. Grassroots forest-watch programs spread from the Rocky Mountain front to the Cascade crest. It was an exciting time. Today thousands of acres are still standing because of the forest-watch movement."

John notes that the need for timber sales appeals continues today with the Bush administration undermining the rights of citizens to review timber sales. "The laws that protect the trees are vulnerable. Some individuals and corporations will stop at almost nothing to get at our public trees. The values of those in power are mirrored in what happens in our forests."

An extensive portion of John's work centers around the checkerboard lands created by the Northern Pacific Railroad Land Grant passed by Congress in 1864. This law gave land to the railroad for the purpose of expanding westward, but ultimately allowed millions of acres of public forests to fall into the hands of private timber companies. John's work in the checkerboard lands began with a drive in the northwestern Rockies. He recalls, "I was up there at sunset. The sun was bloodred on the snow. I drove around a corner and there was a massive clear-cut with big, sharp, chopped corners. I felt like I was kicked in the stomach. I saw the checkerboard pattern of the map becoming clear-cut reality on the ground."

At first, John attempted to entice reporters to the area to document the destruction, but they weren't interested. "Corporations were saying they weren't damaging fish and wildlife, but I saw it happening at Snoqualmie Pass, Pend Oreille, Lolo Pass, everywhere from Yellowstone to the West Coast." John asked himself where this pattern originated. His answer is in the *Railroads and Clearcuts* book he co-authored.

John's question about the checkerboard lands led him to seek remedies for what he believes were gross violations of the law. He asks, "How did thousands of acres intended for homesteaders wind up in the hands of timber companies?" He wrote a grant to fund a team of attorneys who researched congressional and court documents dating back to the 1920s. Legal recourse has not been found, but that has not stopped John from seeking remedy.

In 1996, John's friend, Bart Naylor, asked if John would like to represent him at the Weyerhaeuser annual shareholders meeting. John accepted and used his allotted time to give a brief history of the checkerboard lands and to offer a resolution addressing the problem of overcutting the forests. "I was given ten minutes. When I finished, George Weyerhaeuser grabbed the microphone and said, 'Thank you for that entertaining mixture of fact and fantasy.' As George continued to speak I walked up to the front of the room and presented him with nine copies of my book, one for each board member."

The next year Bart's father asked John to represent him at the Boise Cascade timber company's annual meeting and John used the time to address social justice issues. In 2000 John purchased his own shares of Boise Cascade and presented a resolution to address overcutting at the annual shareholders meeting. With the exposure of fraud within Enron and other corporations, John sees growing public interest in holding corporations accountable. He says, "I want accountability for those companies still benefiting from the land grant."

John's most recent strategy for wildlands protection is rooted in a habit of clipping and filing newspaper articles pertaining to land use and conservation. He began with one newspaper and expanded to six. "In the mid-1980s I cut out stories and put them on an eight-and-a-half-by-fourteen-inch sheet of paper, ran them off on a copy machine, and mailed them out to all the environmentalists I knew." This was the beginning of *Transitions*, a magazine published by the Lands Council from 1988 through 2000. "The articles all together tell a powerful story, an important story that stakeholders need to know. It's our history. You can put history to work to influence the decisions of today. *Transitions* is the history of the national forest, the Columbia River system, fire policy, and mining pollution; a historical archive of profoundly important years at the close of the twentieth century."

John reviewed back issues of *Transitions*, editing them with a focus on Lewis and Clark and was struck by the importance of the expedition. "The bicentennial will occur as a wave of extinction washes over the Columbia River ecosystem. It can be more than a eulogy of what has been lost. We can use the bicentennial to remedy some unresolved problems. It can be an opportunity to preserve ecosystems and make a commitment to the future."

John took this idea to the Northern Rockies chapter of the Sierra Club and the local leadership took it to the regional and national levels. He describes the strategy as "a seven-year campaign to protect and restore salmon runs on the Columbia and Snake Rivers and to protect all at-risk wildlife." In January 2003 the campaign had its official kickoff event, which included a speech delivered by John on the steps of Monticello, where the Lewis and Clark Expedition had been originally conceived in the mind of Thomas Jefferson.

When asked how he deals with the past failures and constant frustrations inherent in preservation of wildlands John attributes his drive to his optimism and patience. He says, "I take care of very sick people—World War II and Korean veterans with chronic disease. I've learned to be more patient, to count victories in inches rather than miles. When I was in Kenya our victories were counted in miles. An infant inflicted with meningitis would come to the clinic at night, receive treatment, and by the next afternoon be sitting up and smiling on her mother's lap. The last seventeen years have been very different and slow both in medicine and conservation." But John persists: "Conservation is the activity of daily living—work that needs to be done and work that will long outlive me."

These and other current leaders bring to the wildlands movement the same levels of energy and determination seen in the earliest days of wilderness preservation, and they know that vigilance is the key to keeping present designations wild. At the same time, such leaders have stepped out on their own with new strategies for restoring and protecting wildlands. Leaders with this kind of insight and innovation have the power to continually renew and revitalize the movement, building ever more momentum for the long-term preservation and regeneration of wild Washington.

CHAPTER 10

The Movement for Wild Washington: Today and Tomorrow

◆ *Ellen Trescott and Tyler Winchell, with Caitlin Houser* ◆

Like the wide-ranging wild areas it strives to protect, today's movement for Washington's wildness is a mosaic. It is a complex and fairly interdependent group of organizations and individuals, representing an evolving network of locally minded and environmentally concerned citizens. From a group working to restrict the development of urban green spaces to one advocating a wild corridor from the Rockies to the Pacific, the passions of active conservationists embody an intangible set of values more than a cohesive, overarching goal.

With this chapter we aim to offer a summary and critique of the movement through a fresh lens, hoping to inform activists yet to be and to provide constructive suggestions for conservationists currently involved. An accurate examination relies on an understanding of the movement's rich past and the changes undergone in the last few decades that have diversified its focus. Voices of involved activists are perhaps the best way to gain insight and perspective about the issues that inform the movement today. Therefore, our analysis draws upon the groundwork laid in the preceding chapters of part 2. Other source materials include academic and environmental publications, personal interviews, conferences and meetings, and campfire discussions.

We begin with an overview of group structures and then discuss the role of professionalism and its effects on the movement's fundraising, legal, scientific, and organizing tactics. We then delve into several of the movement's main goals and strategies, including the campaign for new wilderness designations, emerging dialogues about wildlands regeneration, and motives for direct action and civil disobedience. Finally, we determine that, while the movement's overall goals are expanding and there has been much success in reaching out to new allies, there are still many opportunities for improvement and greater cooperation.

THE SPECTRUM OF GROUP TYPES

One common way to categorize the types of conservation groups found within the movement is by their geographical scope, namely those working on a national or international, a regional, or a local, place-based scale. National conservation groups tend to have political clout with issues concerning congressional legislation and federal policy, and most have offices in Washington, D.C., where they can effectively lobby national decision makers. A few important national groups lobbying for issues affecting Washington State include the Wilderness Society and the American Lands Alliance. Some, like the Sierra Club and the National Audubon Society, have chapters around the state that are accountable to main offices in major cities. The Nature Conservancy is an international organization recognized for large-scale contributions to many aspects of wildlands preservation, especially outside the realm of federal lands. National groups offer valuable resources to regional groups in the state and to the movement as a whole. They often supply political currency and access to decision makers, along with organizing capacity and scientific analysis.

Regional groups work on a smaller scale. They may operate within political boundaries, like Washington State, or they may focus on particular issues, such as management of national forests under the Northwest Forest Plan. They may also operate within bioregions, such as the Greater Columbia Basin or the Okanogan Highlands. A few examples of the numerous regional groups in the Pacific Northwest include the Mountaineers, Kettle Range Conservation Group, Washington Wilderness Coalition, Northwest Ecosystem Alliance, Washington Environmental Council, and the Lands Council. Within a smaller geographical scope, they act as national groups do by providing organizing assistance and regional political power to even smaller organizations.

Place-based groups (also known as spearhead groups or specific defenders) are targeted toward a specific area like a watershed or community. They are a rich source of local, on-the-ground knowledge, which they provide to land managers and larger conservation groups. Though differing in their tactics and objectives, local groups now exist for most national forests in Washington, and a majority of counties now have land trusts or conservancies. These smaller grassroots groups conduct outreach to local citizens and serve as volunteer experts for the areas they know best. Local knowledge does not necessarily require living in the area of concern. Rather, personal experience and commitment to the land is what allows one to know the ground well enough to speak accurately on its behalf.

It would be inaccurate to assume that a lack of specific defenders in parts of the state represents a lack of environmentally minded citizens. In areas east of the Cascades, for example, this type of grassroots organizing is difficult given the great social risks of speaking out for conservation causes.

Although size and organizational structure generally can help delineate a grassroots group from a "mainstream" organization, many other attributes are encompassed by these descriptions. From 1987 to 1988, an analysis of citizen environmental groups in Washington State was conducted by Debra Salazar, the results of which are included throughout the following section about the roles of professionals within the movement. Salazar drew a parallel between the grassroots/mainstream dichotomy on a national scale and that which exists within Washington State. She summarizes, "Grassroots groups are distinguished by class diversity among members, local focus, unconventional political style, the prominence of volunteers, and efforts to democratize environmental science and politics. These characteristics are in contrast to mainstream environmental organizations, which [are] dominated by middle- and upper-class staff and tactics such as lobbying and litigation, and are staffed by professionally trained experts."[1]

 ## PROFESSIONAL TOOLS OF THE TRADE

Most groups in Washington began as strictly volunteer organizations, like the Washington Wilderness Coalition, which had two volunteers in 1979 who were dedicated to working for wilderness preservation with place-based groups across the state (see Karen Fant's interview in chapter 7). Today, the organization has three types of directors, three coordinators, four managers, and one organizer. These individuals are paid staff, working at their jobs full-time, even if they are underpaid for the extra time and effort they spend. As with most groups, the board of directors for the coalition remains volunteer. Those serving on the board often have "professional" abilities and through years of experience have become skilled advisors, fundraisers, and political negotiators.

Professionalism takes on many forms in Washington's movement for wildness, from litigation and science to fundraising and even outreach organizing. As the movement has matured over the past century, the application of these specialized, professional tools can be seen as an evolution of tactics. Without these forms of professionalism, the movement might not have made many important strides, and together they lend strength to its overall effectiveness. In some ways, however, an over-reliance on professionals can stifle the creativity and intrepidness of passionate, less specialized, volunteer activists. Professionalism, then, can both serve the greater good of the movement as well as detract from it.

Fundraising

All organizations within Washington's movement for wildness have a need to conduct fundraising operations in order to maintain their level of activism. In the early days of wilderness campaigns, fundraising often consisted of contributions by members into a general fund in order to purchase simple items like printed letterhead stationary. Today, fundraising has become more professional in nature and requires a considerable focus in most organizations' planning and operations. Methods of fundraising have advanced over time, including increased support from financial foundations, a variety of appeals to wealthy individuals, and a change in the nature of door-to-door outreach. The implications of these methods extend beyond the bankroll, affecting the priorities and decisions that organizations make and the economic classes targeted by many events and outreach tactics.

The most predominant method of financing organizations is to secure foundation grants. Foundations or trusts are well-maintained cash funds that seek out organizations to partially finance. Among Washington groups, the Pew Charitable Trust, and the Rockefeller and Bullitt foundations are important financiers. Kathie Durbin's journalistic report, *Tree Huggers,* confirms that, "Overall foundation grants accounted for 80 percent of the revenue to Northwest [conservation] groups by the mid 1990s."[2] Strikingly, Salazar's survey of environmental groups in Washington State less than a decade earlier (between 1987 and 1988) found that only 10 percent of conservation revenue came from grants and foundations, with three-fourths coming from members. Among the groups in the latter survey, those that were more "institutionalized"—with many members, hired professionals, full-time employees, and a greater degree of organizational bureaucracy—received almost twice as much of their revenue from grants and foundations than smaller, grassroots groups. These institutionalized groups were also most active in the state legislature, though their political actions may have been more constricted by the priorities of their funders.[3]

Foundations provide wonderful financial coverage but often require organizations to use the money given to them in particular campaigns. For example, following the creation of the Northwest Forest Plan in 1994, the

Pew Charitable Trust required its recipients (who were focused on forest and ecosystem issues) to work on the protection of roadless areas. In a more recent example, regional funders of the Northwest Old Growth Campaign directed their recipients to abandon pursuit of protective legislation for old growth in the 108th Congress (2003–4), and instead assume a more defensive approach. Foundations, though generous, can hamper the autonomy of an organization and can often have a powerful influence over decisions concerning political strategy. Nevertheless, most organizations have accepted the additional responsibility in return for the substantial financing that foundations can provide. While an increasing reliance on this type of funding indicates a decrease in the decision-making power of members, some foundations understand the importance of grassroots outreach. Doug Scott, policy director of the Campaign for America's Wilderness, says that the biggest impression on a politician comes not from professional persuasion but from the heartfelt concern of local constituents at the county fair.[4]

Foundation grant writing is time intensive and can be intrusive, and not every foundation's goals will match those of an organization. Therefore, the reliance on member-driven fundraising still continues in Washington. Groups like the Forest Service Employees for Environmental Ethics and the Northwest Ecosystem Alliance proudly claim that their organizations are 60 percent funded by individual donors. These groups hope that efforts to promote member financing will connect members more with the organization and their causes. Because an organization seeks more membership contributions, however, does not imply that it is seeking to be influenced by members' opinions or activism. Take for example the Fund for Public Interest Research, which sends recruiters into the field to generate new contributions for its member organizations like the Sierra Club and Greenpeace. Underlying the conservation goals of these paid canvassers is the need to meet quotas and generate funds, which can interfere with actually empowering members and inspiring new activists for future campaigns. Many of these donors will be offered a membership card and a magazine, but not real participation or connection to the issues the Sierra Club or Greenpeace may be working on.

Furthermore, to compete with groups heavily funded by foundations, member-based fundraising can be targeted toward upper class citizens. An exclusive movie premier with $500 tickets was a creative way for the Cascades Conservation Partnership to finance further purchases of Interstate 90 checkerboard lands. Similarly, infiltrating Microsoft lunch hours with slide shows of the lynx was a successful strategy to raise millions of dollars to save the Loomis Forest (see chapter 12). These examples show the lofty financial achievements and novel acquisition approaches that some conservationists are currently engaged in, though this type of public appeal is markedly different from the traditional community "chili feeds" put on by smaller organizations like the Kettle Range Conservation Group.

Legal Support

As discussed in chapter 8, litigation became both influential and important for the movement for wildness in the last quarter of the twentieth century. Litigation today remains vital for many groups to achieve their goals when the political process becomes insufficient. Many environmental and public interest lawyers are among Washington's fiercest advocates for conservation. Litigation is a powerful tool that has halted or influenced the conduct of timber sales and road and other construction projects, and has shaped the management policies of parks, forests, monuments, and wildlife refuges.

Yet some activists speculate that litigation may have taken on a life of its own. Some worry about the long-term consequences of an increasing dependence on litigation among many organizations. The increased use of litigation by conservationists has fueled a backlash from wise-use groups, conservative think tanks, and some elected officials who see this as "legislating" through the courts. In this view, affecting policy through litigation flies in the face of "original intent," meaning that it contradicts how the U.S. Constitution views the role of the judicial system in public law.[5] In the 108th Congress, legislation was under consideration that would restrict activists' use of appeals and litigation to halt timber sales on federal land. Most of the legislation comes from congressional representatives who want control over the fate of future timber projects. These representatives have claimed that they have the prerogative of "original intent" when it comes to these issues. They also charge that litigation ties up government projects as well as inflating the costs of these operations, although the Government Accounting Office has proven this to be false at least twice in recent years.[6]

There is a legitimate fear by conservationists that current or future governments may dismantle the tools of environmental litigation, including the Endangered Species Act, the National Environmental Policy Act, or the National Forest Management Act, and leave many organizations without effective strategies or legal tactics. In 2002, successful litigation to protect rare species from old-growth timber sales under the Northwest Forest Plan was turned against the conservation movement. Timber industry representatives conducted postlitigation settlement talks "behind closed doors" with the Forest Service, excluding conservationists and moving forward with proposals to dismantle the legal strongholds used by environmental lawyers for several years.

Using a model of "conflict expansion," Salazar defines two types of political resources used among conservation groups: instrumental resources and direct electoral support. Professional lawyers are instrumental resources, in that they are "assets" easily transferred among issues and effective within a closed network of activists. When these resources become ineffective, the resource of direct electoral support has more value, and conflicts are expanded to the general public, or to what Salazar references as the "attentive public."[7] This can be seen with the 2003 attempts to roll back key components of the Northwest Forest Plan. Activists quickly turned to citizens when appeals and litigation came under fire, requiring a mobilization of grassroots resources in an effort to wield the strength of public opinion to influence agency decisions. While professional lawyers will continue to be essential in defending existing environmental standards, the power of a vocal citizenry is just as critical in influencing policy decisions concerning wildlands.

The Role of Science

Science and technology have expanded the traditional conservationist toolbox. The understanding of complex ecosystems has improved, and scientific specialists have become less afraid to engage in advocacy for the protection of wild areas. In turn, citizen conservation groups have been able to develop and argue for policy recommendations. They can utilize ecological research to bolster environmental arguments beyond the time-honored rhetoric of "special places." It is now common for conservation groups to have staff scientists, who educate members and provide scientific information concerning specific wildlands issues and campaigns. Some groups organize hikes into planned timber sales or shrub-steppe areas to allow volunteers to help find rare or endangered plants and animals. The work of both professional and amateur researchers helps to fill gaps in government research and can effect change in the policies and management of wildlands. Often, however, as Loomis forest activist Mark Skatrud aptly says, "Politics influences science more than science influences politics."[8]

The use of scientific arguments to promote wildlands preservation has become quite prominent in the Northwest since the early 1980s, starting with ecologist Jerry Franklin. Using modern scientific findings from the Pacific Northwest Research Station (the Forest Service's regional research branch), Franklin created a traveling slide show about the ecological importance of old-growth forests. Along with scientific data, he incorporated visually aesthetic photographs. This appeal to the public's appreciation for the beauty of an ecosystem, used so often in wilderness protection campaigns, was combined with compelling scientific arguments to create "a pitch" for the protection of ancient forests.[9] Franklin left a legacy for both volunteer and agency researchers to follow. Scientists from the Northwest Research Station still travel with computerized slide shows, promoting the restoration of managed forests to old-growth characteristics through thinning experiments. Although science is perhaps the most objective of conservation tools, it can easily be manipulated to fit different values and desired outcomes, resulting in arguments over the "best science" between conservationists, industry, and management agencies.

A challenge faced by many passionate scientific professionals is deciding the extent to which scientists should be activists. Some, like Peter Morrison of the Pacific Biodiversity Institute, prefer to take an objective stance, insisting on nonadvocacy for reasons of scientific credibility.[10] This can be a wise choice, affirmed by one example, in which activist Mark Skatrud had his ongoing lynx research turned away by the Forest Service due to his commitment to their protection.[11] Yet advocacy informed by science is a powerful tool when used by activists like David Jennings, a volunteer wildlife biologist and chairman of the board for the Gifford Pinchot Task Force. He has undertaken an unprecedented mapping project of the remaining interior forest habitat (forests that are not ecologically affected by roads or clear-cuts) in the Gifford Pinchot. His GIS maps tell a convincing, though saddening, story of the poor habitat contained within the Northwest Forest Plan's late-successional reserves. As a biologist, Jennings is well aware of the ecological consequences of severe habitat fragmentation, and his emotions are visible as he describes it.[12] The scientific analysis shown by his maps has been an effective tool, and they make the dire situation of the forest painfully clear to the average citizen, as well as to local politicians.

The accomplishments of "citizen scientists" like Jennings and Skatrud are increasingly rare in a time when science is more specialized and professional than ever before. Activists use scientific research to both lobby and litigate for policy changes, in a cycle of professional advocacy that can exclude the amateur researcher. The rigorous training and careful methods required of credible research are essential to maintaining the integrity of honest scientific pursuit. Accurate observational data, however, inform many aspects of this process, and can be a successful way for citizens to contribute to protecting the wild.

Communication in a Technological Age

The movement is also able to motivate its citizens through new means of communication that pioneer conservationists could have only dreamed about. Activists now travel the Northwest circuit as Howard Zahniser once traveled the halls of Congress. In the mid-1950s, with his slideshow of Dinosaur

National Monument in one hand and a briefcase full of legal papers and citizen endorsements in the other, this author of the 1964 Wilderness Act tirelessly made presentation after presentation to garner support to stop the Glen Canyon Dam project.

Today, scientific and technological tools can merge pictures with words and graphs, and landscapes with in-depth analyses. Technology-savvy activists can now lobby politicians and talk with large groups of citizens more quickly and effectively than ever before. These tools are impressive and can be effective in reaching many people, but other benefits, such as those achieved though personal grassroots organizing, may be lacking in this form of advocacy. As longtime activist Tim Coleman says, "What works is connecting people to the issue, and wilderness campaigns have taught us a lot about that. If you can talk to people one-on-one, you find that there is a much greater connection to the issue than if you approach them in a group setting."[13]

The Internet has given the movement multiple tools to engage its members and to attain nationwide or global outreach. Many smaller, place-based groups have created professional and informative Web sites that draw members from far and wide. This tool has supplemented the novel approach of the "letterhead strategy" of earlier decades, where even the smallest and newest group gained recognition and political attention by branding all letters and published materials with their name and logo.[14] Today, activists can advertise a forest-action camp, provide links to relevant groups and media, and even discuss the observations of forest-watch volunteers, all via the Internet, using fewer trees and reaching more people. As a mass media tool, an e-mail list is as close to prime-time advertising as most conservationists can get.

Some activists question the increased use of and dependence on electronic communications, however. After receiving a dozen messages about policies and wild places of great concern, it is easy for a person to lose sight of what really matters. With eyes and mind bent on the latest national and regional battles, it may be all too tempting to overlook what is happening in one's own backyard. In addition to sometimes wasting time and energy on the propagation of rumors, e-mail exchanges can isolate citizens who can't afford or who choose not to use a computer.[15] A few activists have taken a step back from using e-mail as their prime source of communication, instead relying on phone calls or face-to-face communication.

Organizing Strategies

Today, there is less personal contact between mainstream national groups and their members, and more marketing toward a particular demographic: middle and upper class, predominately older, well educated, and white.

Members within this target group have a tendency to open junk mail, and they often belong to more than one conservation organization. As a result, national groups routinely buy and sell each other's mailing lists.[16] "Card carrying environmentalist" members must often be content with a regular newsletter highlighting impressive accomplishments and dire threats. The conduit of citizen participation occurs predominantly through the mail or the Internet, with members sending prewritten postcards, form letters, or e-mails to congressional leaders when prompted. This mode of operation generates a high quantity of public comments, but is different from traditional outreach and has, for that reason, been criticized by some in the movement as the generation of "Astroturf" instead of true grassroots involvement.

Increased opportunity to take action may explain why regional groups appeal more to potential activists. Participation in these smaller groups extends beyond the mailbox to meetings and events, outings, and neighborhood outreach. However, most regional groups walk a fine line between the top-down organizing of larger national groups and conventional grassroots organizing. Many of the individuals most targeted for canvassing by regional groups are part of the political swing districts on the outskirts of Washington's major metropolitan areas. This type of organizing is governed mainly by models of efficiency. A large number of people can be contacted through outreach to suburban communities, though regional groups stand apart from national groups by marshalling support beyond these neighborhoods and their associated mailing lists.

Place-based groups have the advantage of developing meaningful relationships with local members, and they tend to use creative grassroots organizing tactics. Activists who frequent local events and gathering places implement a personal outreach that encourages citizens to become directly involved with the issues they care about. These groups can gain more trust and respect in rural areas than their urban-based colleagues. They are also more vulnerable to social and political conflict that can emerge in areas associated with resource extraction and motorized recreation. While outreach organizers are more effective on the grassroots level than policy analysts and lawyers, there is a degree of professionalism within this field as well. Outreach organizers for some of Washington's place-based groups come from a national network of professionals who work on a variety of issues in many states.

In its many forms, the role of professionalism within the conservation movement is a mixed blessing. Activists recognize the continued importance of professional individuals, who devote time and effort far beyond the limits of their salaries, continually putting out brush fires and overseeing the complexities of conservation politics and science. As conservation work evolves into a variety of professions, though, volunteers can inadvertently be pushed to the margins, in part because of meeting times during work-days, the use of acronym-filled "envirospeak" suggestive of a foreign lan-guage, or a general neglect of volunteer development. Citizens and professionals must remember that the "experts" in conservation have al-ways been informed primarily by the places they work to protect, and in this no amount of professional training can supplant the need for concerned people to look out for the wildlands they care about.

 ## ISSUES AND ALLIES

The focus of wildlands advocacy in Washington varies considerably, though several crosscutting trends can be seen among strategies pertaining to a spectrum of diverse issues. Particularly, there is an overall attempt to procure new allies within the movement, as seen in the campaigns described be-low that advocate for new wilderness areas, that focus on regenerating the wild, and that involve tactics of "radical" civil disobedience.

The surge of this current throughout the movement is hardly new, as activists have long attempted to obtain endorsements from local elected officials and other individuals and institutions not readily affiliated with protecting the wild. Recent outreach to new allies is still politically moti-vated, although the cooperative spirit seems to permeate the rhetoric and philosophies of activism to a greater degree than ever before. The effec-tiveness and influence of today's established movement, combined with changing economic and demographic trends (see chapter 4), may explain this style of organizing, though the "battle" metaphor will undeniably res-urrect itself when threats intensify. Nonetheless, if cooperative outreach to new allies is to be a successful long-term strategy, activists will need to surmount considerable challenges to agreement and also consider untapped opportunities to broaden participation.

Wilderness in the Twenty-first Century

Currently, and in the foreseeable future, wilderness proposals for any of Washington's national forests will be coordinated through the Wild Wash-ington Campaign, a unique coalition that is "green" in more ways than one. It is green for the obvious symbolic reason that it is a strong advocate of wildlands protection to promote and preserve biodiversity, threatened eco-systems, and clean air and water for all of Washington's residents. How-ever, the Wild Washington Campaign is also green in the sense that its ability to effectively maneuver through the political landscape in order to pro-tect Washington's roadless areas remains unproven.

The campaign is composed of fourteen organizations from across the state and has its headquarters in Seattle. Though the campaign now has more westside representation on its steering committee, it was jumpstarted in the mid-1990s by two eastside groups, the Kettle Range Conservation Group and the Lands Council, in an effort to protect roadless areas that were left out of the 1984 Washington State Wilderness Act. In 2000, after careful political analysis, a western Washington roadless area was selected as the first wilderness proposal to pursue. This was the precursor to a larger strategy, which would propose several small, politically "easy" bills and build momentum for designations in less wilderness-friendly congressional districts like those on the eastside.

In the initial years of the current campaign, eastside groups acknowledged that a westside proposal would probably be in the best interest of the wilderness community. Jon Owen, former conservation director of the Washington Wilderness Coalition and an active participant in the Wild Washington Campaign until 2003, confirmed that early planning for the first wilderness bill of the new coalition focused entirely on the Mount Baker–Snoqualmie National Forest.[17] The proposed area is named Wild Sky but has been historically known as the Eagle Rock Roadless Area by the Forest Service. Eagle Rock was an area included in the 1984 Washington wilderness proposal, but was taken out of the bill's final incarnation. The Wild Sky Wilderness bill that was first introduced in 2001 would have protected an area that includes low-elevation mature and old-growth forests, is a critical wildlife corridor, and could provide habitat for reintroduced grizzly bears. Having come close to passage in the 107th Congress, it was reintroduced in the beginning of the 108th with full expectations of passage by 2004 or earlier. The Wild Sky proposal is among the most thorough and well assembled in the near forty-year history of national forest wilderness proposals in Washington State.

Senator Patty Murray has pledged to the Wild Washington Campaign that she will be a political champion for this and future wilderness proposals. John Leary, executive director of the campaign, says that he shares Murray's commitment to going the distance for wilderness: "We're in this for the long haul."[18] Senator Murray has shown a new level of congressional leadership in stewarding the Wild Sky bill through Congress, negotiating with snowmobile organizations to set wilderness boundaries that exclude areas favored by motorized recreationists. She was also instrumental in securing the commitment of the nearby town of Index, a former logging community, and its mayor. This collaboration can be seen as an example of shifting land-use trends across the state. The community of Index sees wilderness as a way to propel itself from a resource-based economy to an amenity- or service-based one. While local timber interests did not contest the proposal, as they might have even two decades ago, the challenge of accommodating motorized-vehicle recreation interests is of growing concern for future wilderness designations.

Other implications for new wilderness are also apparent. The Wild Sky bill includes areas of forest that were logged more than a century ago, and the Forest Service requested that this land be dropped from the proposal because it did not meet "pristine" wilderness criteria. This traditional purity argument represents a huge challenge to protecting low-lying areas that have regenerated their wild qualities. Despite the neutrality of a small local lumber mill, the bill was also challenged by the American Forest Resource Council (AFRC), the largest timber lobby in the United States. Believing that too much of the timber base has been "locked up" in wilderness, AFRC representative Bob Dick thinks that there should be no new wilderness designations in Washington. What provokes him most is that the Wild Washington Campaign failed to bring his organization, which represents the local mill, into their original negotiations.[19]

However, even historic wilderness opponents like Senator Larry Craig (R-ID) applauded Murray's work on the legislation, saying at a Senate hearing on the bill, "You [Murray] did it the way it ought to be done. It was an inclusive process."[20] Murray and the Wild Washington Campaign have secured a bill that contains no release language (see chapter 8) that might compromise the chances of other roadless areas to be preserved as wilderness. John Leary emphasizes that from this point forward, "We don't do release in Washington."[21]

With the relatively noncontroversial Wild Sky bill taking at least two sessions of Congress (four years) to pass, the future is uncertain, to say the least, for all of the other Washington wildlands that merit wilderness designation. For example, the campaign is intent on protecting critical eastside areas like the Golden Horn and the Kettle Range, but staff acknowledged that until the political climate changes in the east, they are not willing to undertake any active campaigns. At the original inception of the Wild Washington campaign, it was hoped that momentum could be built for another statewide or omnibus wilderness act. Thus far, however, plans for a future omnibus wilderness bill are not on the table. Nevertheless, the Washington Wilderness Coalition, a predecessor and current member of the Wild Washington Campaign, promotes its statewide Adopt-a-Wilderness network with reference to building momentum for a "Washington Citizen's Wilderness Proposal." It is still unknown whether this piece-by-piece wilderness approach will be as effective as the large wilderness campaigns of Washington's past.

Regenerating the Wild

Surrounding the state's roadless areas and ancient-forest stands are millions of acres of managed public land that have been intensively roaded, logged, and dammed. More than a century of resource use has caused extensive fragmentation of fish and wildlife habitat. A new generation of activists is moving away from traditional preservation strategies (like wilderness designations) and attempting to restore ecological health to these battered lands and the species they harbor. This approach includes aquatic restoration such as road removal and stream passage, as well as terrestrial restoration projects, such as selectively thinning in fire-prone or densely replanted forests.

Restoration techniques are the subject of continuing scientific, economic, and policy debates. Terrestrial restoration in particular has been endorsed by some activists strictly on a precautionary, experimental basis. Regardless of these dialogues about restoration activities, organizations have made unprecedented headway with new allies like labor and industry through the process of collaboration, together working to establish a "restoration economy." Members of these collaborative working groups fit under a modern term, the "blue/green" alliance, an emerging attempt to find common ground between (blue collar) labor activists and (green) environmentalists. The goal is to provide family-wage jobs for struggling rural residents and a transition to a sustainable resource-based economy supported by environmentalists. Such collaborative possibilities have been helped in part by a reprieve on threats to ancient forests. Hailed by many and suspect to some, these efforts are an attempt to include the "human element in the definition of the conservation of biodiversity."[22] Restoration projects are the focus of collaborative rural outreach in three national forests in Washington: the Gifford Pinchot, the Olympic, and the Colville. Examples from two of these forests provide an overview of the emerging possibilities and challenges of regenerating the wild.

Aquatic habitat for fish and other species has been depleted by decades of road building, logging, and grazing. An important element of aquatic restoration is the maintenance and decommissioning of roads. In the Olympic National Forest the ability to do this type of restoration will improve with the implementation of the Access and Travel Management Plan, a final draft of which was released in March 2003. In addition to maintaining many of the more than 2,500 miles of road in the forest, the plan recommends that 36 percent of these roads be decommissioned or converted to trails.[23] Conservationists were glad to see many of their recommendations incorporated into the plan, and these wildlands advocates will further influence decisions through public input once the plan goes into effect.

Along with the repair of failing roads and culverts, activists hope for the conversion of "cherry stem" roads to trails. These roads are often the only entry into otherwise roadless lands, bisecting wilderness areas and negatively affecting key watersheds. As Pacific Rivers Council spokesperson David Bayles explains, areas like these are an opportunity to accomplish a lot of work with a little energy. Recent data on extinction of aquatic species reveals that the initial impact of human disturbance is the most critical, leading Bayles to believe that time and money for aquatic restoration should be spent where the reduction in road mileage gives the most biological results.[24]

While the Olympic National Forest has many wild places that could recover their pristine qualities with the closure of a few roads, other areas have not received such minimal intrusion. The Shelton Sustained Yield Unit, in the Olympic National Forest's Skokomish River watershed, is the most heavily roaded area of all national forests in the United States.[25] Though it may never again possess an "untrammeled" character, conservationists hope to promote terrestrial restoration projects that will improve its habitat, and to train local contractors in new methods of forest management. Representatives from conservation, labor, economic development, and industry groups, as well as from local and tribal government, held a field tour there in 2002, with subsequent roundtable discussions concerning restoration in the area.

A continuous effort will be necessary for the success of this collaboration, and criticism often comes from both sides of the fence. Timber representative Bob Dick has attended these collaborative group meetings and he agrees that in order to find common ground, "antipathy must be overcome." He also believes that activists promoting restoration are "sincere and well-intentioned, but idealistic."[26] Though he has a soft spot for the remaining old-growth areas in the Skokomish watershed, he wants to see timber volume flowing from the forest as "promised" in the Northwest Forest Plan.

Dick is not a stranger to collaborative process, having taken part in the state-initiated forest and fish negotiations concerning salmon protection during the late 1990s. Environmental activist Bonnie Phillips also took part in these talks and has experience in collaborative efforts over several decades, though she is skeptical of their success "on the ground." She writes, "What has amazed me is that so much of the research [on collaboration] is about the beginning of the process—isn't it wonderful that people have gotten together in the same room and are talking to each other!—instead of following the process through to see whether this has really solved problems from both a social and environmental standpoint."[27]

Both of these viewpoints have been expressed with regard to the Northwest

Old Growth Campaign, which is active in collaborative efforts in both the Olympic and Gifford Pinchot National Forests. Dick and Phillips have opposing viewpoints regarding appropriate national forest management. The timber lobby represented by Dick has agreed with the Forest Service on provisions to weaken standards for terrestrial and aquatic protections under the Northwest Forest Plan. Meanwhile, Phillips's conservation group has appealed recent forest thinning projects in the eastern Olympics, citing the harm caused by the construction of "temporary" roads. At least for now, however, both sides are willing to sit down and discuss the ways in which they might see eye to eye. In this respect, the efforts of the Old Growth Campaign are building upon a middle ground that will continue to evolve, albeit slowly.

Though it may be a slow process, steps to achieve solutions to ecological and economic crises are being made. In the Colville National Forest, Jim Doran is a key member of the Colville Community Forestry Coalition. A lifelong resident of the nearby town of Twisp, Doran has witnessed the economic deterioration and related social problems caused by the closure of local mills. He also knows of the deep-rooted tradition of total wildfire suppression in this dry, forest environment, and the associated fears held by rural residents living there. His coalition is made up of diverse stakeholders, similar in representation to those on the Olympic Peninsula. Together, they are implementing projects to restore the health and habitat of densely replanted forests and to reduce the threat of catastrophic wildfires. By thinning trees for fuel reduction and underburning areas that have been denied their natural fire cycle, the coalition hopes to benefit wildlife, watersheds, forest productivity, and nearby residents.

To build trust and areas of agreement between conservationists, industry, and local communities, the coalition has focused its efforts on forests surrounding rural towns, the "wildland-urban interface" (WUI). This has helped to alleviate residential fears concerning wildfire, an attitude shift that is essential to future policy and management changes. However, Doran believes that in order for a restoration agenda to be truly successful, it must expand its focus to watersheds and many more WUI projects that can supply jobs and a larger ecological benefit. "When the local guys drinking beer at the Antlers Tavern talk about their work, because they will, and they are talking about forest restoration in their own terms, then we will change the ethics of small communities across the West. No amount of preaching about 'sustainable communities' will change the ethic as well as will good work that has inherent value."[28] Crucial components of this restoration vision are the infrastructure and labor necessary to perform the work and process the small-diameter trees from fuel-reduction thinning. The locally owned Vaagen Brothers mill remains in operation near the Colville, sub-sisting now more on Canadian logs than nearby timber. This mill will be a tool of restoration efforts in years to come.

Long after the fate of existing roadless areas and ancient-forest stands is decided, citizens in Washington will still be working to devise a model of cohabitation between human communities and the wild. Doran supports traditional preservation campaigns, and his coalition has ground rules that prohibit discussions of logging old-growth trees or creating extensive new roads. But he also feels a deep responsibility to remedy the neglect of de-cades of fire suppression and timber harvest. As historian William Cronon writes, "Idealizing a distant wilderness means not idealizing the environ-ment in which we actually live . . . . We need an environmental ethic that will tell us as much about using nature as about not using it [and] . . . the obligation to take responsibility for our own action that history inescap-ably entails."[29] In Doran's more concise words, "It is one thing to take a stand against things that you don't want. It is a more demanding endeavor to describe and create what you do want."[30]

Collaboration is not an easy task, and even those invited to the table have difficulties agreeing. Hence the current focus on process over prod-uct. There could also be many more voices heard around these tables. Parties involved are representatives of institutions, including paid environmentalists. Insufficient representation can be overcome by including more people with local knowledge about environmental conditions and cultural differences, including local laborers. Native peoples, who have lived in this "state" and practiced their own careful burning practices for millennia, have advocated the modern use of fire and other regenerative processes as essential to pre-serving their natural foods and medicines. As Russell Jim of the Yakama Nation says of campaigns to regenerate lands grazed by livestock, "Your argument stems from economy and recreation, but chances for indigenous cultural reclamation are great."[31] Native tribes have also sided with con-servationists on the Olympic Peninsula, calling for an end to the artificial reinforcement of washed-out roads along rivers. These common beliefs point to many opportunities for the revitalization of not only rural economies and ecological processes, but also indigenous cultures.

A Convergence of Civil Disobedience

Activists committed to the practice of civil disobedience have also branched out, like the larger movement to which they belong. From blockades of gas pipeline construction to urban protests and acts of strip-mall street theater, the "radical" community within the movement has shown variation in the physical places it targets and the larger goals that drive its direct action. As this segment of the movement grows, however, it is faced with the challenge of promoting messages and tactics more accessible to the public, while retaining its anonymity and security.

Perched high above a landscape of fragmented clear-cuts, tree sitters see their actions as a stand against "corporate greed," epitomized by logging the last precious scraps of ancient forest. Perhaps this bird's-eye view from the canopy has made it easier for Washington's direct-action activists to see the metaphorical forest rather than just the ancient trees. Their actions have broken molds over the past several years, from acquiring the first permit from the Forest Service for an "authorized" tree sit, to standing in solidarity with striking unionists. They have denounced the negative impacts of extractive industries, dominated by large corporate conglomerates, and have demanded accountability to the earth, local communities, and laborers. Activists committed to civil disobedience tend to combine participation in the wildlands movement with actions in campaigns to expose the failures of a globalized, unrestrained, and consolidated system of laissez-faire capitalism. One follower of this "radical ecology" contends that "ecological collapse is the central and most visible contradiction in the global system."[32]

To meet their goals, direct-action activists have fostered many new alliances. In December 1998, on the docks of the Port of Tacoma, an unusual set of partners came together in solidarity. Members of the Industrial Workers of the World, striking steelworkers, and Earth First! activists staged a protest of the Kaiser Aluminum Company, attempting to prevent the docking of a barge full of steel bound for Spokane. Activists scaled a crane at the site as if it were an old-growth hemlock, unfurling a large banner that read "Hurwitz cuts trees like he cuts jobs!" The banner was in reference to the Texan whose company, Maxxam, owns a large share in both Kaiser and the Pacific Lumber Company, which has been the target of redwood tree sits and other actions in northern California. Steelworker Don Kegley comments, "All the environmentalists . . . have been an inspiration to us. If a twenty-four-year-old girl can sit in a tree for a year and not even wear shoes for months, then, by God, three thousand steelworkers ought to be able to kick Charles Hurwitz' ass! We really have to thank all the people that are involved for the great inspiration that you've given us. I'm not so sure we'd be as strong as we are without it. It's give and take on both sides and it's an alliance that I'm proud of."[33]

While the action was a milestone in collaboration between labor and environmental activists, it also depicted a convergence of two tactics that are somewhat incompatible: inclusive public demonstration and covert sabotage. While many within the direct-action community think that efforts to reach out to mainstream new allies like labor unions are crucial, other practitioners of direct action think the radical movement should live up to its name. Days after the momentous action on the docks dissipated, and the boat eventually docked in the port, workers were still unable to unload cargo because the conveyor belt had been strategically cut in an act of sabotage. With $50,000 of damage, the entire event gave Maxxam a taste of the negative publicity regularly dished out to radical activists and of the financial woes suffered by thousands of striking workers.

Perhaps owing to their courage in confronting matters directly, and to an underlying vision of both ecological and social justice, issues of gender equity do not go unspoken in these circles. In the spring of 2003, an all-women's forest-action camp took place in the Northwest, with women traveling from across the country to converge, learn, and strategize together. The radical movement has addressed many of the social concerns that are generally avoided by the movement as a whole. However, while its own publicity extols the openness of regional action camps and direct-action trainings, an interested citizen's initial impressions may be very different. With radical forest activists assuming "forest names" that change with the seasons, and growing paranoia about government infiltration, this part of the movement is much less inclusive than it could be. One activist admits that direct-action activism can be "alienating" to a new person interested in the movement, and for the safety of those involved, "you can't just jump right in."[34] Reconciliation of this tension may never fully occur, as the direct-action movement strives to find a balance between personal security and inclusion of strangers within its circles.

Although Washington is not considered the hub of direct action when compared to Oregon and British Columbia, where threats to old-growth forests still loom large, the state has continued to be a nexus of inspiration and creativity. In the summer of 2002, the annual Earth First! Round River Rendezvous was held on the edge of the Dark Divide Roadless Area in the Gifford Pinchot National Forest. A convergence of radical minds came together in a series of discussions, out of which was born a project called SmartMeme that attempts to assess and propel the direct-action movement.[35]

Excerpts from articles that resulted include the following range of opinions about where this part of the movement should be headed: "Traditionally, strategies of direct action have been conceived and enacted within the confines of a specific campaign. Thus we tend to engage in actions tree by tree, mill by mill, store by store . . . a series of strong threads but not woven together across campaigns or across borders."; "A new environmental movement, if it is to catch on outside our current activist circles, must appeal to hopes as well as fears. It must answer the honest concerns of people who think of environmentalism as just another excuse for government manipulation of their lives. It must come from the land and relate to the land, but it must also have something to say to the people who inhabit the land."; "Our revolution(s) will really start rolling as soon as the appeal of disobedience is so clear that it can easily replicate and spread far beyond the limiting definition of 'protester' or 'activist.'" The years to come will show if these more radical wilderness advocates can live out their intentions and ideals in support of preserving wildness.

 EXPANDED HORIZONS

Conservationist Bonnie Phillips has said of her fellow conservationists, "Within the movement, people feel that 'After we're done saving the world, then we'll change our ways and problems.'"[36] As she implies, to avoid recognizing and dealing with important problems will obviously impair the ability of the movement to save the world, or at least to preserve Washington's wild places. It is for that reason that we now offer a summary analysis of some of the problems and opportunities for improvement that we have observed and that others have pointed out in the course of our research. Our critique and advice spring from an abiding faith in the willingness and ability of Washington's wildlands advocates to look carefully in the mirror with us and to act effectively based on what they see.

The Art of Compromise

Throughout Washington's long conservation history, lands have consistently been compromised to gain protection of others. This type of negotiation has always been in the cards for conservationists, beginning with 1890s concessions to railroad companies for lands now within Mount Rainier National Park (see chapter 6) and continuing throughout the century as recently as the I-90 and Gifford Pinchot National Forest land exchange (see chapter 8).

Early compromises continue to resonate throughout the movement. In the early 1950s, the wilderness movement enjoyed its then largest success with the campaign to stop the Echo Park Dam from being erected in Dinosaur National Monument, Colorado. Among the trade-offs was the construction of the Glen Canyon Dam in Utah, a loss that would eventually help spark the direct-action civil disobedience promoted by activist and author Edward Abbey. Memory of this compromise was visible in 1998 when the I-90 land exchange created wilderness study areas near the Alpine Lakes wilderness but also slated ancient forest for logging in the nearby Gifford Pinchot National Forest. To protest the exchange, activists went to the Plum

Creek Timber Company's headquarters, brandishing large, symbolic banners. The words of environmental icon David Brower waved above the crowd, echoing across decades his sorrow over the loss of Glen Canyon: "Never trade a place you've seen for one you haven't."[37]

While the land exchange was not initiated by citizen action, the initial support it received from wilderness advocates in the middle Cascades created animosity between branches of the movement—animosity that still exists today. In the heat of the controversy, direct-action old-growth defenders threw a cream pie in the face of a longtime activist who supported the land exchange. To see such resources spent between activists, when they might be spared and used on common foes, raises questions as to how the movement can better unify its objectives and clarify intended outcomes.

In some cases, activists are promoting better communication between groups to alleviate tensions that occur when compromise is on the table and to better unify the entire movement in service of more effective negotiation. In 2002, the Northwest Old Growth Campaign developed a legislative proposal to permanently protect remaining old-growth stands in federal forests west of the Cascades. Unfortunately, the legislation was redrafted by sponsoring politicians to include the release of timber sales on the eastside. Environmentalists quickly realized the negative implications for eastside forests and the conservationists defending them, and shut down the bill. Today, westside groups in the Old Growth Campaign are making concerted efforts to keep open dialogues with eastside groups about cooperative strategies and issues of mutual concern.

In today's movement, there are more specific defenders (local groups) for Washington's wild areas than ever before, making it difficult to negotiate through compromise without stepping on the toes of colleagues. In campaigns of the past, organizing resources were limited and lands were forfeited in hopes they would be protected by future generations. That future seems to have arrived, like the close of the frontier, and there may be limited chances tomorrow to protect what remains today.

A kind of environmental accountability is increasingly recognized as a component of a successful conservation campaign, whether it assesses the unseen trade-offs of resources around the world or the forest next door. It is doubtful that there will ever be enough pieces of the conservation pie, but by striving to better unify the voice of the movement through substantial communication, activists will improve internal relations and start to tear down the walls that prevent effective cooperation. To do this without backing away from the challenges of negotiating bold, proactive campaigns is a test to which the movement must apply its renowned determination.

Quiet Threats and Overlooked Opportunities

With an overwhelming amount of organizing capability spent on forest issues, it is easy to forget that many of Washington's other ecosystems face
great peril. The most endangered ecosystems in Washington include the
Palouse grasslands, Puget Lowlands (including rare Puget prairies), and
ungrazed sagebrush steppe.[38] Activists struggling to save and regenerate
these remnant wild areas face ecological crises, and conservation success
or failure could determine the fate of an entire native ecotype. Campaigns
to secure private lowlands through conservation easements or to protect
fragile desert landscapes by excluding livestock (see chapters 13 and 14)
are in many ways on the front lines of an uphill ecological struggle that
can be overshadowed within the larger movement for wildlands.

Additionally, there appear to be several other niches in conservation
coverage yet to be filled within Washington. These include lands managed
by the Bureau of Land Management and the Department of Defense. Of
all the western states where the Bureau of Land Management (BLM) manages public lands, the state of Washington has the least land under BLM
jurisdiction. There are less than 400,000 acres, most of which are scattered
across eastern Washington in a complicated and inefficient checkerboard
system. Outstanding examples of ancient pine forests, scablands, shrub-
steppe, Palouse grasslands, and riparian zones are included in the roadless
areas managed by the BLM, including Chopaka Mountain and Escure Ranch/
Rock Creek.

Washington's BLM lands are under the direction of the Oregon BLM,
whose management strategies have recently become more progressive. By
consolidating its holdings and eliminating checkerboard layouts, the BLM
is allowing for easier and more effective management of the lands. This
new policy has given citizens the opportunity to fill critical gaps in wilderness designation. However, a decision by Secretary of the Interior Gale
Norton in 2003 to eliminate the agency's wilderness study area policy leaves
these few roadless BLM areas vulnerable to agency actions taken without
due consideration of wildlands values.

Another major category of federal lands in Washington is Department
of Defense (DOD) lands, which hold some of the best opportunities for
preserving large tracts of semipristine and under-represented ecosystems.
The state's important military installations include the Yakima Training Center
(adjacent to the Hanford Nuclear Reservation), Fort Lewis Military Base
(in south Puget Sound), and the Naval Submarine Base in Bangor (along
Hood Canal). Each base includes ecosystems that are lacking in current
protective designations. The Yakima Training Center has untouched parcels of shrub-steppe lands that have never been grazed, and Fort Lewis

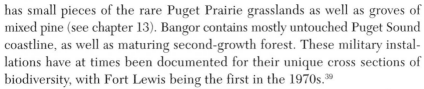

has small pieces of the rare Puget Prairie grasslands as well as groves of mixed pine (see chapter 13). Bangor contains mostly untouched Puget Sound coastline, as well as maturing second-growth forest. These military installations have at times been documented for their unique cross sections of biodiversity, with Fort Lewis being the first in the 1970s.[39]

Recently, Congress has threatened the conservation initiatives of some military installations by giving serious consideration to legislation that could exempt the DOD from the requirements of major environmental laws such as the Endangered Species Act, Marine Mammal Protection Act, Clean Air Act, and the Superfund law governing toxic waste sites. Regional and national groups could do more to advocate for the preservation of rare ecosystems on military bases in Washington, through local outreach and passage of national conservation legislation for military lands.

Partisanship and the Wild

In the last twenty or so years, the problem of political partisanship concerning environmental issues (particularly wildlands) has grown considerably worse. During this time period, the great bipartisan support that helped to create the 1984 and 1988 Washington wilderness acts (for national forests and national parks, respectively) all but collapsed. With the Republican Party's growing alignment with the wise-use movement and many natural resource–based industries, the GOP has earned itself the reputation of being anti-environmental. Also, some organizations have stopped supporting some of the few remaining environmentally friendly Republicans in a short-term political strategy to gain influence and stability in both Congress and the White House.

The (national) Sierra Club has been targeted by some conservationists as well as many pro-environment Republicans as being too closely aligned with the national Democratic Party. Indeed, in the last ten years, the organization has made efforts to endorse Democratic candidates with weaker environmental voting records than their Republican opponents (sometimes even endorsing Democratic candidates with no voting records against Republicans with strong ones).[40] Within the wildlands movement, the issue is divisive. The Sierra Club remains one of few organizations that has the ability to endorse candidates, and no matter who they choose to support, some people will always disagree. However, many activists have resigned themselves to believing that without a Democratically controlled Congress or White House, there will be dramatic rollbacks in environmental protection including wilderness proposals and endangered species protection.

The strongest opposing viewpoint can be found in an organization called Republicans for Environmental Protection (REP America). REP America has decided to initiate a nationwide grassroots campaign to end the hostility towards environmental issues by those in their party (whether they are elected Republicans or national figures who identify themselves as such). REP America has continued to argue that the policies of the Republican Party should reflect those of historic environmental champions like Theodore Roosevelt and Richard Nixon. By forming their own political action committee, they hope to give campaign contributions to pro-environment candidates across America who have been opposed by organizations like the Sierra Club in their political strategies.

Jim DiPeso serves as one of REP America's Washington State representatives as well as serving as the group's national policy director. DiPeso has for the most part been openly received by Washington's wildlands movement (including local Sierra Club chapters), however he and his organization remain the only outlet for encouraging the regeneration of bipartisan support for environmental and wildlands causes in Washington State. Other activists have made attempts to play the role that DiPeso has, such as Mitch Friedman of the Northwest Ecosystem Alliance, but even Friedman has publicly admitted frustration and even bitterness about the slow going when it came to getting Republican support for his organization's projects.

Perhaps the greatest significance of the partisanship issue is that average Republicans have not been able to influence the party's national and regional policies. For example, polls conducted by the Mellman polling group showed that a majority of Republicans and conservatives supported the Roadless Area Conservation Rule (President Clinton's roadless initiative).[41] Yet the majority of western governors challenging the implementation of the Roadless Rule in court were Republicans. A top-down policy-making structure (not unique to the Republican Party by any means) gives greater influence to national wise-use groups and industries opposed to environmental protection, even though the party should be focused on what the majority of its followers want. Washington State's REP America chapter has continued to work with the traditional grassroots model to spread its message. One of its biggest successes was a meeting with state Republican Party chair Chris Vance in 2001, when REP America leaders and representatives were able to get an agreement that, in Washington State, the party would no longer endorse anti-environmental messages by those running for state offices.[42]

Washington's citizen conservation movement now has two models to consider for gaining political power to move important legislation through the state and federal legislative bodies. The first is the model of securing an environmental majority in Congress and in the state legislature, composed mainly of Democrats, as a short-term solution to the issue of overcoming

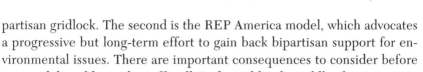

partisan gridlock. The second is the REP America model, which advocates a progressive but long-term effort to gain back bipartisan support for environmental issues. There are important consequences to consider before any model could ever be "officially" adopted by the wildlands movement; however, regardless of political affiliation, emerging activists should actively voice their concerns on the issue to ensure that real reforms and progress can be made.

Diversity: Gender, Race, Age

An initial look at Washington State's conservation movement reveals a considerable, if still unequal, balance of gender. Women direct and staff many important groups in the state and have played a historic role as advocates for wildlands protection. None would accuse the movement of a severe gender bias, although there are striking parallels between perceptions of pioneer women activists and women currently in the movement. In the 1940s, Polly Dyer was often the only woman present at hearings and public meetings on the Olympic Peninsula concerning land management (see her interview in chapter 7). Acknowledging this, she humbly claims that her recognition as a conservation leader was possibly due in part to her discreteness. From her recollection, they probably noticed her hat sticking out in the crowd.[43]

Several of today's women leaders echo these sentiments and, save for the hat, often find themselves sticking out in the conservationist crowd. This seems especially true for councils and meetings of consequence, when important decisions are made, policy or legislation is drafted, or key politicians are conferred with. Dyer admonishes young activists to "start with the scutt work," the mailings, fliers, and phone banks essential to any grassroots campaign. A high ratio of women can be found reinforcing these organizational mainstays today: calling, canvassing, mailing, note taking, organizing agendas for meetings and conference calls, editing newsletters, and the like. New activists of any gender will most likely get their foot in the door this way. But for women activists with longstanding track records, only a handful can be found at power lunches, political shoptalks, or jocular postmeeting barstool congregations. As the gender gap within the movement grows smaller, will certain stereotypes be doomed to repetition? Perhaps progress rests as much on women striving to break away from traditional molds and through the "green ceiling" as it does on men consciously working to tone down the "cowboy mentality."

Washington's movement for wildlands protection has at least made progress in escaping from the "good ol' boys' network within the old wilderness movement"[44] and has almost equal representation of men and women. But critics within and outside of the movement claim that there has been a failure to reconcile the lack of ethnic and racial diversity within its ranks.

When thinking from a historical context, it isn't surprising that the movement presents a predominantly white face. Although society has made some progress in physically and socially integrating people of all races and ethnicities, America has a lamentable history of racism, the evidence of which still exists within its social structure. The follies of past and present separatism have taken their toll: the level of involvement among minority races in the movement to protect public wildlands is visibly minimal. The conservation movement began in a different age, when the term "politically correct" was not yet a cliché or even a catchphrase, and the civil rights movement was in its infancy. In many places races were still separated not only by culture and history, but also by schools, restaurants, drinking fountains, and the like. The conservation movement was spawned from the efforts of recreational clubs and groups with virtually all-white memberships. Since then, very little has been done to engage with communities that have not traditionally been involved in the movement or that looked to wild places as a source of recreation.

Sharon Parker, diversity consultant and a council member of the Wilderness Society, gave a keynote presentation at the North American Wilderness Conference in 2002.[45] In her speech, Parker described the wilderness movement as "monocultural." Her critique emphasized the necessity of racially diversifying the movement, not only for the sake of social justice, but also as a strategically imperative tactic in keeping the movement alive and healthy. To thrive, the wildlands preservation movement must reflect the diversity of the population as a whole. Parker referred to a few historical circumstances wherein diverse factions of support (or lack thereof) made all the difference. For example, she maintained that if an attempt had been made from the beginning to include women of color in the Equal Rights Movement, the Equal Rights Amendment (ERA) would have had a better chance of being ratified by the necessary thirty-eight states in 1982. Southern states were a big reason for the nonratification of the ERA, Parker says, and it was in those same states that African-American and Native American women had the most to gain. Had they been organized early in the campaign, they could have made a great difference. She also pointed out that Bill Clinton's appeals to African-American voters won him the 1992 presidential election. Said Parker, "These are just a few examples of the ways in which our individual and societal prejudices can cripple us, or advance us, as a nation."

Without the support of diverse sectors of society, the wilderness movement could ultimately flounder. One cost of ignoring diversity is the risk of losing potentially critical votes for wilderness by ignoring members of the Black Congressional Caucus, the Latino Congressional Caucus, or the Women's Congressional Caucus until it is too late to secure their votes. Sharon Parker asked her audience, "Do you really want to risk losing wilderness and wildlands, clean air, water, and land because the environmental movement dried up and blew away like topsoil in a drought?" This scenario certainly succeeds in rousing the concern of well-meaning activists but, as Parker contended, "Dreaming is not going to get [you to your goals] any more than you can create and sustain a diverse environmental movement by ignoring the work you have to do on diversity."

How are the efforts of organizations lacking? As Parker aptly put it, "When you can't find the time to study how diversity impacts your work and then plan to address it, you are ignoring the work you have to do. When you can't find the budget dollars to create and sustain programs that will ensure diversity is part of your core work, you are ignoring the work you have to do. When you placate yourself with excuses, you are . . . ignoring the work you have to do on diversity." What Parker is suggesting is that fundamental changes must be wrought within the movement, right down to its very infrastructure. Organizations waste a great deal of time wondering why there are so few people of color involved in the movement when they should be devoting time, money, and, most of all, making a commitment to the goal of ethnic and racial inclusiveness. In order to accomplish this goal, expectations within the movement for its own diversification must be significantly broadened.

Even the outdoor industry has caught on to the need to diversify its clientele. In 1994 the Sporting Goods Manufacturers Association created the Working Group on Diversity: "For the outdoor industry to continue to prosper, we need to broaden the spectrum of those who participate and assume leadership roles in the industry. The first step is to think more broadly and to actively seek out different viewpoints and experiences in order to enrich the environment in which each of us operates."[46] The movement to protect wildlands would be wise to follow suit, exploring reasons, methods, and goals for diversification.

Nearly every American is a potential wildlands advocate, as long as the connections between clean water, clean air, healthful plants and animals, recreation, spiritual opportunities, and other important features of wild places are realized by all. For instance, outreach to urban advocates who recognize that environmental quality in the city is augmented by healthy ecosystems in the countryside can be a good way to bring diverse voices into the fold. There are, of course, many other strategies that can be employed but today's environmental organizations must first see the importance of diversity to their missions in order to commit resources to such strategies.

The movement's future success also depends on young people who know and cherish wildlands. As seen in the interviews with several generations of Washington's influential and committed wildlands advocates (chapters 7 and 9), one of the strongest patterns cutting across the activists' lives is that they all had formative childhood experiences in wild places. As the population of Washington diversifies, it is crucial that children from all backgrounds be given the opportunity to experience the outdoors. The late Ira Spring, photographer and wilderness advocate, was deeply concerned that the variety of activities and technologies available to kids is distracting them from experiencing the outdoors and becoming green-bonded. "Green-bonding is what a person feels as one walks through a forest of ancient trees, finds oneself in a field of wildflowers, takes a dip in a mountain lake, stands at the foot of a waterfall, stops for a dramatic view, or meets the physical challenge of a trail or climbing a mountain," Spring told the room of eager, youthful faces in a lecture to our class a few months before he passed away.[47] We knew very well the feeling he spoke of; as young proponents of wildness, we could all describe personal green-bonding experiences that had prompted us to become active.

Most conservation groups find it outside of their means or goals to sponsor field trips or other activities, but a few organizations can be applauded for their roles in promoting green-bonding and the involvement of youth. The Seattle-based Washington Wilderness Coalition, for instance, partnered up with the Youth Volunteer Corps in 1997 to form the Wilderness Volunteer Corps, "an innovative effort to combine service learning, outdoor education, and leadership development."[48] Groups of ten teenagers of different classes, races, and cultures participate in two weeks of environmental education, trail work, and wildland restoration projects for the Forest Service, ending with a week of backpacking in the wilderness. In the year following completion of the summer program, the students demonstrate their leadership skills by creating service projects that they carry out in their communities. One of this book's authors can sincerely speak for the success of such a program in instilling a penchant for activism among its students: she ventured into her first old-growth forest ever as a fifteen-year-old participant in the inaugural run of the Wilderness Volunteer Corps in 1997, and her experience of being immersed in the wilderness for weeks and learning to live in the woods without trepidation has stayed with her.

Perhaps the most important way to encourage young people to become involved is to offer them proactive opportunities to make change. Young folks want to be active, and they want to be heard. The more accessible and engaging campaigns can be, maintaining a sense of fun and passion over the ominous dread so common in today's movement, the better the chances of catching the next wave of future activists. As political scientist Robert Putnam recommends, "What we need is not civic broccoli—good for you but unappealing—but an updated version of Scouting's ingenious combination of values and fun."[49]

 ## WILD TIMES

If the conservation community in Washington State were analogous to a biological community, it would have its own distinct ecology. The broad membership base for environmental activism can be imagined as soil, rich with viable seeds and nourishing the entire community. Volunteer outreach organizers percolate like water through this layer, supplying nutrients to revitalize the soil and allowing seeds to sprout. Over time, this grassroots layer has grown and been enriched with popular and financial support that has effected change and helped define what the movement is today, for better and worse.

Ancient trees watch over the terrain, their wisdom and experience providing both cover and competition for younger communities. The value of this grove is undisputed, though its legacy depends on the succession of the plants below. This understory, or next generation of activists, is a community of small trees and shrubs, borne of seeds spread from an extended range. The landscape upon which the biological community grows is subject to occasional disturbance, such as fire. Sometimes burning briefly and at other times with intensity, the forces of fire translate into political, social, and economic disturbances that change and renew the landscape. Ancient trees still stand, weathered a bit by such events, and grass regrows vigorously from its steadfast roots. The shrub layer is transformed, some groups perishing while others strive to assert their place among the dominant species. As a natural observer, one should be wary of ever viewing the activist landscape as existing in a "climax" state. Surely, without internal evolution and external disturbance, the movement would stagnate.

The survival and the success of the wildlands movement depend upon its ability to embrace dynamic social change and to adapt to it. It is important to acknowledge the changing roles that citizen activists play within the movement today and how they are influenced by such realities as the rise in professionalism over volunteerism and current methods of communication and grassroots organizing. The limited amount of inclusion and outreach to diverse ethnic and racial populations, as well as the issue of gender equality, are also worthy of attention from the movement as a whole.

By addressing the components of this "social ecology," the conservation community increases its potential for effective advocacy and protection of Washington's wildness.

Similar to the wild lands and processes they look out for, the movement has an amazing adaptability and ability to persevere over time. Shortly before David Brower died in 2000, he gave an interview on the role of activism and activists in the wilderness movement. The last question put to him was, "Any final words of advice?" to which he simply but eloquently replied, "Persevere . . . that's where it's at."[50]

PART III

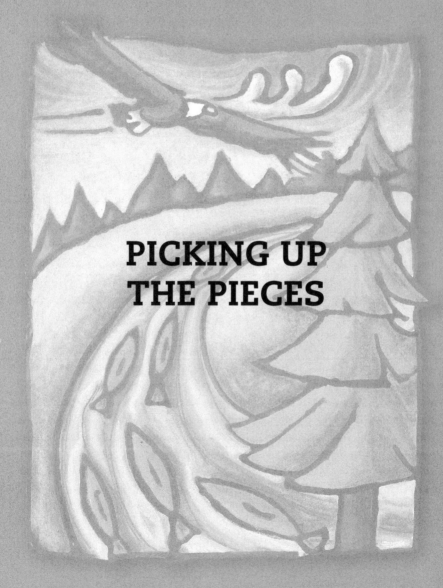

PICKING UP
THE PIECES

CHAPTER 11

Envisioning a Wild Future

◆ *Anthony Bush, Richard Darnell, and Ellen Trescott* ◆

In a Washington computer-mapping lab, where professional activists scientifically analyze the landscape using sophisticated technology, an impressive stack of maps lies on a table in the center of the lab, the products of huge and complex spatial data sets put together with cutting-edge analysis. At the bottom of this pile is an ordinary topographic map with the story of someone's bold vision. It shows the wildlands surrounding the lab, with hand-drawn lines and penned words carefully identifying the landscape. Looking out of the window, a staff member points to a forested peak and back to the map. A dotted line encircles the area, outlining the envisioned boundaries of a future wilderness area with a carefully chosen name. The map shows many other wilderness proposals, along with envisioned road closures, connective corridors, and dismantled remnants of old mining operations. When asked about the significance of this rather simple yet inspiring map, the activist replies, "It's nothing important; just something we like to think about in our spare time."

Assuredly there are counterparts to this private map for many forests, sagebrush seas, and even the populated lowlands. The persistence and passion of most activists are fueled by their larger visions for the lands and waters they love. A wild future relies on citizens' capacities for thinking big, while at the same time seeing each single action as one piece of a larger puzzle, laying the groundwork for future generations to build upon, and bringing seemingly impossible long-range visions that much closer to reality.

This chapter describes citizens' long-range visions for Washington's wild-lands. The following three chapters tell stories of unique places around the state, the citizens working to protect them, and the long-range visions that motivate them to work so hard to protect the places that they know and love. By keeping the big picture in mind as you read those stories, it will become apparent that the citizen conservation movement is working on many fronts to realize its bold visions for a wild Washington.

 ## THE BIG PICTURE

The realization of a wild future starts with a dream for the land itself. Some look beyond the realm of what seems "practical," with goals that encompass vast tracts of protected land supporting a plethora of native species. Such thinking is true to the earliest ideals of visionaries like George Catlin, who in 1832 proposed a park stretching from Canada to Mexico to protect the Great Plains and its Native peoples. Today, scientific knowledge has informed and influenced the design and ecological importance of these visions. The advancing field of conservation biology, among other scientific disciplines, has shown the need for planning on a large scale that encompasses extensive landscapes and regions.

Many wild habitats in Washington have been heavily fragmented, and scientists point out the need to protect not only core wild areas, but also corridors to connect them and buffer zones to surround them. Protected wilderness cores can support wide-ranging species like large carnivores. But the protected corridors are necessary to connect these cores and to provide avenues for migration and dispersal of species. The value of human-managed natural areas that border wildlands is also increasingly being recognized, as suburban development encroaches upon farms and forests. Bold ambitions to protect this range of interconnecting habitats are essential for two reasons: the everyday successes of the conservation movement can be diminished without overall goals that inspire, and ultimately, safeguarding biodiversity requires this scale of foresight.

In 1991, former Earth First! leader Dave Foreman and conservation biologist Michael Soulé formed what is now called the Wildlands Project. The project asserts that large swaths of wildland are necessary for the preservation of biological diversity. The long-term wilderness recovery strategy promoted by the project contains a network of connected reserves across the North American continent. Washington State is home to three of these proposed reserves, including the Rainforest-to-Rockies and Yellowstone-to-Yukon initiatives, and the Central Cascades Wildlands Restoration and Protection Project.[1] Though each of these initiatives is unique, each has in common Wildlands Project goals, including the protection of wild cores like wilderness, which can be connected by habitat corridors. Surrounding the cores and corridors would be wilderness recovery areas or habitat "buffers" and compatible use areas for forestry, grazing, and "active" recreation.

The Wildlands Project differs from traditional wilderness preservation campaigns in its ambitious scope, and the attainment of its goals will be a long process. Several groups in Washington are contributing to the extensive research and planning required by such a large proposal, including the Wilderness Society, the Central Cascades Alliance, and the Northwest Ecosystem Alliance. As impractical as the project's goals may seem, their implication for the future is far reaching. Wilderness Society president Bill Meadows sits on the board of directors for the Wildlands Project. He says, "I am aware of the debate between vision and pragmatism, but if we don't have a vision, we won't get the practical results we deserve. They [the Wildlands Project] have a vision that inspires all of us—the grassroots groups and the big national groups like the Wilderness Society."[2]

Bold models like this help inspire activists of the future, which can be seen in an example from Washington's past. In 1937, a committee of the National Park Service, led by Mount Rainier National Park superintendent Owen Tomlinson, recommended a national park along the mountain peaks of the Cascade volcanoes. What became known as the Ice Peaks proposal contained roughly 5,000 square miles, spanning Washington State from north to south (map 6.1). Ice Peaks, originally called "High Cascades," was conceptualized as a "super park . . . [that] will outrank in its scenic, recreational, and wildlife values, any existing national park and any other possibility for such a park within the United States." Language that was used to describe this vision is notable: "Establishment of this area as one superb park is an inspiring project to fire the imagination . . . worthy of the Nation's efforts."[3] The proposal received much criticism, even from established conservation groups like the Wilderness Society, who sought more protective designations similar to today's wilderness areas. The park never came to fruition, but in retrospect, it offered a baseline for long-term motivation toward a larger goal.

Cores and Corridors

The map of Washington's wild and roadless lands in the color insert shows that there is significant potential for expansion, connection, and buffering of existing protected areas. The vision of the Ice Peaks proposal has largely been achieved in the northern Cascades through protective designations like wilderness and national parks that have secured large wild cores, the likes of which activists in other parts of the state are still working to establish. Many ascribe to models like the Wildlands Project and promote the establishment of corridors to connect these wild mountain cores and

to radiate out from them. For example, David Jennings, board chairman of the Gifford Pinchot Task Force, promotes a vision for Washington's southern Cascades that mixes wilderness areas, protected corridors, managed reserves, and additions to currently protected areas. Together these lands create a contiguous corridor from the Columbia River to Mount Rainier, at the northern end of the Gifford Pinchot. The proposal also addresses the largest remaining gap in achieving the Ice Peaks vision: a corridor in the Gifford Pinchot National Forest.

Other campaigns for habitat corridors are proliferating and the sheer number of inspiring examples illustrates a pattern in conservation visions for Washington. Beginning in the northwestern Cascades, the Mount Baker Wild! group in Bellingham is leading the North Cascades Corridor Project. Activist Ken Wilcox describes it this way: "The Chuckanuts are a range of coastal hills south of Bellingham . . . really the only place where you have foothills of the Cascades extending all the way to salt water. Most of it has been logged over at least once . . . but it still has conservation value in a larger context. When you start looking at landscape-level ecosystems, I think there are opportunities to do something in this corridor that you can't find elsewhere around the inland sea."[4] Also in this region, conservation groups like the North Cascades Conservation Council and the Northwest Ecosystem Alliance are working for the protection of transborder wildlife and forests on both sides of the border.

Moving southward, Jasmine Minbashian, director of the Northwest Old Growth Campaign, describes her vision of renewed corridors of ancient forest stretching through the state. She stands candidly in front of a group of rural stakeholders, holding a map of the fragmented old-growth forests of western Washington. With a modest but ardent smile, she sweeps her hand from the northern through the southern Cascades, and northwest to the Olympic Peninsula. Through protection and regeneration, Minbashian imagines biologically rich, connective forest linking the Cascades from Canada to the Columbia and spanning northwest over Interstate 5 to the Olympic Peninsula and the Pacific. Also within the Cascades, groups like Northwest Ecosystem Alliance and the Cascades Conservation Partnership, are researching and promoting a unique type of wildlife corridor. To connect the protected cores that are bisected by Interstate 90, they envision a "wildlife underpass," which would encourage a different type of traffic to pass below the busy highway. The Partnership spent three years raising almost $16 million from thousands of private donors, and leveraging that into over $50 million more from government funds in order to protect over 35,000 acres of habitat linking the North and Central Cascades of Washington across the I-90 corridor. Now the groups are working with the Washington Department of Transportation to assure that three bridges are constructed as part of an I-90 improvement project, in such a way that wildlife could pass safely beneath, following the habitat corridors.

Activists east of the Cascades look to a future of protection for the "sagebrush sea," flowing from the mountains to the Columbia River and beyond. Long-range goals include assimilating cleaned-up areas at Hanford into the new Hanford Reach National Monument and acquiring lands within and around the Yakima Training Center as they become available. If both are possible, connective lands running from Hanford through the protected Yakima Valley and up Umtanum Ridge into the Cascades could create the largest wildlife corridor in Washington. In the northeastern Cascades, local activist Mark Skatrud paints a visual picture of a corridor extending from the Pasayten Wilderness to unprotected lands eastward. It could potentially connect lynx and grizzly habitat from the Cascades in the United States and Canada to the Kettle and Selkirk ranges in the foothills of the Rocky Mountains.

Buffers and Compatible Uses

The protection of rural lands like farms and "working forests," what the Wildlands Project calls compatible-use areas, becomes ever more important as human development continues to sprawl across Washington. The practical difficulty of protecting critical wildlife habitat that may overlap with human habitation is a challenge now and for generations to come.

Inspiring visions for the management of buffer lands are sometimes held by those who live within them. In the rural town of Packwood south of Mount Rainier National Park, local resident John Squires delivers a handwritten speech to a roomful of rural community members and environmentalists. Squires's family history goes back for generations in the Cowlitz Valley. Bearded, with a wiry build, he is rugged in appearance yet has a friendly attitude. Squires is humble but has a gleam in his eye as he speaks with emotion about his vision for the future of the community and surrounding forest in one hundred years: "I dream of a day when a variety of products will be flowing from the forest in a restrained, environmentally neutral manner . . . . I envision science and Native American traditions coming to the same conclusions and returning fire to the berry fields . . . . I dream that instead of just relying on timber extraction our economy will be diversified . . . . But mostly I just dream of the children of Packwood. I dream that they will grow up as I did, playing amongst 200- to 300-foot firs . . . next to streams teeming with thousands of salmon."[5] The speech is met with a standing ovation, environmental activists and long-time loggers both smiling in sincere agreement. If little else keeps them in the same room, perhaps the future is common ground enough.

Later, Squires's wife and his young daughter, Brook, visit the meeting.

They drive the family's pick-up truck, which Squires uses in his own way to "diversify" his local economy and ecology. He salvages firewood from the national forest to sell at Mount Rainier and can, in certain seasons, be found transporting juvenile salmon to habitat above the upper dam on the Cowlitz River.

PIECES OF THE PUZZLE

Through new and existing legislation and policy, more and more cores, corridors, and buffers are being designated across the landscape, extending from the mountains into the lowlands and the sea. Many conservationists hope that the vision of a wildlands mosaic can be achieved by protecting and enhancing the remaining pieces through an array of designations.

Defending the Cores

With more than 4 million acres in the state designated as wilderness, the National Wilderness Preservation System has definitely contributed to preserving Washington's wild cores. The Forest Service has identified another 2 million acres of roadless areas throughout the state.[6] Additionally, conservationists recognize more than 1 million uninventoried roadless areas. The Forest Service's roadless policy currently regulates only inventoried roadless areas, but it temporarily gives protection for many lands with potential for inclusion in the wilderness preservation system. Amy Schlachtenhaufen, a representative of the Wilderness Society in Washington State says, "The most important essence of the roadless policy is that it creates incredible core areas of habitat for a lot of the large species that we know require a lot more than small islands of wilderness. The other major thing is that by its very nature it protects a lot of low-elevation forest which did not get protected in the history of wilderness to date."[7]

The existence of remaining roadless areas has spurred the conservation movement into developing new wilderness proposals. From the Selkirk range in northeast Washington to the Dark Divide in the Gifford Pinchot National Forest, conservation groups are proposing roadless areas for protection as wilderness. With congressional leadership from Senator Patty Murray and others in the Washington delegation, wilderness will continue to be part of Washington's future.

However, some groups have been working for specific roadless lands to become wilderness areas for a quarter century or longer. Tim Coleman of the Kettle Range Conservation Group remains positive but also sees a certain futility in the constant uphill political struggle. He is optimistic about future possibilities for a national wilderness bill, a larger long-term strategy that could resolve regional conflicts through national legislation. This type of broad wilderness campaign will require significant time and effort. As a first step, Senator Maria Cantwell (D-WA, along with Senator John Warner, R-VA) and Congressman Jay Inslee (D-WA, along with Congressman Sherwood Boehlert, R-NY) have introduced legislation that offers basic protection for inventoried Forest Service roadless areas. While not as secure as the Holy Grail of wilderness designation, the Roadless Area Conservation Act proposes to safeguard 59 million roadless acres nationwide for future wilderness designation.

Creating Corridors

To connect these wild cores in the future, corridors are essential. Rivers are unique because they travel between federal, state, and private lands. Legislative protection under the federal Wild and Scenic Rivers Act provides the flexibility to traverse such borders and can protect critical wildlife corridors. At this time, only three segments of protected rivers are designated in Washington. With the ever-increasing threats to our native salmon and aquatic habitat, conservationists are looking to protect river systems. Organizations like the Pacific Rivers Council and Olympic Park Associates are currently considering Wild and Scenic proposals, which include the Lower Graywolf River on the Olympic Peninsula. With an abundance of rivers in the state, the Wild and Scenic Rivers Act can be better utilized in the future to protect water quality and contiguous wildlife corridors. To supplement protected river corridors, terrestrial wildlife corridors are also needed to link diverse habitats and strengthen the viability of wild species.

Recovering the Fringe

To enhance the compatibility between humans and wild landscapes, it will be necessary to allow managed lands surrounding wilderness cores to regenerate. These buffer lands, previously impacted by human forces, are in need of protective designations that allow wildness to restore itself. Respected conservation biologist Reed Noss has a vision of designated wilderness recovery areas, which he has described in many of his publications.[8] These lands, often adjacent to wilderness areas, have been impacted by logging, mining, and grazing, and could be protected in wilderness recovery status, complementing wilderness designations. National bills to end commercial logging and grazing on federal lands are attempting to create unprecedented buffer lands surrounding wild cores.

In 2003, a new organization, the Evergreen Forest Trust, initiated a novel approach to conservation in eastern King County, where suburban Seattle sprawl has encroached upon nearly 50 percent of the county's forests since 1973.[9] The trust planned to buy the Snoqualmie tree farm from Weyerhaeuser Timber Company with specially approved bonds. The goal was to protect 104,000 acres of forest from development by logging portions of the land over the next fifty years. About 20 percent of the forest would be protected from extraction through conservation easements. Although some see this type of transaction as more of a conservation compromise, maintaining this buffer zone as a working forest is much more wildlife-compatible than the alternative of suburban development. Although the attempted purchase failed to go through because of time constraints, government representatives approved the bond mechanism for acquisitions in the future, and this example could become a trailblazer for future protection of compatible-use areas.

Representing Biodiversity

Although the model of cores, corridors, and buffer lands can protect viable populations and ecological and evolutionary processes, it does not necessarily ensure representation of the broad spectrum of natural communities (see "Assessing Washington's Wildness" in chapter 3). Endangered ecosystems throughout Washington require new measures to preserve these remnant pieces of the puzzle.

Some of the last intact shrub-steppe ecosystems in Washington are being proposed for protection and regeneration through a 2003 citizen initiative to amend public grazing laws by banning livestock on state lands.[10] As will be described in chapter 14, removing livestock from this fragile ecosystem would give more protection to many threatened species. Similarly, the Northwest Old Growth Campaign is contemplating a national bill to protect the last stands of old growth in Washington from future timber harvest. As opposed to protecting one species, such as the spotted owl, this measure would protect a variety of lesser-known species of ecological significance.

To safeguard submerged and endangered ecosystems in the coastal waters and Puget Sound, the Ocean Wilderness Network is campaigning for a series of connected marine reserves or "ocean wilderness areas," from Alaska to northern California. As discussed in chapter 13, such reserves greatly improve the health of marine habitat and sensitive wildlife.

Many of these ecotypes would fall under the protection of the envisioned national endangered ecosystems bill, which many see as a needed protection above and beyond the Endangered Species Act. As continued urban development and resource extraction in Washington persist, conservationists will seek to protect the wild integrity of all regions of the state through new and existing legislation and policy.

Reinstating Ecological Processes

Many conservationists hope for future wildlands management that is designed to reinstate ecological processes that historically have been severely suppressed by human activities. Activists are currently working with agency representatives, taking preliminary steps on this challenging path. Discussed below are three important ecological processes that greatly affect the ability of Washington to naturally regenerate its wild character: a complete food web with top carnivores, free-flowing rivers, and fires regularly rejuvenating large wild areas.

Species Reintroduction

For fully functioning ecological processes to occur in a landscape, a diverse array of species is needed, from small parasites in the soil to the large, top carnivores. Certain keystone and umbrella species are needed for the rest of the ecological community to survive and for the food chain to be complete. Keystone species are those that affect ecosystem function in a unique way that is disproportionate to their numerical abundance. The extirpation (local extinction) of keystone species often triggers other extirpations and significant changes or loss of habitats. Species that generally cover large and ecologically diverse areas in their daily or seasonal movements are called umbrella species because protection of enough habitat to assure a viable population of these organisms would also provide habitat and resources for many other species with more restricted ranges.

Many umbrella species like top carnivores have been eradicated due to fear and commerce. Hardest hit in this state have been the wolf, wolverine, cougar, grizzly bear, fisher, and lynx. Today's domesticated livestock are also indirectly responsible for the low numbers of top carnivores. Many ranchers will shoot a predator that hunts their docile, defenseless animals, because the wild animal is literally eating their livelihood. The predator is not aware of the purpose of artificial boundaries such as fences. The animal sees easy meals and cannot be blamed for humans replacing wild game with domesticated animals and open territory with fragmented, fenced lands.

In Washington, long-ranging thinkers such as volunteer activists David Knibb and Rick McGuire, along with groups such as Northwest Ecosystem Alliance and the Sierra Club, are envisioning the reintroduction of the grizzly to the North Cascades. The latest estimate is that there are ten to twenty resident grizzlies in the Washington Cascades, which is a dangerously low population for the area. The North Cascades have historically been home to strong resident bear populations and are currently capable of harboring 200 to 400 grizzly bears.[11] With numbers as low as ten to twenty, the gene pool is not large enough to sustain a resident population. These bears are doomed to extirpation unless the law that is intended to protect them is fully enforced. The grizzly bear was listed as threatened under the Endangered Species Act in 1975, yet they are still not being fully protected.

In 1982, six national recovery zones were proposed for the recuperation of the grizzly. In Washington State, the North Cascades Grizzly Bear Recovery Zone was later established as part of this proposal. This piece of federal land is one of the biggest contiguous blocks of land left for grizzlies to inhabit in the lower forty-eight states, containing 9,565 square miles of diverse grizzly bear habitat. One important aspect of the recovery zone is that no new trails or roads can be created, keeping many people out of this critical habitat. The North Cascades National Park Service Complex and the majority of the Mount Baker–Snoqualmie, Wenatchee, and Okanogan National Forests fall within the recovery zone, which also includes additional federal, state, and private areas.

The last grizzly killed in the North Cascades was in Fisher Creek in 1967. Over time, it seems that some have managed to migrate south from Canadian populations. Rick McGuire and Jack Wheeler sighted a grizzly bear in the Pratt watershed of the central Cascades in 1998. There have been numerous confirmed and unconfirmed sightings throughout the North Cascades, and evidence of one grizzly near Mount Rainier in the mid-1990s. Without grizzlies how can we call the North Cascades truly wild?

Natural Water Flow
Humans have built many barriers to alter the flow of water across the earth. More than 85 percent of the inland waterways within the continental United States are now artificially controlled.[12] Citizens of Washington are looking to remove key dams, dikes, and levees. Many activists have the grand vision of returning the world's largest salmon nursery, the Columbia and Snake Rivers, closer to their natural state by breaching four dams on the Snake. These dams block fish passage and are posing a great risk to the health of the watershed and those who rely on it.

Between 1955 and 1975 the Army Corps of Engineers built Ice Harbor Dam, Lower Monumental Dam, Little Goose Dam, and the Lower Granite Dam on the Snake River. In the late 1970s, the Corps started to carry juvenile fish around the dams in barges and trucks. After more than twenty years of this practice, salmon and steelhead populations on the Snake are still declining.[13] Societal benefits of the dams in the region include hydroelectric power generation, river transportation, and inexpensive irrigation to farmers. Societal costs of having the dams in place include operations and maintenance of the structures, massive salmon restoration spending, and subsidies for irrigation and transportation.[14] Biologically, the costs include the possible extinction of steelhead and all five native salmon stocks with Snake coho already extinct. The steelhead and spring/summer chinook are both listed as threatened under the Endangered Species Act. Aside from their own inherent value, these Pacific salmon also act as transporting devices for nutrients from the ocean to freshwater and terrestrial ecosystems, providing a beneficial biological ripple effect.

The main reason that the breaching of these particular dams is so necessary is clearly seen in Idaho. Just past the four dams await hundreds of river miles of excellent spawning and rearing habitat. Restoring this area through dam removal would dramatically help save wild salmon and steelhead on the Snake and in turn would potentially revitalize the weak fishing economy and at least end the salmon restoration spending. The Save Our Wild Salmon Coalition leads a large partnership that advocates returning the Snake to its natural flow. The Columbia and Snake Rivers Campaign is a national alliance committed to recovering Pacific Northwest wild salmon and the healthy rivers and habitats upon which they depend. American Rivers, Earthjustice, Friends of the Earth, Idaho Rivers United, Idaho Wildlife Federation, National Wildlife Federation, Northwest Environmental Defense Center, Salmon for All, Sierra Club, Taxpayers for Common Sense, Trout Unlimited, along with tribes, scientists, and individuals all support the breaching of the dams.

Costs of doing so would include removing earthen dams, rerouting roads, replacing power and transportation systems, and compensating irrigation farmers. A 2002 report by the prestigious think tank RAND looks at the economic and employment costs and benefits of lower Snake River dam removal and the alternative energy potential in the Northwest. The report describes ways to diversify the Northwest energy portfolio and how to prevent over-reliance on power sources that are harmful to the environment, such as natural gas and hydroelectricity. The results show that acting on this bold vision to diversify the region's energy sources can help save endangered steelhead/salmon on the Snake, stabilize energy prices, and create up to 1,500 long-term jobs while not hampering economic growth. These jobs would be created through the construction of alternative-energy generation sources, retail, recreation, and real estate. Eventually there could also be a revived fishing economy.[15]

The tribal rights and treaties that have been broken time and again could also be remedied by breaching these dams, restoring Native fishing grounds and a way of life that is essential for Native peoples. Salmon are a spiritual and cultural part of the Warm Springs, Yakama, Umatilla, and Nez Perce Indian Tribes of the Columbia/Snake River basin, not to mention a main source of nourishment. In 1855 and 1856, the U.S. government signed treaties with tribes in the watershed, guaranteeing tribes the "right of taking fish" at their usual and accustomed fishing sites in return for 40 million acres of land. The U.S. Supreme Court has ruled that this entitles the tribes to half of the Columbia Basin salmon harvest.[16] Today, salmon runs in the basin are so low that the tribes are prohibited from fishing. With the dams in place it is not likely that salmon runs will ever return to harvestable levels. This means that the federal government is vulnerable to legal action from the tribes that are affected. If harvestable numbers of fish are not recovered, federal taxpayers could be responsible to compensate the tribes for their lost right to harvest salmon.

There is strong opposition to breaching the dams, making dam removal politically unfeasible to date. Former senator Slade Gorton has said, "Those that want to make a habit of dam removal should understand this. I will never support their proposals to remove Snake or Columbia River dams. Never."[17] Perhaps the question to seriously ponder is whether the greater societal benefits that would arrive with the regeneration of wild Snake River steelhead and salmon runs are worth the disruption to the lives of some Northwest families.

Rekindling the Fire of the Future

Today, many public land managers and citizen activist groups across the state envision letting wildfires burn without human intervention. Understanding that fire is an essential part of ecological processes, especially in arid regions, they no longer believe that it should be suppressed. For example, in the dry forests east of the Cascades, pinecones from several tree species, such as the lodgepole pine, release their seeds only at high temperatures, and the entire ecosystem depends on fire.

For nearly one hundred years the Forest Service has had a policy of spending millions of dollars to aggressively battle all forest fires. This policy has helped create dangerously thick stands of similar-aged trees with extensive ground litter, posing a great fire danger. A century of suppression has also led to the unnecessary loss of human life and valuable resources.

A recent example of such a wildfire in the north central part of the state burned in the bone-dry summer of 2001. This firestorm became known as the Thirtymile Fire in Okanogan County. Many questioned the wisdom of fighting this fire at all, due to the remoteness of the area and the long-term ecological benefits of letting it burn. "This is part of the natural fire regime," said Peter Morrison, director of Pacific Biodiversity Institute. "Fires are meant to burn there."[18] Yet firefighters were sent in to toil against the blazing inferno armed with a poor battle plan; when they came out, four firefighters had died. Morrison said, "It's incredibly tragic to kill teenagers to put out a fire when there is so little at risk."[19]

In remote areas that are ecologically dependent on fires, Morrison suggests simply letting the natural process take its course. This practice, in time, would benefit the whole forest community. Forests become vulnerable when left to grow so long without a natural disturbance cycle. As seen in the aftermath of the 1988 Yellowstone fire, this process regenerates forests, but it takes some time. Yellowstone National Park officials are proud that they stood by and let the fire burn two-thirds of the park, though they endured criticism at the time. Today, the forest is growing back at an impressive rate.

Fears over safety and desires to have an aesthetically pleasing landscape have left Washington's forests in a vulnerable position. People are afraid that if fires are left to burn, their houses or public buildings could be destroyed; worse yet, a friend or family member could be lost to the raging flames. Another common belief about fire is that if left to burn, the forest will no longer be aesthetically pleasing. This may be true if the whole forest burns to the ground, but most fires help create stand diversity, with different ages and species of trees forming a visually pleasing forest. At the same time, a fire in the thick, fire-suppressed forests might be nearly impossible to control, leaving little of the forest left and destroying everything else in its path.

To take a stab at solving this dilemma, agencies and activists have proposed several models. None of the proposals simply allow these hot, damaging fires to burn uncontrolled, nor do they suggest continuing to suppress fire as an adequate solution. The Bush administration addressed this issue with the so-called Healthy Forest Initiative. The initiative advocates building additional temporary roads in order to thin dense forests to fire-safe levels. Opponents argue that this solution masks its true intent, which is to allow timber companies access to timber from public lands.

Using the same prescription for the entire state cannot address the diverse needs of each ecosystem. Each forest should be looked at on a site-by-site basis. Some forest types would suffer from the additional roads built in order to thin forests and reduce fire risk; more roads would create more stream sedimentation and forest fragmentation. The Northwest Ecosystem Alliance points to the model of community-based fire safety programs, like an exemplary one in Roslyn, Washington. The town has thinned only the forests closest to human habitation, creating safety buffers around the community to protect themselves from fire. We should encourage such creative approaches that allow ecological burning processes to return to the land.[20]

Maintaining the "Untrammeled" Wild

Another piece of the wildland puzzle is the question of access. The protected lands of Washington, and the natural heritage they possess, belong to everyone. The future undoubtedly holds challenges for managers attempting to preserve the ecological integrity of wild places while providing continued recreational access to the public. The impact of recreation is perhaps felt most in the "golden triangle" of the Olympic, Mount Rainier, and North Cascades National Parks and the easily accessible places between them, such as the Alpine Lakes and the Issaquah Alps. Pioneers for preservation of these parks used their recreational and aesthetic values to justify protection. Today the recreational demand for such places far exceeds the supply. It is difficult to find solitude and completely untrammeled wilderness within a day's hike from the protective borders of western Washington's mountain playgrounds. Minimizing impacts on these often overpopulated spots has taken various forms, from education and infrastructure development to regulation and mitigation. As human population continues to grow, the future importance of these efforts will be crucial. While the wilderness experience is the foundation of the movement to protect it, some now look to the future and wonder how we can protect the wilderness from ourselves.

Party size in most wilderness areas is now restricted to twelve people in order to reduce the enlargement of campsites and trails. Mitigating the trampling effect of visitors through revegetation began in 1970, when Joe and Margaret Miller, directors of the North Cascades Conservation Council, were given freedom to experiment in a worn-out meadow near Cascade Pass. Reversing the damage to the meadow from the 1960s "backpack fever" was not completed until 1990, and regeneration continues today. The couple won national awards for "pioneering a land healing pattern" that then took hold in other parks.[21] Replanting of side trails with native vegetation will help maintain the integrity of protected wild cores and allow future generations to experience wilderness approximating the condition it was in prior to heavy visitation.

In a few areas, backcountry camping permits are required in order to regulate human impact on wildlands closest to the urban Seattle area. Most permits are free, but they can cost up to $42 per person for a two-week stay in the Enchanted Lakes area of the Alpine Lakes Wilderness. With a limited number of permits issued each day, a quota system regulates the number of campers bound for popular wilderness destinations. Permit schemes will continue to emerge as demand for high-quality recreation grows, as will the arguments for and against them. After all, who wants to buy a ticket for their wilderness experience as if it were a carnival ride? And who wants to hike all day, only to find dozens of people packed into a "remote" campsite?

Some managers see the need for quota systems on a larger scale. In May 2002, Mount Rainier National Park approved a General Management Plan that will direct management for the next twenty years. One of its main tenets is the establishment of a carrying-capacity framework to protect the quality of both resource conditions and visitor experience within the park. By limiting the number of parking spots and wilderness campsites, and by phasing in the use of a shuttle service during peak use, the Park Service will limit the number of people allowed to visit various areas.

In other places less traveled by humans, some conservationists believe that the ultimate vision for the future is the control of certain human-wildlife interactions. A Lakota name for the wolf, *sungmanitu tanka,* means "great dog of the wilderness." Although wilderness is a culturally imposed term, it can be interpreted to mean, "place away from where humans are."[22] Protected wildlands are a refuge for species threatened by development, agriculture, and resource extraction, yet seldom are they off-limits to the presence of people. Although restricting access to tracts of public land may be counter to existing regulations, the idea of establishing "no trail and no people" areas is a future vision held by some environmentalists and agency managers alike. Efforts today to redirect human use away from prime habitats replace the human prerogative for solitude with the needs of wildlife, be they near-extinct species such as the pygmy rabbit or grizzly bear, or endangered species like the sage grouse and spotted owl.

The very notion of keeping people out of wild areas seems contradictory to wilderness activists who encourage green-bonding as a keystone of wildlands advocacy, but varying circumstances on the gound cause positions on this issue to vary as well. Backcountry enthusiasts become passionate spokespeople for solitude-loving creatures when their beloved trails are threatened with conversion to roads, but once protective boundaries are established, local groups often refocus their energy to ensure that wildness is preserved inside them. Members of such groups, including the Olympic Park Associates, the North Cascades Conservation Council, the Alpine Lakes Protection Society, and the Friends of the Hanford Reach, look to the future with an eye toward balancing their advocacy for recreation opportunities with the protection of natural resources like critical habitat. In doing so, they preserve the quality of our natural heritage and the wild character that defines the backcountry experience.

Conflict over Species

The arrival of new species has always been a natural process, yet, with the creation of a highly mobile human society, increasing pathways for species introduction have caused considerable transformation of the landscape. Twenty-four to twenty-eight percent of the vascular plants along Washington's coastline are largely a result of this phenomenon. The concentration of introduced plants gradually decreases inland; however the threat of widescale impacts is just as great.[23] As our landscape evolves with the introduction of new species, certain situations arise that justify active management to preserve historical conditions. Many protective designations, including wilderness areas and natural area preserves, were established to protect their unique natural characteristics. Allowing alien species to replace rare native species is seen by many as a pointless act of destruction. Yet the task of removing threatening species has its own list of difficulties.

In 1969, Washington's Noxious Weeds Control Board was created in an attempt to address the weed problem. A noxious weed is "a plant that when established is highly destructive, competitive or difficult to control by cultural or chemical practices."[24] The limitations of the state's program are illustrated by the case of cheatgrass. Originally introduced in the 1880s with agricultural seed shipped from Europe, it was intentionally introduced again in 1898 by Washington State College as an experimental grass. Initially seen as beneficial for spring cattle forage, the grass is now a threat to both agriculture and the ecology of eastern Washington's shrub-steppe. Many believe this species should be removed; however, it is currently not listed under the state's noxious weed program. Attempts to eradicate this grass are essentially futile due to the extensive range and fragile ecology it inhabits. Scientists like Steve Herman, faculty member at The Evergreen State College, suggest letting natural regeneration take its course, which might be the only solution.[25]

State and federal agencies continue to create new laws, regulations, and policies to restrict the spread of invasive species. Quarantines have been used, yet the incredible volume of transported goods makes containment an extremely difficult task. As society becomes more dependent upon national and global markets, ongoing contamination occurs through shipment of ballast water, soil, car wheels, livestock, agriculture, and imported exotic plants used for home gardening. Congressman Brian Baird, a Democrat from southwest Washington, introduced the National Aquatic Invasive Species bill to address the pathways involved with commercial shipping. Although this bill is supported throughout the scientific community, scientist Phyllis Windle believes the nation's resources still need more adequate protection against invasive species.[26]

Attempts to reduce the cost of controlling invasive plants and to provide more ecologically friendly methods of control have led to the application of biological agents. This method takes advantage of naturally occurring enemies, such as a parasites, pathogens, or predators to reduce the threatening populations. Concern over Scotch broom's nuisance and threat to native prairie grasses and wildflowers has led to the release of Scotch broom beetles in Thurston County. Previous studies have determined that the bugs destroy Scotch broom seeds and provide a slow but successful reduction in the plants' proliferation. Additional studies by the U.S. Department of Agriculture indicate that the beetle will not kill surrounding plants.[27] Nevertheless, the need to more fully understand the negative and even harmful effects of releasing a biological agent within the community has restrained the use of this method.

Public education will always be a significant factor in protecting our wildlands from invasive species. Gardeners who desire exotic species should be aware of the larger implications of choosing such plants for landscaping.

The simple act of spreading common wildflower seeds, marketed in the Pacific Northwest, has been found to release up to thirteen invasive species that threaten to overcome our native plants.[28] Boaters are being asked by the Washington Department of Fish and Wildlife to remove any biological matter from their hulls and props in an attempt to reduce the spread of harmful plants and animals, such as spartina grass and zebra mussels. Early detection by volunteers can also help prevent established colonies of invasive species from forming, such as European green crab and Asian gypsy moth. Finally, support from volunteers like the Clover Creek Council and Tatoosh Sierra Club Group, who are actively removing invasive Scotch broom and blackberries from places like the Clover Creek watershed, allow native wildlife to flourish.

Unmanaged Wild

Deciding on an appropriate level of management for wildlands is a continual dilemma. Some believe that a hands-off approach should be the goal in dealing with Washington's wilderness; they envision large, unmanaged wildlands being autonomous, with as little human interference as possible. These are the blank spots on the map envisioned by Aldo Leopold, in which the complex web of life can thrive unaided by us. Look at a shovel-load of forest soil and humus under a microscope. There, before your eyes, is a world of diversity in which all laws of nature apply. What the earth is losing is this beauty on a grand scale, in part because the dominant Western practice has been to manage and control all of existence, without leaving space for true wildness.

In a world so heavily populated by humans, there must be managed landscapes, but they needn't be Washington's large, roadless wild areas. Some things are better off without human intervention. No matter how good our intentions are or how informed scientists may be, the eternal complexities surrounding us have yet to be understood. Many times, good intentions and science fail when applied in practice. For example, in the 1970s large woody debris was extracted from streams in the name of salmon. We now know that such debris creates critical salmon habitat, cover, and natural stream morphology, which increases watershed health. As a result, vast sums of capital are being spent to place logs back into streams, while we wait for riparian areas to grow coniferous trees large enough to feed the system with naturally occurring debris again.[29]

Because of problems like habitat fragmentation and invasion of harmful, exotic species, management is necessary on some level. Otherwise, areas would be overrun by aggressive, invasive species or could burn to the ground from wildfire. The removal of roads and the thinning of replanted tree plantations are some management activities used to aid ecological recovery. The ultimate goal of management should be to allow nature's autonomous abilities to return—a risky endeavor that will no doubt encounter failures. [30] But if such unsuccessful attempts are learned from and caution is used at all times, perhaps we can tend toward true ecosystem health in which human and natural systems are interdependent and self-regulating.

 ## THE FUTURE IN MIND

Science, legislative tools, and bold citizen visions are laying the foundation for a wild future. Step by step, citizen activists, organizations, and agencies have a long path to travel. Every single act, no matter how seemingly small, is needed to realize these wild visions of Washington. There are endless inspirational stories that pertain to Washington's wild future—some of which are told in subsequent chapters—including innovative and even radical ideas about wildlands.

In 2001, twelve Catholic bishops from across the Pacific Northwest released a unique declaration. Entitled "The Columbia River Watershed: Caring for Creation and the Common Good," this pastoral letter develops a spiritual case for the long-term sustainability of the 260,000-acre watershed and its inhabitants: "We have become concerned about regional economic and ecological conditions and the conflicts over them in the watershed . . . . We hope that we might work together to develop and implement an integrated spiritual, social and ecological vision for our watershed home, a vision that promotes justice for people and stewardship of creation . . . . We ask all people of good will to imagine what they would like the watershed to be like in ten, fifty or one hundred years, and to work conscientiously to make that image a reality."[31]

The people of Washington must ask this same type of question on a state level. Considering the needs of diverse ecosystems and wildlife, and rethinking how human society can accommodate these needs, requires long-term planning. Inspiring proposals of the past have become models for today, improved upon by the latest scientific knowledge and enhanced by new ideas for the future. Many of today's larger visions include connected reserves of wildland buffered by regenerating wildness and compatible human uses. They involve natural processes and species regaining their sovereignty across the wild landscape, and they foresee the eventual control of human-induced impacts such as recreation and invasive species. Activists are working toward these goals right now, in both large and small ways. With today's inspirations moving closer to reality, it is even more exciting to imagine the future visions that will be shaped by generations to come.

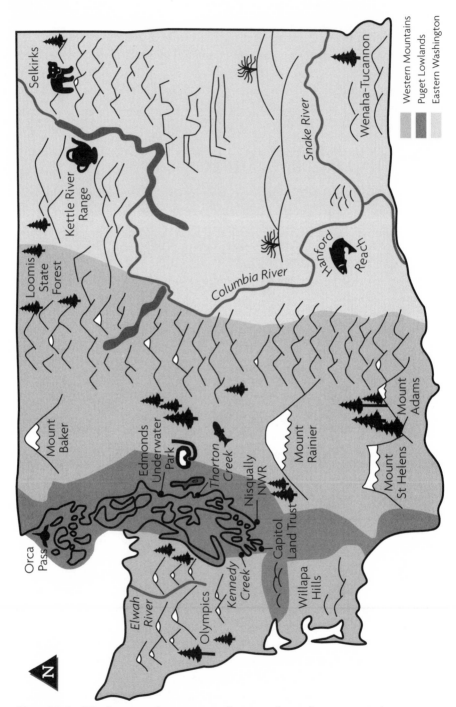

Map 11.1. Washington bioregions discussed in chapters 12 (western mountains), 13 (Puget Lowlands), and 14 (eastern Washington) (Based on drawings by Anthony Bush)

CHAPTER 12

The Western Mountains

◆ *Lana Byal, Connie Czepiel, and Richard Darnell* ◆

The western mountains of Washington State include the Olympic Mountains, the Cascades, and the Coast Range. Together they encompass a vast expanse of western Washington, providing an overwhelmingly beautiful connection between land, sky, and sea. Created from violent forces of the earth, these mountains display a magnificent visual contrast to the western seas of the Pacific Ocean and the eastern flatlands of the Columbia Basin. Both the Coast and Cascade Ranges extend beyond the southern border of Washington State, where the mighty Columbia River forced its way through. To the north, the Cascades continue into Canada. Together, these western mountains are home to ancient temperate rainforests, raging volcanoes, and magnificent wildlife.

Within these western mountains, there exist a variety of species. Rivers flowing from glaciated peaks invite spawning salmon in from coastal waters. Towering evergreen forests provide perches for bald eagles awaiting the incoming fish. Beneath the canopy, elk forage among moss-laden, bigleaf maples at valley edges, while bears forage for thimbleberries along streams. Cascading headwaters flow to meet saltwater estuaries, where migratory birds gather seasonally to feed.

While many wildlands remain intact, the amount of wildness lost to timber and mining interests and to the encroachment of civilization over the years is shocking. Nature has also contributed to its own disruption through volcanic eruptions at places like Mount St. Helens and through fires, floods, and other monumental events.

Early citizen activism led to the progressive protection of natural wild areas through the creation of national parks, imparting the legacy of Mount Rainier, Olympic, and North Cascades National Parks. In later years, the National Wilderness Preservation System became the more effective means of protecting larger "untrammeled" wildlands. Glacier Peak, Alpine Lakes, Mount Skokomish, and twenty-two other areas were designated as wilderness. These designations required committed grassroots political pressure. As activist and author Harvey Manning said, "We couldn't have done it without them [the politicians], they wouldn't have had the idea were it not for us."[1]

In the western mountains, wilderness protection continues to be a strong focus. As of this writing, conservationists are eagerly awaiting passage of the Wild Sky Wilderness bill (see chapter 10). Beyond Wild Sky, additional proposals for wilderness are already in the works. The objective is to pick up pieces of wildlands left out of the 1984 and 1988 wilderness legislation. For example, the Wild Washington Campaign is working to add parcels in the Cle Elum region to the Alpine Lakes Wilderness. The Gifford Pinchot Task Force and the Sierra Club are advocating for a Dark Divide Wilderness Area, and the Olympic Wild organization is dedicated to promoting wilderness for all roadless areas on the Olympic Peninsula.

Wildness is not only a feature of wilderness designations. Many wild areas exist outside of federal roadless areas, and their roads make them ineligible for wilderness designation. As a result, organizations use alternative designations to achieve their preservation objectives. In the Loomis State Forest, critical lynx habitat was saved through the use of Washington State's Natural Resource Conservation Area designation. The Nature Conservancy works to safeguard wildlands on private property, by placing them into land trusts. In the Gifford Pinchot National Forest, Mount St. Helens National Volcanic Monument was created to protect a recovering ecosystem.

Once a wild area is legislatively protected, one might think that the work of the activist is done. However, in order to perpetuate the integrity of the wild, continued efforts are necessary to ensure responsible management. Watchdog groups, like the Olympic Forest Coalition and the Gifford Pinchot Task Force, keep attentive eyes on national forests, where mismanagement can harm an area's wild character. In national parks, groups like Olympic Park Associates are dedicated to promoting the Park Service's adherence to its management policies.

Beyond preserving wildlands through designation and proper management, more and more work is focusing on the regeneration of natural processes. Removal of the Elwha dam is an example of reinstating ecological processes and regenerating the wild Olympics. Throughout the western mountains, citizens play an essential role, stepping forward to promote preservation and natural regeneration. These are a few of their stories.

 ## THE LOOMIS NATURAL RESOURCE CONSERVATION AREA

It is Mark Skatrud's hobby and passion to track lynx in the Loomis State Forest on the northeast slope of the Cascades. In winter, he uses a snowmobile, cross-country skis, or snowshoes to find their tracks. He takes field notes about their young, how far they range, their direction of travel, and any other information that presents itself. They are elusive animals and Skatrud has never seen one himself, but camera shots he has set up throughout the forest have verified their existence. He continues the work, undaunted, because he believes in the lynxs' importance and he lives nearby.

To date Skatrud has gathered more than six hundred bits of information about lynx in this eastside forest. Every year he shares his findings with the U.S. Fish and Wildlife Service, the Forest Service, and the state's Department of Natural Resources (DNR). The agencies do not have the resources to do the amount of fieldwork that Skatrud does. So even though Skatrud is an unpaid volunteer, he has information that no one else has. This gives him power, authority, and credibility to speak on behalf of this rare population.

It is estimated there are only eighteen to twenty-three lynx left in the Loomis Forest, but they are considered to be the best population in the lower forty-eight states.[2] One example of overharvesting occurred in the Kettle Range of northeastern Washington in 1975. In just two years time, two trappers caught sixty lynx. The trappers did not get another lynx for six years and there has not been a population there since.

While Skatrud had some of the best "on-the-ground" knowledge of the lynx population, he wasn't sure how to get them protected. Fortunately, he met Mitch Friedman of the Northwest Ecosystem Alliance (NWEA), who had experience writing petitions to request protection under the Endangered Species Act. Skatrud and Friedman blended their knowledge and expertise to advocate for the lynx by writing the first federal and state petitions to protect them. It took seven lawsuits to accomplish, but the activists finally succeeded in having the lynx listed as threatened by Washington State in 1993 and by the federal government in 2001.

While this effort gained protective status for the lynx itself, its habitat in the Loomis Forest was in grave danger. Skatrud belonged to a local volunteer watchdog group—the Friends of the Loomis Forest—that monitors the DNR's management practices in the Loomis. The DNR not only manages the forest, but also sells timber to support public schools in Washington. In 1996, the Friends sprang into action when they read the new DNR Loomis Forest Landscape Management Plan and determined that it posed a major threat to habitat. Not only was a logging road about to cut through a roadless area, but also lynx, fisher, marten, wolverine, and grizzly bear habitats were threatened by the felling of the trees.

The Friends filed a lawsuit under the Endangered Species Act to block the logging plan. When the case went to mediation, Friends and NWEA came up with a unique proposal that involved using a Natural Resource Conservation Area (NRCA) designation to preserve 25,000 acres of habitat (representing 18 percent of the Loomis Forest). These conservation groups asked if they could reimburse the agency for the value of the timber and land on those 25,000 acres in return for transferring the land from state trust status to NRCA status. The DNR said yes, but stipulated a price of $10 million to $30 million, to be determined by an appraisal, payable within fourteen months. That appraisal was not done for six months and the figure turned out to be approximately $13 million.

While the DNR approved, not everyone was in favor of this preservation effort. As in most cases, opposition to protecting the Loomis arose and compromises were made. Cattle ranchers and recreationists feared they would be banned from the area. They dropped their opposition to the plan when the DNR agreed to allow cattle grazing, hunting, hiking, horse packing, and snowmobiling in the conservation area at traditional levels. Logging and road building, however, were to be banned forever. In return for preserving the 25,000 acres, conservationists agreed to give up their rights to block timber sales based on grizzly-bear issues on the remaining acres of the forest for the next twenty years.

The logging ban highlights a major conflict within the state. Rural, eastside people who make their living off the land were aggravated. The Loomis NRCA project was viewed by some as a westside environmentalist effort to effect policy on lands where they don't live. "Over here, we feel like we are the playground for the westside, and they think we are just in their way. This is our livelihood over here," said Ed Perry, an apple grower and fire chief of the City of Loomis. "It's two different cultures and they are colliding," he said. One logger said, "The more they set aside, the more I'd go hungry. Besides, they need to have something to build their little latte stands and tourist attractions out of."[3] These comments, however, overlook the fact that while contributions were sought from all over the state, the Friends of the Loomis is a local, eastside organization.

While there was predictable opposition, the biggest challenge of all was to raise the money. Such a huge monetary challenge meant that the Friends and NWEA would need to enlist the help of other people who had a similar passion to make a difference for the environment and for threatened species. The nonprofit groups began by setting up a separate fund called the Loomis Forest Fund. They talked to organizations like the Audubon Society, the Nature Conservancy, and the Kettle Range Conservation Group. Their idea had never been tried before and at first it was met with skepticism. But slowly the idea took root. Some foundations had by-laws that prohibited them from giving money for capital projects or land acquisitions, but they gave media money or helped in other ways. More than eighty endorsing organizations and groups throughout Washington State supported the project and let their views be known to state politicians. The issue gained more public attention when the Wenatchee newspaper added its support as well.

In order to garner donations from the public, Skatrud and others took a slide show on the road and talked to anyone who was willing to listen. House parties were conducted throughout the state. On many levels it was an easy sell—the Loomis ranges from 1500 to 7800 feet in elevation and encompasses everything from shrub-steppe to alpine vistas. The variety of plants, wildlife, and habitat offered something for everyone. But the amount of money coming in was not enough and the preservation effort needed to find other supporters.

During this time, the hi-tech industry in Washington was doing well and someone had a friend at Microsoft. Posters were put up inside company facilities and someone was able to get Skatrud into the building during lunchtime. He gave ten-minute slide presentations and showed a ten-minute video. One former employee explained that the company had a matching policy of up to $12,000: if someone gave $1000 the company would add another thousand—all the way up to $12,000. Once employees understood how to donate the Microsoft way, the giving took off.

In addition to workers, ex-Microsoft executives also came on board. Bill Pope, former counsel for Microsoft, donated $320,000. Like others, the sense of place that he had acquired while hiking there motivated his giving: "God is never going to create any more land like this. The vastness of the place . . . just walking there and seeing little evidence of man, I was confirmed in my conviction to save this place."[4] Bruce Jacobsen, another former employee, gave stock contributions estimated at $612,500. The William H. Gates Foundation donated another $250,000.

Two anonymous donors gave $1 million and $2 million gifts. Such amounts would have been huge for any organization, let alone a new organization like the Loomis Forest Fund. The group's small size was advantageous in one respect: their administrative costs were low (6 to 7 percent), ensuring that the bulk of the money was used for the actual land purchase. Miraculously, $13 million was raised, but at the eleventh hour the DNR said that the Loomis Forest Fund had to come up with another $3.3 million for the fair market value of the land. If the money was not raised within ninety days, another appraisal would have to be done. The nearly 6,000 people who had contributed to the cause were devastated. Somehow the money had to be raised. As in most cases, once an organization has proved it can raise significant funds on its own, large corporations are more willing to make a sizeable contribution. In this case, Microsoft co-founder Paul Allen saved the day by contributing this final figure through his Forest Protection Foundation. At the time, it was the largest gift ever given for the environment in Washington State.

Once the area was officially designated, the work of the Friends and others was not done. They continue to monitor draft management plans for the area in order to ensure that the intent of their preservation effort is carried out.

The creation of the Loomis NRCA was an example of using a protected area designation to preserve a wild place. Its success was the result of citizen initiative based on bold, creative ideas. These ideas were carried to completion through a campaign that fired the public's imagination during prosperous times. Perhaps never before was so much accomplished in such a short time by a few people who were able to motivate so many others. This was truly a proud accomplishment within the environmental community. Thanks to all involved, future generations will be able to walk through a healthy forest that harbors a wonderful diversity of species such as lynx, fisher, marten, wolverine, and grizzly bear.

🐻 ONE PIECE OF THE RANGE AT A TIME: PRESERVING THE WILLAPA HILLS

Located in the southwestern corner of Washington State is a portion of the Coast Range known as the Willapa Hills. To the east lie the massive uplifted rock and active volcanoes of the Cascade Range, and to the west the expanse of the Pacific Ocean. Fragmented by the Columbia River at their southern end and shadowed by the Olympics directly to the north, the Willapa Hills appear stranded from a greater legacy. Their tallest peak, at 3,110 feet, is barely high enough to receive much more than an occasional snowfall in the warm, marine climate. Ecologist and natural history writer Robert Michael Pyle described their relation to the surrounding country best when he wrote that the "Willapas simply serve as a lumpy bonding agent between better-defined provinces on three sides."[5]

What the Willapa Hills lack in height and magnitude, however, they make up for in biological diversity. From the magnificent Roosevelt elk to the warty jumping slug, these hills contain some of Washington's rare

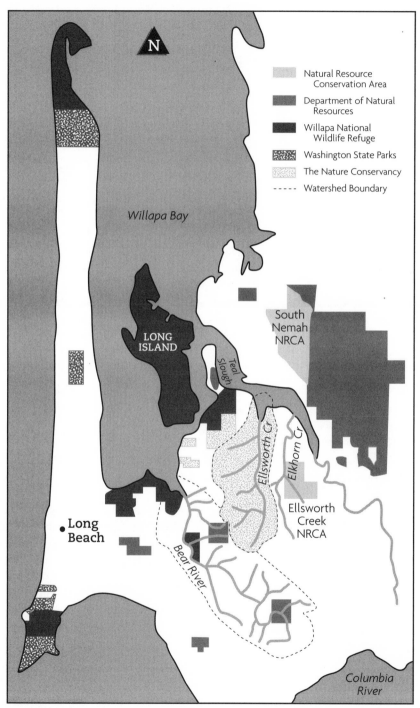

Legend:

- Natural Resource Conservation Area
- Department of Natural Resources
- Willapa National Wildlife Refuge
- Washington State Parks
- The Nature Conservancy
- - - - - Watershed Boundary

Willapa Bay

LONG ISLAND

South Nemah NRCA

Teal Slough

Ellsworth Cr

Elkhorn Cr

Ellsworth Creek NRCA

Long Beach

Bear River

Columbia River

Map 12.1. Land designations and ownership in and around the Ellsworth Creek watershed (Based on drawings by Rick Darnell)

endemic species. Old-growth cedars, hemlock, and Sitka spruce provide nesting habitat for the threatened marbled murrelet. Various species of salmon, including chum and coho, journey up the countless streams. Both the black bear and the cougar call these hills home. With such biological wonders as the tailed frog and Cope's giant salamander, the Willapa Hills have established their own magnificent wonders.

Today only one-half of one percent of the Willapa Hills retains its old growth forests. This drastic reduction has gained the attention of conservationists, the community, landowners, and public agencies. Together they are attempting to preserve the remaining wild characteristics of the Willapa Hills by focusing on the remnant patches of old growth and critical habitat surrounding Willapa Bay.

Some of the first conservation land in the area was held within the Willapa National Wildlife Refuge (see map 12.1). Established in 1937, this refuge now includes four different management areas: the Lewis and Riekkola units, Leadbetter Point, and Long Island. The most impressive is the 7-mile-long, 4700-acre, forested Long Island unit. Although surrounded by an estuarine habitat, the biological characteristics of the island function as part of the Willapa Hills. For more than four thousand years this island has withstood fire and storm, safeguarding some of the most impressive and distinct old-growth trees on the Northwest coast. By the 1950s, much of the island had been commercially logged, but conservationists and politicians joined forces to save some of the last remaining cedars. Today, the island is part of the wildlife refuge, protecting old-growth cedars exceeding 10 feet in diameter and more than a thousand years old. When combined with the other refuge units, 11,000 acres of forest and shoreline provide habitat for many species including bats, bobcats, deer, elk, bear, and upland and migrating birds.

Much of the surrounding Willapa Bay has been heavily logged since the late 1800s. Fire, extensive roadways, clear-cuts, and single-species reforestation have all affected the once biologically diverse landscape. In an effort to reduce the ongoing damage, stewardship programs have been established to work on not only forest issues, but also on the surrounding ecology. Since 1996, the Jobs in the Woods program of the U.S. Fish and Wildlife Service has conduced restoration activities by focusing on watershed degradation and providing job opportunities for displaced natural resource workers. In the Bear River watershed, roads were upgraded to maintain and reduce erosion and sedimentation of streams. Riparian restoration has been focused on the immediate reintroduction and natural maintenance of large woody debris within the river's channel system. During the plan's five-year implementation, 12 square miles of habitat were restored, ensuring the health and functionality of the forest.

Although stewardship activities play a strong role in preserving the health of the forest, they cannot adequately protect wild characteristics over the long term. Vital habitat along the Elkhorn and Smith Creeks are examples of areas that needed protective designation. Their two-hundred-plus-year-old western red cedar and Sitka spruce, some exceeding 8 feet in diameter, provide old-growth habitat for a variety of endangered and rare species, including the marbled murrelet. To protect the site, the Washington State Natural Areas Program acquired 557 acres and has designated it as a natural resource conservation area (NRCA). The South Nemah NRCA has accomplished the same goal with three-hundred-year-old cedars encompassing an uncut drainage and providing 1452 acres of habitat for deer, elk, spotted owls, and an array of amphibians and fish. Combining the two sites with the smaller 8.5-acre Teal Slough NRCA has provided critical habitat protection within a landscape rich in biodiversity that was intensively altered by timber extraction.[6]

Between the Bear River watershed and the Teal Slough NRCA lies the Ellsworth Creek watershed. From sea level to 1600 feet in elevation, the forested valley is home to numerous tributaries, with pristine spawning habitat for the Pacific chum salmon. Within 1.2 miles of Ellsworth Creek, 5600 salmon account for one the thickest runs within the Willapa region. This watershed also contains ancient old-growth cedar, hemlock, and Sitka spruce. With some of the trees exceeding eight hundred years in age, concern over their well-being created a movement for preservation.[7]

In an effort to protect the 300 acres of old growth and other valuable habitat within the watershed, the Nature Conservancy took on an incredible challenge: group members launched a campaign to conserve this 5000-acre watershed as a large functional habitat for old-growth-dependant species such as the warty jumping slug, Cope's giant salamander, and the tailed frog, which could easily disappear if not protected. The Conservancy's intention was to purchase the entire area from the timber management firm, the Campell Group. The firm actually supported the idea, saying, "The Campell Group has a strong stewardship ethic, and part of that is identifying sensitive parcels that are better managed for the broader public interest because they have values that go beyond timber, either for the environment or recreation."[8] The only obstacle was the sale price, estimated at $20 million.

Jump-started through a memorial fund, the money required to purchase the watershed came from the Conservancy's broad-based fund-raising. Donations of $1 million to $2.5 million demonstrated the community's interest in the project. On September 1, 2000, the Conservancy purchased the first 117 acres in the Ellsworth Creek watershed, with an agreement to purchase 1500 more acres in the future. As fund-raising continued, the original goal of purchasing 5000 acres increased to 7100, and by mid-February 2003, 7400 acres of the watershed had been purchased. Owning all but 120 acres of the watershed, the Conservancy can now begin restorative efforts that will hasten the natural regeneration of the old-growth forest.

The efforts of the Nature Conservancy have played a considerable role in the protection of vital habitat within Ellsworth Creek. Focusing on the whole watershed allows for the regenerative processes that will restore a piece of the Willapa Hills' ecological function; when combined with the state's Natural Conservation Resource Areas and the Willapa National Wildlife Refuge, the Ellsworth Creek watershed contributes to the protected cores and corridors so desperately needed by the area's wildlife. With proper stewardship, the surrounding forest can act as a buffer and moderate form of habitat, further enhancing the overall mosaic of the Willapa Hills. The result is a success story of preserving ancient-forest character, brought about by the combined efforts of several parties and hopefully encouraging others to pursue similar protection for other aspects of Washington's wildness.

 MOUNT ST. HELENS

When nature's wildness was on full display during Mount St. Helens's eruption on May 18, 1980, it was a reminder that forces beyond our control can very quickly change the Cascades as we know them. At the time of the blast, the mountain had been silent for 150 years and no one alive had ever witnessed such a cataclysmic event in the western mountains. People were awestruck by the explosion, which was five hundred times more powerful than the first atomic bomb. They were stunned by the sight of huge billows of ash that skyrocketed 17 miles into the atmosphere while red and white lightning screamed to Mount Adams and back. Churning cauldrons of mud, water, and logs choked nearby rivers. Whole houses were seen careening down the Toutle River, and five-hundred-year-old trees fell over like matchsticks. Grey, powdery ash was carried by the wind to eastern Washington, where skies turned black, vehicles and machinery clogged, highways closed, and pasturing cows turned gray. In one week's time the ash reached Boston and in two weeks it had encircled the globe. What remained around the mountain was a silent moonlike landscape.

In order to protect this unique area, Mount St. Helens National Volcanic Monument was created within two years of the eruption. Most people believe that the eruption was the only reason for the designation, but there is more to the story. Efforts to protect Mount St. Helens actually began as early as the 1930s.

Designation: Creating the Mount St. Helens National Volcanic Monument

During the Great Depression, Interior Secretary Harold Ickes suggested that a national park be created that included the entire Cascade Range (see map 6.1). The secretary's idea was inopportune because the country's focus was on economic issues, and his proposal went nowhere. Thirty years later, in 1963, a spelunker named William Halliday wanted to protect lava caves south of the volcano. His idea was to create a 5000-acre national monument and he published his thoughts in *National Parks* magazine. Five years later, Phil Pryde, a geographer at the University of Washington, also wrote an article for *National Parks*, proposing an even bigger monument. His plan was for 80,000 acres and included not only the lava caves, but also the volcano itself and Spirit Lake basin. At about the same time, in 1968, Noel McRae of Kelso and Bob Werner of Chehalis formed the Mount St. Helens Protective Association (MSHPA) and published an even larger proposal for 85,000 acres. Their motivation was to protect the area from mining and logging threats. While none of these proposals resulted in a national monument before the mountain blew, together they contributed to building public support and awareness for protecting the region.[9]

While monument efforts fell short before 1980, the MSHPA had other victories along the way. The organization, with the help of the Sierra Club and Friends of the Earth, worked to stop roads in the Miners Creek and Green River drainages. They waged a six-year campaign and ultimately enlisted the help of newly elected Democratic congressman Don Bonker to bring about a victory. In 1975, the congressman helped facilitate a land exchange between the Forest Service and Weyerhaeuser that resulted in saving the last low-elevation, old-growth forest near Mount St. Helens.

Recreationists such as Susan Saul were also among those who appreciated and wanted to protect Mount St. Helens. Her inspirational story began when she moved to nearby Vancouver, Washington, in 1974. A year later she joined the Mount St. Helens Hiking Club and enjoyed recreating at the club's rustic lodge on the north shore of Spirit Lake. Access to the lodge was by boat or a 4-mile hike beyond the end of a nearby road. She has fond memories of club activities like hiking, snowshoeing, cross-country skiing, canoeing, swimming, and huckleberry picking. But it bothered her that every time she visited the lake it seemed that more and more logging had been done. Clear-cutting was encroaching on the skyline around the lake basin and her activist instincts began to stir.

Saul joined the Willapa Hills Audubon Society and got involved in the committee that was reviewing and commenting on forest unit plans in the Gifford Pinchot National Forest, the forest that included Mount St. Helens.

Through committee work, conversations with fellow members, and hikes with both Audubon and the hiking club, she gained information and familiarity with the Mount St. Helens area and the issues affecting it.

In 1977, Saul first heard about MSHPA through a meeting notice in the newspaper and decided to check it out. She met Noel McRae and Russ Jolley that same evening. In 1978, the Forest Service started work on the unit plan for the Mount St. Helens area, and MSHPA members didn't like what they saw. With the support of the Wilderness Society, the group decided to campaign for the establishment of a national scenic area that would include four wilderness areas in the Mount St. Helens region.

During this time, Saul met Joe Walicki of the Wilderness Society. It was at his urging that Saul first engaged in lobbying her congressman, Don Bonker, to support the scenic area proposal. She took a small delegation of hiking club and Willapa Hills Audubon Society representatives with her and though they were unsuccessful, the lobbying experience was a first step in learning how to engage in the political process.

As time went on, Saul attended fund-raisers and public events that her congressman held. That way, Bonker came to see her as a supporter, not just a nameless face who wanted something from him. This rapport she built with her congressman before the eruption proved invaluable in later preservation efforts. In 1980, to further build public support and awareness about threats to the region, the MSHPA sponsored hikes into the Green River valley so that citizens could see for themselves what was going on. Public support for protection was slowly building, but then, as Saul says, "the mountain itself got involved" when it erupted. The MSHPA believes they were one of the last groups to hike into the area and make it out before the eruption; a week after the group's last hike, several recreationists were killed on the same trail.

A month after the blast, several Seattle-based environmental groups met with the MSHPA in Longview to reevaluate the protection proposals. The first thing they had to figure out was if the various characteristics they had been trying to save even existed anymore. The groups decided to spend the summer researching and to meet again later that year. It was difficult to get into the blast zone, but through collaborative efforts with government agencies, conservationists were able to make some headway gathering data.

By January 1981, a coalition of environmental groups held a press conference and introduced their proposal for a 216,000-acre national monument. They tried to get President Jimmy Carter to designate the monument by executive order in the waning days of his administration, but he was more than preoccupied with the Iran hostage crisis. Since that effort failed, a coalition of environmental groups (MSPHA, Sierra Club, Wilderness Society, National Audubon Society, Friends of the Earth, and others), turned their focus toward designation by congressional legislation. They drafted a bill and asked Congressman Bonker to introduce it into Congress "by request." This was a practice used by congressional representatives to do favors for a constituent. In such cases the representative does not necessarily endorse the bill and does not sponsor it. Still, it was a way forward and Saul's rapport with Bonker—built through the years—led him to agree. Altogether, three related bills with different acreage figures were introduced in the House of Representatives in March 1982: the MSPHA "by request" bill at 216,000 acres; an 84,710-acre bill based on the Forest Service's proposed interpretive area; and a 113,000-acre protective area backed by members of Washington's congressional delegation. Hearings were held in Washington, D.C., in March and in the field in June. Following the field hearings, Bonker introduced a compromise bill for 115,000 acres while Senators Slade Gorton and Henry Jackson introduced a 105,000-acre bill in the Senate. In the end, the House and Senate "split the difference" and passed a 110,000-acre bill that President Reagan signed on August 26, 1982.

People like Susan Saul can and do make a difference when they involve themselves in the process to protect a place they love. But it often takes time to build public support and political will in order to achieve protective designation. Sometimes it takes numerous attempts, varying strategies, and disappointments along the way. The political climate and events taking place in the nation also play a role, and even if there are good reasons for creating an area such as a national monument, designation is by no means a slam dunk.

The Mount St. Helens National Volcanic Monument was designed to protect "geological, ecological, and cultural resources and the natural development of the area." This means that "[m]odifications of natural conditions can only take place in order to ensure public safety, to prevent loss of life or property, to preserve from risk irreplaceable features and to avoid damage to important resources in areas bordering the Monument."[10] The result is that St. Helens will be allowed to recover on its own, while also providing for public recreation and education.

The story does not end with designation; citizen follow-up is required to make sure that the designation goals are met. Susan Saul relates that in the early days, their group threatened to go back to Congress to have the National Park Service take over management of the monument if the Forest Service did not do a better job of protecting the values that the monument was created to safeguard.

Today another serious issue is in need of public attention. Scientific research was a major goal of designating the monument, and right after the eruption, considerable money was made available for research and a lot of baseline data were generated. The National Science Foundation was responsible for much of the funding and universities contributed as well. Follow-up studies were conducted four to five years later and in the biological sciences alone, more than 637 articles were published. But the surprise today is that "funding for biological research on the monument is so scarce that scientists cannot even afford to update long-term studies begun immediately after the eruption."[11] Scientists are looking for a funding base for continued work. According to Forest Service forest ecologist Charlie Crisafulli, only a few scientists are continuing work at the volcano. He points out that new scientists get funded for a time, but their applications for renewal are often denied and the work stops. A handful of people are carrying on long-term work, often at personal expense or by piggybacking off the work of other projects. The monument scientist, Peter Frenzen, once had a seasonal monitoring staff of seven. He is now the only person assigned to the science program and is responsible for public relations and interpretive work besides. As a consequence, scientists are losing the opportunity to examine the long-term environmental results of the volcanic explosion, including information about sediments, outlet channels, natural earthen dams, consequences to fisheries, and other broad subjects.

The latest threat at Mount St. Helens is a proposed tourist road that would cut across critical research locations in the Pumice Plain at the base of the mountain. It would also cut through roadless areas. According to Saul, local groups have been fighting this proposal for the past two years in the "No More Roads at Mount St. Helens Campaign." The campaign is keeping the issue alive in the press and has received the endorsement of more than thirty scientists. Conservationists' many objections include that the road would be exposed to possible eruptions and seasonal flooding, that it would be on top of unstable volcanic rock, and that it would go right through some of the more scientifically valuable and environmentally sensitive parts of the monument. A large coalition of environmental and recreation organizations and several politicians such as Congressman Brian Baird and Senators Patty Murray and Maria Cantwell are supporting the campaign. Some successes have included neutralizing county commissioners and turning others against the road proposal.

Citizen oversight and continued funding will be required to ensure that the monument will embody the values that it was created to protect. Without this oversight, there are no guarantees that future generations will enjoy the benefits of the battles fought in our lifetime.

Regeneration: Nature Takes Its Course Inside theMonument

After the 1980 eruption, people were aghast at the sight of the moonlike landscape and the carnage contained within it. One question on everyone's mind was, how will this ecosystem ever recover? Some said it never would, while others said it would take centuries. At the time no one really knew. Another question being asked was, what role should humans play in the recovery? Controversies over the answers to those questions continue to this day, and an early experiment is instructive in considering human intervention in recovery efforts.

In 1981, the Soil Conservation Service wanted to seed the entire blast zone with grasses in order to halt erosion and start revegetation. Weyerhaeuser was not in favor of this idea, because grasses and clover would compete with their trees, and seeding would attract mice, which gnaw through the tender stem bark of tree seedlings. A compromise was struck and a 20,000-acre experimental plot was seeded by helicopter. The experiment failed near the mountain when the seeds washed away, but some seeds did take root on Weyerhaeuser property. As predicted, the mice population exploded, going from a normal five to ten mice per acre, to one hundred per acre, and the mice began to eat the seedlings. The state's Department of Fish and Wildlife decided to kill the mice by feeding them oats coated with zinc phosphate, and four thousand acres were quickly treated. The result was that gas built up in the bellies of the mice and they literally exploded. Human intervention to solve one problem created a cascade of additional problems in this case.

Mount St. Helens has actually surprised everyone and is farther along on the road to recovery than anyone had imagined. [12] The region now has one of the largest elk herds in the state and one of the largest amphibian populations in the Pacific Northwest. Even Spirit Lake was able to support life within five years of the event. The blast not only destroyed geologic features, but also created new ones. Two new lakes and 120 new ponds now grace the land.

One big reason that recovery has proceeded so well is that far more species survived the eruption than anyone thought possible. Small animals were found in the root wads of overturned trees and frog and salamander populations were protected under the ice and snow of lakes. In the blast zone, burrowing pocket gophers survived because they live underground much of the time.

While the number within each species was often small, the variety of species was enough to make a difference and these survivors played an important role in the recovery. Gophers, for example, ate roots and bulbs of plants whose tops had been blasted off. Their burrowing helped to mix ash with underlying soil and brought up buried forest soil and fungal spores. Seeds blew onto these gopher mounds and took root. Elsewhere, on the barren pumice plain, one lupine started the entire regeneration process. Lupine nodules process nitrogen from the air and when a plant dies, it adds nitrogen to the soil, which lacks this critical ingredient for growth. Colonizing spiders blew into this same region, riding on their webs in the wind. Fireweed and pearly everlasting arrived next. This vegetation attracted insects, which in turn brought birds. Foraging animals then came to the area because there was food to eat.

In some cases, vegetation came back faster in areas that were previously clear-cut than in areas that had been forested. In clear-cut areas, sun-tolerant species had been growing prior to the eruption, and a few survived the blast. The harsh, desertlike, postblast landscape did not adversely affect them, unlike shade-dependent species, which quickly died from exposure.

Large mammals such as the Roosevelt elk were part of the ecosystem before 1980. In fact, hunters were taking one to two hundred per year. The eruption itself killed an estimated 1500 to 2300 elk. But, contrary to expectations, elk recovered in a big way, especially in the early years. Elk were first seen in the blast zone almost immediately. The grass seeding effort by the Soil Conservation Service in 1981 attracted more elk from surrounding forests. Early on, the elk actually assisted plant recovery by stirring up the ash with their hooves and adding fertilizer and seeds through their excrement. Elk herds thrived for a period of time because forage was abundant, there was an absence of predators (hunting was temporarily halted), and winters were mild. There was also a significant increase in the number of calves being born.

However, changes in the availability of food sources both in and around the monument negatively affected elk populations. The winter of 1998–99, was unusually cold and 174 elk were found dead in the valley north of the volcano. Over time, the carrying capacity both inside and outside the monument was reached and elk began to starve. The animals were seen staggering in the monument and, since human intervention was not allowed, they often died a slow but natural death. While this was a bad situation for the elk, another group benefited. Scavengers and predators such as coyote and bear came into the monument from miles around to feed on the carrion. Even an extremely rare wolverine was sighted. And in spite of the difficulties, the monument still boasts the largest elk herd in the state.

The monument's lesson is that if a biological legacy remains when an ecosystem is damaged, then the recovery process is greatly accelerated. This is one reason why Mount St. Helens is recovering sooner than expected.

This discovery has had application to a contentious issue in the West: clear-cutting practices. Fortuitously, Jerry Franklin of the University of Washington was not only heavily involved in scientific research at Mount St. Helens, but he was also an architect of the Northwest Forest Plan (see chapter 8). Franklin wrote logging guidelines into the forest plan that incorporated the importance of leaving a biological legacy when clear-cutting. Loggers are mandated to leave a certain number of trees per acre and to leave woody debris behind. These remnants can then serve as a catalyst for the growth of second- and third-generation trees.

Human Intervention: Weyerhaeuser Reforestation

Adjacent to the monument, the Weyerhaeuser Company took an aggressive and proactive role in restoring 68,000 acres of privately owned timberland that was destroyed by the blast.[13] When the mountain blew, the explosion went sideways instead of skyward, resulting in tremendous damage to surrounding forestland. The explosion sent superheated air (2000–4000 degrees Fahrenheit) screaming across the landscape and trees within the blast zone were blown over, broken, twisted, debarked, and delimbed. Wind pushing rock particles and pebbles sandblasted everything in its path. Farther out, trees were burnt. The wind had stopped at this remove, but the heat was still 500–600 degrees Fahrenheit. Even farther out, trees were left standing, but they were covered with ash. It was not known if these trees would survive the ashfall because the ash prevented photosynthesis and the needles were subjected to high temperatures, so essentially the trees could not breathe. However, because the trees had not yet budded and the snow had not yet melted, the destruction was somewhat mitigated. New needles opened a few weeks after the blast, old needles fell off, and some trees survived.

Weyerhaeuser had operated a tree farm in the area since 1900, and 14 percent of it was destroyed by the blast. Buried under ash or wiped out entirely were 650 miles of roads, nineteen bridges, and 16 miles of railroad. Salvage logging was the company's first step toward recovery. Weyerhaeuser needed to recoup losses by removing fallen trees before they rotted and by preparing to replant. Salvage logging began in September 1980 and was not completed until October 1982. As many as six hundred truckloads of logs per day were taken from the area during this time.

Not only did Weyerhaeuser have to salvage logs from its land, but also from the Toutle River. Twenty million board feet of cut timber had been stacked in log yards when flooding, caused by melting glaciers and snow, swept them into the river. Unfortunately, the logs acted like battering rams and took out many bridges that spanned the river. Weyerhaeuser was able to identify its logs by their end cuts and rescued 12 of the 20 million board feet.

After salvage logging was completed, the next step was to clear the land and replant. From 1981 to 1987, more than 18 million trees were planted. The planting itself was difficult. Research plantings showed that trees would not grow if planted in ash alone. Workers had to dig through 6 inches to 2 feet of ash in order to reach the nutrient-rich soil underneath. The ash was very deep in areas that had been clear-cut before the eruption and sometimes had to be bulldozed before planting could begin. Commercial planting requires hand shoveling and planting, and typically each worker puts in an average of 1000 to 1500 seedlings per day. But because of the difficult conditions at Mount St. Helens, only 400 to 500 seedlings per day could be planted.

The ash had some beneficial effects on growth. It did not allow competitive vegetation to grow and it acted like mulch, keeping moisture levels high in the soil. But the ash was detrimental because it lacked many nutrients required for tree growth. The reflection of the sun off the ash also scorched the underside of seedlings unless they were planted perfectly straight. Still, in spite of the difficulties, the seedlings had an 80 percent survival rate. Trees have grown so well that the company plans to begin commercial logging by 2025.

Contrasting Models of Recovery

The striking contrast between regeneration and reforestation can be observed at the boundary between Weyerhaeuser and national monument land. From the air one can readily see large tracts of green, uniform forests on Weyerhaeuser land, while monument lands are relatively barren. Within the monument, it will be some time before the many millions of conifer seedlings that have taken root around the volcano develop into a mature, coniferous forest. Instead, pioneer plants like fireweed and lupine are growing. In some areas, cottonwood trees and willows have sprung up. These will provide nutrients for the soil that will eventually allow evergreen forests to once again dominate the landscape around the volcano.

Mount St. Helens's story is significant for the conservation movement because more and more conservation organizations are turning from preservation of wildlands to the regeneration of wildlands already destroyed. In order to restore natural processes, however, one must understand how they work in the first place; without accurate information, human intervention may do more harm than good. Mount St. Helens National Volcanic Monument has provided science with far more data than it previously had regarding the recovery of this type of ecosystem, but it has also shown that there is much more to learn.

REGENERATING THE WILD OLYMPICS: REINSTATING WOLVES AND RIVERS

Olympic National Park is a world-renowned Biosphere Reserve and World Heritage Site, recognized by the United Nations Educational, Scientific, and Cultural Organization (UNESCO) for its uniqueness and rich biological diversity. The park, however, is not a complete reserve if important biological components and ecosystem functions are missing. The gray wolf, a powerful predator, once roamed the Olympic Peninsula's steep, forested slopes and fertile valleys, but by the late 1920s there was not a howl left to hear.[14] Soon after the arrival of settlers, a campaign to systematically eliminate wolves from the peninsula began. Early hunters' overwhelming desire for robust elk and settlers wishing to protect their livestock led to federally endorsed trapping, poisoning, and hunting of wolves to the point of extirpation. Wolves are now the only missing predator from the Olympics ecosystem, and without this keystone predator, important ecological processes are lost from the park's wilderness. As top predators, wolves regulate deer and elk populations, strengthening the genetics of herds by selecting weaker individuals as prey and keeping the animals from overgrazing their habitats.

Olympic National Park's wild character has also been significantly disrupted by the introduction of the nonnative mountain goat. Hunters introduced mountain goats at about the same time they were eliminating wolves from the peninsula. The goats do most damage in the fragile subalpine and alpine meadows, where in creating wallows for dusting themselves the goats erode soils and destroy delicate plant communities. The goats also forage on rare and endemic plant species, such as Cotton's milk-vetch, which is now listed as endangered in Washington State.

The disruption of ecological processes has prompted visions for the removal of the mountain goats and reintroduction of the western gray wolf. As early as 1935, wildlife biologist Adolf Murie proposed reintroducing the wolves on the peninsula they once roamed, including the Olympic valleys and wildlife-rich prairies. Such hopes continue, drawing on the success of reintroduction projects within Yellowstone National Park and the northern Rockies, where wolves have reestablished their territories and are regulating both ungulate and coyote populations, which had soared in the absence of natural predators. Balancing ecological processes can also be applied to the park's compromised alpine habitat. Removing mountain goats would allow alpine meadows to reestablish their endemic and rare plant species, such as Piper's bellflower, Olympic Mountain groundsel, and Olympic Mountain aster. Without goats, soil-stabilizing lichen and moss communities would also be able to recolonize and regenerate alpine soils.

Olympic Park Associates (OPA) supports these visions, encouraging their implementation by actively participating in the park's general management planning process. OPA president Tim McNulty notes that the management plans are supposed to be reviewed and updated every fifteen to twenty years. The revised plan is now nearly thirty years overdue, but is finally in the beginning stages of revision. The Park Service is required to reintroduce extirpated species when possible for the reestablishment of ecological relationships and processes. OPA wants the new plan to address the regeneration of wildness for Olympic National Park by removing the damaging, nonnative mountain goats from the park's alpine peaks and by reintroducing the western gray wolf.

On the mountain goats issue, park wildlife biologist Patti Happe has affirmed that the Park Service will attempt to remove the goats using nonlethal reproductive control methods; it is just a matter of time and federal funding before the project is underway. But the wolves are a different story.

In 1997, Defenders of Wildlife united with OPA to promote reintroducing wolves. They were met with support from Congressman Norm Dicks, who was able to allocate federal funds for a feasibility study. Habitat assessments revealed that the park's wilderness provides sufficient range and enough deer and elk to support a population of fifty to sixty wolves.

To determine public support for wolf reintroduction, in 1998 Defenders of Wildlife hired Seattle-based consulting firm Evans/McDonough Company to conduct a telephone survey. The firm polled residents on the Olympic Peninsula and throughout western Washington, asking their opinions of wolf reintroduction. Results showed that 51 percent of peninsula residents and more than 60 percent of western Washington residents were in favor of wolf reintroduction. After hearing about the western gray wolf's role in the park's ecosystem, the percent of peninsula residents in favor of reintroduction increased to 56 percent. These survey results exhibit the potential public support for wolf reintroduction, which could be strengthened by educating people concerning wolf ecology to alleviate fears about this poorly understood predator. But because of perceived local opposition and inadequate federal funding, reintroduction of wolves is an ongoing fight needing active public participation.

Until wolf reintroduction and goat removal are implemented under the new general management plan, OPA will continue to press for the regeneration of Olympic National Park and the agency's adherence to federal regulations.

Elsewhere in the park, rivers are the arena for regeneration. In 1912, the Lower Elwha hydroelectric dam ended one of Washington's most abundant salmon runs. By preventing fish passage, more than 180 miles of vital spawning habitat became inaccessible to migrating salmon. The effects of this blockage decreased the river's unusually diverse and multiple runs by more than 90 percent. Ten original migratory fish runs once proliferated within these waters, totaling an estimated 380,000 returning fish every year, but with the dams in place, the native Elwha sockeye are now extinct. Both the pink and spring chinook are so low in numbers that extinction of these historical runs is almost assured.[15]

Once abundant within the river, summer/fall run chinook, coho, and chum, and winter/summer steelhead are now heavily managed by hatchery programs. Even with the hatchery program, the construction on the upper river of Glines Canyon Dam in 1926 further exacerbated problems for the surviving fish. The combination of dams has altered stream flow and decreased the amount of shaded water available, resulting in a seasonal increase in water temperature. In the event of drought or extended warm periods, the water temperature increases beyond normal. Consequently, spawning fish have been susceptible to abnormal parasitic infection. In 1987, this situation became evident when 26 percent of returning salmon died from an outbreak of two specific parasites that coated the gills of spawning fish and resulted in suffocation. It is feared that with the continued decline of suitable habitat and increased parasitic infections, all wild Elwha salmon may face extinction.

Beginning in the icy snowfields of the Olympics, the river is fed by high-gradient tributaries spilling from 6000-foot-tall peaks into the gradually sloping Elwha Valley. It is this combination of two gradients and ancient forests that provides the needed gravel, woody debris, and nutrients for productive salmon habitat. Before the dams were introduced, this habitat supported an unusually high number of salmon species, but perhaps the most unusual were the "June hogs." Tales of these fish are not fictional, but rather describe the unusually large chinook that would return only to the Elwha. Normal chinook salmon average approximately thirty pounds, with some of the largest fish exceeding sixty pounds. The Elwha's chinook were not only kings, they were the king of kings. Imagine a run of salmon where the fish reach an incredible one hundred pounds. These fish were truly a wonder of nature.

Even before completion of the two dams, Native peoples expressed their desire for the Elwha to remain a free-flowing river; and ever since the dams started taking their toll on Elwha fisheries, the Lower Elwha Klallam Tribe has fought for the return of the river's fish runs. Individuals outside the Native community share this vision—a vision that requires dam removal. Species return and river health are not the only incentives for removal. The dams have created other problems from the very beginning. After construction of the 1912 dam, the base of the dam blew out, draining a significant portion of the reservoir. Repaired with branches and concrete, the dam's safety has always been in question. Crown Zellerbach (a timber and paper company) acquired the dam and afterward an independent engineering firm studied it, concluding that during high flood levels the structure could fail. Eventually, the Army Corps of Engineers became aware of the condition and advised that safety precautions must take place before downstream development could commence.

Along with public-safety concerns and the desire for the historic Elwha salmon runs, citizen activism played a key role in addressing the relicensing of the two dams. In 1986, the Lower Elwha Klallam Tribe filed a motion to remove both dams and to allow fish restoration. Conservation groups also filed a motion that year for removal of the dams and restoration of the watershed. The conservation movement was reflecting the general population's concern over the declining fish population and the lack of wild rivers. Support for dam removal soon came from the National Marine Fisheries Service, the U.S. Fish and Wildlife Service, and the National Park Service. With the majority of the Elwha River and the Glines Canyon Dam in Olympic National Park, it turned out that relicensing could violate the 1988 Washington Park Wilderness Act. Still, even with much heated debate, the licenses of the dams continued on yearly extensions. Finally, in 1992, President Bush signed the Elwha River Ecosystem and Fisheries Restoration Act. This legislation called a halt to relicensing and required a federal study outlining the restoration of the Elwha River ecosystem and fisheries.

In 1994, the final report outlining the restoration of the Elwha concluded that both dams should be removed to adequately restore the river ecosystem and anadromous fisheries. Six years later, both the Elwha and Glines Canyon dams were acquired and are now operated by the U.S. Department of Interior. Based on the findings within the record of decision, dam removal and sediment management will begin by the year 2007.

What was once predominately an issue for the Lower Elwha Klallam Tribe became an opportunity for Natives and non-Natives to work together. The tribe's initiative, motivated by concern about safety and the desire to reestablish wild salmon, eventually generated enough momentum to ensure that the Elwha River will be left to regenerate its wild character in the foreseeable future.

The western mountains have long been the center of conservation action. Washington's national parks began here in the 1890s and that work continues to this day, with a wide variety of conservation designations under consideration to protect even more areas from the Coast Range and Olympic Mountains to the Cascades. In modern campaigns, creative approaches have been used in response to new circumstances and obstacles, as illustrated by citizen efforts to protect the Loomis National Forest, the Willapa Hills, Olympic National Park and Forest, and Mount St. Helens. These campaigns have not only relied upon the old tool of protected-area designations, but they have made regeneration of the wild a centerpiece of their strategies as well. Bringing back old-growth forests, healthy wolf, lynx, and salmon populations, and the regeneration of the full complement of ecological processes in the western mountains, have been promoted and advanced by spirited volunteers and conservation organizations all over western Washington. The work continues in the areas we have described, as well as in many other portions of the western mountains.

CHAPTER 13

The Puget Lowlands

◆ *Glenn Thomas Burkhart, Anthony Bush, and Katherine Jones* ◆

On September 20, 1890, the year when the U.S. frontier ended according to the Census Bureau, urbanites in downtown Seattle were reminded that their city had not completely banished the wild. At 9:30 a.m. as people were beginning their workday, they were joined on busy Pine Street by a 160-pound cougar. More than a century later, Seattle had spread in all directions as it joined with other port towns along the banks of Puget Sound, urbanizing and domesticating most of the lowlands south to the capital city, Olympia. Yet in the early morning hours on May 28, 2003, a security guard for Washington's Department of Ecology office in Lacey, 60 miles south of Seattle, reported seeing a cougar prowling the urban woods, showing the region's wild face in the midst of intensive development.[1]

Where water meets land, society flourishes. Rich natural resources, dramatic scenery, mild climate, and a diverse economy attract millions of people to the Puget Lowlands. With continual expansion of the cities along Interstate 5, from Vancouver, Washington, in the south to Bellingham in the north, our open spaces in the Puget Lowlands are being devoured. This region is, arguably, one of the most trammeled places in the state.

Noted nature photographer and founder of the Washington Trails Association, Ira Spring, used to canoe from Olympia along Puget Sound wilderness beaches with his family in the 1920s. Paddle out into the Sound today and you will see the effects of human efforts to separate the land from the sea. The Department of Natural Resources claims that "[s]ince the mid-1800s, about 75 percent of Puget Sound's estuaries and adjacent habitats . . . have been modified so significantly they no longer provide their original functions."[2] Degradation of many natural habitats surrounding the Sound is an effect of bulkheads, dikes, and other structures, which have transformed nearly one-third of the interior coastline.[3]

Today, most residents of Washington State would readily argue that the Puget Lowlands is a place where development and concrete have won over nature. However, a minor lapse in maintenance anywhere in the region opens the door for wildness to reestablish itself. The lowlands are some of the most fertile, productive lands in the state and are capable of regenerating themselves. What is necessary now is to encourage these remnants to persist, allowing them to expand naturally.

Where water meets land, wildness also flourishes. The lowlands historically included dense coniferous forest of western red cedar, western hemlock, and Douglas fir. These familiar westside old-growth forests were broken up, in the South Sound, by grasslands, camas prairies, and oak forests more typical of eastside dry forests. The line between land and water was not always so well defined. A series of boggy, dynamic wetlands transitioned the salty waters of the Pacific into the freshwater streams and solid ground in the lowlands. None of these landscapes has been wholly lost.

Everything from caterpillar-like sea cucumbers to charismatic and powerful orca whales reside here. The Puget Sound, despite heavy pollution, still maintains a healthy population of giant Pacific octopuses, the largest species of octopus in the world. Wild Pacific salmon continually rejuvenate the area's waters. As salmon run up streams, spawn, die, and decay, they replenish the watersheds of their birth with ocean-derived nutrients. This exchange between ocean and land systems produces the qualities that characterize the lowlands.

These qualities have typically been underprotected; wildlands protection in Washington State has traditionally focused on public lands, large areas, pristine landscapes, or dramatic rocky peaks. There are no national forests, national parks, or designated wilderness areas in the lowland bioregion, and more than 90 percent of the lowlands is in private ownership.

Protected areas currently in place in the lowland region include natural area preserves, natural resource conservation areas, marine reserves, city, county, and state parks, national wildlife refuges, private conservation easements, and parts of military installations. The resulting landscape is a mosaic of island wildness interspersed throughout a sea of human-dominated geography. Because of the unique circumstances of the Puget Lowlands,

motivated and well-informed citizens are not fighting for federal wilderness designation but instead seek alternative methods of protection to regenerate and preserve wildness.

URBAN WILDNESS

A businesswoman in a pleated skirt and taupe pumps walks down a busy street in Seattle, negotiating a path through the crowd of people. Her double-tall vanilla latte cools in her left hand while her right palms a cell phone, holding it gently to her ear. As she passes the Washington Mutual branch on Third Street, she yells out her conversation, fighting to be heard over the whir of downtown traffic. Directly above, a wild peregrine falcon falls into a two-hundred-mile-an-hour dive to catch a pigeon midflight. With her kill in tow the falcon returns to her nestlings who are waiting hungrily atop the fifty-four-story Tower Financial Center. Every spring since 1995, she and her mate have met on this very roof. Every spring they send off young. As one of only seventy-three pairs of nesting peregrine falcons in the state in 2002, this couple is partially responsible for the regeneration of their species. As pigeon down floats to the street below, not a single person looks up. Busy shoppers, commuters, and business people are each preoccupied with what they are doing at that moment while rushing to one of the city's shops, offices, or parking lots. Not one takes notice as the fastest bird in the world—a state treasure that until last year was listed as endangered in Washington State—hunts, lives, and thrives above their heads.

Only a few miles away from bustling Third Street is Leschi Natural Area. This tiny park protects a 3.5-acre hilltop in an east Seattle neighborhood. Visible to the northeast, over the waters of Lake Washington, are the skyscrapers of downtown Bellevue. Each building towers thirty or forty floors above the streets, but the streets themselves are invisible. In fact, the first eight floors of some buildings are obscured from a hilltop viewer; they hover above a carpet of green. Houses radiate in all directions but appear as little more than tips of rooftops, sinking below the ocean of cedar, fir, and maple. This mosaic fades to solid evergreen as the landscape rolls over Cougar Mountain and back to the Cascade Crest. To the south is the floating Interstate 90 bridge that delivers people between mainland Seattle and Mercer Island. Bailey Peninsula and the 299 acres of Seward Park old growth stand silhouetted behind the highway as an unbroken green mound of majestic trees. Mount Rainier provides the final backdrop; it towers over everything, reflecting pinks and oranges from the sunset on its glacial peak.

City parks, greenways, backyards, and sidewalk-bound trees all contain aspects of wildness in which humans do not control much of what happens and natural processes still dictate how and what is able to survive. Many wetlands that once covered the Seattle area are today parking lots and super markets; the forests have given way to streetlights and powerlines. But the cement mixers have not found all such spaces. What remain are the remnants of wildlands that have managed to withstand urbanization in the Puget Lowlands, and urban environmental groups are preserving and fostering this wildness literally in their backyards.

Seattle Urban Nature Project

The Seattle Urban Nature Project (SUNP) is a nonprofit organization that is using the tools of science, geographic information systems, satellite imaging, aerial sensors, and ground surveys to map out public lands within Seattle city limits. The group collects both quantitative and qualitative information about public green spaces for use by ecological advocacy organizations in Seattle. The data that they generate are available to anyone as a public service.

Motivated by a lack of information about urban public lands, Seattle resident Ann Lenartz organized the founding of SUNP in 1998. The organization's first set of maps was released as a large-format atlas in 2000. The maps contain detailed information about the size and shape of Seattle green spaces, including classifications of habitat type, quality and natural-ness of the environment, as well as presence and extent of invasive species.

Of the 58,000 acres of land within city limits, 7800 acres (or about 13 percent) are classified as public property; of this public property, undevel-oped areas of old-growth conifer stands, deciduous stands, beach dunes, and emergent wetlands account for 4156 acres within the city.[4] The remaining public green spaces are places like recreational areas within parks, such as soccer fields and rose gardens, or planted medians in roads—places that have been heavily impacted, do not retain their original character, and are currently maintained by human activity (lawn mowing, weeding, planting, and the like).

Since the completion of its initial mapping of public lands, SUNP has taken the next step: using its information to make policy recommendations and to aid urban conservation efforts. Its first project is a cost-benefit analysis of wildlife habitat quality with east-west connectivity in mind for wildlife movement across Seattle. The current project is a test, to estimate the cost and time requirements of this type of survey, done in hopes that SUNP may offer it to other groups in the future.

Thornton Creek: Wildness Beneath the Asphalt

The Seattle community of Northgate has been center stage for an ongoing controversy between gung-ho developers and concerned citizens. Northgate Mall is one of Seattle's centers of consumerism. In fact, the city of Seattle identified this area as an urban center in its 1993 overall comprehensive plan. Urban centers are defined in the state's Growth Management Act as places where higher density, pedestrian-friendly development is expected to occur. To address this issue, in 1999 the Simon Property Group, current owners of the Northgate Mall, wrote a fifteen-year redevelopment plan. The estimated $125-million-dollar plan included enlarging existing department stores, building a thirty-screen movie complex, and adding 450 new apartment units, a two-story underground parking lot, a hotel, and offices to the sixty-eight-acre shopping complex.[5]

Beneath the asphalt in the south end of the Northgate Mall, Thornton Creek still flows. Thornton Creek is part of the Thornton watershed, the largest watershed completely within Seattle city limits.[6] The creek runs through 7485 acres, with about 7 miles of open stream and just over 2 miles buried in culverts and pipes. More than 50 percent of the watershed is covered with impervious surfaces such as streets and sidewalks, channeling rainwater and urban runoff into the flow. Despite the desperate condition of this creek, five species of wild salmon and two species of wild trout are found within the watershed. The watershed is also home to many wildlife species, including blue herons, bald eagles, and chorus frogs. Just three years ago, North Seattle residents saw an otter and spawning coho salmon in the upper reaches of the watershed.

Bob Vreeland, a retired fisheries biologist from the National Marine Fisheries Service, and Janet Way, a North Seattle resident, were among the founding members of Thornton Creek Alliance, an organization involved in neighborhood preservation and restoration projects throughout the watershed. They later created Thornton Creek Legal Defense Fund (TCLDF) in order to file a legal appeal of the Northgate General Development Plan. They have developed a network of citizens and organizations that support rehabilitating the watershed, including the Washington Department of Fish and Wildlife, local chapters of the Sierra Club, the Audubon Society, the Washington Conservation Voters, and Yes for Seattle. Neighborhood organizations such as Citizens for a Livable Northgate, Twin Ponds Fish Friends, and Ravenna Creek Alliance have also joined in. Way says that "it's all about showing up."[7] The way to find and offer broad support is by involving yourself in a variety of organizations; coalition building is key to running a successful campaign.

Thornton Creek Legal Defense Fund is fighting for the health of the entire watershed and is unwilling to make deals that do not work toward that end. According to its Web site, TCLDF's mission is to "represent all individuals, organizations and community groups in Seattle and Shoreline who have an interest in the livability, health and restoration of Thornton

Creek through all legal means possible." The group is working to convince the city of Seattle to "daylight" (unbury) the creek and, through a series of lawsuits against the city and the Simon Property Group, TCLDF has drawn attention to this cause. The aim is to require Northgate Mall to remove the asphalt atop Thornton Creek and to provide for collection and retention of stormwater runoff from the property. The group's bold legal actions have been documented in every major newspaper in the city, and public opinion has continually been in its favor.

The suit against the city was based partially on the definition of a creek. Proponents of the development plan and the city of Seattle claim that Thornton Creek is merely a drainage ditch, not a creek, and therefore potential developers are not required to adhere to any environmental regulations concerning the flow. TCLDF has provided historical photos from as early as 1929, which show the creek prior to its diversion through culverts, and has presented the testimony of people who remember fishing in the creek in the 1930s and '40s. The defense fund has also cited the city's own 1992 environmental impact statement of the Northgate Area Comprehensive Plan, which acknowledged this portion of the stream. Despite the name given to the flow—creek or drainage ditch—the state's Department of Fish and Wildlife has identified suitable fish habitat on either side of the Northgate pipe and enough flow to support significant populations of coho salmon and cutthroat trout. It is unclear whether fish are using this stretch of Thornton Creek, yet their presence throughout the watershed is a testament that the potential is great.

Because of the opposition they faced from the defense fund and Citizens for a Livable Northgate, the Simon Property Group is not currently pursuing further development of the Northgate south parking lot but is, instead, trying to sell portions of the property. TCLDF continued restoration efforts and became involved in the campaign for Initiative 80, "Save our Creeks," spearheaded by the citizen group Yes for Seattle. The initiative called for habitat restoration of historic and existing creeks on public and private lands citywide in order to "protect our urban environment and help recover threatened salmon within our city."[8] The plan would uncover buried creeks as well as impose bans on the use of pesticides, herbicides, and fungicides within 200 feet of creeks on city land. Though the initiative encountered legal challenges that kept it off the ballot, activists have promised to continue working for the health of the Thornton watershed. Such opportunities to preserve and restore wildness within city limits demonstrate that an urban environmentalist does not have to turn to the mountains for the chance to engage in conservation activism. Sometimes, all that is required is to look into the cracks in the asphalt.

WILDNESS ON THE URBAN FRINGE

All over the Puget Lowlands, large tracts of private land are being subdivided to accommodate the ever-increasing demand for suburban development. In areas of critical concern, land trusts are working to acquire conservation easements to help defend the wild from untamed development. Such easements are used to restrict development and protect healthy and somewhat intact ecosystems that provide habitat for native species, conserve open space, and retain forest cover. This nonpolitical, nonconfrontational alternative is preserving some of the last remnants of lowland wildness.

A conservation easement is a tool used to gain developmental rights on a property, usually in perpetuity. Benefits to landowners may include tax breaks and/or monetary compensation. These incentives, plus a steadfast love of the land, have inspired many ecologically conscientious landowners in the South Sound to make valuable contributions to their community and its wild character.

Joann Kaiser-Harper is one of those people. In 1905, a German immigrant named August Kaiser moved his family and herd of dairy cows from Copalis Beach, north of Gray's Harbor, to homestead the uplands of Cooper Point, northwest of Olympia. The family operated a dairy farm for nearly seventy years until August's son (and Joann's father) Elmer passed away in 1972. Since then, Joann has owned the property and a few years ago she sold the development rights.[9]

Joann was raised on her family's farm. She raised her children there, and now they are raising their families there. Joann's connection to the place is very strong, but overwhelming property taxes forced her to reluctantly place twenty-one acres of her pioneer family's homestead up for sale in 2001. The property was a prime candidate for development, Joann recalls. "I was approached several times by timber companies, and all around I could see land being developed."[10]

Over the years the Kaiser family had maintained a healthy stand of trees by selectively logging. They built a house early on and in the 1940s Joann remembers her father building the hay barn with trees harvested from the property. "Then we didn't have power saws," Joann says. "Dad and the hands would go out with the old cross-cuts." Evidence of the old-growth trees used for the barn can be seen on the property today: stumps more than 4 feet across still bear the old springboard notches used to support their fellers.

Despite historic land use, the remaining 64 acres of the original 200-acre homestead still exhibit many wildland characteristics. The property contains extensive wetlands, forested riparian areas, and deciduous and coniferous forests that collectively support a variety of species. The distinctive *who-whooo* of a band-tailed pigeon, the screech of a red-tailed hawk, or the loud *clack-clack-clack* of a pileated woodpecker can be heard while walking through the upland area. Frogs singing an evening chorus serenade the great blue heron, poised for a supper of tadpoles. White-tailed deer browse the forest floor and raccoons scavenge the waters' edge for food. Downstream, beavers diligently work on jumbled piles of willow and alder branches, contributing to the vibrant uniqueness of the site.

Perhaps more significant is that Green Cove Creek basin hosts the best run of wild coho salmon within the Olympia city limits, and migrating salmon have been located well upstream of the Kaiser property.

In addition to the abundance of wildlife on the old homestead property itself, the basin is full of wildlife moving up and down the creek, which has been designated a critical wildlife corridor. Joann's property provides a buffer that benefits other protected wildlands within the drainage because species throughout the area benefit from the contiguity of forest cover and lack of fragmentation. Without protective cushions, the nearby 164-acre Grass Lake Reserve and the 1100 acres of The Evergreen State College land can become ecological islands isolated by suburban development.

In the summer of 2001, the nonprofit Capitol Land Trust (CLT) and area residents decided that Joann's property was a high conservation priority, partly because it was the largest amount of land in the basin with only one owner. After seeing her "For Sale" sign, the CLT negotiated to give Joann $5000 in earnest money, and Joann agreed not to sell the property for six months.

Then the CLT approached Thurston County as a partner (the county's management plan for the creek basin calls for conservation of 60 percent forest cover for stormwater retention). CLT suggested purchasing a conservation easement on 63 acres of Joann's property using $160,000 from the Conservation Futures Fund, a state program authorizing counties to collect money for conservation. The county fund derives from a 6.25¢ tax levied countywide on each $1000 of property value.

Just two days before the earnest-money offer expired, county commissioners approved the purchase of the CLT-negotiated easement. The easement forbids all future subdivision, construction of new homes, cutting of trees, mining, grazing, and other detrimental uses of the sensitive habitat. For Joann this was a way to protect open space she loved, make a contribution to conservation, and enjoy significant tax benefits allowing her to stay on her family's farm.

Further protection of the basin came with amendments to Olympia's Comprehensive Plan under the state's Growth Management Act (see appendix A for a description of the act). The plan designates Green Cove

Creek and its watershed as a sensitive drainage basin, removing it from within the Urban Growth Boundary and further restricting development. Joann's property now lies just outside of the adjusted boundary.

In *A Sand County Almanac,* Aldo Leopold wrote, "A land ethic reflects the existence of an ecological conscience, and this in turn reflects a conviction of individual responsibility for the health of the land."[11] Joann had such conscience and conviction, and she weighed her individual rights with the needs of the larger ecosystem. By selling the developmental rights of her property, Joann acted out of a sense of stewardship for the commons and has ensured that activities on the property will not adversely affect the environment.

"Joann's contribution to this community is immeasurable," wrote Eric Erler, executive director of CLT, in the trust's newsletter. "Joann chose the rewards of diverse habitat, natural character, and open space over development and logging transactions that would have yielded a much greater financial reward."[12] "It's beautiful land," maintains Joann. "It means that much to me to see it saved; I couldn't, in good conscience, wake up in the morning and see the land stripped of the trees."

 ## MARINE AND AQUATIC WILDNESS

In focusing on wildlands, the state's protection efforts often overlook the Sound itself. Less than 1 percent of Washington's marine and coastal waters is preserved by a patchwork of protections, including designated marine protected areas.[13] Leading scientists have called for 20 percent of oceans around the world to be designated as marine reserves. Washington State could make a significant contribution to that effort by establishing marine reserves in appropriate places along its shores.

As with land, there are many valid reasons to protect marine areas. The wildness of the Sound has declined due to many sources of degradation, including overfishing and artificial salmon hatcheries. Other dangers to the Sound include pollution of estuaries, uncontrolled stormwater, and the risk of a ship collision caused by increasing traffic. Many species are threatened, endangered, or locally extinct. Puget Sound has higher levels of highly toxic PCBs than Chesapeake or San Francisco Bays. Other contaminants in the Sound include mercury, arsenic, dioxins, lead, crude oil, motor oil, untreated sewage, pesticides, among hundreds of other pollutants. However, Puget Sound enthusiasts are finding ways to make sure this ecological treasure is protected for future generations. Designations and education are two tools they are using to regenerate and raise awareness of marine and aquatic ecosystems in the region.

An Underwater Park

On the Edmonds shoreline, cars load on and off ferries while a train rumbles quickly through the otherwise quiet town. Just offshore a man in full scuba gear slowly submerges, head first, into the cold waters of Puget Sound. In the distance, heads of divers pop up and down like sea otters surfacing for gasps of air. The thousands of commuters that float by everyday have no idea of the wildness that dwells in the waters below, nor do many of them know that underwater creatures live and breed in the safety of marine preservation. This is Edmonds Underwater Park, the first marine reserve in Puget Sound to ban fishing.

In the 1960s, local marine life was depleted in this area due to over-harvest by spear fishers. In 1970, Edmonds Underwater Park was established when local divers and citizens requested that the city, and later the state's Department of Fish and Wildlife, protect the area from harvest so that divers could actually see fish. Edmonds is one of more than one hundred marine protected areas throughout the Sound and encompasses almost 23 acres of subtidal zone and 6.5 acres of upland area. Only nineteen of the Sound's marine protected areas ban some or all fishing. Many only ban marine development such as docks or dredging.

Edmonds Underwater Park is unique in that it is devoted to both preservation and recreation. While allowing divers, this city marine reserve prohibits boating in the park, as well as the extraction of any resource. There are large signs by the parking lot and bathrooms that warn the visitors of these regulations. The perimeter is clearly marked with buoys to keep out boaters, and all regulations of harvest apply to uplands as well as tidal zones.

For the last twenty-five years, local volunteer and grassroots organizer Bruce Higgins and other dedicated divers have spent their Saturdays at the underwater park to oversee visitor safety, park security, and park preservation. When time allows, new structures are sunk for habitat and diving locations. These enhancements include sunken wooden boats, archways for viewing, and a complete trail system of ropes that lead divers to the main structures. Every enhancement made is well thought out and has a purpose for the enjoyment of the estimated twenty thousand divers who visit the park each year. At the same time, marine wildlife can thrive because they are protected from harvest. The carbon in the wood of the sunken boats nourishes worms that are food for the fish, and the artificial structures become home to rockfish, lingcod, shrimp, anemones, and crabs, to name a few common species. Others, including rare species, are found within the park boundaries at one time or another. A thirty-pound lingcod that nests in the park is one of many fish that benefit from these enhancements.

The ban on fishing and boating, combined with the artificial enhancements of the underwater environment, have led not only to a large population of marine life in the park itself, but also to fish populations spilling out into neighboring waters, contributing to the regeneration of wildlife in Puget Sound. A Washington Department of Fish and Wildlife research program, started in 1992, examined whether or not lingcod, rockfish, and other bottom fish respond to the protection from harvest provided by marine refuges. The study clearly showed that copper rockfish and lingcod were larger and more plentiful at the Edmonds refuge than at any of the similar, fished areas in central Puget Sound. Statistics show that copper rockfish populations at the long-standing Edmonds refuge were fifteen times greater than at the unprotected, fished sites.[14]

The state's first marine protected area set a precedent for the Sound, and activists are hopeful that such protective measures will gain popularity. Groups like the Ocean Wilderness Network and the Natural Resources Defense Council have taken to calling Edmonds Park an "ocean wilderness" in hopes that marine areas will become valued as wilderness like their terrestrial counterparts. But most important will be the many hours of dedicated volunteer support and cooperation between several key entities that made the Edmonds Underwater Park a reality.

Saving Orcas by Protecting the Sound

The pod of orca whales that lives around the San Juan Islands and in the northern Puget Sound has recently lost more whales than it has gained: the population slid from ninety-eight to seventy-nine between 1995 and 2002.[15] Any new orca calves will not be ready to breed for nearly twenty years, essentially creating another mouth to feed for the pod for some time. Without Endangered Species Act protection, these whales are in danger of eventual extirpation. But, according to the National Marine Fisheries Service (NMFS), this pod's genetic layout is not distinct enough from other orcas to meet the act's stringent requirements. The Sound's resident orcas were designated as a "depleted stock" in the summer of 2002, which required the NMFS to prepare a conservation plan to promote orca recovery and to identify agencies to be held responsible.

The high level of toxins in the Sound is a major cause of the orcas' demise. The Sound's toxins increase as they accumulate in the food web, a process called biomagnification. For an orca to gain one pound of weight, it must ingest ten pounds of food, such as salmon. For a salmon to gain 10 pounds, it must eat more than one hundred pounds of other fish. These fish, in turn, eat thousands of pounds of invertebrates and zooplankton, which themselves consume thousands of pounds of phytoplankton. Toxic chemicals become more and more concentrated as they are carried, molecule-by-molecule, through the food web from the phytoplankton to the top predators such as the orca whales. Accumulation of these toxins during the lifespan of an orca, which is similar in length to a human life, can result in reproductive dysfunction, weakened immunity, and increased mortality.[16]

In order to help these orcas—the wild wolf packs of the sea—vast tracts of marine environments must be preserved. The Orca Pass International Stewardship Area is a collaborative, grassroots effort attempting to preserve fourteen identified "richness zones" of nearshore, critical habitats and areas of high biological diversity. This conservation initiative focuses on the waters surrounding Washington's San Juan Islands and British Columbia's Gulf Islands, a major pathway of migration for orcas. The effort is a prime example of a citizen-based approach to preserving an important piece of wild Washington.[17]

A Wild Alternative to Hatcheries

At least twenty rivers flow into Puget Sound, connecting the rugged mountains with the sea. They vary in length from several miles to 135 miles long. In some of these lowland freshwater habitats, salmon hatcheries have long been established to supplement fish stocks for commercial harvest. Over the years, hatcheries have poured millions of fish into the region, yet salmon stocks are still waning, indicating that there are many problems associated with hatcheries.[18]

For one thing, they disrupt the genetics of wild salmon stocks. This occurs when salmon are transferred across watersheds without acknowledging the coevolution of a stock with its home stream. Often the genetic source for hatchery salmon is one healthy wild stock from a particular watershed. These same genes are used in hatcheries across the Northwest, which weakens and homogenizes the overall genetic pool of salmon. Hatcheries also contribute to higher levels of exploitation of wild salmon runs: there are so many hatchery fish that a 90-percent exploitation rate is allowed, even though the wild salmon that are intermingled with the targeted hatchery fish are too vulnerable to be caught at this rate.

Hatcheries are hiding the real causes behind the decline of wild salmon, which include overharvest, habitat degradation, genetic alteration, and blocked access to spawning territory. Developers and hydropower companies make financial contributions to hatcheries in an attempt to show the public that they are supporting the battle to save the salmon. This leads people to believe that their native stocks are being replenished, when, in reality, wild salmon stocks are in danger along with Puget freshwater, marine, and terrestrial ecosystems.

However, some hatcheries are using native stocks in an attempt to regenerate wild runs of salmon. By allowing some returning salmon to spawn in the creeks, following generations will be considered wild. The Nisqually

Tribe's Clear Creek hatchery rears and releases coho and chinook smolts into the upper watershed in hopes that the adult salmon will return to the streams to spawn. The tribe is also practicing other methods at hatcheries to create a more natural rearing environment. For instance, every year the tribe returns nutrients to the upper watershed by having a salmon toss, returning carcasses to the river. What is still missing is the high percentage of eggs that naturally would not hatch in the wild and would nourish aquatic insects and birds such as the water ouzel.

At the same time, the lowlands region still harbors rivers with no hatcheries. These gems provide opportunities for human inhabitants to observe wildness in their urban backyards. Kennedy Creek, in the Capital State Forest, is one salmon-bearing stream free of a hatchery. Located near Olympia in Totten Inlet, this creek is home to many salmon runs, including the largest run of chum in southern Puget Sound. At times the returning salmon resemble the runs of historical significance, described as so thick that one could walk across the river on the backs of the fish. Indeed, between 1992 and 2001 an average of 41,000 wild chums returned to the creek every year.[19]

In November, chum return to the rocky spawning beds nestled in the cedar and alder-shaded streams. Here, females build redds and spawn with purple-striped, hook-toothed males. Competition amongst males sometimes elevates to violence, and the wild salmon often splash their surroundings during this spawning ritual. To encourage understanding of this process essential to our ecosystem, the Washington Department of Natural Resources designated Kennedy Creek as a natural area preserve for education, research, and preservation. Then, thanks to the inspiration of one person committed to salmon restoration, the Kennedy Creek Salmon Trail was created in 2000.

The brainchild of fisheries scientist Jeff Cederholm, the trail took shape through the efforts of many groups and individuals, including the Squaxin Island Tribe, Taylor United Shellfish Company, Mason Conservation District, the Department of Fish and Wildlife, the Department of Natural Resources, The Evergreen State College, and Trout Unlimited. The trail supplies interpretive signs around the preserve and several viewing sites along the creek. At the main stations, South Sound Salmon Stewards, along with South Puget Sound Salmon Enhancement Group volunteers, are found on the weekends to answer any questions about salmon throughout the spawning season. Viewing stations have fences to keep people at a safe distance, and some stations are designed to handle large groups of people. Busloads of schoolchildren from as far away as Seattle are seen at the park on most weekdays, and salmon enthusiasts such as Cederholm are heard throughout the riparian area passionately engaging the young and curious minds with information about salmon. Experiences to view wild salmon such as this can create an awareness and respect for the wildness that still remains in the Puget Lowlands.

 ## THE NISQUALLY RIVER BASIN: A MODEL FOR COOPERATIVE WATERSHED MANAGEMENT

Stretching 73 miles from the glaciers on the southwestern flanks of Mount Rainier to the tidal mud flats east of Olympia, the Nisqually River basin is one of the healthiest watersheds in our state. The basin covers 720 square miles and contains many productive habitats, from alpine meadows and old-growth forests to oak woodlands and saltwater marshes. Although the marshlands have been modified for agricultural purposes, the Nisqually and its cohorts, McAllister and Red Salmon Creeks, have one of the largest intact estuaries in Washington. Wild salmon and steelhead rely on the estuary for passage to upriver spawning areas, and thousands of migratory birds on the Pacific Flyway use the area to rest, nest, breed, and feed. Bald eagles and osprey perch in 100-foot-tall cottonwood trees along the riverbanks and farther upriver, deer and elk roam the open prairies foraging on the lush grasses. In spite of the presence of dams and other human impacts, the watershed is a unique and diverse landscape that provides clean water and air; a place to live and recreate and a place where wildness still prospers.

Management of the river's resources is complicated because it flows through eleven governmental jurisdictions. But despite the potential for conflict, many citizen groups; city, county, and state governments; and the Nisqually Indian Tribe have taken a holistic approach to protecting the basin's economic, natural, and cultural resources. Their watershed management approach is a technique that recognizes the basin as one ecological unit. From a biological standpoint this sounds reasonable; however, from a planner's perspective it seems an overwhelming task.

The Delta

The Nisqually Delta is preserved as one of the largest estuaries in Washington State, in large part because of citizen opposition to development proposals. Urban infrastructure for the growing Puget Sound metropolis has been expanding across the landscape since the post-World War II building boom. Industrial developers began looking toward the delta for projects as early as 1949, when the Port of Olympia included it in its development plan. Fortunately, the plan was not implemented and the delta was spared for fifteen years until, in 1964, the city of Seattle explored the possibility of using the Nisqually Delta as a municipal landfill. In 1965, the Port of Tacoma considered installing a $65 million super port at the Nisqually River's mouth. Detailed plans were developed, the Port of Olympia was brought on board, and a public hearing on the plan was held August 25, 1965. The public outcry was astonishing. So many people showed up to voice their opinions that a second hearing had to be scheduled to accommodate the rest of the people.[20]

Many citizens saw the need to organize against the proposed threats. Margaret McKenny of Olympia formed the grassroots citizen organization known as Washington Citizens Committee for Outdoor Resources. The purpose of this group was to preserve the Nisqually Delta from any industrial use, including the establishment of a deep-water port. McKenny (1885–1969) was an educator, author, and conservationist and was widely known as a great naturalist. She wrote letters to Lady Bird Johnson and Senators Henry Jackson and Warren Magnuson, as well as the U.S. Fish and Wildlife Service and the Department of the Interior, all calling for the preservation of the educational, ecological, and cultural resources of the delta. She also recruited citizens to write to their elected officials and local governments about the issue.

After McKenny died in 1969, many conservationists were inspired by her cause and continued her work, including Florence "Flo" Brodie (1915–1992), who had moved to Olympia in the 1940s and had been a great friend of McKenny. Equipped with McKenny's original vision to save the delta, Brodie and others established the Nisqually Delta Association in 1969 to fight the industrial threats to the delta.

The overwhelming public opposition to the development plans spurred local political response. In 1970, the Washington Legislative Council was authorized to undertake an interim study of the Nisqually Delta area, and a forty-three-member Nisqually River Task Force was appointed by Governor Dan Evans. The task force commissioned future governor Dixie Lee Ray and Gordon Alcorn to perform a special study to determine whether it was "possible to have a clean super port with limited industrial development and a wildlife game preserve side by side on the Nisqually Delta." The resulting report concluded that deep-water port development was incompatible with the well-being of the natural resources in the delta.[21]

Buoyed by this finding, the Nisqually Delta Association continued its opposition and was ultimately successful. The Shoreline Management Act (SMA) and the creation of the Nisqually National Wildlife Refuge were eventual outcomes of the group's sustained grassroots effort. In 1971, the Nisqually River's banks and the shoreline stretching across the Nisqually Reach were designated as a "Shoreline of Statewide Significance" under the SMA. This was the first shoreline in the state placed under this designation, drawing much attention to the watershed and its delta. Finally, in 1974, the Nisqually National Wildlife Refuge was established and now hosts more than 100,000 visitors each year.

The Watershed

Over the years, a variety of management plans were proposed for the Nisqually River basin. In 1971, Governor Dan Evans again turned to his task force of citizens and officials to explore the idea of a national park. The grandiose scale of the park idea alarmed many local residents and the task force instead suggested that the river basin be managed as open space with a core green belt stretching its full length. The task force's second report, *The Nisqually Plan: From Rainier to the Sea,* proposed that the delta be maintained as a wildlife refuge and supported establishing a team to develop a comprehensive management plan for the river basin. Although not enough momentum was generated to implement the recommendations, this report would lay the groundwork for what was to come.[22]

As an aide to Governor Dan Evans in the early 1970s, Jennifer Belcher of Olympia, along with others in the Evans administration, promoted the plan to manage the entire river basin as one ecological unit. Later, in 1985, Representative Belcher introduced Substitute House Bill 323, which passed the state house and senate that year. The act mandated that the Washington Department of Ecology develop a comprehensive river management plan.

The Department of Ecology then sponsored the Nisqually River Task Force to develop what became the Nisqually River Management Plan, which was subsequently approved by the legislature in June 1987. The plan created two new entities: the Nisqually River Council and the Nisqually Basin Land Trust. The council is an interagency body committed to the protection and enhancement of the Nisqually ecosystem through education, advocacy, and coordination. A separate Nisqually River Citizens Advisory Committee was also created within the council to assure citizen representation during implementation of the management plan. The land trust is a nonprofit group of farmers, business owners, homemakers, and others working to protect the basin through private, nongovernmental means. In the last fourteen years the land trust has acquired more than 645 acres of critical habitat for permanent protection.

Citizen input, neighborly trust, and compromise have supported the management plan from its inception. Enthusiastic stakeholders can now act on their plans to restore salmon, protect water quality, and allow wildness to reestablish itself. To date nearly 67 percent of the habitat in the main stem of the river outside of Mount Rainier National Park is protected by Fort Lewis, the Nisqually Basin Land Trust, the Nisqually Tribe, or the Nisqually National Wildlife Refuge.[23]

Tribal Action

Nisqually Indian conservation efforts are key to protecting the watershed as a whole. The Nisqually and their ancestors, the Squalli-absch people, have lived in the basin for thousands of years. The name *Squalli* means "the people of the grass country." They have historically lived off of the camas prairies and open grasslands of the southern Puget Lowlands. The Nisqually culture has also depended on the life of the river. From the headwaters to the delta, the river supports not only an abundance of native salmon and steelhead, but also many other aquatic species: freshwater mussels and clams, edible crustaceans, amphibians, and a wide variety of edible and medicinal plants. Today, the reservation is 1,500 acres in size, along the river southeast of the wildlife refuge. Tribal influence, however, extends well beyond the political boundaries of the reservation.[24]

Billy Frank Jr., a Nisqually elder, is one of the state's best-known Native American activists. For more than fifty years he has worked to defend tribal fishing rights. Frank's style of activism focuses on building connections rather than making enemies, and he strives to find solutions that are mutually acceptable to all interested parties. Frank has established working relationships between the Nisqually Tribe, the National Wildlife Refuge, and Fort Lewis. He has also chaired the Northwest Indian Fisheries Commission since 1977. Nineteen tribes throughout Puget Sound and the Olympic Peninsula participate in the commission, which works with biologists, ecologists, policy analysts, and lawyers to improve native fish runs in the Northwest.

The current tribal strategy for habitat protection and restoration has been simply to buy land and manage it to protect and restore ecological process. "Buying and protecting land is better protection than federal rules and regulations," says Georgiana Kautz, the tribe's natural resource manager.[25] The tribe is buying as much land as possible along the edges of the reservation and on the banks of the Nisqually River. David Troutt, the director of natural resources for the tribe, reinforces this sentiment, "We cannot count on regulations alone; we need to work together with a common vision. It is going to take people willing to learn what to do to help fish and then doing the right thing on their lands. It is going to take concerned citizens throughout Puget Sound following the lead of the Nisqually Basin community."[26]

Nisqually tribal restoration projects began in 1996 with the breaching of a dike surrounding an 8-acre plot of pastureland near Red Salmon Slough. Today, native salt marshes are returning naturally, as saltwater grasses fill in the mud and juvenile chinook seek refuge there while preparing for ocean conditions. In 1999, the tribe bought 410 acres of the Ken Bragit Farm, and a dike surrounding a 31-acre portion of it was removed in late summer of 2002. The site is currently a tidally influenced mud flat; with every tide, seeds from the adjacent intact marsh, managed by the U.S. Fish and Wildlife Service, are washing into the new site and recolonization is beginning. Marsh restoration will continue acre by acre, with the goal of bringing salt marsh to the 110-acre portion of the Bragit Farm along the banks of the Nisqually River.[27]

In a conservation movement used to thinking about preservation in terms of hundreds of thousands or millions of acres, restoration of 39 acres seems insignificant. But it is estimated that rehabilitation of the estuary would double the number of wild chinook salmon returning to the Nisqually Delta every year. In this case, protecting and regenerating a few acres can have major impacts on the health of the entire watershed.

Rewilding the land from a Native perspective is not an issue that demands immediate results. The Nisqually people have seen much of the land destroyed throughout the tribe's long history in the area, but they have also seen the regenerative abilities of this fertile region. The estimated time span for complete regeneration of the salt marshes is thirty to fifty years. Conventional restoration projects would consider that a long time and would probably impose a more active management scheme. However, five decades is only a moment in the eyes of people who have been there for thousands of years and intend to be there when the salmon fully return.

Fort Lewis

Much of the ancestral lands of the Nisqually people has been usurped and parceled out to a variety of new owners. One of the largest parcels is the Fort Lewis military installation. With more than 60,000 of its 86,000 acres within the Nisqually watershed, the U.S. Army is the single largest land manager in the watershed. Fort Lewis accounts for 12 percent of the watershed, while the U.S. Forest Service comes in second at 10 percent. Army-base acreage is half again greater than that of Mount Rainier National Park and the Nisqually Wildlife Refuge combined; its ability to affect the well-being of the watershed as a whole is undeniable.

Though the Department of Defense is a wing of government often overlooked by today's wildland movement, military lands like Fort Lewis are unorthodox refuges, containing some of the last and largest examples of the state's native ecosystems. The largest remaining parcel of Puget Sound prairie lies within the fort, and biologists have documented about eight plant and animal species on army land that are listed as threatened or endangered.[28] Fort Lewis commanders have voluntarily adapted many of their land-use policies to accommodate sensitive species. For example, they have imposed no-fly zones over known bald-eagle nesting sites, reinforced creek beds to minimize erosion from armored-vehicle crossings, and restricted off-road-vehicle use around sensitive wetlands where the federally protected water howellia grows.

Though somewhat ironic, the fort's 7,000-acre artillery range provides a good deal of protection for sensitive species and habitats. The grasslands remain primarily intact because heavy logging, grazing, cultivation, irrigation, and settlement have been excluded from the range for nearly a century. The army has also designated the lands between the range and the edge of the Nisqually River as buffer lands to reduce noise and potential safety impacts on the surrounding area.

The Pentagon has been pressuring Congress to ease environmental laws on military installations, claiming that restrictions placed on exercises due to environmental concerns degrade the quality of training. Fort Lewis, in particular, has been recognized as a place where environmental regulations inhibit training. The deputy commander in chief of the U.S. Army, Lt. General William Tangney, complained to a House committee that troops were not able to train properly at Fort Lewis because 70 percent of the fort's training grounds is recognized as critical habitat for the spotted owl.[29]

Despite efforts to reduce the military's responsibility to enforce environmental laws, Fort Lewis continues to impose even stricter guidelines for its future impacts. In February 2002, a meeting was held to begin the planning process for the Installation Sustainability Program, whose purpose is to set environmental goals for the next twenty-five years on Fort Lewis lands. Participants included representatives from Fort Lewis, surrounding communities, environmental regulatory agencies, and other agencies. According to the *Seattle Times*, their discussions led to the current goals of the fort "generating its own electricity from renewable sources, reducing water consumption by 75 percent and recovering all endangered species on the post by 2025."[30] The same article quoted former Fort Lewis commander General James Hills's statement to the U.S. Senate committee: "I am a good steward of the environment for two reasons: It's the law and it's the right thing to do."

 ## WILDNESS PREVAILS

Although much of the Puget Lowlands has been degraded by industrialization and urbanization, much wildness remains. Concerned citizens have fought to preserve those yet untrammeled places and to encourage the regeneration of potential wildlands. Such efforts—and continued persistence—have resulted in creative strategies and widespread collaboration. As the

Puget Sound metropolis expands, it is imperative that the people of the Puget Lowlands continue to fight for wildness. The task of wildland advocates is to demonstrate how much wild is left and what the possibilities for the future may be. But activists must first help Washingtonians understand that this region is not beyond repair.

The lowlands are the stepping stones between the Olympic Mountains and the Cascade Range; their wildlands are what unifies the western portion of the state. Marine protected areas, conservation easements, and city parks connect urban landscapes with wild ones. The icon of the Northwest, the wild Pacific salmon, connects oceans to lowlands to mountains, symbolizing the dependence that each ecosystem has on the others. Efforts in the salmon-bearing Nisqually watershed exemplify how collaboration and creative techniques preserve wildland connections. Statewide, this holistic approach would achieve the connectivity that residents, advocates, and wildlife desire and need.

CHAPTER 14

The Wild East

♦ *Caitlin Houser, Oliver Smith, and Wayne Warrington* ♦

Washington State is widely recognized for a variety of attributes unique to the Pacific Northwest. The mention of Washington calls to mind the misty city of Seattle, the smell of coffee, and sea air drifting through rain-shrouded streets. Minutes away from Seattle, verdant forests thrive and mountain peaks tower over wild green places. This is the picture of Washington most commonly envisioned by prospective visitors and other nonlocals considered conversant with the geography of the Pacific Northwest. For many in the region, wildlands are most often associated with trees—colossal trees strengthened by age, serving as majestic examples of life before Manifest Destiny. Yet, just east of the Cascade mountains lies an exceptionally different Washington.

Few can recognize aging sagebrush or have even heard of the delicate cryptogamic crust of algae and lichen characteristic of desert soil that has gone undisturbed for decades. Even the dry ponderosa pine forests of eastern mountain ranges, many of which contain acre upon acre of ancient trees, are left out of the stereotypical picture of Northwest woodlands.

Within these arid ecosystems there are wild places of great beauty and diversity. In spring, wildflowers bloom and ignite the desert landscape. Come winter, lynx prowl through snow-swept lodgepole pine forests, stalking snowshoe hares. Ponderosas withstand summer wildfires that sweep

320

through and rejuvenate the understory of grasses and shrubs. Indeed, the dry lands east of the Cascades harbor a wealth of life amid some of the most challenging living conditions in the state. There is profound beauty to be found, not only in the visual aesthetics of these ecosystems, but also in the resiliency of the creatures and organisms that reside there.

Tragically, only a fraction remains of what were once endless vistas of thriving shrub-steppe and old-growth ponderosa forests. In little more than a century, most of the pristine habitat has been replaced by farms, degraded by cattle, or razed for the valuable timber. Just as a culture that is stereotypically "Northwest" developed in response to the economy and locale of the Seattle area, the lifestyle of eastern Washingtonians has engendered a set of values and perspectives that grew from decades of toiling the land to survive. Not surprisingly, a rift developed between environmentalists who live and work on the west side of the state and those who represent the interests of rural communities on the eastside. However, history has shown that there is significant local support for conservation throughout eastern Washington.

While extensive tracts of land in eastern Washington have been culti-vated and developed, wild areas do remain intact thanks to unique historical or geographical circumstances. Three of these, the Hanford Reach National Monument in the Columbia Basin, the northwestern reaches of the Rocky Mountains, and the Wenaha-Tucannon Wilderness in the Blue Mountains, exemplify the controversies of conservation in eastern Washington, exhibit the strategies employed by local activists, and serve as paragons of suc-cess from which readers can derive inspiration. These eastern Washing-ton wild areas are part of unique desert, river, and mountain ecosystems less well-known than their western Washington wilderness counterparts, but equally deserving of protection.

THE COLUMBIA BASIN

When Lewis and Clark ventured eastward from the Pacific's coastal rainforests into the wide-open spaces of the Columbia Basin in 1806, they found a valley flourishing with life. Meriwether Lewis wrote in his jour-nals, "The plain is covered with a rich verdure of grass and herbs from four to nine inches high and exhibits a beautiful scene, particularly pleas-ing after having been so long imprisoned in mountains and these almost impenetrably thick forests of the seacoast."[1] The wide clear sky and fluid grasses and wildflowers relieved the explorers from confinement in an im-mense realm of giant timber, and they found solace in a land unjustly dis-regarded by later visitors as too dry, sterile, and uninhabitable.

The Columbia Basin, sculpted over tens of thousands of years from dozens of cataclysmic hydrologic events (see chapter 2), is composed of a rich volcanic soil distributed by countless lava flows over the whole region. The basin's general borders extend south to Oregon, north above the Columbia River into the Colville Indian Reservation, west to the crest of the Cascades, and east to the edges of Lincoln, Franklin, and Adams Counties. Due to the rain-shadow effect of the Cascades, the yearly precipitation averages 6 to 9 inches, with half falling as snow, creating a dry region hospitable to the native shrub-steppe landscape.

The basin once contained 10.5 million acres of shrub-steppe, an intricately woven ecological unit composed of sagebrush, an abundance of shrubs, an understory of perennial grasses and forbs, and a protective ground layer called cryptogamic crust. The prevailing plant in the region is big sagebrush, which grows to an average height of 3 to 5 feet, and the predominant grass is Washington's state grass, bluebunch wheatgrass. Other common plants include bitterbrush, green rabbitbrush, greasewood, Sandberg's bluegrass, and Indian rice grass. Washington's shrub-steppe is home to a variety of animal species as well; deer, coyotes, jackrabbits, porcupines, raptors, mice, badgers, and even elk shelter in the ubiquitous sagebrush.

An intact shrub-steppe ecosystem is easily identified by the presence of undamaged cryptogamic crust. Cryptogamic, or cryptobiotic, crusts are composed of algae, lichens, mosses, and fungi that create a living carpet between stands of shrubs and bunches of grass and forbs. A healthy crust can be several inches thick and serves a variety of functions vital to an arid environment. An intact crust promotes soil stability by creating a barrier over the delicate soil, inhibiting wind and water erosion. Healthy crust also increases water infiltration, absorbing moisture and distributing it into the soil while providing shade for the underlying earth, thereby decreasing temperature and water evaporation. During the winter, freezing temperatures cause the crust to expand and crack, creating homes for dispersed seeds.

When the crust is disturbed by domestic livestock or adventurous off-road-vehicle (ORV) users, the vital topsoil underneath becomes susceptible to arid conditions and often blows away. Once airborne, the dried soil covers neighboring areas of cryptogamic crust and hinders the crucial photosynthetic processes needed for its survival. While the crust is tailored to extreme environmental conditions, it evolved in the absence of livestock, ORVs, and modern agriculture and is highly vulnerable to disturbances from these widespread activities. Depending on the severity of the disturbance it can take crust up to one hundred years to regenerate. (See the contrasting photographs of grazed and ungrazed shrub-steppe in the color insert.)

PUBLIC LAND AND LIVESTOCK GRAZING

On those public lands where the preservation and regeneration of wild shrub-steppe and grassland ecosystems are management objectives, the removal of domestic livestock grazing is of paramount importance.  Sheep and cattle trample cryptogamic crust and eliminate native grasses, leaving the landscape exposed to invasion by nonnative vegetation. Cattle also denude streamsides of vital plant life, erode streambanks, and contaminate waterways by defecating directly into and around streams. Still, only a handful of conservation groups, including the Northwest Ecosystem Alliance and the Kettle Range Conservation Group, are aggressively addressing the issue within Washington.

Several agencies are charged with regulating grazing on public lands, including the Washington Department of Natural Resources (DNR) and the federal Bureau of Land Management (BLM). While the BLM manages less than 400,000 acres in Washington, more than 70 percent of it is open to grazing. And while the DNR manages more than a million acres for agricultural use, it estimates that 800,000 acres, or 73 percent, are covered by grazing leases or permits. Regardless of the agency, all grazing leases or permits have a "use it or lose it" policy; all public lands managed for grazing must have livestock roaming and feeding off of the land or else the lease is revoked. Though efforts are made by land managers to ease the impacts of grazing on public lands and though some lands may lose grazing permits through disuse, endangered species like the pygmy rabbit and sage grouse, who depend on wild, undamaged shrub-steppe environments, continue to lose habitat.

During the intervening years, exposed areas are susceptible to invasive weedy species such as cheatgrass, which take root and kill some of the already-established native flora. Consequently, widespread grazing and agricultural conversion has turned a formerly diverse landscape into a patchwork of separated ecosystems. Regardless, according to John Zelazny, a former researcher for the Northwest Ecosystem Alliance, "A century of domination by those predisposed to grazing livestock, cultivation and irrigation has not completely altered an ecosystem that once thrived here; the energies of devoted conservationists can, through appreciating and understanding arid lands ecology, protect the intact vestiges that remain and work to restore some of what has been lost."[2]

Hanford Reach National Monument

Near the southwestern corner of the Columbia Basin lies Washington's newest national monument, the Hanford Reach. [3] Blessed with generally flat terrain and deep soils, it would have been a prime location for agricultural use. Nevertheless, this reach (or segment) of the Columbia River, along with approximately 170,000 acres of shrub-steppe, has been set aside because of a unique history and a concerted effort by environmentally and historically concerned individuals (see chapters 6 and 9).

Native Americans inhabited the area for thousands of years, as evidenced by the area's 120 recognized archaeological sites. The Army Corp of Engineers highlights the importance of native cultural resources within the reach: "The prehistoric sites within the Hanford Reach of the Columbia River represent the best preserved complex of mid-Columbia cultural resources. Evidence to date indicates that these sites span approximately 6,000 years of occupation and represent a wide variety of activities for the Columbia Plateau culture area which are poorly documented elsewhere."[4] Sheep ranchers and farmers had attempted to settle the area since the 1800s, but its dry, windy weather and remoteness hampered success. It was only in the first two decades of the 1900s, with the arrival of the railway and irrigation, that the two small towns of Hanford and White Bluffs managed to establish themselves along the Reach.

The towns survived until World War II when, in response to growing concerns about a nuclear Germany, the U. S. War Department mounted the unprecedented, secret Manhattan Project to develop nuclear weapons.[5] The government used six criteria to identify a suitable location for the safe production and hiding of nuclear materials: the project needed an area of at least 12 by 16 miles; a remote setting with no populations greater than 1000 within 20 miles; an abundant water supply of at least 25,000 gallons per minute to cool the reactors; a dependable hydroelectric power source to supply at least 100,000 kilowatts of electricity; a relatively flat landscape; and an available fuel and concrete aggregate.

The lands to the north of Richland, Washington, overwhelmingly qualified, and construction of the Hanford Engineer Works began in 1943. Residents were given notice to vacate their homes and relocate within ninety days; some were forced out in the first two days. The Army Corps of Engineers—the contractor for the project—decided which buildings were of use in each town and demolished the rest. The land on which the original town of Hanford had been established became the temporary home for approximately 51,000 members of Hanford's construction team, and Richland grew into a city to house the administrators of the project.

At 5:30 a.m. on July 16, 1945, the success of Hanford's secret project was established with the world's first atomic explosion in Alamogordo, New Mexico. Named the Trinity test, the explosion was made possible by plutonium produced at Hanford's B Reactor less than two years after construction began on the nuclear site. Just under a month later, the two atomic bombs credited with ending World War II were dropped on Japan: Little Boy over Hiroshima on August 6, 1945, and Fat Man over Nagasaki, three days later. The latter bomb was fueled with plutonium created at Hanford.

The Hanford Reach runs right along the north and east sides of the nuclear reservation. Specifically, it is the stretch of river that begins one mile below Priest Rapids Dam at river mile 396 and extends 51 miles to the slack waters behind McNary Dam at river mile 345. The Hanford Reach is one of only four significantly intact stretches in the entire length of the Columbia; 51 miles of the 1,214-mile flow from British Columbia to the Pacific represents a dismal 4 percent of this once mighty river.

The lands adjacent to the river are home to some of the most extensive, intact shrub-steppe habitat left in Washington and provide critical habitat to shrub-steppe obligate species—species like the sage grouse, sage thrasher, pygmy rabbit, and sagebrush vole that are either entirely dependent on the sagebrush for food or shelter or require the deep, soft soils specific to shrub-steppe for burrowing.

The White Bluffs along the eastern shore of the Reach rise 400 to 600 feet above the river and are rich in prehistoric fossils of extinct species of camel, mastodon, deer, bear, and rhinoceros. They not only provide nesting sites for swallows, but also claim the only known habitat in the world for the rare White Bluffs bladderpod.

Conservation of the Columbia's Hanford Reach became a subject of great contention as early as the 1960s, when fly-fishermen Richard Steele, Jack DeYoung, and Lowell Johnson discovered that the Army Corps of Engineers was planning yet another dam.[6] The Ben Franklin Dam, named for Benton and Franklin counties, was to provide additional hydroelectricity to the Northwest and allow barge access to Wenatchee, Washington, by raising the level of the river approximately 60 feet and drowning the last remaining, nontidal, free-flowing stretch of the Columbia in the United States. Steele, a resident of the Tri-Cities (Richland, Kennewick, and Pasco), brought the proposal to the attention of local eastside conservation groups, while DeYoung, a reporter for the *Seattle Post-Intelligencer,* began writing articles to inform the general public. A coalition called the Columbia River Conservation League, which included the Mid-Columbia Archeological Society, the Lower Columbia Audubon Society, the Sierra Club, and the Steelheaders, formed to answer the call. The conservation league discovered that the economics of the dam were so poor, that only public opposition was needed to defeat it. Faced with accurate economic statistics and the combined membership of the coalition, the Army Corps of Engineers was forced to temporarily shelve the proposal.

Throughout the next decade and into the 1980s, the Ben Franklin proposal was resurrected every few years, along with canal construction and river-dredging proposals. Rick Leaumont of the Lower Columbia Basin Audubon Society, Richard Steele, Nick Paglieri and Laura Smith of the Nature Conservancy, along with local conservation groups, decided that a federal Wild and Scenic River designation was necessary to provide permanent protection for the Hanford Reach. They recruited the help of Senators Dan Evans and Brock Adams and Congressman Sid Morrison to bring the issues of the Reach to the attention of Congress, which in 1988 resulted in Public Law 100-605, authorizing a study of the Reach.

A National Park Service–directed task force was created in April 1989 that included relevant state, federal, and local organizations representing a variety of interests. In three years they managed to produce a draft study and environmental impact statement, and in 1992, public meetings were held throughout Washington to allow for comments and discussion of the draft report. In 1994, the National Park Service recommended including the Hanford Reach as a recreational river in the National Wild and Scenic Rivers System, a designation supported by the small group of active conservationists working to save the Reach.

That same year, Rick Leaumont, Mike Lilga, and Richard Steele were desperately eager for increased public involvement when Bob Wilson, inspired by the beauty and natural flow of the Reach, decided to involve himself in its protection (see Wilson's interview in chapter 9). Soon after, the foursome established Save the Reach with like-minded citizens of the Tri-Cities area. The group's goal was a Wild and Scenic River designation of the Hanford Reach. In order to garner widespread support for the campaign, it was necessary to educate the public about the varied ecological and historical values of the Reach. This was done by creating a newsletter, coordinating guided river tours, conducting numerous public speaking engagements, and encouraging public letters to the editor of the *Tri-City Herald*. By 1996, the *Tri-City Herald* listed the Save the Reach campaign as one of the top ten issues in eastern Washington.

As the group gained momentum, it attracted the attention of other parties interested in the Reach. Recognizing their efforts, Senator Patty Murray, in 1995 and 1997, introduced legislation to designate a federal Wild and Scenic River. In fervent opposition, local congressman Doc Hastings introduced his own bill, H.R. 1811, which would turn federal lands in the Hanford area over to the local counties of Benton, Franklin, and Grant.

The two opposing bills created enough debate to require a hearing before the Committee on Energy and Natural Resources in Mattawa, Washington, on June 21, 1997. Approximately two thousand people showed up for the 9:30 a.m. meeting, creating the largest event ever held in Mattawa.

Save the Reach chartered a bus and brought people in from all over eastern Washington. Supporters of both bills were prepared with their own arsenal of experts and concerned local citizens. Commissioners for Benton, Franklin, and Grant Counties all testified in support of the Hastings bill and local control—this despite the fact that, according to Hanford land-use surveys distributed by the counties themselves, the counties' citizens overwhelmingly supported federal control of the Hanford Reach. Leaumont, Smith, Wilson, Steele, and several other concerned citizens made speeches supporting Senator Murray's legislation. Senator Slade Gorton, who chaired the hearing and supported local control of the Reach, concluded by assuring attendees that he would work with the ideas presented to secure the common good.

Leaumont and Lilga met with Senator Murray in Washington, D.C., later in 1997 and apprehensively requested that she consider seeking administrative support for federal designation if Congress continued to stall on a decision, warning that such a move could be politically harmful so close to her run for reelection. Regardless, Murray reaffirmed her support and agreed with their suggestion of possible administrative action. The following day she visited the House asking that they pass her bill and detailing the damage Hastings's bill would do to the Reach. Immediately after leaving the House, she publicly announced that if Congress did not act on her bill she would ask for an administrative solution. When recalling her courageous decision, Leaumont praises her as a true statesman.

Unfortunately, in 1999 the two opposing sides were still locked in a stalemate and Murray again introduced legislation for a Wild and Scenic designation. This time, regrettably, it looked like a Republican Congress favored Hastings's bill, leaving Save the Reach and Senator Murray struggling for congressional support. In the fall of 1999, county commissioners approached Save the Reach members and asked to initiate a series of private meetings. It took six months for representatives to come to an agreement pleasing both sides, whereby the Hanford Reach would be designated a Wild and Scenic River and the counties would receive monetary compensation. However, upon hearing that the commissioners had arrived at an agreement with the Reach group, Senator Gorton sent his assistant to kill the agreement. This gave local conservationists the impression that the private meetings had been originally intended to fail so that it could be publicly stated that environmentalists were impossible to work with.

Luckily, while Hastings was promoting his bill, the Clinton administration was also taking an interest in the area. Save the Reach was encouraged by a contact within the Department of Energy to consider pursuing a national monument designation, which, under the Antiquities Act, could be established by presidential proclamation. Such a designation required that an area under consideration have historical or cultural significance, a spectacular natural landscape, and be threatened with degradation. The Hanford Nuclear Site's history, archeology, and remnants of Euro-American settlement all established important historical and cultural significance. The intact shrub-steppe, free-flowing Columbia, and White Bluffs provided the natural landscape requirements. With the publication of the county commissioner's plans to sell the north slope to agricultural interests, Hastings's own bill ironically became the threat needed to satisfy the final requirement for national monument designation.

Save the Reach was well prepared with polls, flyers, fact sheets, and other relevant information for a complete proposal for monument consideration. Within months, Secretary of the Interior Bruce Babbit toured the Reach and returned to Washington, D.C., with a formal recommendation to President Clinton supporting monument designation. The first week of June 2000, Bob Wilson received an exhilarating and long-awaited call: Vice President Al Gore was coming to the Tri-Cities to formally announce designation of the Hanford Reach National Monument. After a demanding and protracted battle to protect the Reach from exploitation and destruction, the monument designation came as a swift and welcome reward.

Rick Leaumont and Rich Steele, alongside local conservation groups, fought for more than thirty years to maintain the Reach in its free-flowing condition. Bob Wilson and Mike Lilga supported them through the final stretch of political turmoil. Now the four can stand confidently on the edge of the federally protected White Bluffs and reminisce about a volunteer campaign that brought them together and saved not only a treasured stretch of river but also created a national monument that can serve as a testament to what future citizen activists can accomplish.

 ## THE NORTHEASTERN MOUNTAINS

In the northeast reaches of the state, there are two distinct mountain ranges rising from the shrub-steppe below: the Kettle River Range and the Selkirk Mountains. Farthest west is the Kettle Range, which derives its name from the river that has slowly separated it from the larger Monashee Mountains to the north. The Kettles contain the largest area of untouched montane forests in the region, as well as harboring a number of important species such as lynx, grizzly bear, wolverine, and western cutthroat trout.

Farther east lie the Selkirk Mountains, rising higher than the Kettles and beginning just north of Spokane. These are the southernmost extension of the Canadian Selkirks, and they spread across Washington and Idaho. The south-facing slopes of the Selkirks are dominated by ponderosa pine, while other areas mimic the wet, cedar-laden hillsides and valleys of the western mountains of the state. There is an incredible amount of diversity here, where Rocky Mountain species intermingle with the maritime-influenced habitat. The woodland caribou, a highly endangered species in the lower forty-eight states, is found only here and in the Idaho reaches of the range. The Washington Selkirks are also part of a grizzly-bear recovery area that reaches across northern Idaho and into Montana.

Local conservation groups in this lesser-known part of the state are determined to preserve habitat and species in both the Kettle Range and the Selkirks. The Kettles contain more than 300,000 acres of roadless wildlands—none of it formally protected. The Selkirks have fared better, with designated wilderness and wildlife refuge protections. Still, for the unique habitats and the multiple threatened and endangered species to thrive, far more protection is needed—and that means far more attention from all of Washington's wildlands advocates.

Wildlands Conservation in the Kettle River Range

While sharing many ecologic attributes with the central Rockies, the Kettle River Range is, as Harvey Manning states, "a place between, geologically and ecologically distinct from both the Cascades and the Rockies."[7] The Kettles reside in the western Colville National Forest, as well as in lands of the Confederated Tribes of the Colville. Leading up to these mountains is the arid shrub-steppe ecosystem. Traveling north, it becomes a landscape of rolling hills, with forests and meadows rising from river basins below.

The unique diversity apparent in the Kettles stems from a meeting of both the Pacific maritime climate and the dryer continental climate. The high peaks in the range include 7135-foot Copper Butte and 7258-foot Mount Bonaparte. The two major rivers carving through the Kettles are the San Poil River and the range's namesake, the Kettle River. The Kettle River watershed in its entirety covers approximately 750,000 acres of this terrain.

Within the forests of the range, there are eight inventoried national forest roadless areas, totaling approximately 104,850 acres, plus more than 200,000 acres of roadless lands that went unrecognized by the Forest Service. Because of this significant amount of wildland, many pristine forests can be found in the range, as well as an abundance of wildlife. The Kettles are home to many endangered, threatened, and sensitive species, as well as those close to achieving such dubious state or federal status. At-risk species include six birds, four mammals, one amphibian, and twenty plants. Mammals in the Kettle Range include grizzly bear, wolverine, lynx, marten, river otter, cougar, bighorn sheep, and moose. Because of the range's unique climate, western larch, Engelmann spruce, whitebark pine, subalpine fir, lodgepole pine, and ponderosa pine grow along with sagebrush. In 2001, the Kettles were named one of the fifteen most endangered wildlands in America by the Wilderness Society.

Nestled next to the Kettle Range and literally surrounded by the Colville National Forest is the small rural community of Republic, Washington, just shy of one thousand residents. The town sprang up because of a nearby gold mine, and the downtown now boasts a half-mile of local businesses—a feed/hardware store, a grocery store, a handful of hotels and restaurants, a natural foods store, and a public library. There are no fast food restaurants, and Radio Shack is the sole chain outlet in the town, save for gas stations. Home to both the Vaagen Brothers Lumber Company mill and the Kettle Range Conservation Group (KRCG), this community is no stranger to controversy, especially in the form of the jobs-versus-environment debate.

The Kettle Range Conservation Group has its headquarters on main street. Founded in 1976 by Dick Slagle, a lifelong resident of Republic, the KRCG is dedicated to regional wildlands protection. Up until 1997, when it opened its Republic office, the group consisted of an all-volunteer member base. Now it also has an office in Spokane, as well as seven staff members. Over the years the KRCG has successfully stopped timber sales in important roadless areas and ancient forests throughout the Kettle Range, as well as disputing hundreds of other threatening projects in the region. In the late 1970s and early 1980s, the KRCG was considered one of the best-organized conservation groups in Washington.

Though the KRCG, along with other groups, fought to include the Kettle Range in the 1984 Washington State Wilderness Act, the region was dropped from the bill before passage, leaving the Kettles with no official wilderness areas designated. This came as a hard blow to the KRCG. Meetings became fewer and farther between, and it seemed as though the group was falling apart. Tim Coleman and Mike Peterson had moved to the area a few years prior and were a part of the group at the time. During the mid-1980s they had the drive to revamp the group and Coleman is now its executive director.

The KRCG has been quite successful at protecting area forests from the saw, but this success has brought much opposition from members of local communities. Although Coleman is blamed for many community woes attributed to a lack of timber, many do not know that Coleman himself is not diametrically opposed to logging, even within the mountains he has fought to protect. While he would like to see about half the Colville National

Forest saved from cutting, he acknowledges that logging has a place in our national forests. Coleman believes both job losses and environmental degradation could be avoided if the timber industry and Forest Service could agree to a "logging program that is gentle on the woods and does not create new roads."[8]

Coleman and the KRCG employ many tactics to pursue their goal of preservation and have been especially successful in appealing national forest timber sales. These appeals slow down the sale process, as well as forcing the Forest Service to reconsider its sales. Some recent examples include the 1995 Trout Timber Sale, which would have sacrificed 2000 acres of ancient forest in the Colville National Forest; the 1997 Deer Timber Sale in the Colville, which would have punched 9 miles of new roads into a 7000-acre roadless area; the 1998 Long Draw Timber Sale in the Okanogan National Forest, which was to be in one of the largest roadless areas in Washington; and the 1998 Tonata Timber Sale in the Colville's Bodie Mountain Roadless Area.[9]

Because the Kettle Range has no lasting protection from logging and road building, the KRCG, the Pacific Biodiversity Institute, and American Lands proposed the Columbia Mountains National Monument in late 2000.[10] The proposal covers approximately 420,000 acres in the Kettle Range, with about 97 percent on Colville National Forest lands, 0.6 percent on BLM land, and 2.2 percent on private lands. Approximately 311,325 acres (72 percent) of the proposed monument retain their natural integrity: the Washington Department of Fish and Wildlife has confirmed sightings of gray wolf, wolverine, lynx, great grey owl, three-toed woodpecker, and grizzly bear. Right now more than 300,000 acres (nearly 90 percent) within the proposed area are open to logging and road building. Unfortunately, when presented with the protection plan in 2001, local congressman George Nethercutt opposed it.

The KRCG is still actively pursuing wilderness designation in the Kettles, which would afford the highest level of protection. In 1996 the group brought together five eastern Washington organizations to form a coalition that later led to the creation of the Wild Washington Campaign (see chapters 8 and 10 for more about the Wild Washington Campaign). In August 2002, four groups within the campaign, including the KRCG, presented Republican Congressman Nethercutt and Democratic Senators Patty Murray and Maria Cantwell with 7000 signatures requesting that there be more wilderness designations in the Colville and Umatilla national forests of eastern Washington. These persistent conservationists continue working for their goal to protect roughly 1.2 million acres within the Okanogan, Colville, and Umatilla National Forests as wilderness, including 225,000 acres in the Kettle Range that were dropped from the 1984 wilderness act.

Grizzlies of the Selkirks

East from the Kettle Range another set of mountains dominates the sky-line: "The Selkirk Mountains offer the silence of old-growth groves of cedar and hemlock, the solitude of high mountain trails and the hope of wildness in a lone wolf's howl."[11] The northwesternmost limit of the Rockies in the United States, the Selkirks begin within Spokane city limits at a popular local rock climbing area called Minnehaha Park. Looking north, however, the mountains rise in elevation, with nearby Mount Spokane at 5,867 feet. The highest peak in the Washington Selkirks is 7,309-foot Gypsy Peak, found a few miles south of the Canadian border. National forests in the Selkirks are the Colville and Idaho Panhandle. Protected areas include the Little Pend Oreille National Wildlife Refuge and the Salmo-Priest Wilderness. The major rivers winding their way through this landscape are the Pend Oreille, Salmo, Colville, and Columbia.

The Selkirks share many habitat types and wildlife species with the Kettle Range and are also home to the most endangered mammal south of the forty-ninth parallel—the woodland caribou. Also present in the Selkirks, though mainly confined (in Washington) to the Salmo-Priest Wilderness, is the rare, gray wolf. Grizzlies are found here as well, altogether making this a wild place with enough remnant areas of habitat to support these umbrella species.[12] Interestingly, this region lies within the path of an interior storm track, which results in much wetter and more biologically diverse habitats, including wet cedar forests that mimic those of the Cascades.

The Selkirk Mountains, though fragmented, still retain significant strongholds of wildness. The Salmo-Priest Wilderness, established through the 1984 Washington State Wilderness Act and located in the extreme northeast corner of the state bordering Idaho and Canada, contains 41,335 acres of pristine wildlands. This wilderness spills over into Idaho, which contains an additional 9,440 acres of designated wilderness.

The Washington Selkirks are part of the Selkirk/Cabinet-Yaak Grizzly Bear Recovery Area, which extends from the Cabinet-Yaak region in extreme northwestern Montana, through northern Idaho, and into the Washington Selkirks. The grizzly is listed as threatened in these areas, but many are working for stronger protection for the bear and its needed habitat.

The U.S. Fish and Wildlife Service has been reprimanded for breaking the law a number of times by failing to adequately protect grizzly bears. A judge ruled twice in a four-year period that Fish and Wildlife neglected to implement measures necessary to provide protection for the threatened Selkirk grizzly population. Because of this continuing negligence, conservation groups throughout the region have been fighting to have the grizzlies' listing upgraded from threatened status to endangered. If endangered status is achieved, areas of core, critical habitat will have to be designated and protected for the bear. Because grizzlies require large ranges to survive, the preservation of these habitats will invariably foster protection for most flora and fauna within these ecosystems.

Groups involved the protection of the grizzlies in the Selkirks include the Kettle Range Conservation Group, the Lands Council out of Spokane, the Owens Foundation for Wildlife Conservation, Vital Ground, the Sierra Club (Inland Northwest chapter), and the Alliance for the Wild Rockies, among others. In early 2003, largely through these groups' efforts, legislation to create the Northern Rockies Ecosystem Protection Act was brought before Congress. This bill is based on a comprehensive, far-reaching vision of connected ecosystems that, if protected, would provide habitat for a multitude of species, including the grizzly bear, gray wolf, and woodland caribou. If passed, it would create many needed habitat corridors, providing linkages from one core area of wilderness to another. This, in turn, would facilitate species movement and lessen the current isolation of "island habitats" scattered across the northern Rockies landscape.

Though this bill covers wildlands in Washington, Idaho, and Montana, it proposes more than 140,000 additional acres for protection in the Selkirk Mountains alone, and approximately 190,000 acres in the Kettle River Range. This would be long-awaited and welcome protection for both of these ranges, but equally if not more exciting is the ecosystem scope of the entire bill. If great creatures like the grizzly bear, a living symbol of the wild character of the American West, are to survive in our state, it is going to be through collaboration with Idaho and Montana to the east and with our northern neighbor, Canada. The Selkirks in Washington still retain much of their wild character, yet their wildness (at least in the form of charismatic megafauna) is dependent upon habitat connectivity with out-of-state ecosystems such as the Cabinet-Yaak in Montana and the Selkirks of Canada. A bioregional perspective must be adopted in order to realistically protect and preserve this wild landscape that is the Washington Selkirks.

THE BLUE MOUNTAINS

In southeastern Washington, small rural towns pepper the landscape. The drive between towns is breathtakingly scenic, with the rolling hills of golden grassland known as Palouse shimmering in the sun. The Palouse Hills rise abruptly to become the craggy basaltic ridges of the Blue Mountains, the slopes of which are covered with dry forests, chaparral, mountain meadows, and grasslands.

In addition to displaying dramatic geological features, such as looming basaltic ridges and crumbling mesas cut by deep river gorges, the Blue

Mountains act as a refuge for a wealth of well-known wildlife: cougars, bob-cats, fishers, bald eagles, and northern spotted owls reside in the dry for-ests. Marmots whistle from mountainside scree while black bears pull chinook and steelhead salmon from the Wenaha and Tucannon Rivers below, and coyotes can be heard howling at night. Pine martens, small creatures be-longing to the weasel family, and several other historically or currently threat-ened species depend on the old-growth forests of this region as habitat. Large herds of Rocky Mountain elk and chattering gaggles of wild turkey roam the hills of the Wenaha-Tucannon, attracting more hunters than hikers to the Blue Mountains.

Only a finger of the Blue Mountains extends into Washington State; the rest of the range is situated in the northeastern corner of Oregon. Within Washington, the Wenaha-Tucannon Wilderness is the only major protected area, with a total of 111,048 acres. The Tucannon River is a proud feature of the wilderness and is home to four federally listed, threatened and en-dangered fish species.

Moving away from the water and up the hillsides, the forests become drier and shift in appearance from lush understory to parkland, with open meadows, and clumps of trees growing sparser with elevation, rising above patches of bunchgrass. Ponderosa pines dominate the lower elevations, transitioning into lodgepole pine forests above 4,500 feet with some larch, fir, and spruce. Crowning the sharp grassy inclines are spectacular ridges of jagged basalt that tower like ancient fortress walls. A quick hike up one of these steep hills rewards the viewer with a panorama of velvety hills, often crosscut by parallel outcroppings of basalt cliffs. The landscape is both severe and nurturing to an extensive array of plants and wildlife, in-dicating a long legacy of endurance and adaptation in the harsh conditions of the region.

The Wenaha-Tucannon Wilderness

When the rugged, tree-laden canyonlands known as Wenaha-Tucannon were signed into law as wilderness in February 1978, a man named Bill Arthur was on site to celebrate. Arthur and a friend, arriving inside the new bound-aries just before midnight, braved a chilly winter night in the mountains so they could be known as the first people to hike in the Umatilla National Forest's new Wenaha-Tucannon Wilderness. As chairperson of the regional Palouse branch of the Sierra Club, Arthur (then a young college student) played an important role in gaining local support for the bill in the years before the area was designated as wilderness.

The Wenaha-Tucannon Wilderness, which was created as part of the 1978 Endangered American Wilderness Act, is located in the Blue Mountains of southeastern Washington and northeastern Oregon. The Blue Mountains possess the same regional issues and political climate that make the question of conservation an embittered dispute in other places in the Inland Northwest. Much of the area around the Wenaha-Tucannon Wilderness has been severely impacted by logging, grazing, and agricultural cultivation. The land faced a grim future of logging roads and clear-cuts if the movement to protect it had failed to catch on. According to Arthur, the factor that ultimately led to the success of conservationists' efforts was the visible presence of public support.[13]

The Sierra Club knew that in order to gain the support of Congressman Tom Foley, who was then the local Democratic representative, they would have to show that more than students and hikers backed a wilderness area; the endorsement of key members of the community was vital. Knowing this, and knowing that sportsmen clubs were a large and respected interest group in the area, Bill Arthur set out to recruit hunters and fishermen. Arthur traveled from town to town, visiting with local hunting and angling groups. Many residents, although wary of his Sierra Club affiliation, found common ground with Arthur, who had grown up in rural northwest Montana.

The Palouse Sierra Club chapter, along with the Spokane chapter and the Wenaha-Tucannon Wilderness Council, a group of local supporters who did not want to be affiliated with a national environmental organization, all collaborated to garner the attention of Congressman Foley. Arthur says these efforts were, "sufficient enough to get on Foley's radar screen. He acknowledged support [for a wilderness], but compartmentalized it and minimized it by noting who we were and who we weren't and making it clear we didn't have enough support from more average constituents of the district." This led to Arthur's next move.

With Jim Kittrick, co-chair of the Wenaha-Tucannon Wilderness Council, Arthur visited the head of the Inland Empire Big Game Council, Art Solomon. "Jim and I went up to meet with him just to get acquainted. I think once people meet you as a person, you can get past what people think you are and start figuring out who you really are. He [Solomon] knew who we were, but was a little suspicious of the Sierra Club and what we were all about." Solomon had a shooting range in his backyard and he invited Arthur and Kittrick to join in black powder target practice. "Jim had a whole bunch of hunting stories to tell and I had one good one; one dead deer to my credit and I got the maximum mileage out of that dead deer."

The importance of this time spent with Solomon was significant: "We established a comfort zone," says Arthur. "Art still didn't agree with everything the Sierra Club did, but we were okay people. We talked about habitat for elk and deer and the key elk calving habitat [in the Wenaha-Tucannon]."

Arthur explained to Solomon that if the Wenaha-Tucannon area was not protected, a major elk calving area called Moore Flat would most likely be sacrificed to logging. The only option that would protect the place from chain saws and bulldozers was wilderness designation. Before Arthur left the meeting, Solomon had agreed that the Inland Empire Big Game Council would support the wilderness designation. "That put us over the hump with Foley," Arthur says.

During his work in the community, Arthur found that correcting widespread misinformation was important in strengthening the movement on a local level. A misconception exists among some conservationists that residents of the state's east side must not love their wild places; so much has been lost, and many of the places that have retained their natural character are still vulnerable to resource-extracting interests.

But in reality, it is not an aversion to wildness or even the legacy of resource extraction that is responsible for the lack of protected areas; it is often an eastside aversion to designations like "wilderness" that plagues the movement. Arthur has indicated that the Forest Service "intentionally or unintentionally fostered misperceptions" by spreading false purist doctrine about what is and is not permitted in wilderness. Residents of the area fall victim to myths that horse packing, hunting, or even trailside signs are not allowed in wilderness areas.

The influence of libertarian political ideology is also responsible for some of the local wilderness designation resistance. In Arthur's words, "You can love this area—and a lot of them did—and they would still either fear or hate the word wilderness because of [its affiliation with] the federal government." If the "Feds" represent a threat to independence, then most forms of federal land management are suspect or cause for resentment. In spite of such problems, by engaging with the community and presenting the prospect of wilderness designation as the only option for beloved local lands, Arthur was able to rally the support of the public.

While there is currently a lack of political leadership for expanding protected areas in the Blue Mountains, organizations such as the Umatilla Forest Watch are maintaining visions for the future. The group's current proposal includes two additions to the Wenaha-Tucannon Wilderness totaling 58,100 acres. The largest addition follows the Tucannon River north from the current wilderness boundary encompassing 38,600 acres. This addition would protect important geologic, cultural, and biological resources, including the only known mountain mahogany in Washington State. The other proposed section extends from the Wenaha-Tucannon's eastern boundary, on the Washington side, covering 19,500 acres in the Wenatchee Creek and Devils Canyon areas. Deep, river-cut canyons in this parcel harbor year-round freshwater springs that feed salmon-bearing streams.

OUT OF THE RAIN: DEFENDING THE WILD EAST

A beautiful and diverse landscape exists in Washington's eastern reaches, with many threats and challenges to its ecological integrity. Some of these lands have retained their natural character because of unusual circumstances, as with the Hanford Nuclear Site. Other places have stayed out of the spotlight because of their stronger association with other states, such as the Selkirk/Cabinet-Yaak Grizzly Recovery Area. Still others have remained relatively intact because they are simply out of the way in low-population areas, as with the Wenaha-Tucannon Wilderness in the Blue Mountains. The overarching reason, however, that there are wild places left in the Columbia Basin, the northwestern reach of the Rockies, and the Blue Mountains is because there are dedicated citizens who have worked hard, made sacrifices, and devoted their time and energy for the cause. It is because they feel so strongly for these wildlands and the need for their protection that they are willing to give so much of themselves to protect the land they love.

In western Washington, there are many like-minded people who share appreciation of untrammeled wilderness. Preservation is quite popular in the western part of the state, and at times it can feel like preaching to the choir when speaking about the benefits of wildlands preservation. There is certainly less personal risk associated with criticizing old-growth logging, protecting roadless areas, opposing clear-cuts, or even advocating removal of dams.

On the east side, things are different. Conservationists still face challenges that hearken back to an earlier era in which opposition was fierce and wildlands preservation was still considered a "wild" idea. It calls for the truly dedicated to speak out and organize to effect change under these circumstances, the likes of which many younger conservationists have not had to face. When it is time to defend the ecosystems you love, where you live and what the popular vote happens to be become irrelevant. What matters is that committed citizens step up and speak out against harmful practices that destroy the wild integrity of the lands they cherish.

CHAPTER 15

The Reclamation of Washington

◆ *Edward Whitesell* ◆

The preservation and regeneration of Washington's wild places is a story that continues to unfold. After millennia of compatible human cohabitation with the wildlife, wild rivers, old-growth forests, mature shrub-steppe and native grasslands of this region, radical landscape transformations were introduced by non-Native peoples in the short span of a few generations. These interventions were so extreme and came so rapidly that residents throughout the state found themselves forced into open resistance to defend Washington's lands and waters as they knew and loved them.

At the initiation of the frontier, this resistance came from the Native peoples, for whom the frontier meant not development and progress but invasion of their ancestral lands and violation of a sacred relationship with their natural community of life. The political movement to restrain and direct frontier development came into its own in the twentieth century, just as the frontier economy was attaining an unprecedented scale and intensity of resource extraction and environmental alteration. Because of this movement, the landscape of Washington gradually took on a more mixed character than would have been produced by frontier development alone. National parks and monuments, wilderness areas, and private land trusts multiplied across the map, safeguarding pieces of a natural heritage that would otherwise have been cut down, dug up, plowed over, or drowned from one end of the state to the other.

The story of how small, determined, audacious and resourceful groups of people have accomplished so much against such daunting opposition is an inspiration to those who must assume this difficult charge today and tomorrow. When Karen Fant, one of the two founders of the Washington Wilderness Coalition, was asked what would be one of the most important messages she would like us to share with our readers, she responded right away, "that the work will never end." If the citizens of Washington ever lose their footing as they traverse what Ben Shaine calls the political wilderness, not only will they themselves fall, but so will the wild places that depend upon a mobilized and powerful citizenry for their defense.

Our greatest source of hope and inspiration for the future is the remarkable extent to which citizens of Washington have already made a difference. Had it not been for their courageous work and many sacrifices, protected areas in twenty-first-century Washington would be limited to little more than scattered offshore islands and a handful of icy mountain peaks. Indeed, the protected areas of Washington would be so small and isolated by now that they would serve only as decorations in a thoroughly domesticated and commercialized landscape. Setting aside scenic vistas saves places that are pleasant to look at, but this sustains the living wild no more than makeup, hairstyling, and fine clothes bring to life the embalmed remains of a loved one; each is a purely cosmetic response to death.

Washington's current protected areas did not come easily. Smokey the Bear did not hand them down to us, and neither did environmentally conscious business leaders or farsighted politicians. The history of conservation in Washington certainly includes influential resource managers like the Forest Service's Bob Marshall and its former chief, Mike Dombeck, magnanimous corporate figures like those who gave millions of dollars to save the Loomis Forest, and deeply committed statesmen like Dan Evans. Nevertheless, at each step of the way, when Washington's most outstanding natural areas were on the chopping block, it took a citizen movement to stand up to the tremendous and seemingly unstoppable momentum of the development frontier. In chapter after chapter, we have read the stories and heard the voices of Washington residents, from diverse walks of life, who said to the land management agencies, corporations, and politicians: Enough is enough. We do not have to blast mines, bulldoze roads, plug up rivers, level forests, and chew up bunchgrass in every single place where there is profit to be made. We must save some of it as it is.

The early conservationists in this state shaped a movement that has continued to evolve. For the outdoor clubs that turned toward the political wilderness in the early and mid-twentieth century, saving it "as it is" meant wilderness preservation. Toward the end of the twentieth century, saving it "as it is" also came to be called old-growth or ancient-forest protection. Now, increasing numbers of conservation groups are going even further, working with notable success to save it like it was, to reverse the damage of frontier developments like the Elwha and Snake River dams, which decimated wild salmon populations that once seemed limitless. All of these actions and others like them constitute the movement for the preservation and regeneration of wild Washington.

The legacy of citizen conservation work is glorious but it should not be glorified—not if a similar legacy is to be established by current and future citizen activists. This book seeks to inform and better prepare conservationists to learn from their movement's past successes, avoid past mistakes, and carry on with the work of creating innovative solutions and pushing bold agendas. We do not learn from past successes when conservation victories are told as epoch battles between superhuman forces of good and evil or when earlier conservationists' actions are judged from the perspective of today's circumstances, possibilities, and values. Neither do we learn from past mistakes when information about these mistakes is jealously guarded. That is why a constructive critique of the movement is necessary.

The most important conclusion we reached in our research for this book is that the citizen movement for the preservation and regeneration of the wild in Washington is not effectively tapping into the large public support for its cause. Consequently, insufficient progress is being made to realize the visions and dreams of conservationists around the state. There is no more obvious demonstration of this fact than the narrow scope of current congressional work to designate additional wilderness areas in the state.

At the turn of the present century, Congress finally showed interest in resuming the designation of new Washington wilderness areas—work that it abandoned after the Washington Park Wilderness Act of 1988. But Washington's congressional delegation has, so far, only entertained the idea of one wilderness bill at a time, over a period of many decades. The plan is to slowly add to the National Wilderness Preservation System a few of the national forest lands that were left out of the 1984 Washington State Wilderness Act, one wilderness area at a time. Judging from the track record of the first of these, the relatively noncontroversial Wild Sky Wilderness, designating only a dozen top priority, isolated wilderness areas on that timetable would take half a century. This agenda not only takes too long to safeguard the areas in question, but it completely leaves out millions of acres of other wildlands where citizens around the state are working hard to fend off unnecessary developments and ongoing environmental degradation. This very narrow wilderness agenda is, no doubt, being complemented by other strategies such as campaigns for old-growth forest protection, campaigns to stop the damage of livestock on public lands, campaigns to remove the most devastating dams and so on. Nevertheless, the research conducted in the preparation of this book clearly shows that today's movement as a whole does not promise to fully realize the visions for the preservation and regeneration of the wild that are currently being expressed by citizens around the state.

Although there is no easy way for the movement to rise to the challenge, the solution can nevertheless be simply stated: as conservationists we must politically mobilize and empower the vast numbers of Washingtonians who care about their wild places and wild creatures. Favorable public opinion polls will only translate into bold and timely accomplishments if the public becomes meaningfully involved. As we have seen in the book's final chapters, grassroots organizing is currently being done, but as we have also seen in this book, there are critical gaps that are internally recognized but which are not being effectively addressed. The movement has become increasingly partisan (Democratic) and encompasses a narrow demographic profile (overwhelmingly white, increasingly urban and suburban, and with some important gaps regarding representation of youth, as well as in power sharing between men and women at upper levels of some groups). Moreover, some conservation groups prefer to mobilize people as donors and as names on postcards and e-mail messages to decision makers, rather than to empower them to lead their own separate and autonomous conservation groups where they live. More than a few conservation leaders recognize these trends as troublesome, yet within significant portions of the movement there is still little evidence of a resolve to spend the money and the time necessary to do things differently.

Lacking the vast financial resources and pervasive political connections of large corporations and the political elite, activists depend for their strength and effectiveness on a mobilized and empowered citizenry. Mobilization and empowerment mean more than getting large numbers of people to make financial contributions and respond to action alerts (although those things are necessary). Mobilization means getting sympathetic people from all sectors of society to fully participate, including people of all socioeconomic classes, both genders, all races and ethnic backgrounds, all occupational fields, and in every locality of the state. Empowerment requires assisting people in the acquisition of the knowledge and tools they need to fully develop their inherent potential as activists in the true sense of that term—as people who are actively making history themselves rather than furnishing a proxy for other people to act in their stead.

What is needed is good, old-fashioned, grassroots organizing designed to empower broad sectors of the public to defend wild places, wildlife, and wild ecological processes where people live, work, and play. This is what produced the movement we have today, as we have seen in the stories of countless people throughout the state. Four decades ago, when three fly fishermen in the Tri-Cities heard that the Army Corps of Engineers was going to finish the job of taming the wild Columbia River by damming up the last free-flowing stretch in the United States, they set to work talking with everyone they could find in their communities about standing up to this governmental Goliath, no matter how tiny their band was at first. Pulling together a hardy crew of local people from many walks of life, they repeatedly forced the Corps to back down. Eventually, they got the endorsement of the Park Service for their Wild and Scenic River proposal. In the second half of the 1990s, they even succeeded in mounting a congressional campaign led by Senator Patty Murray, despite the fervent opposition of local congressman Doc Hastings, who introduced a bill to turn federal lands in the Columbia Reach over to the counties. With this move, Save the Reach violated a cardinal rule for wilderness campaigns, which is that the local congressional representative must go along or at least remain neutral for a conservation bill to be worth fighting for. But that didn't stop the people in Save the Reach. They were breaking all the other rules anyway, like trying to save sagebrush country instead of old-growth forest; going for a wild river designation, which is just not done in Washington; and trying to apply a congressional protective designation to something other than a national forest (this area was managed by the Department of Energy, for crying out loud!). But the grassroots organizers of Save the Reach did not care about any of this. All they knew was that they loved that stretch of river and they were going to keep right on meeting with local hunters, fishers, farmers, business people, and others, because that is what it would take to protect one of the most endangered and neglected ecosystems in the state and, of course, the place they liked to fish. Ultimately, breaking all the rules worked. With spunk, determination, creativity, luck, and good, old-fashioned grassroots organizing, they protected the last free stretch of the Columbia as a new national monument.

Spending years working face-to-face with people who know the land; developing sincere friendships, trust, and powerful working relationships among wildlands supporters from all walks of life; helping to start scrappy new organizations and then stepping back to relinquish control and responsibility to these local defenders of the wild—these may be old-fashioned techniques, but they are also radically democratic when the objective is to redistribute power in the movement from a centralized to a decentralized pattern. No movement will achieve anything close to its full potential if its members are sought by professional activists simply for their money and to create political capital for the professional activists to use as they see fit in their dealings with elected officials and other decision makers. Because this approach centralizes power and knowledge, it actually undercuts the very source of power upon which any true citizen movement depends, namely a mobilized and empowered citizenry.

Another important conclusion of this book is that the movement for the preservation and regeneration of the wild in Washington still suffers from deeply ingrained predilections when it comes to its issues and priorities. The top two priorities of the movement have long been wilderness designation and the protection of old-growth forests. When these priorities are mapped out, the result is a distorted picture of the future of wild Washington, in which protection coincides almost entirely with the location of roadless national forest and national park lands. The vast majority of the state is ignored by that agenda. Left out are scores of rivers deserving of inclusion in the Wild and Scenic Rivers System, along with the highly endangered shrub-steppe and grasslands of the Columbia Basin. Also left out of the top two priorities are the wild places left in pockets of the Puget Lowlands and in the depths of Puget Sound itself. We have made it a point to show in this book, that wildness exists in all of these places and that important work is being done by citizen groups to preserve what is left and to bring back some of what has been lost. We do this as a way to challenge the dominant viewpoint that protecting wildness is all about protecting roadless national forests and charismatic megaflora (big old trees). Though all victories are hard fought, the roadless areas in the national forests and the inspiring old-growth forests of Washington will be the easiest places to protect, given the widespread public recognition and support that has already been generated by citizen campaigns focused on such areas. This means that much greater citizen attention is required to preserve wild places in the rest of the state, in order to achieve a truly balanced system of protection.

Right now is an exciting time for those grassroots organizers who are out working with people in their communities, because this period in Washington's history is full of undreamed-of potential for the movement. This may seem incomprehensible to those who are staving off current attacks on environmental policy and legislation at the national level. Yet, the fact remains that our state is undergoing major and irreversible economic restructuring and social transformations that bode extremely well for the preservation and regeneration of the wild. As shown in the first part of this book, the movement is now poised to catch a favorable political wave, if its participants prove to be sufficiently astute to understand this and to start paddling in the right direction. It is now possible for community organizers to find much more common ground with business leaders, city councils, and politically conservative recreation groups than they could during the heyday of the frontier's extractive economy. Because the movement for wilderness and wild areas accomplished so much at the height of the frontier economy, it only stands to reason that sustained organizing in the twenty-first century should yield results beyond the wildest dreams of those earlier activists.

A few years ago, the Nisqually Tribe purchased a farm by a river mouth near Washington's capital city, Olympia. Yet instead of farming or building on it, they proceeded to breach the former owner's dikes. Non-Natives had constructed these dikes after they had assumed ownership of this place in the frontier days, when drying up wetlands was called "reclamation." With this recent purchase and others to come, the Nisqually people are now in the process of reclaiming pieces of the Nisqually River, in the true sense of the word. Not only is their act of reclamation a return of ownership to Native peoples, but by breaching the dikes they have deliberately set free wild processes brought with the rise and fall of tidal waters, allowing wild creatures and plants to reclaim the land too. The people came to watch and celebrate as the first tide bathed the land, regenerating the environment needed by wild salmon and their entire wetland community of life. As some people danced and everyone gave thanks, one of the tribal biologists stood in the rising water, watching it rapidly advance across the slightly inclined tidal plain. Gazing down between his rubber boots, his eye was attracted to the sight of a hermit crab scrambling along just behind the leading edge of the flowing water. This tiny, wild creature was a pioneer, but it was a new sort of pioneer because it was not a foreign immigrant in this land. It was one of the very first wild creatures taking part in the reclamation of a wild wetland, nearly one hundred years after this place had been domesticated. With every passing year, growing populations of wild salmon will follow suit in this watershed as their estuarine rearing habitat is regenerated.

Wildness will reclaim the frontier landscape throughout Washington as soon as the imprint of humanity is lightened. Great swaths of the state, from east to west, from the mountains to the deserts and the sea, can be preserved and regenerated by simply expanding and strengthening citizen efforts already in progress throughout the state. We can reclaim for future generations the natural heritage that has been denied to our own, if we take action to pick up the wild pieces that are left, allowing them to flourish once more. It is our responsibility as citizens to do so because only a broad and inclusive movement of informed, dedicated, and empowered citizens can make this come to pass.

APPENDIX A:
Laws and Regulations

FEDERAL LAWS AND REGULATIONS
Laws and regulations listed chronologically below are important tools for activists in guiding the administration and management of our federal public lands and for ensuring proper protection and management of species and ecosystems. Public Laws (PLs) and subsequent amendments are incorporated into the U. S. Code (USC) every six years. The USC is ordered by title, then chapter, and finally section (§). Statutes are described below, including the agencies affected. Reference information is given by title and section, followed by any additional relevant title sections. For example, the Wild and Scenic Rivers Act is section 1273 of title 16, or 16 USC § 1273. Title sections that apply to this act include sections 1271 through 1287, so the full reference reads 16 USC § 1273 (§§ 1271–1287). Statutes that have not yet been published in the USC are identified by PL number (e.g., PL 106-393). Laws passed after 1972 can be accessed at *http://thomas.loc.gov* using the PL number. You can search the USC at *http://uscode.house.gov/ usc.htm*; the Cornell Law School also makes the USC available online at *www4.law.cornell.edu/uscode*. For guidelines to implementing these laws, see the Code of Federal Regulations at *www.gpoaccess.gov/cfr/index.html*. Text of all laws and regulations is also available at public libraries.

Federal Agency Abbreviations
BLM: Bureau of Land Management
FWS: U.S. Fish and Wildlife Service
NOAA: National Oceanic and Atmospheric Administration
NPS: National Park Service
USFS: U.S. Forest Service

Wilderness Act (1964)
Created the National Wilderness Preservation System, allowing Congress to designate wilderness areas on federal public land, to be managed by the agency with jurisdiction. USFS, NPS, BLM, FWS. *16 USC § 1131 (§§ 1131–1136).* **More information:** Wilderness Information Network, *www.wilderness.net.*

National Wild and Scenic Rivers Act (1968)

Allows designation of free-flowing river segments for public access and recreation with three different classifications: wild, scenic, or recreational. These correspond to varying degrees of preexisting development. Candidate rivers can be proposed for study by citizen groups or local governments with the help of a willing representative who introduces a study bill for congressional approval. A river accepted for study is protected from development for up to six years. USFS, NPS, BLM, FWS. *16 USC § 1273 (§§ 1271–1287)*. **More information:** National Wild and Scenic Rivers System, *www.nps.gov/rivers*.

National Environmental Policy Act (1969)

Established a national policy for incorporating environmental protection and public participation into federal land-management decisions. Requires environmental assessments and draft and final environmental impact statements to be submitted before actions are taken that would significantly impact the environment. Allows administrative appeals of decisions by individuals or organizations. Created the Council on Environmental Quality. All federal agencies, including the Depts. of Defense and Energy. 42 USC § 4321 (§§ 4321–4370). **More information:** Council on Environmental Quality, *http://ceq.eh.doe.gov/nepa/regs/ceq/toc_ceq.htm*; USFS NEPA site, *www.fs.fed.us/emc/nepa*.

Endangered Species Act (1973)

Species listed under the ESA are considered threatened or endangered (T&E), and the law forbids their "taking" (killing, harassing, harming, or removing). Some species have critical habitat designated under the ESA, but not many. Landowners conducting activities that may result in takings, like federal agencies, must consult with the FWS and NOAA. In addition, state and private resource lands are required to develop habitat conservation plans, which outline steps for T&E species protection but also exempt managers from further legal restrictions. A congressional moratorium on listing new species ended in 1996, and there is a large backlog of species that need listing. FWS, NOAA. *16 USC § 1533 (§§ 1531–1544)*. **More information:** FWS ESA site, *http://endangered.fws.gov/policies/index.html*; FWS list of wildlife laws, *http://laws.fws.gov/lawsdigest/reslaws.html*.

Federal Land Policy and Management Act (1976)

This BLM "Organic Act" established a management framework for the BLM based on multiple-use principles. Requires BLM managers to develop a comprehensive planning process that involves public input. Areas of critical environmental concern can be established, and natural resources must be protected and managed to ensure their integrity and viability. BLM. 43 USC § 1701 (§§ 1701–1782). **More information:** BLM FLMPA site, *www.blm.gov/flpma;* overview of the act, *www.wilderness.net/nwps/legis/flpma_legis.cfm.*

National Forest Management Act (1976)

The primary law concerning national forest administration, requires the USFS to implement a resource management plan for each unit, guided by multiple-use, sustained yield principles. Established public participation standards for involvement in national forest planning procedures. USFS. 16 USC §§ 1600–1614.

Washington State Wilderness Act (1984)

Established eighteen new wilderness areas in the national forests throughout WA along with one wilderness area within BLM jurisdiction (Juniper Dunes). Also sought to assure that other national forest roadless areas would be available for more intensive use, by allowing USFS to develop them without reviewing their potential for future wilderness designation until the expiration of existing forest-management plans (which were expected to be revised roughly every ten years). Of the thirty wilderness areas in the state at the writing of this book, three were established by the 1964 Wilderness Act, three were created by the 1988 WA Park Wilderness Act, and nineteen were established by the 1984 WA State Wilderness Act (the other five were designated in other legislation). USFS, BLM. 16 USC § 460pp.

Washington Park Wilderness Act (1988)

Established wilderness within the Olympic and Mount Rainier National Parks and the North Cascades National Park Service Complex. Created 1.7 million acres (roughly 40 percent) of the state's current 4.3 million acres of designated wilderness. NPS. 16 USC § 90 note.

Appeals Reform Act (1992)

Enacted an administrative appeals process that allows individuals or organizations to file appeals of USFS natural resource management. Allows citizens to challenge legality of projects without going to court. On June 5, 2003, new regulations revised the USFS appeals process (*Federal Register* vol. 68, p. 33581) in ways that significantly reduce the public's ability to administratively challenge USFS management decisions. USFS. 16 USC § 1612. **More information:** USFS appeals and litigation site, *www.fs.fed.us/emc/applit/36cfr215.htm;* review of new regulations at the Wilderness Society site, *www.wilderness.org/OurIssues/Forests/reform.cfm.*

Northwest Forest Plan (1994)

Also known as Option 9, a land management plan affecting national forests and BLM lands in WA, OR, and CA, developed as an ecological and economic compromise to the timber wars of the late 1980s and early 1990s concerning decreasing timber jobs and the listing of the northern spotted owl as endangered. Goals were to establish sustainable timber production and the protection of biological diversity, initiatives for providing assistance and job retraining to displaced timber workers and affected communities, and avenues of agency coordination and public input in decision making. Set aside designated use areas in the forests, most notably late-successional reserves, adaptive management areas, and matrix lands. USFS and BLM within the range of the northern spotted owl (five national forests in WA). The plan is not yet legislated. **More information:** Background, record of decision, guidelines, and current amendments and reviews, *http://pnwin.nbii.gov/nwfp.shtml*; current happenings: *www.or.blm.gov/nwfpnepa*.

Secure Rural Schools And Community Self-Determination Act (2000)

Also know as the Payments to Counties Act, provides funding to rural counties with a high federal land base in lieu of taxes and timber sale receipts. Established eleven resource advisory committees (RACs) in WA (composed of industry, environmentalists, and local elected representatives) to allocate money for resource improvement/restoration projects, and sets aside funds for rural community institutions and services. Payments are issued to the state, which allocates funding to counties. PL 106-393. **More information:** USFS RAC information, *www.fs.fed.us/r6/RAClinks.htm*.

WASHINGTON STATE LAWS AND REGULATIONS

Environmental laws and regulations specific to Washington are a spotlight on the most pressing issues concerning state, local, and private lands. Those presented chronologically below are only a partial list, though together they showcase citizen priorities concerning responsible forest management, salmon and watershed health, rare endemic species and ecosystems, and the ever-increasing pressures of urbanization. The *Revised Code of Washington* (RCW) contains all laws. Each title (e.g., 43) contains specific chapters (e.g., 43.21). The *Washington Administrative Code* (WAC) also has titles and chapters, composed of complementary rules and guidelines for implementation of laws. Full text of laws and regulations can be obtained at *www.leg.wa.gov* or at public libraries.

State and Federal Agency Abbreviations

DFW: Department of Fish and Wildlife
DNR: Department of Natural Resources
DOE: Department of Ecology
FWS: U.S. Fish and Wildlife Service
USDA: U.S. Department of Agriculture

Forest Practices Act (1946, 1974)

Original 1946 act required reforestation after timber harvest. Newer act created the Forest Practices Board, which presides over rule making to protect wildlife, fish, soil, and water quality on state timber lands. Administered by DNR. RCW 76.09 (many amendments since). **More information:** DNR Forest Practices site: *www.dnr.wa.gov/forestpractices*.

Conservation Easement Laws (1971, 1979, 1984)

Laws allowing purchase or conveyance of development rights and conservation easements by local governments or nonprofit organizations. The Conservation Futures Program allows property taxes to be levied for acquisition funds by local governments. The DNR Forest Legacy Program, under the USDA federal program, protects working forests near urban areas. Nonprofit land trusts work directly with landowners, mostly on the county level. RCW 84.34.200–250 (acquisition), RCW 64.04.130 (easements/conveyances), RCW 84.36.500 (tax exemptions for conservation of farm land). **More information:** Many counties have nonprofit land trusts and Conservation Futures programs, so check with county offices or Web sites; DNR Forest Legacy Program, *www.dnr.wa.gov/htdocs/amp/forest_legacy/legacyhome.html;* List of WA land trusts, *www.lta.org/findlandtrust/index.html.*

Shoreline Management Act (1971)

Regulates development on shorelines of the Pacific, Puget Sound, Straight of Juan de Fuca, rivers, streams, and lakes of a certain size, and associated shoreline wetlands. Local cities and counties regulate through shoreline master programs (SMPs). An August 2001 lawsuit resulted in repeal of 1972 (with 2000 additions) SMP guidelines. Settlement announced in December 2002 by Governor Gary Locke with support from WA Environmental Council and Association of WA Business. Updated rules expected to be developed and implemented between 2003 and 2014. RCW 90.58 **More information:** Background and guidelines repeal, *http://textonly.mrsc.org/Subjects/Environment/shorelin.aspx.*

State Environmental Policy Act (1971)

Modeled after and similar to the federal act (NEPA). Pertains to state and local government projects or plans and is intended to incorporate environmental values and public participation into decision making by agencies. Requires a scoping and/or public comment process and submission of draft and final environmental impact statements before action is taken. Amended in 1983, requiring state agencies to follow guidelines under SEPA rules. Administered by DOE and affecting DNR, DFW, and DOE. RCW 43.21C (2003 amendments pending). **More information:** DOE SEPA home page: *www.ecy.wa.gov/programs/sea/sepa/e-review.html.*

Natural Area Preserves Act (1972)

Established the natural area preserve (NAP) designation under DNR administration. A 1982 amendment established the DNR Natural Heritage Program, which now selects and nominates areas for NAP status. The heritage program also monitors native ecosystems and rare species; amendment outlined six categories to describe the status of rare plants in WA. RCW 79.70. **More information:** DNR Natural Areas Program, *www.dnr.wa.gov/ nap/;* DNR Natural Heritage Program, *www.dnr.wa.gov/nhp;* University of WA Rare Plant Care and Conservation Program, *http://courses.washington. edu/rarecare/index.htm.*

Scenic River System (1977)

Prohibits many development activities in and along river corridors designated as state scenic rivers. Can serve as the first step toward federal Wild and Scenic River protection. There are only a few protected riverways in WA. Administered by State Parks and Recreation Commission. RCW 79A.55 (amended 1999). **More information:** American Rivers list of state river protection programs, *www.amrivers.org/wildscenictoolkit/stateprograms.htm.*

Natural Resource Conservation Areas Act (1987)

Established the natural resource conservation area (NRCA) designation and four initial NRCAs. Managed by DNR Natural Areas Program (see Natural Areas Preserve Act). The Trust Lands Transfer Act (RCW 79.71.050) allows purchase of lands or development/extraction rights to establish NRCAs. RCW 79.71 (amended 1991, 2000).

Endangered Animal Species (1990)

Under state regulation (not law), several classifications exist for listing species of concern, including endangered, threatened, and sensitive. The Fish and Wildlife Commission (in the DFW) is charged with listing and delisting wildlife species in coordination with the federal FWS. WAC 232-12-297 (wildlife). **More information:** DFW species of concern: *www.wa.gov/wdfw/wlm/diversity/soc/concern.htm.*

Growth Management Act (1990)

A statewide comprehensive land-use planning law requiring counties and cities to develop twenty-year comprehensive plans to address both urban and rural development. There are thirteen key goals of the plan, which include reducing sprawl, protecting greenspace and the environment, encouraging citizen participation, and maintaining natural resource industries. Local planning efforts identify urban growth areas and conservation areas such as greenways, open space, and critical habitat designations. RCW 36.70A, WAC 365-195 (procedural criteria for adopting comprehensive plans and development regulations), WAC 365-190 (guidelines to classify natural resource and critical areas). **More information:** State Growth Management Program, *www.ocd.wa.gov/info/lgd/growth;* WA Research Council reports, *www.researchcouncil.org/Briefs/2001/PB01-29/WAGMAGoalsPromises.htm;* 1000 Friends of WA smart growth site, *www.1000friends.org/smart_growth/smart_growth.cfm.*

Puget Sound Water Quality Protection Act (1996)

Created the Puget Sound Action Team and Puget Sound Council to represent diverse interests and negotiate a biennial work plan for protecting Puget Sound through watershed planning and restoration activities. Broad public information sharing and participation are delineated. These and other activities are funded by the Governor's office. RCW 90.71. **More information:** Puget Sound Action Team, *www.psat.wa.gov.*

Salmon Recovery Act (1999)

After the listing of sixteen endangered salmon species, the Forests and Fish negotiations began in 1996 between industries, environmentalists, tribes, and others to create new rules guiding habitat conservation plans for state and private timberlands. These were influential if unsuccessful, as conservation groups pulled out of the negotiations in protest, but the resulting report was used for the forestry module of the act. The act delineated seven Salmon Recovery Areas in the state and created the Governor's Salmon Recovery Office, as well as a forest riparian easement program that gives tax credits to responsible small-forest landowners. RCW 77.85 (formerly 75.46). **More information:** Governor's Salmon Recovery Office, *www.governor.wa.gov/gsro;* DFW salmon recovery site, *www.wa.gov/wdfw/recovery.htm.*

APPENDIX B:
Land-Use Planning

INFORMATION AND CONTACTS

In order to effectively participate in land-use planning decisions, citizens must inform themselves of agencies' proposed activities. The *Federal Register* *(http://fr.cos.com/)* is the official daily publication for rules, proposed rules, and notices of federal agencies and organizations, as well as executive orders and other presidential documents. Individual agencies produce documents containing proposals and environmental impact statements, as with the Forest Service's *Schedule of Proposed Actions* and the National Park Service's *General Management Plans*. The following listings of federal, state, and local agencies should help you to stay informed.

FEDERAL
Army Corps of Engineers

The Corps provides engineering services to the nation through a civilian and military workforce. It develops and manages water resources on military installations and public lands.

Seattle District
PO Box 3755
Seattle, WA 98124
(206) 764-3742
www.nws.usace.army.mil

Walla Walla District
201 N 3rd Avenue
Walla Walla, WA 99362
(509) 527-7700
www.nww.usace.army.mil

Bonneville Power Administration

Under the Department of Energy, the BPA markets wholesale electricity and transmission to the Pacific Northwest's public and private utilities as well as to some large industries. For this purpose, the BPA uses thirty-one federally owned dams in the region, one nuclear power plant at Hanford, and a nonfederal wind-energy program.

Street address:
905 NE 11th Avenue
Portland, OR 97232

Mailing address:
PO Box 3621
Portland, OR 97208-3621
(800) 282-3713
(503) 230-3000
www.bpa.gov/corporate/kc/home/index.cfm

Bureau of Land Management

The BLM, within the U.S. Department of the Interior, manages roughly 400,000 acres of grazing and recreation lands in Washington, as well as more than one million mineral leasing sites.

Spokane District Office
1103 N Fancher
Spokane, WA 99212
(509) 536-1200
www.or.blm.gov/Spokane

Bureau of Reclamation

Operating under the U.S. Department of the Interior, the Bureau is the largest wholesaler of water in the country and the second largest producer of hydroelectric power. The Bureau has thirty-nine projects in its Pacific Northwest Region.

Eastern Washington
Upper Columbia River Area Project
1917 Marsh Road
Yakima, WA 98901
(509) 575-5848, ext. 202

Western Washington
Lower Columbia Area Office
825 NE Multnomah Street, Suite 1110
Portland, OR 97232
(503) 872-2795
www.pn.usbr.gov

Environmental Protection Agency
The EPA works with other agencies, state and local governments, and Native American tribes to develop and enforce regulations under existing environmental laws. Washington is included in Region 10, the Pacific Northwest.

U.S. EPA, Region 10
1200 6th Avenue
Seattle, WA 98101
(800) 424-4EPA
(206) 553-1200
www.epa.gov/region10

Washington Operations Office
300 Desmond Drive SE, Suite 102
Lacey, WA 98503

Fish and Wildlife Service
The FWS is part of the Department of Interior and is charged with conserving, protecting, and enhancing fish, wildlife, and plants and their habitats. The agency manages more than thirty national wildlife refuges, fish hatcheries, and other areas in Washington State.

Regional Director, Pacific Region
911 NE 11th Avenue
Portland, OR 97232
(503) 231-6828
http://pacific.fws.gov

Hanford Reach National Monument
3250 Port of Benton Boulevard
Richland, WA 99352
(509) 371-1801
http://hanfordreach.fws.gov

Forest Service

As part of the U.S. Department of Agriculture, the USFS manages forests under the sustained yield, multiple-use concept, planning timber sales and managing federally designated wilderness. Within the agency's Region 6, the USFS manages a scenic area, a national monument, and eight national forests in Washington (including two that share land with neighboring states).

Colville National Forest
765 S Main Street
Colville, WA 99114
(509) 684-7000
www.fs.fed.us/r6/colville/forest

Gifford Pinchot National Forest
10600 NE 51st Circle
Vancouver, WA 98682
(360) 891-5000
www.fs.fed.us/r6/gpnf

Idaho Panhandle National Forest
3815 Schreiber Way
Coeur d'Alene, ID 83815
(208) 765-7223
www.fs.fed.us/ipnf

Mount Baker–Snoqualmie National Forest
905 64th Avenue W
Mountlake Terrace, WA 98043
(425) 775-9702
www.fs.fed.us/r6/mbs

Okanogan National Forest
1240 2nd Avenue S
Okanogan, WA 98840
(509) 826-3275
www.fs.fed.us/r6/oka

Olympic National Forest
1835 Black Lake Boulevard SW
Olympia, WA 98512
(360) 956-2402
www.fs.fed.us/r6/olympic

Umatilla National Forest
2517 SW Hailey Avenue
Pendleton, OR 97801
(541) 278-3716
www.fs.fed.us/r6/uma

Wenatchee National Forest
215 Melody Lane
Wenatchee, WA 98801
(509) 662-4368
www.fs.fed.us/r6/wenatchee

Columbia River Gorge National Scenic Area
902 Wasco Avenue, Suite 200
Hood River, OR 97031
(541) 386-2333
www.fs.fed.us/r6/columbia

Mount St. Helens National Volcanic Monument
42218 NE Yale Bridge Road
Amboy, WA 98601
(360) 449-7800
www.fs.fed.us/gpnf/mshnvm

National Oceanic and Atmospheric Administration

As part of the U.S. Department of Commerce, NOAA deals with oceanic and atmospheric issues through five major organizations, including the National Marine Fisheries Service and the National Ocean Service (both listed below). For a list of all NOAA offices and field stations in Washington see *www.legislative.noaa.gov/noaainyourstate/washington.html*.

National Marine Fisheries Service

The NMFS states that its three goals are to rebuild and maintain sustainable fisheries, promote the recovery of protected species, and protect the health of coastal habitats.

Northwest Regional Office
7600 Sand Point Way NE
Seattle, WA 98115
(206) 526-6150
www.nmfs.noaa.gov/www.nmfs.gov

National Ocean Service
The NOS governs the National Marine Sanctuary Program, implements Coastal Zone Management Plans through its Office of Ocean and Coastal Resource Management, and works to prevent and mitigate harm to coastal resources through its Office of Response and Restoration.

Olympic Coast National Marine Sanctuary
115 East Railroad Avenue, Suite 301
Port Angeles, WA 98362
(360) 457-6622
www.oceanservice.noaa.gov

National Park Service
Under the U.S. Department of the Interior, the NPS preserves the natural and cultural resources and values of the national park system for enjoyment, education, and inspiration.

Mount Rainier National Park
Tahoma Woods, Star Route
Ashford, WA 98304
(360) 569-2211
www.nps.gov/mora

North Cascades National Park Service Complex
  (including Lake Chelan and Ross Lake National Recreation Areas)
810 State Route 20
Sedro-Woolley, WA 98284
(360) 856-5700
www.nps.gov/noca

Olympic National Park
600 E Park Avenue
Port Angeles, WA 98362
(360) 565-3130
www.nps.gov/olym

Lake Roosevelt National Recreation Area
1008 Crest Drive
Coulee Dam, WA 99116
    or
1368 S Kettle Park Road
Kettle Falls, WA 99141
(509) 633-9441
www.nps.gov/laro

San Juan Island National Historical Park
125 Spring Street
Friday Harbor, WA 98250
(360) 378-2240
www.nps.gov/saj

U.S. Geologic Survey
The USGS is a scientific agency that manages water, biological, energy, and mineral resources. In Washington the USGS deals with geologic and hydrologic hazards, monitoring river nutrient transport, salmon and other fish issues, groundwater contamination, and water resources data.

Washington State USGS Representative
1201 Pacific Avenue, Suite 600
Tacoma, WA 98402
(253) 438-3600, ext. 2602
www.usgs.gov

STATE
Department of Ecology
The DOE promotes the wise management of Washington's air, land, and water for the benefit of the public. It is Washington's principle environmental management agency and deals with pollution clean up and prevention, as well as the support of sustainable communities and natural resources.

Headquarters
PO Box 47600
Olympia, WA 98504
(360) 407-6000
www.ecy.wa.gov

Department of Fish and Wildlife
The DFW is the steward of Washington's fish and wildlife, managing species and habitat for the well-being of populations as well as for recreational interests.

Olympia Office (Main Office)
600 Capitol Way N
Olympia, WA 98501
(360) 902-2200
www.wa.gov/wdfw

Department of Natural Resources

The DNR manages more than 5 million acres of public land in Washington: forests, farms, commercial properties, and underwater lands. Much of the land is managed to support public institutions like schools and universities through timber and agricultural production. Lands are also managed for recreation and to protect public resources.

Olympia Headquarters
1111 Washington Street SE
PO Box 47000
Olympia, WA 98504
(360) 902-1000
www.dnr.wa.gov

Department of Transportation

The DOT manages statewide transportation systems and services. A seven-member Transportation Commission appointed by the governor is responsible for developing long-range plans and partnerships, overseeing operations, and enabling the public to participate in transportation decisions.

Street address:
310 Maple Park Avenue SE
Olympia, WA 98501

Mailing address:
PO Box 47308
Olympia, WA 98504
(360) 705-7070
www.wsdot.wa.gov/commission

Parks and Recreation Commission

Parks and Recreation acquires, operates, enhances, and protects a system of recreation, cultural, historical, and natural sites, including 120 parks. A board of commissioners is appointed by the governor to set policy for the agency.

Street address:
7150 Cleanwater Lane
Tumwater, WA 98504

Mailing address:
PO Box 42650
Olympia, WA 98504
(360) 902-8844
www.parks.wa.gov

LOCAL

City Web sites directory: *www.mrsc.org/byndmrsc/cities.aspx*
County Web sites directory: *www.mrsc.org/byndmrsc/counties.aspx*
County land-use planning information: *www.evergreen.edu/library/govdocs
/wastate/countygovt.html*
Growth Management Act–related information for counties: 1000 Friends
of Washington, *www.1000friends.org*

GOVERNMENT OFFICIALS

Federal

President and Vice President of the United States
1600 Pennsylvania Avenue NW
Washington, DC 20500
Switchboard: (202) 456-1414
president@whitehouse.gov
vice.president@whitehouse.gov

U.S. Senate and U.S. House of Representatives
Washington, DC 20515
Switchboard: (202) 224-3121
www.senate.gov
www.house.gov

Secretary of Agriculture
U.S. Department of Agriculture
Washington, DC 20250
(202) 720-4623
agsec@usda.gov

Secretary of the Interior
U.S. Department of the Interior
1849 C Street NW
Washington, DC 20240
(202) 208-7351
www.doi.gov/secretary

State

Office of the Governor
PO Box 40002
Olympia, WA 98504
(360) 902-4111
www.governor.wa.gov

Washington State Senate and House of Representatives
(800) 562-6000
www.leg.wa.gov

Secretary of State
520 Union Avenue SE
PO Box 40220
Olympia, WA 98504
(360) 902-4151
www.secstate.wa.gov

Commissioner of Public Lands
Department of Natural Resources
PO Box 47001
Olympia, WA 98504
(360) 902-1004
www.dnr.wa.gov

Attorney General
1125 Washington Street SE
PO Box 40100
Olympia, WA 98504
(360) 753-6200
www.wa.gov/ago

APPENDIX C: Advocacy Contacts

Conservation Organizations

See chart legend on page 365

ORGANIZATION	ISSUES	SCOPE	CONSERVATION AGENDA
American Lands Alliance 726 7th St., Washington, D.C. 20003 202-547-9400 www.americanlands.org; wafcdc@americanlands.org		National	Dedicated to protecting forest, grassland, and aquatic ecosystems, preserving biological diversity, restoring landscape and watershed integrity, and promoting environmental justice with these goals. Supports grassroots activists nationwide.
American Rivers 150 Nickerson St., Ste. 311 Seattle, WA 98109 206-213-0330 www.amrivers.org arnw@amrivers.org		National w/ regional offices	Dedicated to protecting and restoring rivers using the National Wild and Scenic Rivers System. Opposes the construction of large dams in potential Wild and Scenic Rivers. Focuses on coalition building, promoting public awareness.
Audubon Society 1063 Capitol Way, Ste. 208 Olympia, WA 98501 360-786-8020 http://wa.audubon.org/new/audubon audubonaudubonwa@olywa.net		National w/ local chapters	Conserves and restores natural ecosystems, focusing on birds, other wildlife, and their habitats for the benefit of humanity and earth's biological diversity.
Biodiversity Northwest 4649 Sunnyside Ave. N., Ste. 321 Seattle, WA 98103 206-545-3734 www.biodiversitynw.org; info@bioidiversitynw.org		Western Washington	Dedicated to forest protection in the Pacific Northwest through public outreach and advocacy, policy analysis, coalition building, timber sale comments, field monitoring and, when appropriate, non-violent direct action. Currently (early 2004) inactive.
Business for Wilderness 3775 Iris Ave, Suite 5 Boulder, CO 80301 303-444-3353 www.businessforwilderness.org B4Winfo@outdoorindustry.org		National	Outreach program that engages outdoor businesses in efforts to protect public lands.

ORGANIZATION	ISSUES	SCOPE	CONSERVATION AGENDA
Campaign for America's Wilderness 705 2nd Avenue, Suite 203 Seattle, WA 98104 206-342-9212 www.leaveitwild.org dscott@leaveitwild.org		National	Supports campaigns of state coalitions and citizen groups across the country to press for adoption of locally-developed citizen proposals that will increase the amount of land included in the National Wilderness Preservation System. Supports state coalitions by contributing resources and expertise to local efforts to help make their work more effective.
Capitol Land Trust 209 E 4th Avenue, #205 Olympia, WA 98501 360-943-3012 www.olywa.net/trust/ trust@olywa.net		South Puget Sound	Olympia-based land trust that works with landowners in South Puget Sound to protect and conserve critical habitats and open spaces by offering non-regulatory opportunities for land management.
Cascades Conservation Partnership 3414 Fremont Avenue N Seattle, WA 98103 206-675-9747 www.ecosystem.org/tccp/ partnership@ecosystem.org		Central Cascades of Washington	Three-year campaign to purchase and protect over 75,000 acres of privately owned forests that link the Alpine Lakes to Mount Rainier in order to protect critical wildlife habitat and old-growth forests on private land. Campaign projected to end sometime in 2004.
Cascadia Forest Alliance 1540 SE Clinton Street Portland, OR 97202 503-241-4879 www.cascadiaforestalliance.org cfa@spiritone.com		Pacific Northwest	Works to inspire non-violent grassroots involvement in regional forest protection through education, creative expression, alliance building, and action.
Defenders of Wildlife 1101 14th Street NW, #1400 Washington, DC 20005 202-682-9400 www.defenders.org info@defenders.org		National	Dedicated to the protection of all native wild animals and plants in their natural communities and protection of entire ecosystems and interconnected habitats.
EarthFirst! Greg03a@earthfirst.org		International decentralized groups	A decentralized movement that advocates a direct action approach to protecting wildlands.

ORGANIZATION	ISSUES	SCOPE	CONSERVATION AGENDA
Earthjustice Washington Office 203 Hoge Building, 705 2nd Avenue Seattle, WA 98104 206-343-7340 www.earthjustice.org info@earthjustice.org		National	A public interest law firm that represents clients, free of charge, who are working through the courts to protect public lands, reduce pollution and preserve endangered species and wildlife habitat while shaping and enforcing environmental law.
Evergreen Forest Trust 615 2nd Avenue, Suite 525 Seattle, WA 98104 206-686-2992 www.evergreenforesttrust.org eft@cofen.com		Washington	Design easements and land management plans to protect natural resources and ecosystems on private land while maintaining jobs in forest-dependent communities. Provides for some commercial logging on acquired land. All proceeds go toward the repayment of bonds issued to buy land.
Forest Service Employees for Environmental Ethics P.O. Box 11615 Eugene, OR 97440 www.fseee.org; fseee@fseee.org		National	An organization of government employees and concerned citizens holding the Forest Service accountable for responsible land stewardship to ensure ecologically and economically sustainable resource management.
Friends of Loomis Forest PO Box 36 Loomis, WA 98827 www.loomisforest.org info@loomisforest.org		Loomis Forest in northeastern Cascades	Volunteer forest watch group working to ensure that the Washington State Department of Natural Resources sustainably manages the Loomis State Forest, protecting native flora and fauna, water, recreation, soils, scenic views, and timber.
The Gifford Pinchot Task Force 917 SW Oak Street, Suite 410 Portland, OR 97205 503-221-2102 www.gptaskforce.org info@gptaskforce.org		Southwest Washington	Employs grassroots commuity-based organizing with other strategies to protect ecosystems and local communities in the forests of southwest Washington, with a particular focus on the Gifford Pinchot National Forest.

Legend: Wildlife Rivers Forests/ecosystem Land trust Ancient forests Other Wilderness

ORGANIZATION	ISSUES	SCOPE	CONSERVATION AGENDA
Issaquah Alps Trails Club P.O. Box 351 Issaquah, WA 98027 206-328-0480 www.issaquahalps.org david_langrock@yahoo.com	★	Seattle and surrounding municipalities	Founded in response to the urbanization of the Puget Sound region, in order to "protect, preserve, promote and enhance open space lands, hiking trails, recreational opportunities and environmental qualities of the Issaquah Alps area." Encourages increased accessibility to trails for public use.
Kettle Range Conservation Group P.O. Box 150 Republic, WA 99166 509-775-2667 www.kettlerange.org tcoleman@kettlerange.org	↻ ⬠	Eastern Washington and South-central British Columbia	A grassroots environmental organization focusing on obtaining wilderness protection for eastern Washington's roadless national forests and encouraging sustainable ecosystem management and protection in the Colville, Okanogan and Wenatchee National Forests, federal and state shrub-steppe ecosystems, Washington Department of Natural Resources land, and forests in south-central British Columbia.
The Lands Council 423 W 1st Avenue, Suite 240 Spokane, WA 99201 509-838-4912 www.landscouncil.org tlc@landscouncil.org	↻ ★	The Inland Northwest (E. Washington, N.E. Oregon, N. Idaho and W. Montana)	Working to end commercial logging of federal forests of the inland Northwest, to train citizens to monitor and intervene in USFS activities, to restore the Spokane-Coeur d'Alene watershed from effects of mining pollution, to assist rural communities with wildfire protection, and to restore and protect urban forests.
League of Conservation Voters 1920 L Street NW, Suite 800 Washington, DC 20036 202-785-8683 www.lcv.org	★	National	An organization devoted solely to shaping a pro-environment Congress and White House. Runs campaigns funded only by LCV members and other individuals to support environmentally friendly political candidates and watchdog activities of the current administration.
Lighthawk PO Box 653 Lander, WY 82520 307-332-3242 www.lighthawk.org info@lighthawk.org	★	North and Central America (with Northwest Program Manager in Oregon)	Group of 100+ volunteer pilots who donate time, expertise, and use of their aircraft to groups for flights for environmental causes. They provide educational flights for local villagers, community leaders, or members of Congress; media flights for people working on environmental stories; technical flights for scientists gathering data or images; and surveillance flights to document environmental crimes and land conditions.

ORGANIZATION	ISSUES	SCOPE	CONSERVATION AGENDA
Mount Baker Wild! c/o Ken Wilcox, Northwest Ecosystem Alliance 1208 Bay Street, #201 Bellingham, WA 98225-4304 360-671-9950; 360-671-8429 fax www.mtbakergroup.org ken@parksandtrails.com	↻ ⬠	Skagit and Whatcom Counties	Volunteer group of wilderness enthusiasts working to protect roadless areas in the northern Mount Baker Snoqualmie National Forest. Advocates for federal wilderness designation and works on ecosystem health issues. They host hikes, slide shows, and other public events to educate the community on environmental issues affecting the area.
Mountains to Sound Greenway Trust 1011 Western Avenue, Suite 606 Seattle, WA 98104 206-382-5565; 206-382-3414 fax www.mtsgreenway.org mtsgreenway@tpl.org	★	King and Kittitas counties	A coalition of 68 parties including major land owners and managers along Interstate 90, foresters, business representatives recreation groups, environmentalists, community activists, elected leaders, and government agencies working to protect and enhance a 100-mile corridor of permanent open space lands along Interstate 90 for recreation and wildlife habitat.
The Mountaineers 300 3rd Avenue W Seattle, WA 98119 206-284-6310; 206-284-4977 fax www.mountaineers.org clubmail@mountaineers.org	⬠ ↻ ★	Washington	Volunteer-based organization geared to preservation and conservation by organizing and promoting outdoor recreation.
National BLM Wilderness Campaign 1473 South 1100 East Salt Lake City, UT 84105 801-486-2728 www.blmwilderness.org	⬠	Western United States	Pew Wilderness Trust project, working to preserve BLM lands in the western United States as federally designated wilderness.
National Forest Protection Alliance PO Box 8264 Missoula, MT 59807 406-542-7565 www.forestadvocate.org nfpa@forestadvocate.org	↻	National w/ State delegates	A coalition of 130 organizations and 27 state delegates dedicated to ending comercial logging on public lands.

ORGANIZATION	ISSUES	SCOPE	CONSERVATION AGENDA
National Public Lands Grazing Campaign c/o The Larch Company 1213 Iowa Street Ashland, OR 97520 541-201-0053; 541-201-0065 fax www.publiclandsranching.org www.permitbuyout.net andykerr@andykerr.net		Western United States	A multi-organization effort to end abusive livestock grazing on the nation's public lands through public education, enforcement of environmental protection standards, and legislative or administrative reform.
The Nature Conservancy 217 Pine Street, Suite 1100 Seattle, WA 98101 206-343-4344 http://nature.org/		International	Non-confrontational organizaton working to preserve ecosystems and plant and animal species that represent the diversity of life on Earth. Works with private land owners, public land managers, non-profit partners and corporate partners to achieve these goals.
Nisqually River Basin Land Trust PO Box 7444 Olympia, WA 98507 360-357-3792 www.nisquallylandtrust.org staff@nisquallylandtrust.org		Nisqually River Basin	Seeks to protect wetlands and associated wildlife habitat in the Nisqually Basin through donations of land, conservation easements, and the purchase of land with donated funds.
Nisqually River Council PO Box 7444 Olympia, WA 98507 360-357-3792 www.nisquallyriver.org/nrc.html info@nisquallyriver.org		Nisqually River Basin	Broad-based organization composed of federal, state, and local governments along with private citizens committed to the protection and enhancement of the Nisqually watershed through advocacy and education. Seeks to do so by integrating history, culture, environment, and economy of the watershed to promote a sustainable future. Responsible for implementing the Nisqually River Management Plan.

Legend:  Wildlife   Rivers   Forests/ecosystem   Land trust   Ancient forests   Other   Wilderness

ORGANIZATION	ISSUES	SCOPE	CONSERVATION AGENDA
North Cascades Conservation Council P.O. Box 95980 Seattle, WA 98145 206-282-1644; 206-684-1379 fax www.northcascades.org		Greater North Cascades Ecosystem (of Washington and British Columbia)	Works to protect and preserve wildlands in the North Cascades through legislative and legal processes, and by informing the public of issues affecting this area.
Northwest Ecosystem Alliance 1208 Bay Street, #201 Bellingham, WA 98225-4304 360-671-9950; 360-671-8429 fax www.ecosystem.org		Pacific Northwest	Works to protect and restore wildlands in the Pacific Northwest, and supports these efforts in British Columbia. Uses both science and advocacy to inform and collaborate with activists, policy makers, and the public.
Northwest Old Growth Campaign P.O. Box 2492 Bellingham, WA 98227 360-714-0572; 360-671-8429 fax www.nwoldgrowth.org		Ancient forests affected by the Northwest Forest Plan	A coalition of 10 conservation organizations focused on protecting mature, old-growth forests on federal public lands in western Washington and Oregon.
Ocean Wilderness Network 202 San Jose Avenue Capitola, CA 95010 831-462-2550; 831-462-2542 fax www.oceanwildernessnetwork.org info@oceanwildernessnetwork.org		U.S. Pacific Coast	Non-profit coalition of regional and national organizations dedicated to establishing a system of protected areas along the U.S. Pacific Coast.
Olympic Forest Coalition c/o Bonnie Phillips 606 Lilly Road NE, #115 Olympia, WA 98506 360-456-8793 www.olympicforest.org info@olympicforest.org		Olympic Peninsula	Works to protect, preserve, and restore federal and state forests on the Olympic Peninsula. Strives to educate the public, local communities, government agencies, and other environmental groups. Runs the Olympic Wild Campaign (www.olympicwild.org), which works to secure federally designated wilderness on the Olympic Peninsula.

ORGANIZATION	ISSUES	SCOPE	CONSERVATION AGENDA
Olympic Park Associates 168 Lost Mountain Lane Sequim, WA 98382 360-681-2480 mcmorgan@olypen.com www.drizzle.com/~rdpayne/opa.html		Olympic National Park and the Olympic Peninsula	Volunteer-based organization working since 1948 to preserve and restore Olympic National Park's wilderness integrity and ecosystem.
Pacific Biodiversity Institute P.O. Box 298 Winthrop, WA 98862 509-996-2490; 509-996-3778 fax www.pacificbio.org info@pacificbio.org		National	Conducts scientific research in conservation biology, ecology, and natural resources management. Develops advanced analytical tools (specializing in GIS maps and scientific reports) which are then made available to environmental groups, educational institutes, governmental agencies, and the public to aid in the conservation of biodiversity.
Pacific Rivers Council P.O. Box 10798 Eugene, OR 97440 541-345-0119; 541-345-0710 fax www.Pacrivers.org		Rivers in Washington, Oregon, and Idaho	With offices throughout the West, PRC strives to protect and restore rivers, their watersheds, and their native aquatic species. Focusing on the link between land management and watershed health, their strategies follow the idea "protect the best, restore the rest."
Republicans for Environmental Protection 325 Washington Ave. S., #206 Kent, WA 98032 253-740-2066; 206-417-1878 fax www.repamerica.org dipeso@repamerica.org		National	REP America is the national grassroots organization of Republicans for Environmental Protection. Founded in 1995 to restore the Republican Party's conservation tradition, REP America educates citizens and advocates strong environmental legislation consistent with traditional Republican values of stewardship, fiscal responsibility, and protecting America's national heritage.
Save Our Wild Salmon Coalition 424 3rd Avenue W, Suite 100 Seattle, WA 98119 800-SOS-SALMON 206-286-4455; 206-286-4454 fax www.wildsalmon.org sos@wildsalmon.org		Columbia/Snake Rivers in Washington, Oregon, and Idaho	A national collaboration of conservationists, commercial fishing families, sportfishers, businesses, and taxpayer advocates committed to recovering Pacific Northwest wild salmon and the healthy rivers and habitat upon which they depend, including the removal of the 4 lower Snake river dams.

ORGANIZATION	ISSUES	SCOPE	CONSERVATION AGENDA
The Sierra Club *Northwest Field Office* 180 Nickerson Street, Suite 202 Seattle, WA 98109 206-523-2147; 206-378-0034 fax www.sierraclub.org/wa/ www.cascade.sierraclub.org nw-wa.field@sierraclub.org *Inland NW Field Office* 10 N Post Street, Suite 447 Spokane, WA 99201 509-456-8802; 509-456-8803 fax http://idaho.sierraclub.org Chase.Davis@sierraclub.org		National with regional chapters and local groups	The nation's oldest and largest grassroots environmental organization provides local support through 9 national field offices. The Sierra Club works to protect wild areas, to promote responsible resource use, and to educate the public about the protection and restoration of our natural environment through all lawful means.
South Puget Sound Salmon Enhancement Group 6700 Martin Way E., Suite 112 Olympia, WA 98516 360-412-0808; 360-412-0809 fax www.spsseg.org spsseg@qwest.net		South Puget Sound	Formed by the legislature in 1990 to increase salmon populations in the South Puget Sound region through habitat restoration and community education.
Spring Family Trust for Trails 5015 88th Ave SE Mercer Island, WA 98040 http://www.springtrailtrust.org		Washington	Non-profit established by the late photographer Ira Spring to fund the construction and maintenance of trails in order to enhance opportunities for the public to come to know and love Washington's great outdoors.
Washington State Public Interest Research Group 3240 Eastlake Avenue E, Suite 100 Seattle, WA 98102 206-568-2850 www.washpirg.org info@washpirg.org		Washington (part of national network)	Focused campaigns include cleaning up the Hanford Nuclear Site, protecting Washington's roadless areas in national forests, and other public service activities.

ORGANIZATION	ISSUES	SCOPE	CONSERVATION AGENDA
Washington Trails Association 1305 4th Avenue, Suite 512 Seattle, WA 98101 206-625-1367 www.spsseg.org spsseg@qwest.net	(star)	Washington	Works to increase the number of trails across all lands, advocates greater funding for trail construction and maintenance. Does outreach to young people in the belief that, once "greenbonded", they will be the next generation of conservationists.
Washington Wilderness Coalition 4649 Sunnyside Avenue N, Suite 520 Seattle, WA 98103 206-633-1992; 206-633-1996 fax www.wawild.org	(pentagon)	Washington	Largest member-based wilderness group in Washington. Advocates for wilderness protection of federal roadless areas in Washington.
Western Environmental Law Center 1216 Lincoln Street Eugene, OR 97401 541-485-2471; 541-485-2457 fax www.westernlaw.org eugene@westernlaw.org	(icons)	Western U.S.	Non-profit legal firm working on behalf of Native Americans, citizen activists, and local governments to conserve and restore western ecosystems and communities.
Wild Washington Campaign 4649 Sunnyside Avenue N, Suite 520 Seattle, WA 98103 206-633-1992, ext. 108 www.wildwashington.org	(pentagon)	Washington	State-wide coalition to support and coordinate efforts to expand wilderness designation in Washington.
The Wilderness Society— Pacific Northwest Region 1424 4th Avenue, Suite 816 Seattle, WA 98101 206-624-6430 www.wilderness.org info@twsnw.org	(icons)	National with Regional Offices	Large-scale effort to preserve, protect, and restore wilderness in the United States including the Pacific Northwest. Uses methods of public education, scientific analysis, and advocacy. Founded in 1935 and instrumental in passage of the 1964 Wilderness Act. Vision is to develop a nationwide network of wild lands and to gain lasting protection for another 200 million acres of public wildlands.
The Wildlands Project PO Box 455 Richmond, VT 05477 802-434-4077; 802-434-5980 fax www.twp.org; info@wildlandsproject.org	(icons)	North America	Network of regionally-focused citizen groups working to preserve, restore, and connect extensive wild areas across the continent, using the insights of conservation biology along with political activism.

NOTES

ACKNOWLEDGMENTS:
Doug Goodman and Daniel McCool, eds., *Contested Landscape: The Politics of Wilderness in Utah and the West* (Salt Lake City: The University of Utah Press, 1999).

CHAPTER 1:
Preservation and Regeneration of Wildness at the Close of the Frontier

[1] Frederick Jackson Turner, "The Significance of the Frontier in American History," *Annual Report of the American Historical Association for 1893* (Washington, DC: U.S. Government Printing Office, 1894).

[2] In common parlance, as in this chapter, "wild" refers to whatever is undomesticated, and "wild places" or "wildlands" are those landscapes that are characterized by relatively little human alteration as perceived by an untrained eye.

[3] Throughout this book we refer to "citizens" in the broad sense, as residents with a commitment to place and democratic processes, who work to defend wild Washington, thereby including residents who may not fit the legal definition of "citizen."

[4] When we use the terms "conservation" and "conservationist" in this book it is important to remember that we are discussing the citizen movement for the preservation and regeneration of wild places, wildlife, and wild ecological processes. There is, of course, an important distinction between utilitarian conservation, which emphasizes utilization of natural resources, and natural area preservation, which emphasizes limiting human uses in some places. Nevertheless, the citizens and citizen organizations discussed in this book commonly use the term "conservation" to label their work for the preservation and regeneration of wildness. They do so in a nonexclusionary way, recognizing that there are obviously many other important forms of conservation action, ranging from pollution prevention and clean-up to combating global climate change. We have adopted the widespread usage of "conservation" within the movement for wild Washington except when discussing an important distinction between the views of utilitarian conservationists and preservationists.

[5] The data in this paragraph come from the Washington State Department of Natural Resources, *Our Changing Nature: Natural Resource Trends in*

Washington State (Olympia: Washington State Department of Natural Resources, 1998).

6 Lee Clark Mitchell, *Witnesses to a Vanishing America* (Princeton: Princeton University Press, 1981), xiv.

7 Ibid., 7.

8 Henry George, *Our Land and Land Policy* (1871; rpt. New York: Doubleday Page and Co., 1904), 11. Cited in Mitchell, *Witnesses*, 54.

9 Douglas W. Scott, *A Mandate to Protect America's Wilderness: A Comprehensive Review of Recent Public Opinion Research* (Washington, DC: Campaign for America's Wilderness, 2003).

10 A widely read example is the collection edited by J. Baird Callicott and Michael P. Nelson, *The Great New Wilderness Debate* (Athens: University of Georgia Press, 1998).

11 Thomas R. Vale, ed., *Fire, Native Peoples, and the Natural Landscape* (Washington, DC: Island Press, 2002).

CHAPTER 2:
A History of Washington's Landscape Transformations

1 Our discussion of Washington's geologic formation is informed primarily by David Alt and Donald W. Hyndman, *Northwest Exposures: A Geologic Story of the Northwest* (Missoula, MT: Mountain Press Publishing Company, 1995); William N. Orr and Elizabeth L. Orr, *Geology of the Pacific Northwest*, 2e (New York: McGraw Hill, 2002); and Patrick Pringle, personal communication with Molly Arrandale, 24 June 2003.

2 Russell C. Evarts and Donald A. Swanson, "Geologic Transect Across the Tertiary Cascade Range, Southern Washington," in *Geologic Field Trips in the Pacific Northwest*, vol. 2 (Seattle: University of Washington Department of Geological Sciences, 1994), 6–7.

3 Alt and Hyndman, *Northwest Exposures*, 223–25.

4 Adapted from a figure in Orr and Orr, *Geology of the Pacific Northwest*, 243.

5 Information on glaciations in Washington is derived primarily from Robert Burns, *The Shape and Form of Puget Sound* (Seattle: University of Washington Press, 1985); and Alt and Hyndman, *Northwest Exposures*.

6 Our discussion of faunal migration during the Pleistocene is informed primarily by Björn Kurtén, *Before the Indians* (New York: Columbia University Press, 1988).

7 For more information on tribal stories, see Rodney Frey, *Landscape Traveled by Coyote and Crane: The World of the Schitsu'umsh (Coeur d' Alene Indians)* (Seattle: University of Washington Press, 2001); Vi Hilbert, *Haboo: Native American Stories from Puget Sound* (Seattle: University of

Washington Press, 1985); Jacilee Wray, ed., *Native Peoples of the Olympic Peninsula: Who We Are* (Norman: University of Oklahoma Press, 2002).

[8] Quoted in Michael Parfitt, "The Floods that Carved the West," *Smithsonian Magazine* 95 (April 1995), 56.

[9] U.S. Geological Survey, "Columbia Plateau–Columbia River Basin–Columbia River Flood Basalts," *http://vulcan.wr.usgs.gov/Volcanoes/ColumbiaPlateau/summary_ columbia_plateau.html.*

[10] For more information on the region's post-glacial environments, see H. E. Wright Jr., ed., *Late-Quaternary Environments of the United States*, vols. 1 and 2. (Minneapolis: University of Minnesota Press, 1983).

[11] Information about the early humans, coastal settlement, and cultural change is taken primarily from Douglas Deur, "Salmon, Sedentism, and Cultivation: Toward an Environmental Prehistory of the Northwest Coast," in *Northwest Lands, Northwest Peoples*, ed. Dale D. Goble and Paul W. Hirt (Seattle: University of Washington Press, 1999); Douglas Deur, personal communication with Raelynn Rinehart, 27 March 2003; and Alvin M. Josephy Jr., *500 Nations: An Illustrated History of North American Indians* (New York: Alfred A. Knopf, Inc., 1994).

[12] Eugene S. Hunn, "Mobility as a Factor Limiting Resource Use," in *Northwest Lands, Northwest Peoples*, ed. Goble and Hirt (Seattle: University of Washington Press, 1999), 163–65.

[13] Thomas Vale, *Fire, Native Peoples, and the Natural Landscape* (Washington, DC: Island Press, 2002), 10.

[14] Eric O. Bergland, *Summary Prehistory and Ethnography of Olympic National Park, Washington* (Seattle: National Park Service, Pacific Northwest Region Division of Cultural Resources, 1983), 72. For more information about western Washington village locations and descriptions see Richard White, *Land Use, Environment, and Social Change: The Shaping of Island County Washington* (Seattle: University of Washington Press, 1980), 15; and Richard D. Daugherty, "People of the Salmon," in *America in 1492: The World of the Indian Peoples Before the Arrival of Columbus*, ed. Alvin M. Josephy Jr. (New York: Alfred A. Knopf, 1992).

[15] Information about eastern Washington village locations and descriptions is from Madge L. Schwede, "The Relationship of Aboriginal Nez Perce Settlement Patterns to Physical Environment and to Generalized Distribution of Food Sources," *Northwest Anthropological Research Notes* 4, no. 2 (1970): 129–35; Emory Strong, *Stone Age on the Columbia River* (Portland, OR: Metropolitan Press, 1959), 91–93; Deur, personal communication; and Daugherty, "People of the Salmon," 74-76.

[16] Vale, *Fire, Native Peoples, and the Natural Landscape*, 12.

[17] White, *Land Use, Environment, and Social Change*, 20.

[18] Justine E. James Jr. and Leilani A. Chubby, "Quinault," in *Native Peoples of the Olympic Peninsula: Who We Are*, ed. Jacilee Wray (Norman: University of Oklahoma Press, 2002).

[19] Helen H. Norton, Robert Boyd, and Eugene Hunn, "The Klikitat Trail of South-Central Washington: A Reconstruction of Seasonally Used Resource Sites," in *Indians, Fire, and the Land in the Pacific Northwest*, ed. Robert Boyd (Corvallis: Oregon State University Press, 1999), 65–67.

[20] Daugherty, "People of the Salmon," 52; Bergland, *Ethnography of Olympic National Park*.

[21] Information about eastern Washington fishing is primarily from Hunn, "Mobility as a Factor Limiting Resource Use," 164; and Daugherty, "People of the Salmon," 75.

[22] Jim Lichatowich, *Salmon without Rivers: A History of the Pacific Salmon Crisis* (Washington, DC: Island Press, 1999), 28.

[23] William C. Sturtevant, ed., *Handbook of North American Indians*, vol. 7, *Northwest Coast* (Washington, DC: Smithsonian Institution, 1990), 507.

[24] See Wray, *Native Peoples of the Olympic Peninsula*.

[25] Information concerning tidal marsh cultivation is from Douglas Deur, "Plant Cultivation on the Northwest Coast: A Reconsideration," *Journal of Cultural Geography* 19, no. 2 (spring/summer 2002): 9–27; Deur, "Salmon, Sedentism, and Cultivation," 142–46; and Deur, personal communication.

[26] Information about prairies and controlled burning in western Washington is from, White, *Land Use, Environment, and Social Change*, 14–34; and Helen H. Norton, "The Association Between Anthropogenic Prairies and Important Food Plants in Western Washington," *Northwest Anthropological Research* Notes 13, no. 2 (1979): 175–200.

[27] Information about controlled burning and plant encouragement in eastern Washington is primarily from Alan G. Marshall, "Unusual Gardens: The Nez Perce and Wild Horticulture on the Eastern Columbia Plateau," in *Northwest Lands, Northwest Peoples*, ed. Goble and Hirt, 175–80; John Alan Ross, "Proto-Historical and Historical Spokan Prescribed Burning and Stewardship of Resource Areas"; and David French, "Aboriginal Control of Huckleberry Yield in the Northwest," both in *Indians, Fire, and the Land*, ed. Boyd.

[28] Information about hunting is primarily from Daugherty, "People of the Salmon," 55, 82; and Ross, "Proto-Historical and Historical Spokan," 284.

[29] Information about fire precautions and ecological consequences of Native controlled burning is from Ross, "Proto-Historical and Historical Spokan,"

279, 282–83; French, "Aboriginal Control of Huckleberry Yield in the Northwest," 32; Norton, Boyd, and Hunn, "Klikitat Trail," 79; Deur, personal communication; and White, *Land Use, Environment, and Social Change*, 25.

30 White, *Land Use, Environment, and Social Change*, 36.

31 Ibid., 25.

32 Eugene S. Hunn, *Nch'I-Wána: The Big River* (Seattle: University of Washington Press, 1990), 27.

33 Lancaster Pollard, *A History of the State of Washington*, vol. 1 (New York: The American Historical Society, 1937).

34 This discussion of the fur trade is from Philip L. Jackson and A. Jon Kimerling, *Atlas of the Pacific Northwest*, 8e (Corvallis: Oregon State University Press, 1993), 13.

35 Quoted in Nancy Langston, *The General Riot of the Natural Forest: Landscape Change in the Blue Mountains* (Seattle: University of Washington, 1994), 76.

36 Lichatowich, *Salmon without Rivers*, 55.

37 Robert Bunting, *The Pacific Raincoast: Environment and Culture in an American Eden*, 1778-1900 (Lawrence: University Press of Kansas, 1991), 37.

38 Pollard, *History of the State of Washington*, 40.

39 Both quoted in Bunting, *Pacific Raincoast*, 105, 106.

40 Quoted in Langston, *General Riot of the Natural Forest*, 83.

41 Quoted in Jean Johnson, *Farm, Range, Forest, and Salmon: The Tucannon Watershed of the Columbia River Basin, 1850-1995* (Pullman: Washington State University, 1995), 16–17.

42 Pollard, *History of the State of Washington*, 42.

43 Quoted in Bunting, *Pacific Raincoast*, 112.

44 Ibid, 75–76.

45 Pollard, *History of the State of Washington*, 190.

46 Quoted in Bunting, *Pacific Raincoast*, 145.

47 Carl Abbott, "Footprints and Pathways: The Urban Imprint on the Pacific Northwest," in *Northwest Lands, Northwest Peoples*, ed. Goble and Hirt, 119–20.

48 Quoted in Dorothy Zeisler-Vralsted, "Cultural Perceptions of an Irrigated Landscape in the Pacific Northwest," in *Northwest Lands, Northwest Peoples*, ed. Goble and Hirt, 393.

49 The following information about land-use changes is based on Pollard, *History of the State of Washington*, 44, 51, 65, 264, 276.

50 Nancy Langston, "Environmental History and Restoration in the Western Forests," *Journal of the West* 38, no. 4 (1999): 47.

51 Quoted in Bunting, *Pacific Raincoast*, 148.
52 Thomas R. Cox, "Changing Forests–Changing Needs: Using the Pacific Northwest's Westside Forests, Past and Present," in *Northwest Lands, Northwest Peoples*, ed. Goble and Hirt, 466.
53 Nancy Langston, *General Riot of the Natural Forest*, 105.
54 Derrick Jensen and George Draffan, with John Osborn, *Railroads and Clearcuts: Legacy of Congress's 1864 Northern Pacific Railroad Land Grant* (Sandpoint, ID: Keokee Co. Publishing, Inc., 1995), 10.
55 Richard M. Highsmith, *Atlas of the Pacific Northwest: Resources and Development*, 2e (Corvallis: Oregon State University Press, 1957); A. Jon Kimerling and Phillip L. Jackson, *Atlas of the Pacific Northwest*, 7e (Corvallis: Oregon State University Press, 1985).
56 See Michael C. Blumm, "The Northwest's Hydroelectric Heritage," in *Northwest Lands, Northwest Peoples*, ed. Goble and Hirt, 267.
57 Washington State Department of Natural Resources, *Our Changing Nature: Natural Resource Trends in Washington State* (Olympia, WA: DNR, 1998), 41.
58 Richard M. Highsmith, *Atlas of the Pacific Northwest: Resources and Development*, 1e (Corvallis: Oregon State College, 1953), 33.
59 Kimerling and Jackson, *Atlas of the Pacific Northwest*, 7e, 100.
60 Kimerling and Jackson, *Atlas of the Pacific Northwest*, 8e, 32.
61 DNR, *Our Changing Nature*, 20, 31, 32, 43, 47.

CHAPTER 3:
Current Protected Areas and Geographical Assessment
1 Due to space limitations, this chapter is primarily focused on public protected areas. However, private land is critically important for threatened species and ecosystems, and it may be protected in several ways. For example, land trusts are nonprofit organizations that acquire land through purchases, donations, or through partnerships between private landowners and government agencies in order to withhold lands from development. Landowners who sell or donate their property to a land trust are provided with monetary incentives, such as tax deductions that are based on the value of their land. Land trusts and governments can also acquire conservation easements on private property when a landowner donates or sells the right to use an area for specific purposes, such as for subdivision or oil drilling. The property remains in private ownership, but the land trust or governmental agency that acquired the easement enforces the terms of the original agreement forever. Land trusts and conservation easements are important tools for conservationists, even if they usually protect small areas of land. These and other alternatives

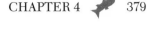

for wildlands protection will be further explored throughout parts 2 and 3 of this book.

2 Stan Stevens, "The Legacy of Yellowstone," in *Conservation through Cultural Survival: Indigenous Peoples and Protected Areas*, ed. Stan Stevens (Washington, DC: Island Press, 1997), 13–32, has a good discussion of the IUCN Protected Area Guidelines on pages 14–19.

3 Washington Department of Natural Resources, *State of Washington Natural Heritage Plan* (Olympia, WA: DNR, April 2003), 18.

4 Peter Morrison, executive director, Pacific Biodiversity Institute, personal communication with Edward Whitesell, July 2003.

5 DNR, *Washington Natural Heritage Plan*, 18.

6 Judd Slivka, "Park's Future at Risk: Overuse, Underfunding Threatens National Treasures," *Olympian*, 18 May 2003.

7 U.S. Forest Service, "Concepts in Ecosystem Management: Forest Edges," *www.fs.fed.us/r6/olympic/ecomgt/unecosys/edges.htm*.

8 Robert E. Frenkel, "Vegetation," in *Atlas of the Pacific Northwest*, 8e, ed. A. Jon Kimerling and Philip L. Jackson (Corvallis: Oregon State University Press, 1993), 60.

9 Tim McNulty, *Washington's Wild Rivers: The Unfinished Work* (Seattle: Mountaineers Books, 1990).

10 Daniel J. Evans, foreword to Washington's Wild Rivers, 7.

11 Peter Morrison, Susan Snetsinger, and George Wooten, *Unprotected Wild Lands in Washington State: An Analysis of Their Current Status and Future under Current Management Direction* (Winthrop, WA: Pacific Biodiversity Institute, February 1998).

12 Ibid., 1.

CHAPTER 4:
Surfing the Tides of Change

1 Paul Campbell, *Population Projections: States, 1995–2025*, Report P25-1131 (Washington, DC: U.S. Department of Commerce, Economics and Statistics Administration, May 1997).

2 The terms "urban" and "rural" are commonly based upon the Census Bureau definition in the literature on these topics. That definition is at *http://factfinder.census.gov*. However, the terms often become arbitrary as the line between urban and rural areas become blurred with changing demographics, infrastructure, and communication technologies. As a result, the reader is warned against strict definition of the terms urban and rural for the purposes of this chapter. Instead, view "urban" and "rural" as little more than commonsense reference points.

3 Information about suburban growth and urban flight is from Joel Kotkin, *The New Geography* (New York: Random House, 2000).

[4] Ibid., 45.

[5] Harriet H. Christensen, Wendy J. McGinnis, Terry L. Raettig, Ellen Donoghue, *Atlas of Human Adaptation to Environmental Change, Challenge, and Opportunity: Northern California, Western Oregon, and Western Washington*, General Technical Report PNW-GTR-478 (Portland, OR: U.S. Department of Agriculture, Forest Service, Pacific Northwest Research Station, May 2000), 38.

[6] Thomas M. Power, *The Economic Impact of Protecting Washington's Roadless National Forests* (13 June 2000), 13, *www.kettlerange.org/power/powerreport.htm*.

[7] For information on shifting rural demographics, see Karl N. Stuaber, "Why Invest In Rural America—and How? A Critical Public Policy Question for the 21st Century" (Center for the Study of Rural America, 2001), *www.kc.frb.org/RuralCenter/ruralstudies/studiesmain.htm*.

[8] Gundars Rudzitis, *Wilderness and the Changing American West* (New York: John Wiley & Sons, Inc., 1996), 107.

[9] Ibid., 93.

[10] See David T. Herbert and Colin J. Thomas, *Urban Geography: A First Approach* (Chichester, NY: John Wiley & Sons, Inc, 1982) for a discussion of this trend.

[11] David North, "Rural Industrialization," in *The Geography of Rural Change*, ed. Brian Ilbery (Essex, UK: Addison Wesley Longman Limited, 1998), 170–72.

[12] Matthew S. Carroll, *Community and the Northwest Logger* (Boulder, CO: Westview Press, 1995), 4.

[13] Martha Henderson Tubesing, interview by book authors, 13 February 2003.

[14] U.S. Department of Agriculture, National Agricultural Statistics Service, Census of Agriculture, *www.usda.gov*.

[15] Carroll, *Community and the Northwest Logger*, 5.

[16] Thomas M. Power, "Mill Closures: Rational but Painful Adjustment to Low Prices and Excess Supply" (University of Montana, Department of Economics, photocopy, 10 January 2003).

[17] Unless stated otherwise, all information in this paragraph is from Power, *Economic Impact of Protecting Washington's Roadless Forests*.

[18] Christensen et al., *Atlas of Human Adaptation*, 34.

[19] Jason Henderson, "Building the Rural Economy With High-Growth Entrepreneurs," *Economic Review*, Federal Reserve Bank of Kansas City (third quarter 2002): 6.

[20] Thomas M. Power, "Economic Structure, Economic Density, and Pay in the Pacific Northwest." Paper presented at 35th Annual Pacific Northwest Regional Economic Conference, Victoria, British Columbia, 16–18 May 2001, *www.umt.edu/econ/papers/PNREC2001.pdf*.

[21] Henderson, "Building the Rural Economy," 7.

[22] Power, executive summary, *Economic Impact of Protecting Washington's Roadless Forests*, 3.

[23] Power, "Mill Closures," 1; and Rudzitis, *Wilderness and American West*, 132.

[24] Peter E. Daniels and William F. Lever, *The Global Economy in Transition* (Essex, UK: Addison Wesley Longman Limited, 1996), 375.

[25] Rudzitis, *Wilderness and American West*, 94, 96.

[26] Ibid., 95.

[27] Martin Phillips, "Social Perspectives," in *Geography of Rural Change*, ed. Ilbery, 39.

[28] T. Harvey, "The Changing Face of the Pacific Northwest," *Journal of the West* 37, no. 3 (1998): 22-32.

[29] Quoted in William Dietrich, *The Final Forest: The Battle for the Last Great Trees of the Pacific Northwest* (New York: Penguin Books, 1992), 190.

[30] Jeremy Clegg, "The Development of Multinational Enterprises," in *Global Economy in Transition*, ed. Daniels and Lever, 104.

[31] Daniels and Lever, *Global Economy in Transition*, 1.

[32] Joseph Collins and John Lear, *Chile's Free Market Miracle: A Second Look* (Oakland, CA: Institute for Food and Development Policy, 1995), 203–17.

[33] U.S. Census Bureau, Census 2000 Redistricting Data (Public Law 94–171) Summary File, Tables PL1, PL2, PL3, and PL4; Campbell Gibson and Kay Jung, *Historical Census Statistics on Population Totals by Race, 1790 to 1990, and by Hispanic Origin, 1970 to 1990, for the United States, Regions, Divisions, and States*, Population Division Working Paper No. 56, U.S. Census Bureau, September 2002. Statistics of this sort are problematic due to changes in Census Bureau methodology between 1990 and 2000. These figures are conservative estimates of the growth in each population group.

[34] U.S. Census Bureau, Population Division, Population Paper Listing No. 47, Population Electronic Product No. 45, *www.census.gov/population/projections/state/9525rank/waprsrel.txt*. Data are from Series A as reported in Paul R. Campbell, *Population Projections for States, by Age, Sex, Race and Hispanic Origin: 1995 to 2025*, Report PPL-47 (Washington, DC: U.S. Census Bureau, Population Division, 1996).

[35] Information about political participation of minorities is from Megan Brokaw, *Permanently Protected Parks for a Dynamic Society* (masters thesis, The Evergreen State College, 2002). See especially 42–43.

[36] Campaign for America's Wilderness, *A Mandate to Protect America's Wilderness* (Washington, DC : Campaign for America's Wilderness, 2003), 22. Also at *www.leaveitwild.org/reports/index.html*.

[37] D. E. Taylor, "Meeting the Challenge of Wild Land Recreation Management: Demographic Shifts and Social Inequality," *Journal of Leisure Research* 32, no. 1 (2000), quoted in Brokaw, *Permanently Protected Parks*, 59.

[38] Brokaw, *Permanently Protected Parks*, 55.

[39] For more information about the 1995 Nationwide Personal Transportation Survey, visit *www.cta.ornl.gov/npts/1995/Doc/index.shtml*. To learn how the Census Bureau uses variable income thresholds to define poverty according to family size and composition, see *www.census.gov/hhes/poverty/povdef.html*.

[40] Linda L. Swanson, "Minorities Represent Growing Share of Tomorrow's Work Force," *Rural Conditions and Trends* 9, no. 2 (February 1999): 9–13.

[41] Brokaw, *Permanently Protected Parks*, 60.

[42] U.S. Department of the Interior, *The National Park Service Comprehensive Survey of the American Public* (Washington DC: National Park Service, 2001), cited in Brokaw, *Permanently Protected Parks*, 61.

[43] Brokaw, *Permanently Protected Parks*, 53–55.

[44] Robert D. Putnam, *Bowling Alone: The Collapse and Revival of American Community* (New York: Simon and Schuster, 2000).

[45] Ibid., 60–61.

[46] Ibid., 107.

[47] Ibid., 283.

[48] Brad Edmondson, "In the Driver's Seat," *American Demographics* (March 1998), quoted in Putnam, *Bowling Alone*, 213.

[49] Kenneth T. Jackson, *Crabgrass Frontier: The Suburbanization of the United States* (New York: Oxford University Press, 1985), quoted in Putnam, *Bowling Alone*, 211.

[50] Putnam, *Bowling Alone*, 213.

[51] J. Eric Oliver, "The Effects of Metropolitan Economic Segregation on Local Civic Participation," *American Journal of Political Science* 43 (January 1999), quoted in Putnam, *Bowling Alone*, 210.

[52] Putnam, *Bowling Alone*, 215.

[53] Ibid., 204.

[54] Ibid., 204.

[55] Ibid., 223–24.

[56] Ibid., 229.

[57] Tannis MacBeth Williams, ed., *The Impact of Television: A Natural Experiment in Three Communities* (Orlando, FL: Academic Press, 1986), quoted in Putnam, *Bowling Alone*, 236.

[58] Putnam, *Bowling Alone*, 224–25.

59 Ibid., 231.

60 Ibid., 257–58.

61 Ibid., 241.

62 Ibid., 262, 239.

63 Ibid., 265.

64 Edelman Public Relations press release, "'Echo Boomers' Face Millennium Condemning Government and Media while Believing in Themselves as Agents of Change," 1 December 1998.

CHAPTER 5:
Entering the Political Wilderness

1 Ellen Trescott, personal communication with Ben Shaine, March 2003.

2 Quoted in Lin Nelson, "Remembering Rachel," *Cooper Point Journal* 31, no. 22 (10 April 2003): 6.

3 I had the pleasure of working with Harry while he was writing his book, *Commonwealth: A Return to Citizen Politics* (New York: Free Press, 1989).

4 Harry C. Boyte, "Reinventing Citizenship," *Kettering Review* (winter 1994): 2.

5 Quoted in Boyte, *Commonwealth*, 121.

6 Harry C. Boyte, "Builders of the Commonwealth: Citizenship as Public Work," Center for Democracy and Citizenship Working Paper, n.d., 2, *www.publicwork.org/3_1_papers.html*.

7 Boyte, "Builders of the Commonwealth," 4.

8 Bernard Crick, *Democracy: A Very Short Introduction* (Oxford: Oxford University Press, 2002), 1.

9 Winston Churchill, speech in House of Commons, 11 November 1947.

10 Crick, *Democracy*, 12, 5. Emphasis in the original.

11 Boyte, *Commonwealth*, 5.

12 See, for example, Robert Bellah, ed., *Habits of the Heart: Individualism and Commitment in the American Experience*, 2e (Berkeley: University of California Press, 1996), which asserts the prevalence of this ethos.

13 Hannah Arendt, *The Human Condition* (Chicago: University of Chicago Press, 1958), 189.

14 Steven E. Daniels and Gregg B. Walker, *Working through Environmental Conflict* (Westport: Praeger, 2001), 4.

15 Quoted in Arendt, *Human Condition*, 175.

16 David Jennings, chairman of the board, Gifford Pinchot Task Force, class lecture at The Evergreen State College, Olympia, Washington, 27 February 2003. We observed the agency shift he describes during our class visit with state wildlife and federal Forest Service staff at the Sinlehekin Wildlife Area in October 2003.

[17] David Jennings's maps graphically illustrate this trend. See, for example, "Continued Logging of Old Growth is Based on False Assumptions" and "Roadless Areas and Threatened Native Forests of the Gifford Pinchot National Forest, Gifford Pinchot Task Force," January 2003.

[18] Michael Frome, *Battle for the Wilderness* (New York: Praeger/Wilderness Society, 1974).

[19] Brock Evans, "Brockie Bulletin #10 Valentine's Day 2003," *http://b-team.org/brock/bb-10.htm*.

[20] William Ury, *Getting to Peace: Transforming Conflict at Home, at Work, and in the World* (New York: Viking, 1999), 140.

[21] Tim McNulty, The Evergreen State College field trip to Quilcene River, 3 December 2002.

[22] Elliot Marks, class lecture at the Nature Conservancy offices, Seattle, 12 November 2002.

[23] Roger Fisher, Elizabeth Kopelman, and Andrea Kupfer Schneider, *Beyond Machiavelli: Tools for Coping with Conflict* (Boston: Harvard University Press, 1994).

[24] Ury, *Getting to Peace*, 198.

[25] See, for example, the work of Buddhist peace activist Thich Nhat Hanh, especially *Being Peace* (Berkeley: Parallax Press, 1988).

[26] Boyte, "Builders of the Commonwealth," 232–33.

[27] For example, Tenzin Gyatso (the Dalai Lama) reports that the work of University of Wisconsin neuroscientist Richard Davidson supports the conclusion that meditative practices "cultivating compassion, equanimity or mindfulness . . . strengthen the neurological circuits that calm a part of the brain that acts as a trigger for fear and anger. This raises the possibility that we have a way to create a kind of buffer between the brain's violent impulses and our actions." Op-ed, *New York Times*, 26 April 2003.

[28] I owe many thanks to Paul Becker, teacher, and my fellow practitioners at the Port Townsend Aikido dojo for this training, which has given me insight into my political activism in recent years.

[29] Marks, class lecture.

[30] Daniels and Walker, *Working through Environmental Conflict*, 16.

[31] Quoted in ibid., 1.

[32] Steven Nachmanovitch, *Free Play: The Power of Improvisation in Life and the Arts* (New York: Jeremy P. Tarcher/Putnam, 1990), 86–87.

CHAPTER 6:
Climbers to Conservationists

[1] John C. Miles, *Koma Kulshan: The Story of Mount Baker* (Seattle: Mountaineers Books, 1984), 59.

2 Ruth Kirk, *Sunrise to Paradise: The Story of Mount Rainier National Park* (Seattle: University of Washington Press, 1999), 47.

3 Dyan Zaslowsky, *These American Lands* (Washington, DC: Island Press, 1994), 17–18.

4 "16th Annual Outing Announcement," The Mazamas, 2–16 August 1909, 2.

5 Jim Kjeldsen, *The Mountaineers: A History* (Seattle: Mountaineers Books, 1998), 118.

6 See "Brief History of the Spokane Mountaineers," *www.spokane mountaineers.org/public_html/ history.htm*.

7 Kjeldsen, *Mountaineers*, 118.

8 For the original mission of the Park Service, see the *National Park Service Organic Act*, 16 *U.S. Code* §§ 1, 2, 3, 4 (1916).

9 Masthead on stationary of the Federation of Western Outdoor Clubs, Manuscripts, Special Collections, University Archives, University of Washington Libraries, accession no. 1886-2, boxes 1 and 2.

10 Doug Scott, *A Wilderness Forever Future* (Seattle: Pew Wilderness Center, 2001), 4.

11 National Park Service, "Northern Cascades Area Report," November 1937, 3, quoted in chapter 1 of David Louter, *Contested Terrain: An Administrative History of the North Cascades National Park Service Complex* (1998), *www.nps.gov/noca/adhi-1a.htm*.

12 See Craig W. Allin, *The Politics of Wilderness Preservation* (Westport, CT: Greenwood Press, 1982), especially pp. 87–88, for the effects of World War II on wilderness.

13 Kjeldsen, *Mountaineers*, 130.

14 Max Oelschlaeger, *The Idea of Wilderness* (New Haven: Yale University Press, 1991), 283.

15 "The Cascadians and Conservation," *The Cascadians* (1959), 52.

16 North Cascades Conservation Council newsletter, circa 1957, Manuscripts, Special Collections, University Archives, University of Washington Libraries, accession no. 1414, box 2.

17 Ibid.

18 Harvey Manning, *Conservation and Conflict: The U.S. Forest Service and National Park Service in the North Cascades, 1892–1992* (Seattle: North Cascades Conservation Council, 1992), 59.

19 Richard Steele, Bob Wilson, Rick Leaumont, and Mike Lilga, interview with book authors, Richland, Washington, 10 May 2003.

20 Ben Hayes, personal communication with Shawn Olson, 20 February 2003.

21 For further information, see David Knibb, *Backyard Wilderness: The Alpine Lakes Story* (Seattle: Mountaineers Books, 1982).

CHAPTER 7:
Pathfinders in the Political Wilderness

1 For a variety of reasons, it was not possible to interview all of the Washington State pathfinders; however twelve interviews are archived and available in The Evergreen State College library, and five of these are summarized in this chapter.

2 Polly Dyer, interview by chapter authors, minidisc recording, Olympia, Washington, 13 January 2003.

3 Harvey Manning, interview by chapter authors, minidisc recording, Bellevue, Washington, 26 February 2003.

4 When Harvey Manning and others involved with NCCC refer to their organization, they say "N3C." However, since the abbreviated name is written "NCCC," we have used that conventional acronym spelling.

5 Harvey Manning, *Footsore: Walks and Hikes around Puget Sound* (Seattle: Mountaineers Books, 1977), 100.

6 Harvey Manning, *How We Got the Park* (unpublished, n.d.).

7 Harvey Manning, Harvey Manning Papers, Manuscripts, Special Collections, University Archives, University of Washington Libraries, accession no. 2097-2.

8 Patrick Goldsworthy, interview by chapter authors, minidisc recording, Seattle, 28 February 2003.

9 Karen Fant, interview by chapter authors, minidisc recording, Seattle, 14 February 2003.

10 Tim McNulty, interview by chapter authors, minidisc recording, Lost Mountain, Clallam County, Washington, 16 January 2003.

CHAPTER 8:
On the Trail from Wilderness to Wildness

1 Quoted in Ted Kerasote, ed., *Return of the Wild: The Future of Our Natural Lands* (Washington, DC: Island Press, 2001), v.

2 Kathie Durbin, *Tree Huggers: Victory Defeat, and Renewal in the Northwest Ancient Forest Campaign* (Seattle: Mountaineers Books, 1996), 15.

3 Senate Subcommittee on Public Lands and Reserved Water, *The Washington State Wilderness Act of 1983: Hearings on S. 837*, 98th Cong., 1st sess., 1983, part 1, p. 1.

4 Karen Fant, interview by Glenn Burkhart and Lin Skavdahl, minidisc recording, Seattle, 14 February 2003.

5 Denis M. Roth, *The Wilderness Movement and the National Forests: 1964–1980*, Publication FS 391 (Washington, DC: U.S. Department of Agriculture, Forest Service, 1984), 52.

6 Quoted in Durbin, *Tree Huggers*, 61.

[7] Senate Subcommittee, *Washington State Wilderness Act Hearings on S. 837*, part 1, pp. 437–40, and part 2, pp. 1709–12.

[8] David Jennings, chair, Gifford Pinchot Task Force, Evergreen State College class lecture, 27 February 2003.

[9] Matthew S. Carroll, *Community and the Northwestern Logger: Continuities and Changes in the Era of the Spotted Owl* (Boulder, CO: Westview Press, 1995), 13.

[10] Gifford Pinchot Task Force, "Historical Logging on the Gifford Pinchot National Forest," *www.gptaskforce.org*.

[11] Durbin, *Tree Huggers*, 59.

[12] Jerry Franklin et al., *Ecological Characteristics of Old-Growth Douglas-Fir Forests*, General Technical Report PNW-GTR-118 (Portland, OR: U.S. Department of Agriculture, Forest Service, Pacific Research Station, 1981).

[13] Forsman's findings were published in the Wildlife Society's journal in 1984 and in the Audubon Wildlife Report in 1985, exposing the decline of the northern spotted owl population.

[14] *National Forest Management Act*, 16 *U.S. Code* §§ 1600–14 (17 August 1974), as amended 1976, 1978, 1980, 1981, 1983, 1985, 1988, and 1990.

[15] Janine Blaeloch, "Earth First! Cracks the Elwha Dam," *Voice of the Wild Olympics*, Olympic Park Associates newsletter (December 1987). Reprinted in Sally Warren Soest, ed., *Voice of the Wild Olympics 50th Anniversary Edition* (Seattle: Olympic Park Associates, Spring 1998), 57.

[16] Martha F. Lee. *Earth First!: Environmental Apocalypse* (Syracuse, NY: Syracuse University Press, 1995), 81.

[17] Lee, *Earth First!*, 121.

[18] Christopher Manes, *Green Rage: Radical Environmentalism and the Unmasking of Civilization* (Boston: Little Brown and Company, 1990), 102.

[19] Manes, *Green Rage*, 103–4.

[20] For projections of jobs lost and the spotted owl controversy, see Sarah Hines, "Trouble in Timber Town," *University of Washington Columns Online* (December 1990), *www.washington.edu/alumni/columns/top10/timber_town.html*; and Forest Historical Society, "Northern Spotted Owl Timeline" (19 March 2002), *www.lib.duke.edu/forest/usfscoll/policy/northern_spotted_owl/timeline.html*.

[21] Hines, "Trouble in Timber Town."

[22] Durbin, *Tree Huggers*, 124.

[23] H. Michael Anderson, *Citizen Guide to the Northwest Forest Plan* (Washington, DC, and Seattle: The Wilderness Society, Bolle Center

for Ecosystem Management, September 1994), 9.

24 "Forest Plan Revisions Could Cut Protections; Critics Decry Ending Search for Dozens of Species Before Logging," *Seattle Post-Intelligencer*, 24 May 2003, *http://seattlepi.nwsource.com/local/123465_species24.html*.

25 Senate Subcommittee on Public Lands, National Parks, and Forests, *The Washington Parks Wilderness Act of 1988: Hearings on S. 2165*, 98th Cong., 1st sess., 1983, 40.

26 *Washington Park Wilderness Act of 1988*, Public Law 100-668, 100th Cong., 2d sess. (16 November 1988).

27 "Facts on the 1995 Salvage Rider" (Oregon Natural Resource Council, 2002), *www.onrc.org/info/fire/srfacts.html*.

28 Bonnie Phillips, personal communication with Edward Whitesell, 6 October 2003.

29 Elizabeth Manning, "Forests Worth Fighting For," *High Country News*, 2 September 1996, *www.hcn.org/servlets/hcn.Article?article_id=2756*.

30 Linda V. Mapes, "New Plum Creek Land Exchange Pleases Environmentalists," *Seattle Times*, 4 November 1999, *www.westlx.org/assets/NewPlumCreek.pdf*.

31 Mike Matz, "The Politics of Protecting Wild Places," in *Return of the Wild: The Future of Our National Lands*, ed. Ted Kerasote (Washington, DC: Island Press, 2001), 88.

32 Jon Owen, field director, Washington Wilderness Coalition, electronic correspondence, "Forest Campaign-Final Update #8," 10 July 2000.

33 Gifford Pinchot Task Force, "Old Growth Protection," *www.gptaskforce.org*.

CHAPTER 9:
Leaders in Today's Movement

1 Susan Jane Brown, interview by chapter authors, minidisc recording, Olympia, Washington, 22 January 2003.

2 Susan Jane Brown, personal communication with Lin Skavdahl, 9 June 2003.

3 Georgiana Kautz, interview by chapter authors, minidisc recording, Nisqually Delta, Thurston County, Washington, 8 April 2003.

4 Charles Wilkinson, *Messages from Frank's Landing* (Seattle and London: University of Washington Press, 2000), 27.

5 Ibid., 12.

6 Robert McClure, "Tribes Reignite Legal Battle over State's Fish Catch," *Seattle Post-Intelligencer*, 17 January 2001.

7 Mitch Friedman, interview by chapter authors, minidisc recording, Bellingham, Washington, 20 January 2003.

8 William Dietrich, *The Final Forest: The Battle for the Last Great Trees*

of the Pacific Northwest (New York: Simon and Schuster, 1992).
9 Bob Wilson, interview by chapter authors, minidisc recording, Richland, Washington, 28 January 2003.
10 Dr. John Osborn, interview by Lin Skavdahl, minidisc recording, Spokane, Washington, 16 April 2003.
11 Derrick Jensen and George Draffan, with John Osborn, *Railroads and Clearcuts: Legacy of Congress's 1864 Northern Pacific Railroad Land Grant* (Spokane, WA: Inland Empire Public Lands Council, 1995).

CHAPTER 10:
The Movement for Wild Washington
1 Debra Salazar, "Political Resources and Activities of Environmental Groups in Washington State," in *Public Lands Management in the West: Citizens, Interest Groups, and Values*, ed. Brent S. Steel (Westport, CT: Praeger, 1997), 65.
2 Kathie Durbin, *Tree Huggers* (Seattle: Mountaineers Books, 1996), 214.
3 Salazar, "Political Resources and Activities," 1.
4 Doug Scott, class lecture at The Evergreen State College, Olympia, Washington, 4 December 2002.
5 Bernard Bailyn, ed., *The Great Republic: A History of the American People* (Lexington, MA: D.C. Heath and Company, 1992), 632.
6 The Wilderness Society, "Forest Service Continues to Blow Smoke: Latest GAO Report, University Study, Show McInnis Wildfire Bill Based on Flawed Assumptions" (20 May 2003), *www.wilderness.org*.
7 Salazar, "Political Resources and Activities," 67.
8 Mark Skatrud, field tour of the Loomis National Resource Conservation Area, Washington, 21 November 2002.
9 Andy Stahl, director, Forest Service Employees for Environmental Ethics, interview by Ellen Trescott and Tyler Winchell, minidisc recording, Eugene, Oregon, 31 January 2003.
10 Peter Morrison, class lecture at Pacific Biodiversity Institute, Winthrop, Washington, 20 November 2002.
11 Mark Skatrud, field tour.
12 David Jennings, class lecture at The Evergreen State College, Olympia, Washington, 27 February 2003.
13 Tim Coleman, interview by Glenn Burkhart and Lin Skavdahl, minidisc recording, Republic, Washington, 23 January 2003.
14 Harvey Manning, class lecture at Issaquah Trail Center, Issaquah, Washington, 29 October 2002.
15 Karen Coulter and Jasmine Minbashian, personal communication with Ellen Trescott at a Northwest activist meeting, Spokane, Washington,

8 February 2003.

[16] Andy Stahl, interview.

[17] Jon Owen, interview by Ellen Trescott and Tyler Winchell, minidisc recording, Seattle, Washington, 21 January 2003.

[18] John Leary, interview by Ellen Trescott and Tyler Winchell, not recorded, Seattle, Washington, 28 January 2003.

[19] Bob Dick, interview by Ellen Trescott and Tyler Winchell, minidisc recording, Olympia, Washington, 25 February 2003.

[20] Quoted in Jon Owen, "Wild Sky on the Political Trail," *Washington Wildfire* (fall/winter 2002): 6.

[21] John Leary, interview.

[22] Pete Nelson, policy director, Biodiversity Northwest, interview by Melissa Carter, Ellen Trescott, and Tyler Winchell, minidisc recording, Seattle, 21 January 2003.

[23] U.S. Department of Agriculture, Forest Service, *Olympic National Forest Access and Travel Management ATM Final Plan Summary*, www.fs.fed.us/ r6/olympic/aboutonf/atm_web/Final_docs/final_atm_summary_040103.pps.

[24] David Bayles, comments during the panel presentation "Beyond Preservation: Visions of Westside Forest Restoration," Public Interest Environmental Law Conference, Eugene, Oregon, 8 March 2003.

[25] Durbin, *Tree Huggers*, 2.

[26] Dick, interview.

[27] Bonnie Phillips, personal communication with Edward Whitesell, 10 February 2003.

[28] Jim Doran, comments during the panel presentation "Forest Resource Management: Moving from Neglect to Active Management," Public Interest Environmental Law Conference, Eugene, Oregon, 8 March 2003.

[29] Quoted in William A. Shutkin, *The Land That Could Be: Environmentalism and Democracy in the Twenty-first Century* (Cambridge: MIT Press, 2000), 120.

[30] Doran, "Forest Resource Management" panel.

[31] Russell Jim, audience comment to participants on the panel "Ending Public Lands Grazing Equitably," Public Interest Environmental Law Conference, Eugene, Oregon, 8 March 2003.

[32] "The Next Environmental Movement," *Earth First! Journal* (January/ February 2003): 32.

[33] Mikal Jakubal, "On Strike Against MAXXAM: Striking Kaiser Employees Say Hurwitz is the Real Problem," *River & Range* 1, no. 3 (1999). Available at *http://bari.iww.org/iu120/local/Jakubal1.html*.

[34] Undisclosed activist, comments at a "security culture" training, Olympia, Washington, 29 May 2003.

[35] "The SmartMeme Project," parts 1–3, *Earth First! Journal* (November/

December 2002, December/January 2003, January/February 2003).

[36] Bonnie Phillips, class lecture at The Evergreen State College, Olympia, Washington, 30 January 2003.

[37] Alexander Cockburn, "The Original Green Activist Keeps Going: An Old Fighter for the Environment is Still a Thorn in the Side for Many," *Los Angeles Times*, 20 May 1999: 9.

[38] R. Noss, E. T. LaRoe III, and J. M. Scott, *Endangered Ecosystems of the United States: A Preliminary Assessment of Loss and Degradation*, Biological Report 28 (Washington, DC: U.S. Department of Interior, National Biological Service, February 1995), 47.

[39] Don Easterbrook and Susan March, *Potential Geologic Natural Landmarks: North Pacific Border Province* (Bellingham: Western Washington University Press, 1978).

[40] "Our Endangered Moderates," *The Green Elephant* 6, no. 2 (2002): 3.

[41] The Mellman Group, *Report on Issue among Registered Voters Concerning President Bush's Rollback of the Clinton Roadless Initiative Protection of National Forest Lands*, memorandum to the Heritage Forests Campaign, 30 April 2001, 4.

[42] "Washington Activities: State GOP," Republicans for Environmental Protection Web site, *www.repamerica.org.*

[43] Polly Dyer, class lecture at The Evergreen State College, Olympia, Washington, 24 October 2002.

[44] Amy Schlachtenhaufen, class lecture at the Wilderness Society's Northwest office, Seattle, 10 December 2002.

[45] Sharon Parker, keynote presentation to the North American Wilderness Conference, Seattle, 3 May 2002.

[46] The Working Group on Diversity, "Outdoor Diversity Resource Guide" (1996), *www.outdoorindustry.org/market-research-articles/diversity/ message.html.*

[47] Ira Spring, class lecture, "Healthy Trails for Healthy People," The Evergreen State College, Olympia, Washington, 13 February 2003.

[48] Wilderness Volunteer Corps Web site, *www.wawild.org/youthvolunteer/ page_1.htm.*

[49] Robert D. Putnam, *Bowling Alone: The Collapse and Revival of American Community* (New York: Simon and Schuster, 2000), 406.

[50] David Kupfer, "The Archdruid's Parting Shots," *Backpacker* 29, no. 3 (2001): 24.

CHAPTER 11:
Envisioning a Wild Future
[1] The Wildlands Project, "Wildlands Conservation Planning Efforts," *Wild*

Earth 10, no. 1 (2000): 84–90.

2 Quoted in Greg Hanscom, "Visionaries or Dreamers?," *High Country News* 31, no. 8 (1999): 12.

3 Quoted in David Louter, *Contested Terrain: North Cascades National Park Service Complex, An Administrative History* (Seattle: Department of the Interior, National Park Service, 1998), 20.

4 Ken Wilcox, interview by Glenn Burkhart and Lin Skavdahl, minidisc recording, Bellingham, Washington, 3 February 2003.

5 John Squires, speech to the Packwood Collaborative Working Group, Packwood, Washington, 7 February 2003.

6 U.S. Department of Agriculture, Forest Service, "Appendix A Inventoried Roadless Area Acreage Categories of NFS Lands Summarized by State," *http://roadless.fs.fed.us/documents/feis/data/sheets/acres/appendix_state_acres.html.*

7 Amy Schlachtenhaufen, comments during a panel at the conference, "Looking Ahead: Models for Protecting National Forests," The Evergreen State College, Olympia, Washington, 10 May 2003.

8 See, for example, Reed Noss, "Sustainability and Wilderness," *Conservation Biology* 5, no. 1 (1991): 120–22.

9 Craig Welch, "Conservation via Capitalism: Two Men's Novel Idea Could Forever Alter Land Protection," *Seattle Times*, 24 March 2003.

10 John J. Anderson, sponsor, Initiative 812: An Act Relating to Grazing; amending RCW 16.24.065, 79.01.076, 79.01.096, 79.01.244, and 79A.05.070; adding a new section to RCW 279.01; and repealing RCW 79.01.295, 79.01.2951, 79.01.2955, 79.01.296, 79.28.040, 79.28.050, 79.28.070, and 79.28.080.4, submitted to the secretary of state 1 January 2003.

11 Information on grizzly populations comes from David Knibb, class lecture at The Evergreen State College, Olympia, Washington, 21 February 2003; Northwest Ecosystem Alliance, "A Word for the North Cascades Grizzly" and "Background on the North Cascades Ecosystem Grizzly Recovery Zone" (both 2002), *www.ecosystem.org/grizznorthcascades.html*; and Rick McGuire, personal communication with chapter authors, May 2003.

12 LeRoy N. Poff and David J. Allan, "The Natural Flow Regime," *BioScience* 47, no. 11 (1997): 769–84. See also National Research Council, *Restoration of Aquatic Systems: Science, Technology, and Public Policy* (Washington, DC: National Academy Press, 1992).

13 Discussed in detail in Blaine Harden, *A River Lost: The Life and Death of the Columbia* (New York: W. W. Norton and Company, 1996).

14 For a discussion of the benefits and costs of the dams versus those of dam removal, see Eve Vogel and Phillip S. Lansing, *Restoring the Lower*

Snake River: Saving Snake River Salmon and Saving Money (Portland: Oregon Natural Resources Council Fund, 1998).

[15] Save Our Wild Salmon, "Overview of RAND's Northwest Energy Report: Wild Salmon and Clean Energy; A Vision of the Future for the Pacific Northwest" (2003), *www.wildsalmon.org*.

[16] American Rivers, "Treaty-Reserved Fishing Rights," *www.american rivers.org/snakeriver/snaketreaty.htm*.

[17] Slade Gorton, press release, 15 September 1997, quoted in Vogel and Lansing, *Restoring the Lower Snake*, 10.

[18] Quoted in Mike Lewis et al., "More Questions Than Answers over Killer Wildfire: Amid Investigation, Some Wonder Why It Was Fought At All," *Seattle Post-Intelligencer*, 14 July 2001.

[19] Ibid.

[20] For more information on the history of forest fire policy, see *Fire in the West: A High Country News Special Report* (Paonia, CO: *High Country News*, 2003).

[21] Harvey Manning, *Conservation and Conflict: The U.S. Forest Service and National Park Service in the North Cascades 1892–1992* (Seattle: North Cascades Conservation Council, 1992), 110.

[22] Linda Moon Stumpff, *Protecting Restorative Relationships and Traditional Values* (unpublished, 2001), 15.

[23] See the discussion of species introduction in Taylor H. Ricketts and Eric Dinerstein, *Terrestrial Ecoregions of North America: A Conservation Assessment* (Washington, DC: Island Press 1999).

[24] Washington State Noxious Weed Control Board, "Overview of Washington's Noxious Weed Laws" (2001) *www.wa.gov/agr/weedboard/weed_laws/overview*.

[25] Steve Herman, class lecture at The Evergreen State College, Olympia, Washington, 14 November 2003.

[26] Union of Concerned Scientists, testimony before U.S. House of Representatives, Phyllis N. Windle, Ph.D.: *Regarding Reauthorization of the National Invasive Species Act*, 107th Cong., 1st sess., 14 November 2002.

[27] See Mina Vedder, "Imported Beetles Gnaw on Scotch Broom 'Young'," (Tacoma) *News Tribune*, 26 May 2001, B1.

[28] Elizabeth Murtaugh, "Wildflower Packets Found Loaded with Invasive Species," (Vancouver, Washington) *Columbian*, 1 May 2002.

[29] See Larry Dominguez and Jeff Cederholm, "Rehabilitating Stream Channels Using Large Woody Debris With Considerations for Salmonid Life History and Fluvial Geomorphic Processes" (unpublished draft, 1997), published in *Sustainable Fisheries Management: Pacific Salmon*, ed. E. Eric Knudsen et al. (Boca Raton, FL: Lewis Publishers, 2000).

[30] For a discussion of management alternatives and cautions, see Bill Willers, preface to *Unmanaged Landscapes: Voices for Untamed Nature* (Washington DC: Island Press, 1999).

[31] Columbia River Pastoral Letter Project, *www.columbiariver.org*.

CHAPTER 12:
The Western Mountains

[1] Harvey Manning, class lecture at the Issaquah Trail Center, Issaquah, Washington, 29 October 2002.

[2] Mark Skatrud, class lectures at the Sinlahekin Wildlife Refuge and the Loomis State Forest, 20 November 2002.

[3] Both quoted in Lynda V. Mapes, "Fund Raising Effort to Save Loomis Forest Highlights Values Clash," *Seattle Times*, 1 June 1999, *http://archives.seattletimes.nwsource.com*.

[4] Quoted in Lynda V. Mapes, "High-Tech Moguls Give $1.7 Million for Forest," Seattle Times, 3 March 1999, *http://archives.seattletimes.nwsource.com*.

[5] Robert Michael Pyle, *Wintergreen: Listening to the Land's Heart* (Boston: Houghton Mifflin, 1986), 23.

[6] For additional NRCA information, see Washington State Natural Areas Preserve Program, "NRCA Descriptions," *www.dnr.wa.gov/nap/nrcadesc.html*.

[7] For a description of the Ellsworth Creek ecosystem and actions to preserve it, see Friends of the Willapa National Wildlife Refuge, "Willapa National Wildlife Refuge History," *www.wilapabay.org/~fwnwr/refugehistory*; U.S. Fish and Wildlife Service, "Bear River / Ellsworth Creek Watersheds, Pacific County, WA," *www.pacific.fws.gov/jobs/wwojitw/bear_ellsworth*; Pamela McAllister, "Ellsworth Creek," *Washington Wildlands* (fall 2000/winter 2001): 2–4; Dave Wortman, "Ellsworth Creek," *Washington Wildlands* (fall 2000/winter 2001): 5; Joe Connelly, "In the Northwest: It's Up to Us to Preserve Ellsworth Creek Old Growth," *Seattle Post-Intelligencer*, 31 October 2001; and Erik Robinson, "Pristine Coastal Forest Secured," [Vancouver, Washington] *Columbian*, 28 March 2003, C1.

[8] Quoted in Lynda Mapes, "Conservancy Aims to Buy Watershed in Willapa Hills," *Seattle Times*, 27 September 2000.

[9] All historical information about monument designation efforts is from Susan Saul, interview by Lin Skavdahl, Vancouver, Washington, 23 April 2003, and from e-mails received from Saul by Connie Czepiel during May and June 2003.

[10] Hubertus L. R. Preusser, "Planning Procedures on Different Levels for a Protected Area Around Mount St. Helens," in *Mount St. Helens: Five*

Years Later, ed. S. A. C. Keller (Cheney: Eastern Washington University Press, 1986), 411.

[11] Rob Carson, *Mount St. Helens: The Eruption and Recovery of a Volcano*, 20th anniversary edition (Seattle: Sasquatch Books, 2000), 141.

[12] For descriptions of Mount St. Helens's recovery, see Evelyn Merrill, Kenneth Raedeke, and Richard Taber, *The Population Dynamics and Habitat Ecology of Elk in the Mount St. Helens Blast Zone* (Seattle: Wildlife Science Group College of Forest Resources, University of Washington, 1987); *Mount St. Helens: The Turmoil of Creation Continues*, dir. Steve Brantley, Cinescope Enterprises (a Panorama International Production), 1989, videocassette; and Carson, *Eruption and Recovery*.

[13] Most of the information about Weyerhaeuser recovery operations as well as eruption facts are from Dick Ford, director, Weyerhaeuser Forestry Learning Center, interview by Connie Czepiel, Longview, Washington, 27 February 2003.

[14] Read about gray wolf reintroduction in Janine Blaeloch et al., "Toward Ecosystem Conservation: Case Studies of Single-Species management," in *Cascadia Wild: Protecting an International Ecosystem*, ed. Mitch Friedman and Paul Lindholdt (Bellingham, WA: Greater Ecosystem Alliance, 1993); Tim McNulty, "Wolves in the Olympics: An Historical Perspective," in *Voice of the Wild Olympics*, 50th anniversary edition, ed. Sally Warren Soest (Seattle: Olympic Park Associates, 1998), 81–82; and Tim McNulty, "Gorton Ignores Data," *Voice of the Wild Olympics* (summer 1998), 7.

[15] For information on the Elwha dams and salmon in the river, see the Elwha River Restoration Project, *www.elwha.org/river.htm*; "History and Timeline—Elwha River Recovery," *www.nps.gov/olym/elwha/history.htm*; Roger Oakes, "Historical Background on the Elwha River Dams," online at American Field Guide Teacher Resources: Salmon vs. Dams, *www.pbs.org/americanfieldguide/teachers*; Larry Lange, "Battle of the Elwha Dams Heads to Federal Court: 'Bring Back The Salmon' Groups File Suit," *Seattle Post-Intelligencer*, 1 June 1991; David Foster, "Pressure Is On for Removal of Dam from Elwha River" *Seattle Times*, 6 October 1991; Dave Birkland, "State Frantic to Save Salmon in Elwha River—Parasites, Heat Threaten Chinook," *Seattle Times*, 29 August 1992; "Bush OKs Study of Elwha Projects," *Seattle Times*, 26 October 1992; Mark Munn, *An Assessment of Stream Habitat and Nutrients in the Elwha River Basin: Implications for Restoration*, Water-Resource Investigations Report 98-4223 (Tacoma, WA: U.S. Geological Survey, 1999); and Adam Burke, "River of Dreams," *High Country News* 33, no. 18 (24 September 2001).

CHAPTER 13:
The Puget Lowlands

1. Greg Lange, "Cougar Wanders into Downtown Seattle and Creates Excitement on September 20, 1890," *Seattle Post Intelligencer*, reprinted 25 February 1999; and N. S. Nokkentved, "Lacey Guard Reports 2 a.m. Cougar Sighting," *Olympian*, 29 May 2003.

2. C. D. Levings and R. M. Thom, "Habitat Changes in Georgia Basin: Implications for Resource Management and Restoration," Canadian Technical Report of Fisheries and Aquatic Sciences no. 1948 (1994), quoted in *Changing Our Water Ways: Trends in Washington's Water Systems* (Olympia: Washington State Department of Natural Resources, 2000), 57.

3. For the conservation status of the lowland ecoregion, see the Conservation Biology Institute's online report, "Pacific Northwest Conservation Assessment, Section 30: Puget Lowlands Forest," *www.consbio.org/cbi/pacnw_assess/er30/setting.htm*.

4. See Seattle Urban Nature Project, *Habitats on Seattle Public Lands* (Seattle: SUNP, 2000).

5. See Kathy Mulady, "Northgate Shopping Center Takes Shape, but Mall Expansion Is Stuck," *Seattle Post-Intelligencer*, 28 March 2000.

6. Descriptions of the watershed can be found in Robert Vreeland, "Thornton Creek Watershed Committee Minority Report," at the Seattle Public Utilities Web site, *www.cityofseattle.net/util*; and in " Otter and Spawning Salmon Spotted in Thornton Creek," *Seattle Press*, 18 October 2000.

7. Janet Way, interview by Katherine Jones, Seattle, 16 April 2003. For more information about the campaign, see the Thornton Creek Alliance Web site, *www.scn.org/earth/tca/*; Kery Murakami and Kathy Mulady, "Northgate Expansion is Delayed," *Seattle Post-Intelligencer*, 19 May 2000; Matthew Treusch, "Mayor Seeks to Sell Vision for Northgate Area," *Seattle Sun* 7, no. 2 (February 2002); Roberta Cruger, "Plans for Northgate South Lot: Up in the Air or up the Creek?," *Seattle Press*, 25 April 2002; and Kathy Mulady, "Mayor Sets Up Salmon Battle," *Seattle Post-Intelligencer*, 17 December 2002.

8. "Initiative 80: Save Seattle Creeks," *http://yesforseattle.org*.

9. Information about the Kaiser homestead, its ecosystem, and the path to its preservation is from the *Green Cove Creek Comprehensive Drainage Basin Plan* (Olympia: Thurston County and City of Olympia, December 1998); Eric Erler, "Habitat and Homestead: A Story of Success in Green Cove," *Capitol Ideas* (winter 2002); and John Dodge, "3-Way Deal to Protect Prime Land," *Olympian*, 17 February 2002.

10. All Joann Harper-Kaiser quotations are from an interview by Glenn Burkhart at the Kaiser homestead, March 2003.

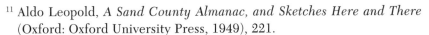

[11] Aldo Leopold, *A Sand County Almanac, and Sketches Here and There* (Oxford: Oxford University Press, 1949), 221.

[12] Erler, "Habitat and Homestead."

[13] For the state of the Sound and efforts to protect it, see People for Puget Sound, *Sound and Straits* 12, no. 3 (2002): 1, 18; and Robert McClure and Lisa Stiffler, "PI Special Report: Our Troubled Sound," *Seattle Post-Intelligencer*, 18–22 November 2002.

[14] Wayne Palsson, "Marine Refuges Offer Haven for Puget Sound Fish," *Fish and Wildlife Science: An Online Science Magazine*, from the Washington Department of Fish and Wildlife (April 2001), *www.wa.gov/wdfw/science/current/marine_sanctuary.html*.

[15] Eric Sorensen, "Federal Protection Denied for Puget Sound Orcas," *Seattle Post-Intelligencer*, 26 June 2002.

[16] Dan Wandersee, "Chart on Biomagnification," in *The Sea, the Strait, and the Sound: Preserving Washington's Marine Communities* (Seattle: People for Puget Sound, Surfrider Foundation Northwest, and Ocean Wilderness Network, 2002), 7.

[17] "Stewardship and a Network of Protected Areas," in *The Sea, The Strait, and the Sound*, 21.

[18] Hatcheries are discussed in detail in Gary K. Meefe, "Techo-Arrogance and Halfway Technologies: Salmon Hatcheries on the Pacific Coast of North America," *Conservation Biology* 6, no. 3 (1992): 350–54. Further information about salmon is from Charles Wilkinson, *Messages from Frank's Landing: A Story of Salmon, Treaties, and the Indian Way* (Seattle: University of Washington Press, 1984); and Jeff Cederholm, class lecture in the course "Salmon Ecology: A Watershed Perspective," The Evergreen State College, Olympia, Washington, 7 August 2002.

[19] Washington Department of Fish and Wildlife, "Viewing Chum Salmon: Kennedy Creek," *www.wa.gov/wdfw/fish/chum/viewingchum_kennedy.htm* 2001. See also Bill Young, "Kennedy Creek: Wild Salmon in Mason County's Backyard," *Shelton-Mason County Journal*, 23 May 2002.

[20] History of preservation in the basin is from Jill Schropp, *Nisqually Delta Controversy: A Question of Significance* (master's thesis, The Evergreen State College, 1981); and the "Our People: Empowerment" article in the *Olympian* series celebrating 150 years of Olympia, 19 July 2000.

[21] Gordon Alcorn and Dixie Lee Ray, *Future of the Nisqually Delta Area*, report to the House of Representatives, State of Washington (November 1970).

[22] See Kaia Anne Petersen, *An Analysis of the Development and Implementation of the Nisqually River Management Plan*, Washington State (master's thesis, The Evergreen State College, 1990).

[23] Georgiana Kautz, Nisqually Tribe natural resource manager, personal communication with chapter authors, May 2003.

[24] For more information about tribal presence and management within the watershed, see Ariona, *The Effectiveness of a Watershed Council: The Nisqually River Council* (master's thesis, the Evergreen State College, 1998); and the Georgiana Kautz interview in chapter 9 of this book.

[25] Georgiana Kautz, interview by Lin Skavdahl and Katherine Jones, minidisc recording, Nisqually Delta, Thurston County, Washington, 8 April 2003.

[26] David Troutt, "Nisqually River Chinook Recovery Efforts," *www.NisquallyLandTrust.org/learnaboutnisqually.html*.

[27] See Elizabeth M. Gillespie, "Nisqually Tribe Welcomes the Tides at Newly Finished Salmon Recovery Site," *Seattle Post-Intelligencer*, 18 November 2002.

[28] For Fort Lewis species and management, see U.S Fish and Wildlife Service, "Nisqually National Wildlife Refuge Comprehensive Conservation Plan," draft (2002), *http://pacific.fws.gov/planning/draft/docs/wa/docsnisqually.htm*; and Craig Welch and Katherine Pfleger, "Fragile Species, Military Might Strain to Co-Exist at Fort Lewis," *Seattle Post-Intelligencer*, 19 January 2003.

[30] Welch and Pfleger, "Fragile Species, Military Might."

[31] Ibid.

CHAPTER 14:
The Wild East

[1] Quoted in Lee E. Rogers, *Shrub-Steppe Seasons: A Natural History of the Mid-Columbia Basin*, US DOE PNL-10691 (Richland, WA: Pacific Northwest Laboratory, 1995).

[2] John Zelazny, *Arid Lands of Eastern Washington: History, Ecological Condition and Conservation Strategies* (Bellingham, WA: Northwest Ecosystem Alliance, 1996).

[3] For information about the monument see the U.S. Fish and Wildlife Service Hanford Reach National Monument and Saddle Mountain National Wildlife Refuge Web site, *http://hanfordreach.fws.gov*; and National Park Service, *Hanford Reach of the Columbia River: Comprehensive River Conservation Study and Environmental Impact Statement: Final* (Seattle: NPS, 1994).

[4] U.S. Army Corps of Engineers, *Hanford Reach Study Report: Impacts of Ben Franklin Dam* (Seattle: Corps, 1981).

[5] For a history of Hanford see U.S. Department of Energy Hanford Cultural and Historic Resources Program, *History of the Plutonium Production Facilities at the Hanford Site Historic District, 1943–1990* (Richland, WA: U.S. Department of Energy, 2002).

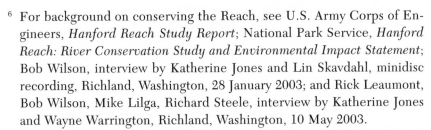

[6] For background on conserving the Reach, see U.S. Army Corps of Engineers, *Hanford Reach Study Report*; National Park Service, *Hanford Reach: River Conservation Study and Environmental Impact Statement*; Bob Wilson, interview by Katherine Jones and Lin Skavdahl, minidisc recording, Richland, Washington, 28 January 2003; and Rick Leaumont, Bob Wilson, Mike Lilga, Richard Steele, interview by Katherine Jones and Wayne Warrington, Richland, Washington, 10 May 2003.

[7] Harvey Manning, *Washington Wilderness: The Unfinished Work* (Seattle: Mountaineers Books, 1984). For more about this ecosystem, see Timothy Coleman, "Emerald Islands—The Kettle River Range," *Wild Rockies Networker: The Quarterly Journal of Alliance for the Wild Rockies* 12, no. 3 (2000).

[8] Interview by Dan Hansen, *Spokesman-Review*, 16 February 2003.

[9] See the Kettle Range Conservation Group Web site for details of the group's campaigns, *www.kettlerange.org*.

[10] See Pacific Biodiversity Institute, *Scientific Justification for the Proposed Columbia Mountains National Monument* (2000), *www.pacificbio.org/pubs/pubs.html*.

[11] Derrick Knowles and Hal Rowe, "Washington's Southern Selkirk Mountains: The Inland Northwest's Wilderness Backyard," *Protect Eastern Washington Wilderness Newsletter*, Kettle Range Conservation Group (2002). For information about protecting the Selkirks, see the Lands Council Web site, *www.landscouncil.org/selkirks/selkirks.htm*.

[12] Umbrella species are megafauna that require such significant amounts of habitat as to provide, by default, habitat for most other species within the ecosystem.

[13] All information and quotations from Bill Arthur are from an interview by Lin Skavdahl, Seattle, 5 February 2003.

INDEX

ABOUT THE AUTHORS

Molly Arrandale was born and raised in Albuquerque, New Mexico, and moved to Washington to attend The Evergreen State College in 2000. As an undergraduate, she has focused on environmental studies and plans to pursue her master's degree in the same subject. An avid equestrienne, she enjoys heading out on the trails with her horse and she has volunteered at two wildlife rehabilitation centers. On her trips to see her family in Montana she always visits the wolves in Yellowstone National Park.

Glenn Thomas Burkhart is a twenty-seven-year resident of Washington State. He grew up in the heart of volcano country, where he naturally became an avid outdoorsman and explorer. Glenn is a former wilderness ranger in the Gifford Pinchot National Forest, where he toured the rugged Goat Rocks, Tatoosh, Glacier View, and William O. Douglas Wilderness Areas. Although an engineer by trade, he works to promote healthy forests, salmon restoration, and wildlands preservation in the Northwest. Glenn holds an associates in technical arts degree in civil engineering from Centralia College and a bachelor of science degree from the Evergreen State College.

Anthony Robert Bush was born and raised near the Rocky Mountains in Denver, Colorado. He moved to Olympia, Washington, to attend The Evergreen State College and to study ecology and the environment. Tony grew up watching as urban sprawl took over formerly wild areas of his youth. This propelled him to work on preserving and regenerating what wildness is left, especially in more urbanized areas.

Lana Byal is originally from Eugene, Oregon, and is now a resident of the Olympic Peninsula. Her focus of study is forest ecology and her passions are all that wildness provides. She enjoys hiking in the mountains, exploring tropical and temperate rainforests, and swimming in cold clean rivers. Lana is committed to a future in conservation work, environmental education, and perfecting the Spanish language.

Melissa Carter moved to Olympia, Washington, with her cat in the summer of 2002 and is finishing her undergraduate degree at The Evergreen State College. The Protecting Washington Wildness program introduced her to different wild areas across the state, and as she continues her academic education she will continue to explore the wildness of Washington.

Connie Czepiel returned to college as a senior after raising a family and pursuing a career. She is the mother of twin sons and a daughter, is an Air Force veteran, and has been an accountant for twenty-four years. Connie loves the outdoors, especially the ocean, and hopes to produce outdoor videos; she has begun work on a video about the writing of this book.

Richard Darnell has lived in Washington all of his life. Raised on a small farm in Thurston County, he spent the majority of his free time fishing, camping, and playing outdoors. Six years after earning a degree from Washington State University in environmental science, he returned to college to prepare for the graduate program in environmental studies at The Evergreen State College. If Rick isn't training with the National Guard, studying, or volunteering for the Olympic Forest Coalition, he's either leaving for a fishing trip, out fishing, coming back from fishing, or wondering why he isn't fishing.

Caitlin Houser grew up on Cougar Mountain and has spent many hours hiking and jogging in the Issaquah Alps. During her adolescence, she witnessed the rapid transition of small-town Issaquah and nearby areas into sprawling suburbs, which opened her eyes to the plight of the region's wild places and planted the seeds for her environmental activism. Caitlin's love affair with wilderness areas began when she first experienced them as a teenage participant in the Wilderness Volunteer Corps. She strongly believes in the need to expose youth to wildness and environmental education and is proud to represent her generation in the movement to protect Washington's wild places.

Katherine Jones is a member of the Blackfeet Tribe, a former air force brat, and a recent graduate of The Evergreen State College. Katie draws on a variety of perspectives in her approach to life, and her lifelong travel addiction ensures a constant supply of new experiences and ideas. She hopes to combine her cultural background, her education, and her enthusiasm to motivate and help people establish positive connections with wildlands.

Travis Keron is a junior at The Evergreen State College, where he has focused on environmental studies, economics, and political science. He participated in an internationally sponsored conference on climate change held in Vancouver, British Columbia, and was part of a team that created a timber harvest management proposal for the director of the Natural Resources Department of the Skokomish Indian Tribe. Except for a five-year hiatus in a small agricultural town in South Dakota, he has lived most of his life in western Washington, where he enjoys hiking, fishing, and scuba diving.

Shawn Olson is a graduating senior at The Evergreen State College with a self-titled bachelor's degree in environmental studies and social movements. A native Washingtonian, Shawn transferred to Evergreen in 2001 and has focused her studies around historical and current political movements across the Americas, concentrating on the impact that social upheavals have on human relationships with the natural world. She is a passionate outdoorsperson and plans to hike the Pacific Crest Trail from Mexico to Canada in 2004.

Raelynn Rinehart will graduate from The Evergreen State College in spring 2004. Her studies have focused on environmental disciplines, natural sciences, and writing. She hopes to establish a career as an environmental writer, eventually freelancing a series of educational creative nonfiction books for young readers. From her birth state of California, to her adopted state of Washington, hiking, fishing, and just enjoying the outdoors have been a large part of her life.

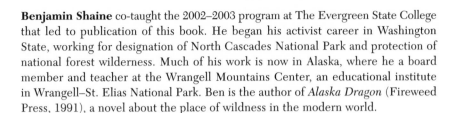

Benjamin Shaine co-taught the 2002–2003 program at The Evergreen State College that led to publication of this book. He began his activist career in Washington State, working for designation of North Cascades National Park and protection of national forest wilderness. Much of his work is now in Alaska, where he a board member and teacher at the Wrangell Mountains Center, an educational institute in Wrangell–St. Elias National Park. Ben is the author of *Alaska Dragon* (Fireweed Press, 1991), a novel about the place of wildness in the modern world.

Lin Skavdahl, after twenty-five years as a teacher and counselor in public education, once again became a student in order to participate in the Protecting Washington Wildness program at The Evergreen State College. Interviewing the leaders, past and present, who devote their lives to preserving and restoring wildness was the most educational and inspiring process she has ever experienced. She is a seasonal park ranger for the Wilderness District of the North Cascades National Park Complex and plans to return to school counseling in the off-season.

Oliver Smith is a graduate of The Evergreen State College with a bachelor of science degree. He is a lover of all places wild and, if not writing or with his nose stuck in a book, can usually be found traveling with his dog Sadie in his old green bus going backpacking, climbing, surfing, or camping on a river somewhere out West where there aren't many other folks around.

Oscar Soule, project advisor, has taught environmental studies at The Evergreen State College since it opened in 1971. His comfort in nature began with summer trips to northern Wisconsin as a youth. His eyes were opened to ecology at Colorado College and his graduate studies in the Sonoran Desert at the University of Arizona made him a scientist. More than a thousand of his students dot the world trying to make it a better place. Oscar will retire in June 2004 and continue his special interest in urban ecology.

Ellen Trescott traveled to Washington in 1998 from the tamed wilds of upstate New York and has lived, worked, played, and studied in the wild and agricultural lands of the Northwest ever since. She hopes to continue her involvement with conservation groups focused on education, collaborative restoration stewardship, and wilderness protection. She plans to devote her energy to life experiences that will enhance her ability to defend environmental and social causes.

Wayne Warrington hails from the desert Southwest. His twenty-six years' experience as a human being has given him an appreciation for the delicate ecological balance of Earth and a passion to become better entwined within it. Since relocating to Washington in 2002 to attend The Evergreen State College, Wayne has enjoyed and continues to explore the Pacific Northwest wildlands that are in constant need of more defenders.

Edward Whitesell, while a freshman at the University of Colorado, co-founded the CU Wilderness Study Group in 1970. After graduation, Ted ran the Colorado Wilderness Workshop, the only statewide wilderness preservation organization at the time. From 1975 to 1985, he was an activist with the Southeast Alaska Conservation Council, campaigning to secure designation of the first wilderness areas in the Tongass National Forest. Later, he earned a Ph.D. in geography from the University of California, Berkeley, investigating grassroots proposals for conservation and development in the Amazon rainforest of Brazil. He now teaches environmental studies at The Evergreen State College.

Tyler Winchell is a near lifelong resident of Washington State and an avid admirer of its wildlands and seascapes. He enjoys hiking around his "backyard backcountry," in northwestern Mason County at the edge of the Olympics, including the Mount Skokomish Wilderness and the unprotected Upper-Skokomish River Roadless Area east of Lake Cushman. A recent graduate of The Evergreen State College, he will be returning for work on a master's degree in the school's Masters of Environment Studies program and hopes one day to enter law school and later practice environmental law here in the Northwest.

Front row (left to right): Caitlin Houser, Melissa Carter, Lana Byal, Raelynn Rinehart, Lin Skavdahl, Connie Czepiel, Oliver Smith, Shawn Olson. Back row (left to right): Glenn Burkhart, Katherine Jones, Travis Keron, Ellen Trescott, Molly Arrandale, Wayne Warrington, Benjamin Shaine, Tyler Winchell, Anthony Bush, Richard Darnell, Edward Whitesell

ABOUT THE SPONSORS

The Evergreen State College
The Evergreen State College is a public, liberal arts college serving Washington State. Its mission is to help students realize their potential through innovative, interdisciplinary educational programs in the arts, social sciences, humanities, and natural sciences. In addition to preparing students within their academic fields, Evergreen provides graduates with the fundamental skills to communicate, to solve problems, and to work collaboratively and independently in addressing real issues and problems. Various "green" projects on campus model ways to learn about incorporating concepts of sustainability in daily life. Evergreen works to build relationships with local communities, organizations, and agencies that share this commitment to sustainability. Its commitment to sustainability manifests itself in many unique ways, including taking responsibility for its food sources, following through with waste management, incorporating eco-friendly designs into its buildings, using responsible resources for cleaning supplies and paper sources, and providing academic programs in which students learn more about sustainable living. For more information, please visit the Olympia or Tacoma campuses and also check out *www.evergreen.edu*.

The Mountaineers Foundation
The Mountaineers Foundation is a public foundation established in 1968 to promote the study of the mountains, forests, and streams of the Pacific Northwest, and to contribute to the preservation of its natural beauty and ecological integrity. The Mountaineers Foundation fulfills its mission by stewardship of important preserves and by grant making. Through these means, it actively supports conservation in the Pacific Northwest. Although the Mountaineers Foundation has close ties to The Mountaineers, the foundation is a separate corporation with separate volunteer officers and trustees. The Mountaineers Foundation gratefully welcomes your financial contribution to continue and extend its vital conservation work. Because The Mountaineers Foundation is a 501(c)(3) charitable organization, contributions are tax deductible to the extent allowed by law. Please contact *www.mountaineersfoundation.org* for more information.

Patagonia, Inc.
Patagonia, Inc. designs, markets, and distributes technical outdoor apparel through its mail order, Internet, retail, and wholesale divisions. The company's purpose statement is to "use business to inspire and implement

solutions to the environmental crisis." Toward that end, Patagonia pursues a variety of environmental initiatives. As a member of "1% Percent for the Planet," Patagonia donates 1% of its sales for the protection and restoration of the natural environment and has contributed $19 million to grassroots activist organizations since 1985. Patagonia's definition of product quality includes minimizing environmental harm wherever possible. Since 1986 the company has used 100% organic cotton in all of its cotton apparel, and Patagonia offers various products made with PCR® (Post-Consumer Recycled) plastic bottles, including its Synchilla® jacket. Through its various channels, the company runs environmental communications campaigns to educate its consumers and the general public on critical issues, such as habitat protection and the plight of wild salmon. For more information on Patagonia's environmental initiatives, please refer to: *www.patagonia.com/enviro*.

Friends of The Evergreen State College Library
Friends of The Evergreen State College Library works to support the college library as a community resource. The Friends organizes programs and events to bring the campus and the community together, it holds regular membership meetings in conjunction with readings, and it works to raise funds to help the Library provide the best service possible for both campus users and the surrounding community. Go to http://*www.evergreen.edu/library/admin/friends.htm* for more information.

THE MOUNTAINEERS, founded in 1906, is a nonprofit outdoor activity and conservation club, whose mission is "to explore, study, preserve, and enjoy the natural beauty of the outdoors . . . . " Based in Seattle, Washington, the club is now the third-largest such organization in the United States, with seven branches throughout Washington State.

The Mountaineers sponsors both classes and year-round outdoor activities in the Pacific Northwest, which include hiking, mountain climbing, ski-touring, snowshoeing, bicycling, camping, kayaking, nature study, sailing, and adventure travel. The club's conservation division supports environmental causes through educational activities, sponsoring legislation, and presenting informational programs.

All club activities are led by skilled, experienced instructors, who are dedicated to promoting safe and responsible enjoyment and preservation of the outdoors.

If you would like to participate in these organized outdoor activities or the club's programs, consider a membership in The Mountaineers. For information and an application, write or call

The Mountaineers, Club Headquarters, 300 Third Avenue West, Seattle, WA 98119; 206-284-6310. You can also visit the club's website at *www.mountaineers.org* or contact The Mountaineers via email at clubmail@mountaineers.org.

The Mountaineers Books, an active, nonprofit publishing program of the club, produces guidebooks, instructional texts, historical works, natural history guides, and works on environmental conservation. All books produced by The Mountaineers Books fulfill the club's mission.

Send or call for our catalog of more than 500 outdoor titles:

The Mountaineers Books
1001 SW Klickitat Way, Suite 201
Seattle, WA 98134
800-553-4453
mbooks@mountaineersbooks.org
www.mountaineersbooks.org

The Mountaineers Books is proud to be a corporate sponsor of The Leave No Trace Center for Outdoor Ethics, whose mission is to promote and inspire responsible outdoor recreation through education, research, and partnerships. The Leave No Trace program is focused specifically on human-powered (nonmotorized) recreation.

Leave No Trace strives to educate visitors about the nature of their recreational impacts, as well as offer techniques to prevent and minimize such impacts. Leave No Trace is best understood as an educational and ethical program, not as a set of rules and regulations.

For more information, visit *www.LNT.org*, or call 800-332-4100.

OTHER TITLES YOU MIGHT ENJOY FROM
THE MOUNTAINEERS BOOKS:

55 Hikes Around Stevens Pass: Wild Sky Country,
Rick McGuire & Ira Spring
The Wild Sky Country is proposed as a new Wilderness Area—explore the land and see what is at stake

Exploring Washington's Wild Areas,
Marge & Ted Mueller
The most comprehensive reference available to all of Washington's wildernesses and roadless areas

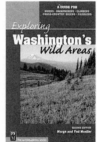

Best Old-Growth Forest Hikes:
Washington & Oregon Cascades,
John & Diane Cissel
Discover 100 paths to enchantment among the ancient old-growth forests of the Northwest

Predators At Risk in the Pacific
Northwest, *Dan Nelson*
An insightful look into the background of current predator controversies

Arctic National
Wildlife Refuge:
Seasons of Life and Land,
Subhankar Banerjee
Photographic documentation of the necessity to preserve this precious area

---

THE MOUNTAINEERS BOOKS